Sugar Princess
Skating to Win

Story & Art by
Hisaya Nakajo

Vol. **2**

Sugar Princess
Skating to Win

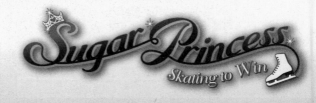

Vol. 2

Contents

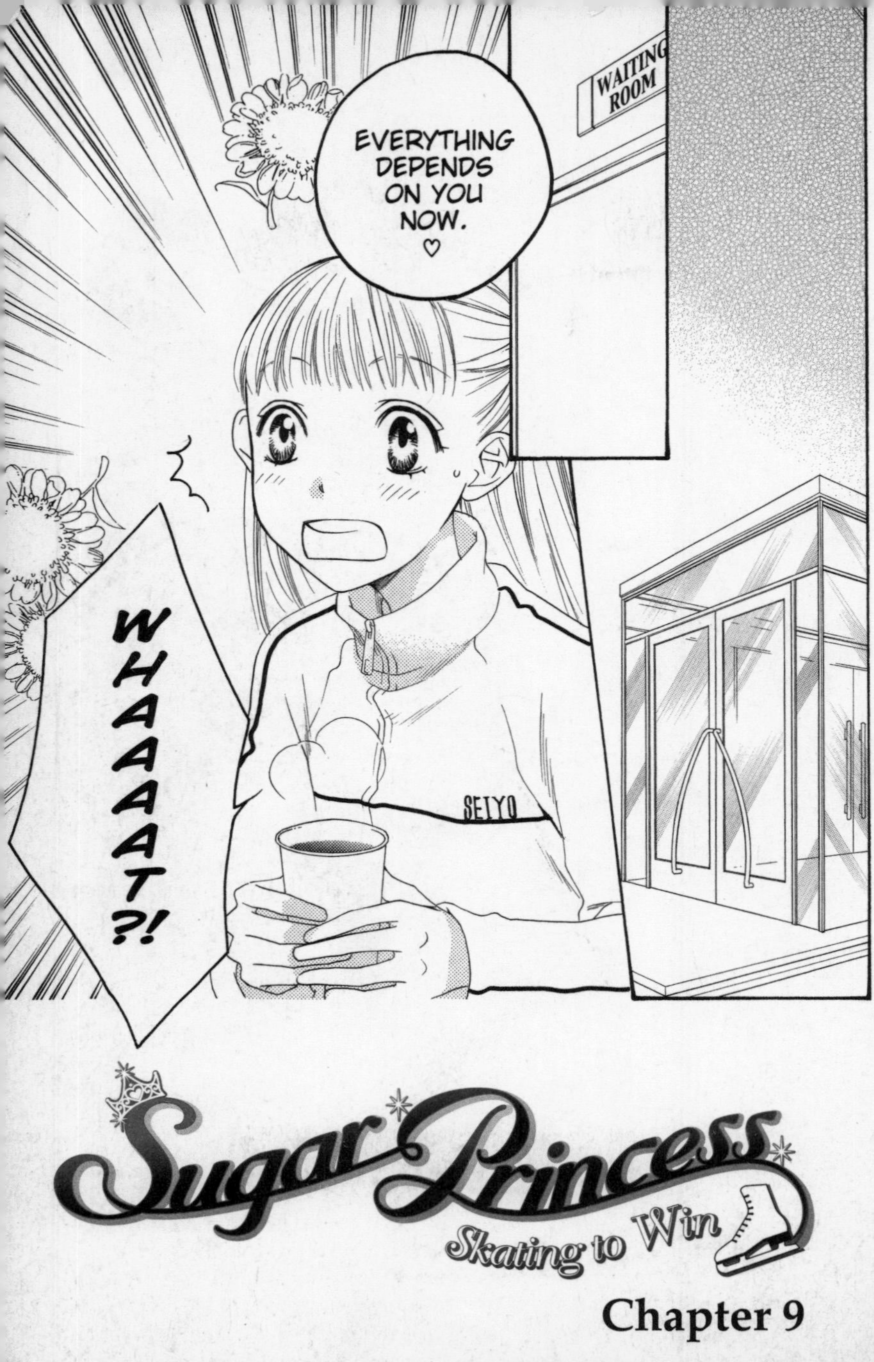
WAITING ROOM
EVERYTHING DEPENDS ON YOU NOW. ♡
WHAAAAT?!
SEIYO

Sugar Princess
Skating to Win

Chapter 9

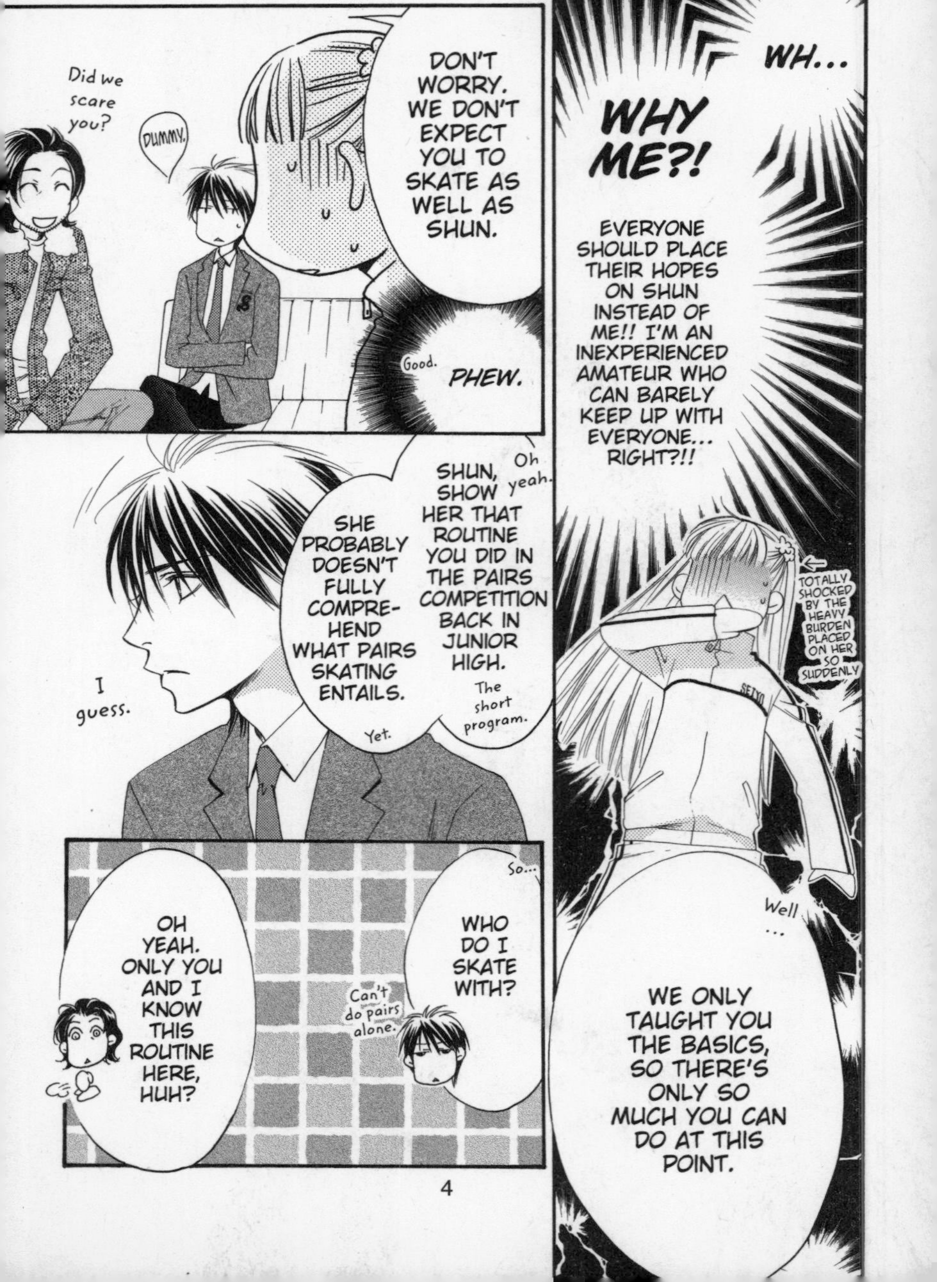
WH...
WHY ME?!
EVERYONE SHOULD PLACE THEIR HOPES ON SHUN INSTEAD OF ME!! I'M AN INEXPERIENCED AMATEUR WHO CAN BARELY KEEP UP WITH EVERYONE... RIGHT?!!
TOTALLY SHOCKED BY THE HEAVY BURDEN PLACED ON HER SO SUDDENLY
Well...
WE ONLY TAUGHT YOU THE BASICS, SO THERE'S ONLY SO MUCH YOU CAN DO AT THIS POINT.
DON'T WORRY. WE DON'T EXPECT YOU TO SKATE AS WELL AS SHUN.
Did we scare you?
DUMMY.
PHEW.
Good.
Oh yeah.
SHUN, SHOW HER THAT ROUTINE YOU DID IN THE PAIRS COMPETITION BACK IN JUNIOR HIGH.
The short program.
SHE PROBABLY DOESN'T FULLY COMPRE-HEND WHAT PAIRS SKATING ENTAILS.
Yet.
I guess.
So...
WHO DO I SKATE WITH?
Can't do pairs alone.
OH YEAH. ONLY YOU AND I KNOW THIS ROUTINE HERE, HUH?

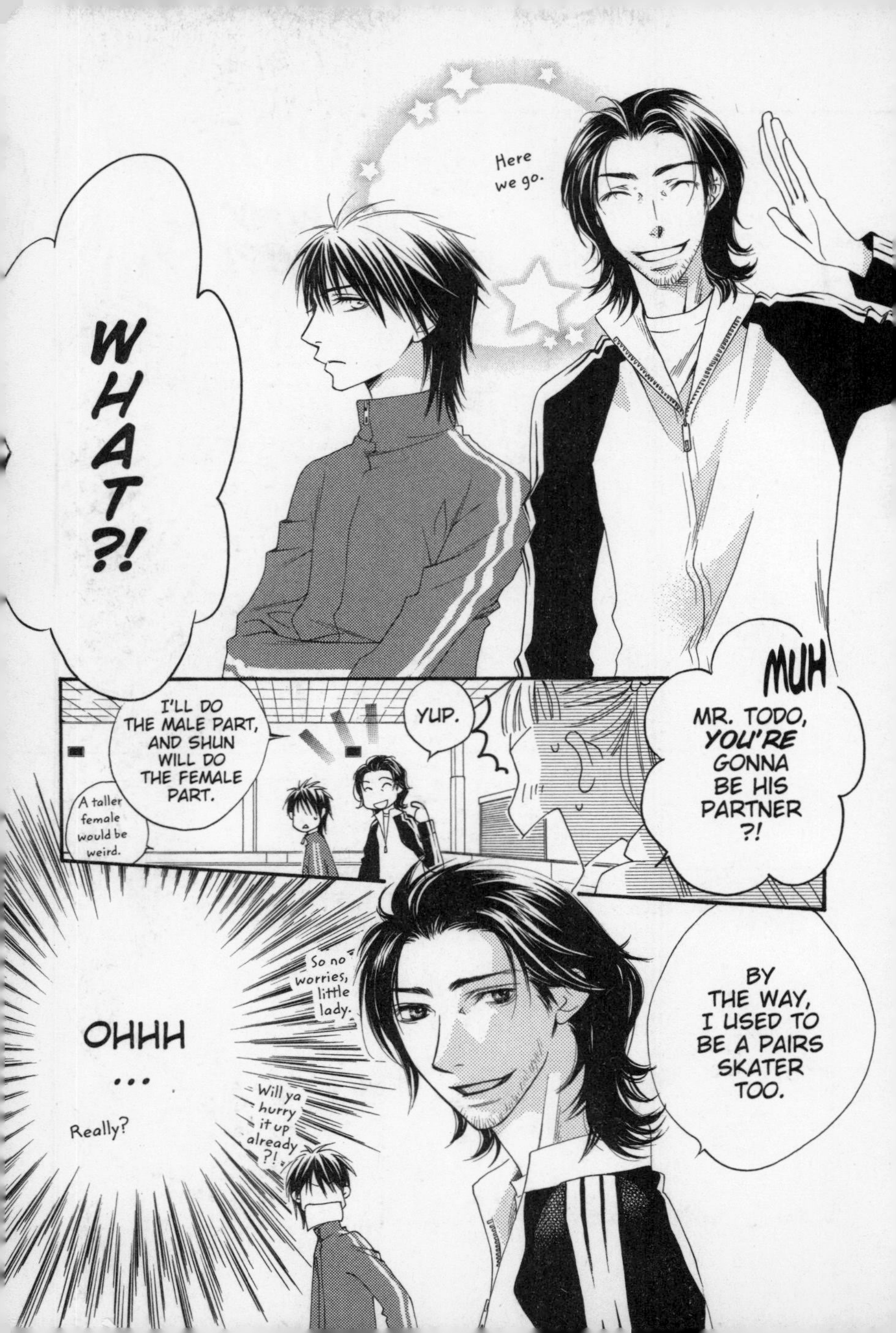
Here we go.
WHAT?!
MUH
MR. TODO, YOU'RE GONNA BE HIS PARTNER?!
YUP.
I'LL DO THE MALE PART, AND SHUN WILL DO THE FEMALE PART.
A taller female would be weird.
BY THE WAY, I USED TO BE A PAIRS SKATER TOO.
So no worries, little lady.
Will ya hurry it up already?!
OHHH...
Really?

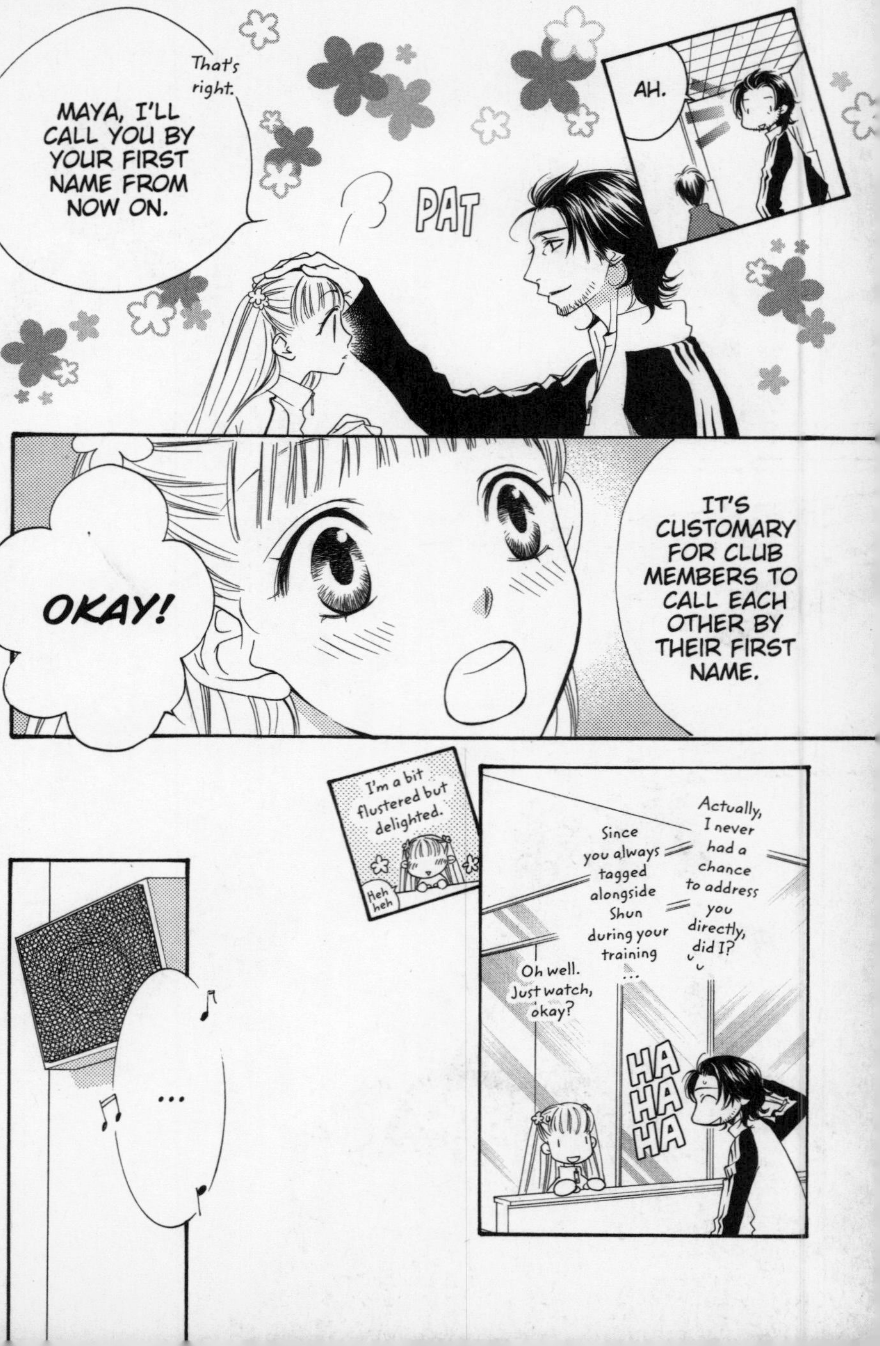

AH.
That's right.
MAYA, I'LL CALL YOU BY YOUR FIRST NAME FROM NOW ON.
PAT
IT'S CUSTOMARY FOR CLUB MEMBERS TO CALL EACH OTHER BY THEIR FIRST NAME.
OKAY!
I'm a bit flustered but delighted.
Heh heh
Actually, I never had a chance to address you directly, did I?
Since you always tagged alongside Shun during your training...
Oh well. Just watch, okay?
HA HA HA
...

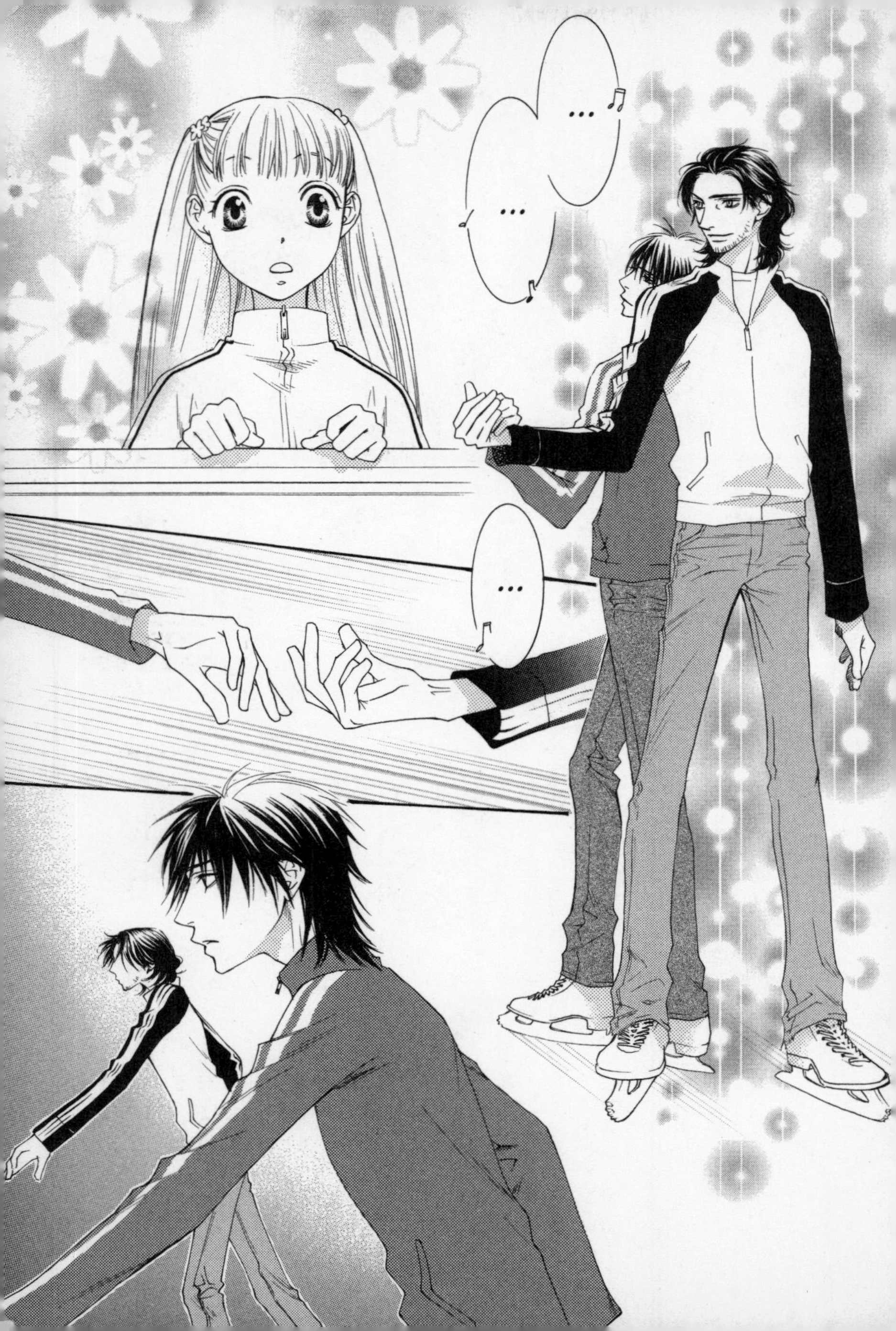
…♪
…♪
…♪

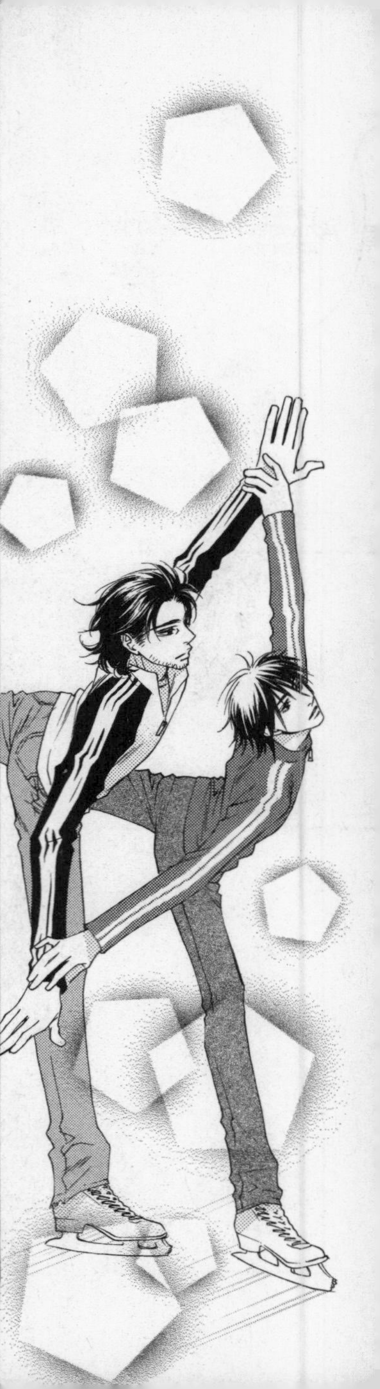

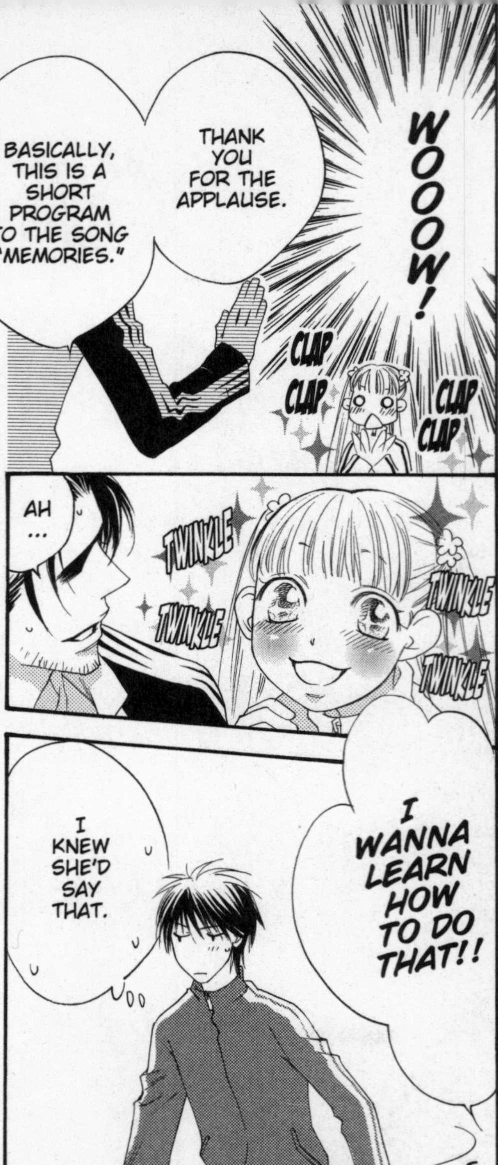
WOOOOW!
THANK YOU FOR THE APPLAUSE.
BASICALLY, THIS IS A SHORT PROGRAM TO THE SONG "MEMORIES."
CLAP CLAP
CLAP CLAP
TWINKLE
TWINKLE
TWINKLE
TWINKLE
AH ...
I WANNA LEARN HOW TO DO THAT!!
SKRRSH
I KNEW SHE'D SAY THAT.

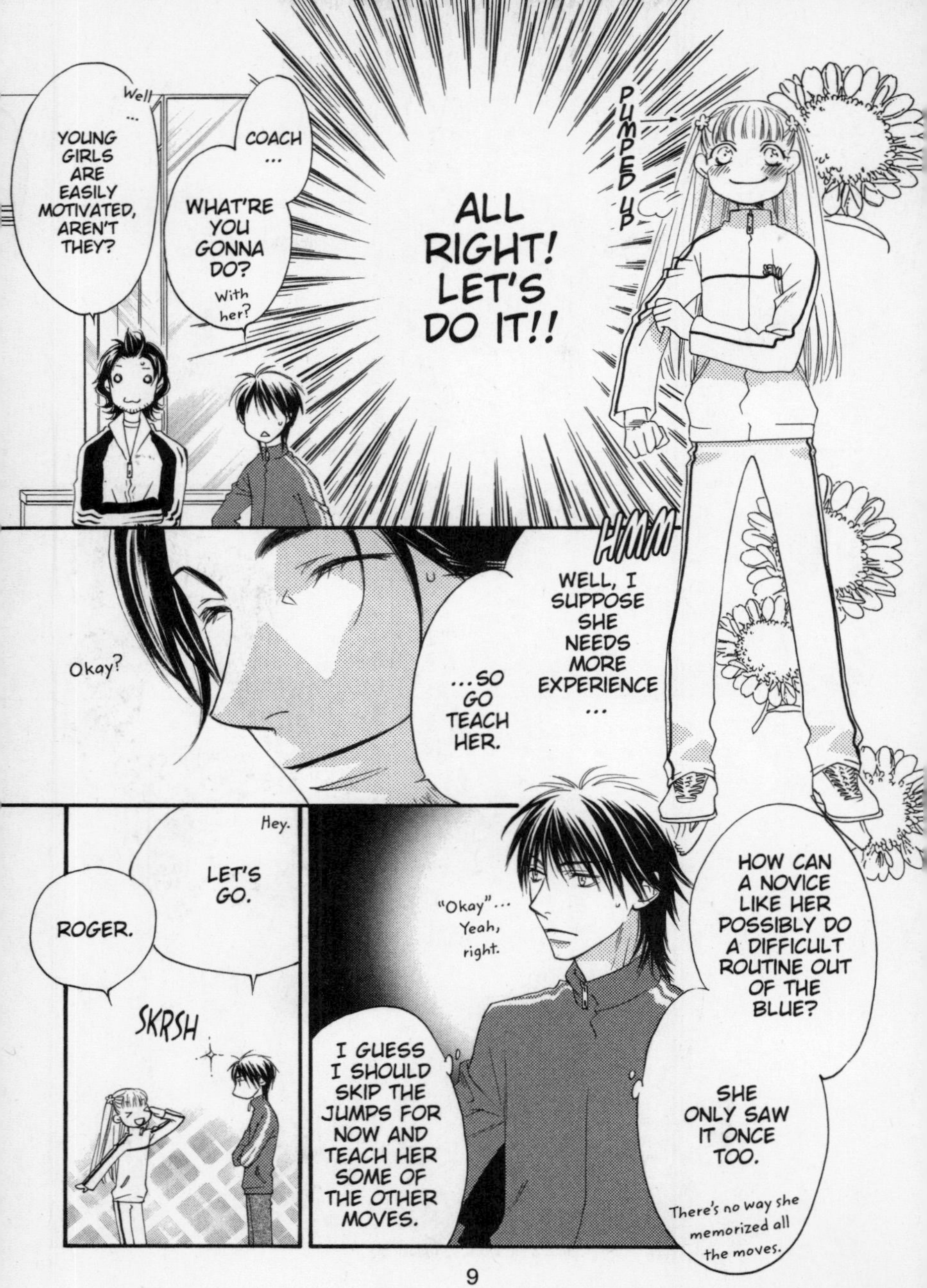
PUMPED UP
ALL RIGHT! LET'S DO IT!!
COACH... WHAT'RE YOU GONNA DO? With her?
Well... YOUNG GIRLS ARE EASILY MOTIVATED, AREN'T THEY?
HMM
WELL, I SUPPOSE SHE NEEDS MORE EXPERIENCE...
...SO GO TEACH HER.
Okay?
HOW CAN A NOVICE LIKE HER POSSIBLY DO A DIFFICULT ROUTINE OUT OF THE BLUE?
SHE ONLY SAW IT ONCE TOO.
There's no way she memorized all the moves.
"Okay"... Yeah, right.
I GUESS I SHOULD SKIP THE JUMPS FOR NOW AND TEACH HER SOME OF THE OTHER MOVES.
Hey. LET'S GO.
ROGER.
SKRSH

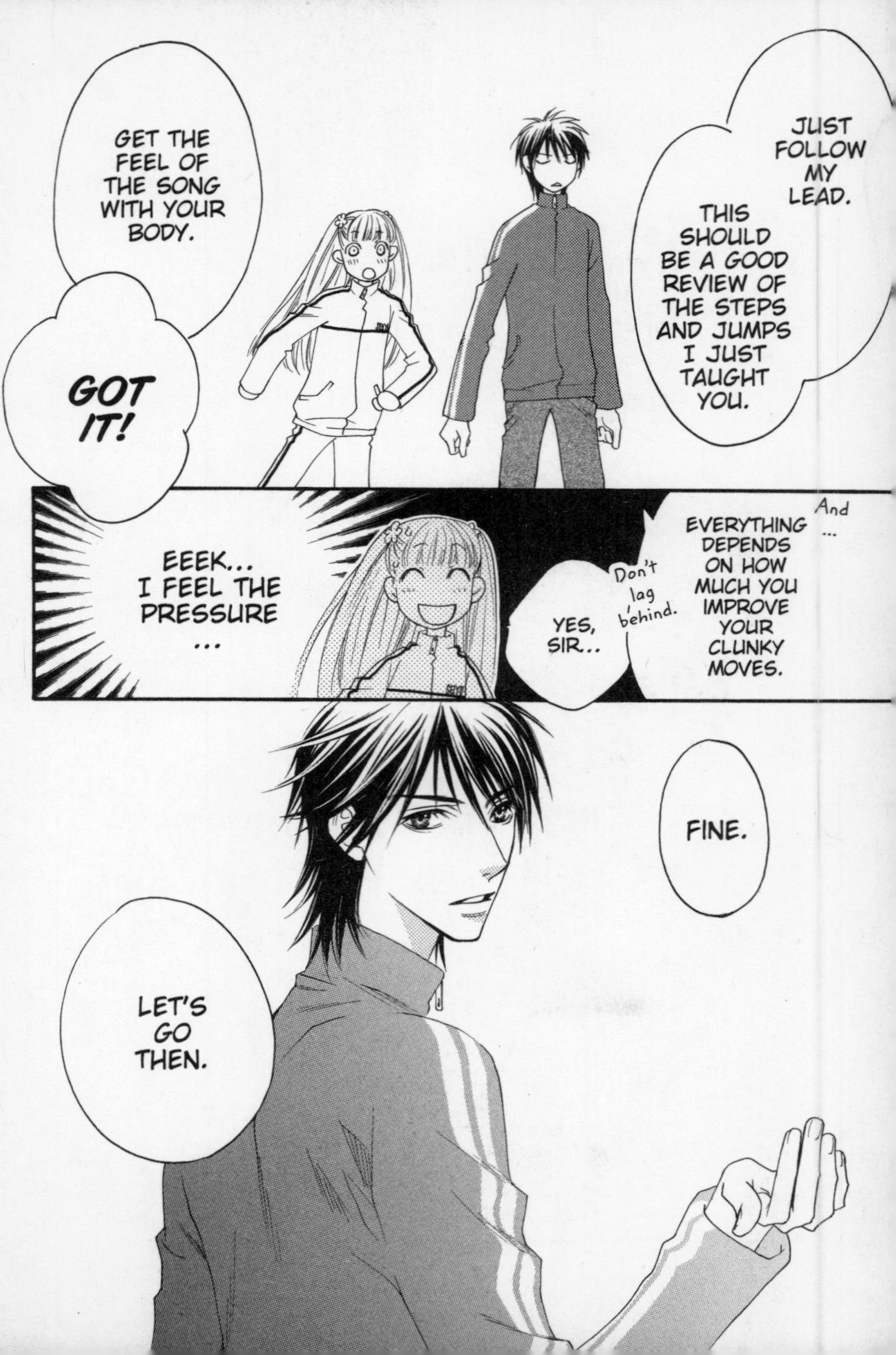
JUST FOLLOW MY LEAD.
THIS SHOULD BE A GOOD REVIEW OF THE STEPS AND JUMPS I JUST TAUGHT YOU.
GET THE FEEL OF THE SONG WITH YOUR BODY.
GOT IT!
And ...
EVERYTHING DEPENDS ON HOW MUCH YOU IMPROVE YOUR CLUNKY MOVES.
Don't lag behind.
YES, SIR...
EEEK... I FEEL THE PRESSURE ...
FINE.
LET'S GO THEN.

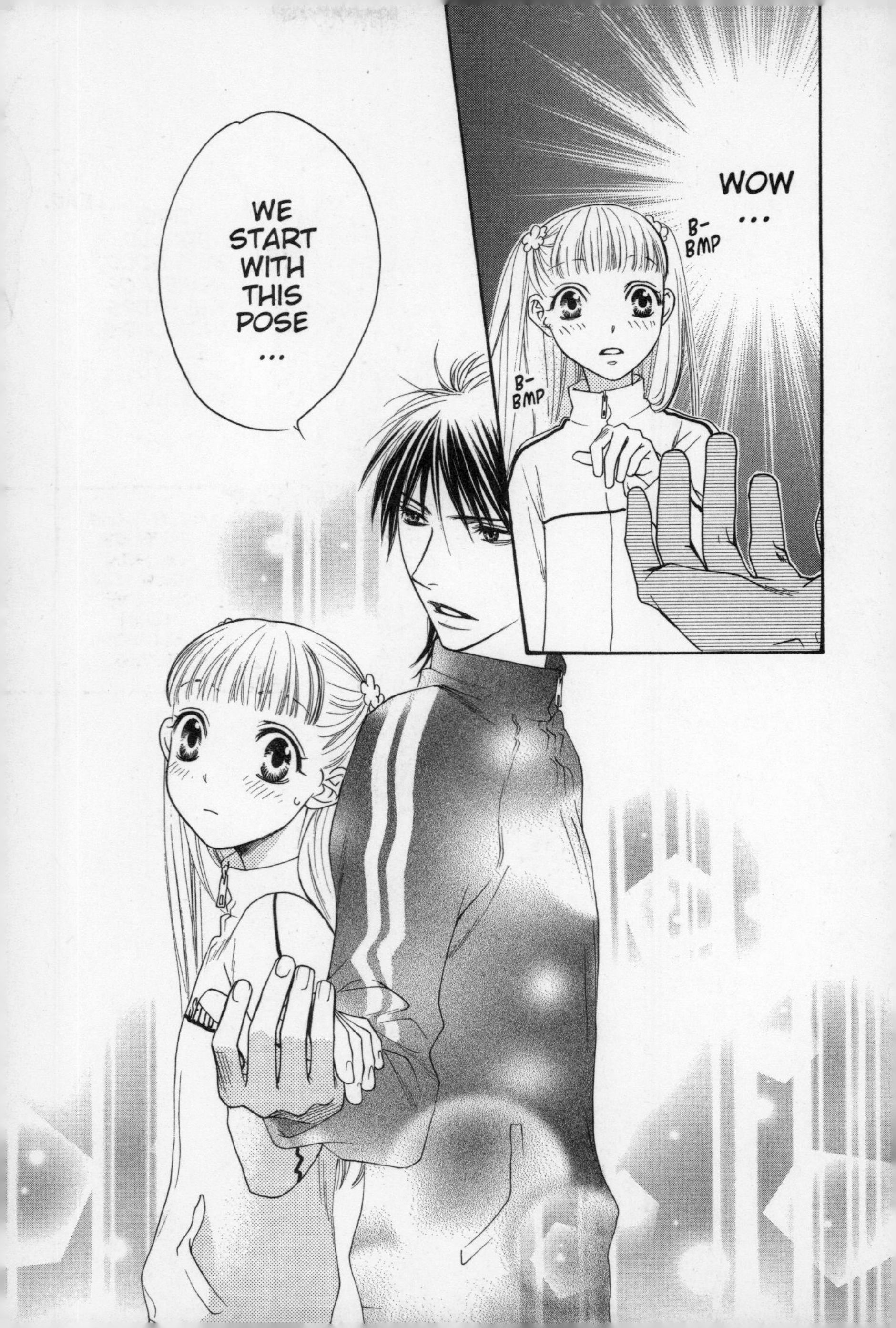
WOW ...
B-BMP
B-BMP
WE START WITH THIS POSE ...

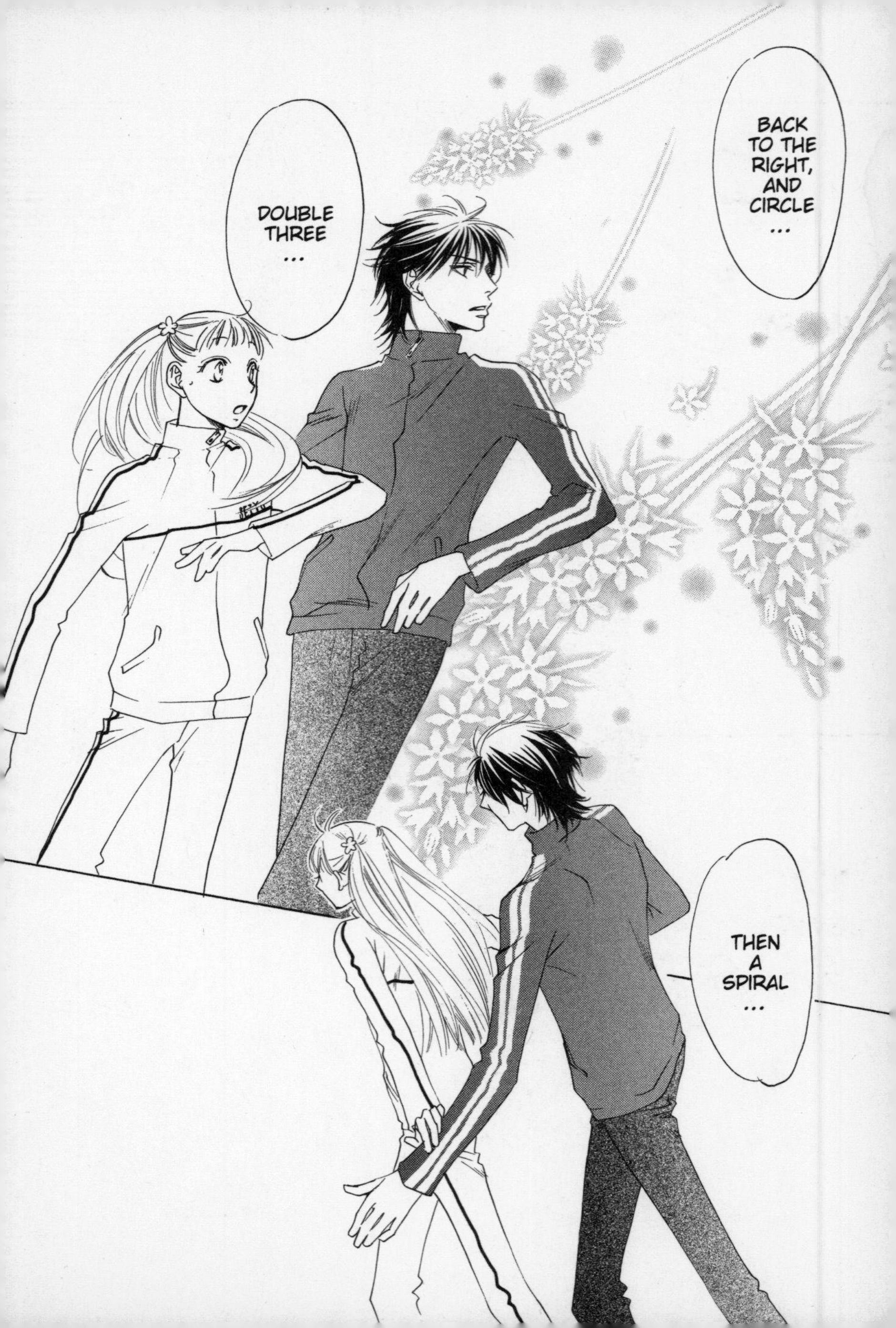
BACK TO THE RIGHT, AND CIRCLE...
DOUBLE THREE...
THEN A SPIRAL...

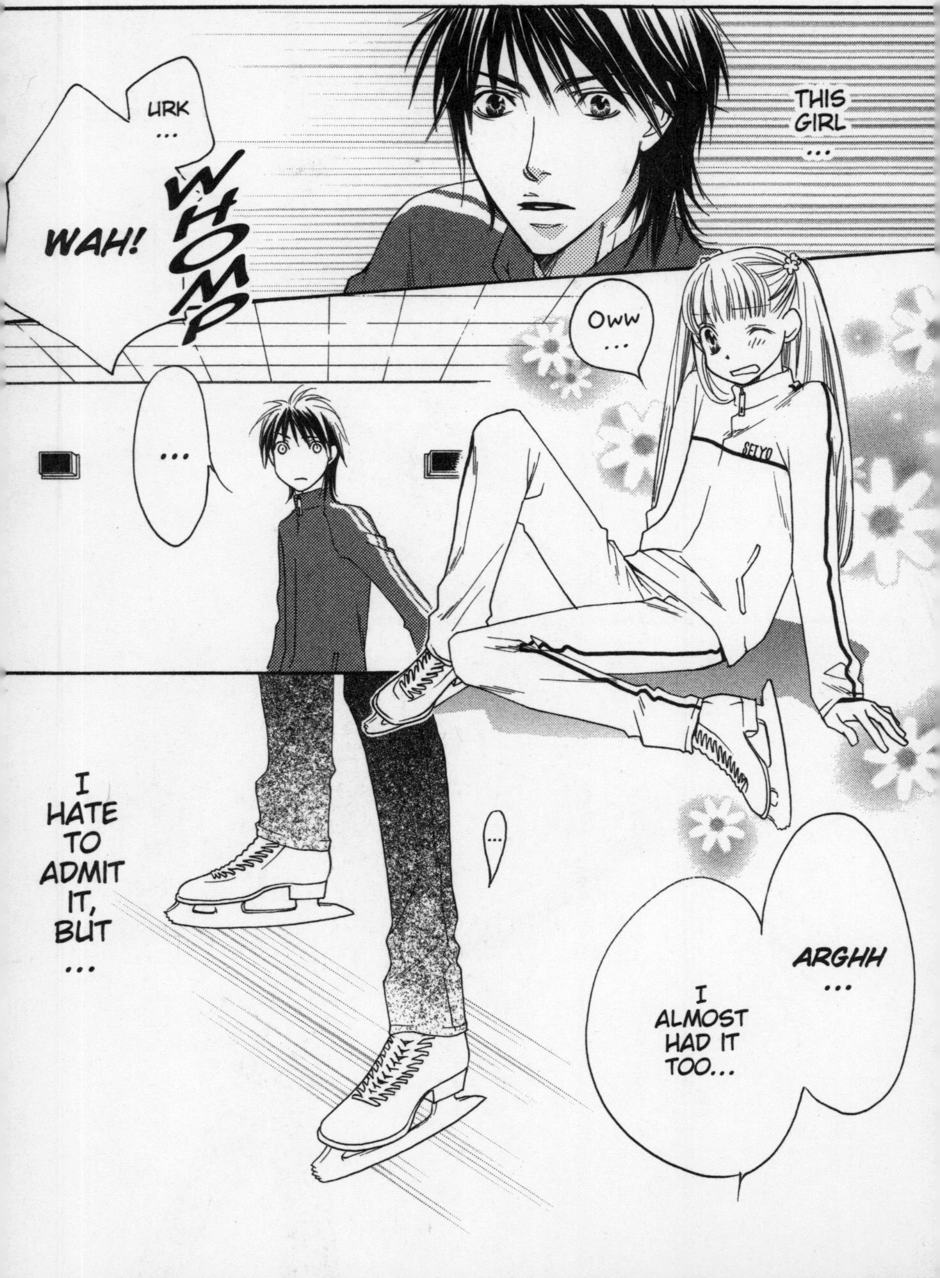
THIS GIRL ...
URK ...
Oww ...
WHOMP
WAH!
...
SEIYO
ARGHH ...
I ALMOST HAD IT TOO...
...
I HATE TO ADMIT IT, BUT ...

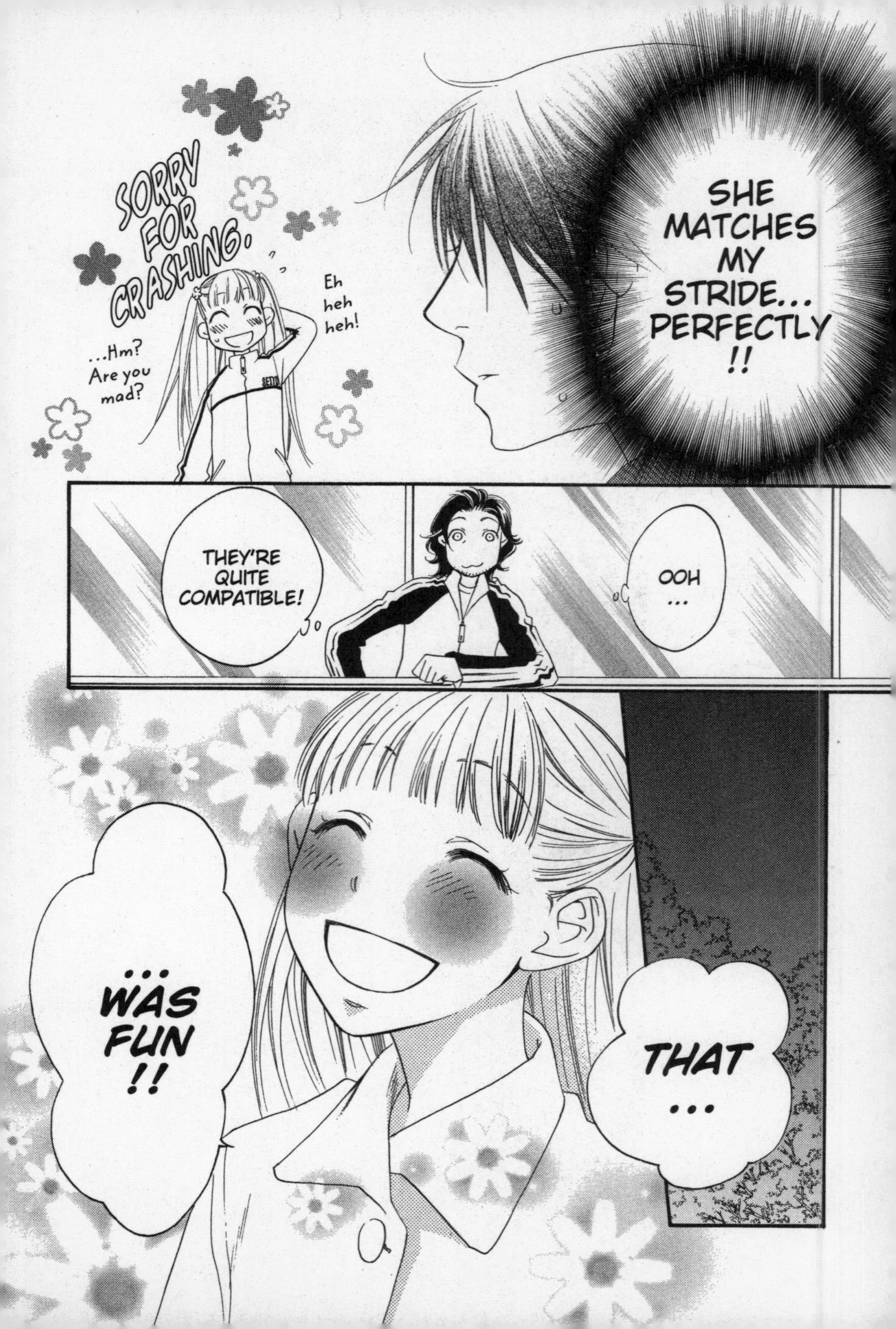
SHE MATCHES MY STRIDE... PERFECTLY!!
SORRY FOR CRASHING.
Eh heh heh!
...Hm? Are you mad?
OOH ...
THEY'RE QUITE COMPATIBLE!
THAT ...
... WAS FUN!!

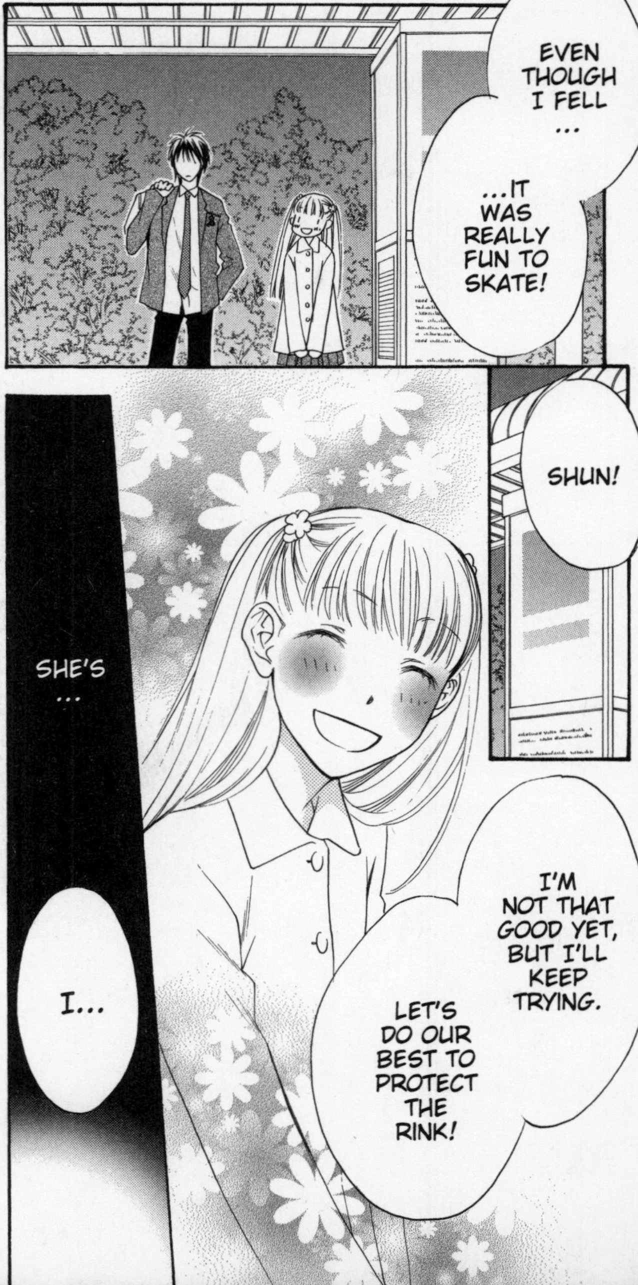
EVEN THOUGH I FELL ...
...IT WAS REALLY FUN TO SKATE!
SHUN!
I'M NOT THAT GOOD YET, BUT I'LL KEEP TRYING.
LET'S DO OUR BEST TO PROTECT THE RINK!
SHE'S ...
I...

SUGAR PRINCESS VOLUME 2!

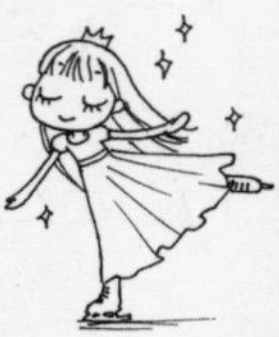

PLEASE READ IT ALL.

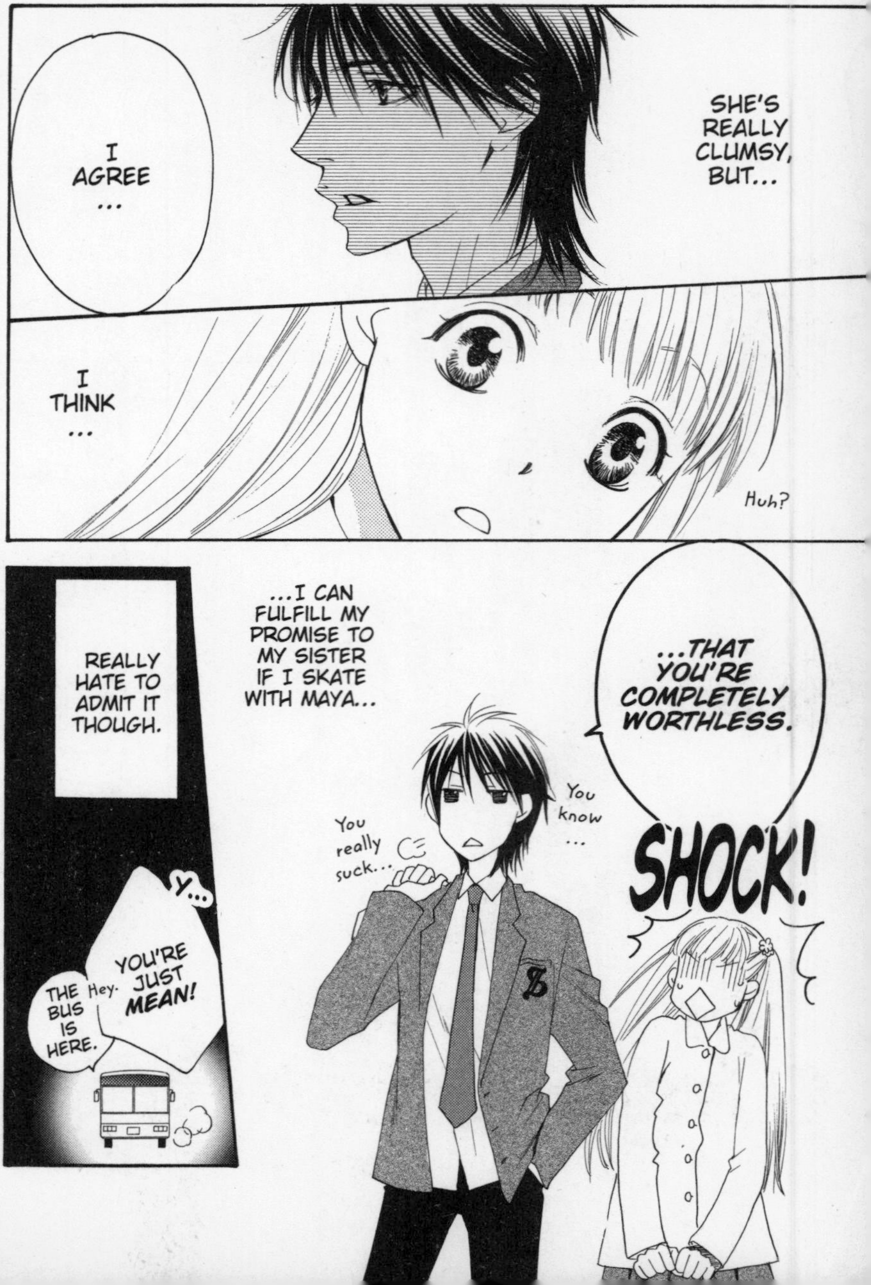
SHE'S REALLY CLUMSY, BUT...
I AGREE ...
Huh?
I THINK ...
...THAT YOU'RE COMPLETELY WORTHLESS.
...I CAN FULFILL MY PROMISE TO MY SISTER IF I SKATE WITH MAYA...
SHOCK!
You know ...
You really suck...
REALLY HATE TO ADMIT IT THOUGH.
Y...
YOU'RE JUST MEAN!
Hey.
THE BUS IS HERE.

Chapter 10

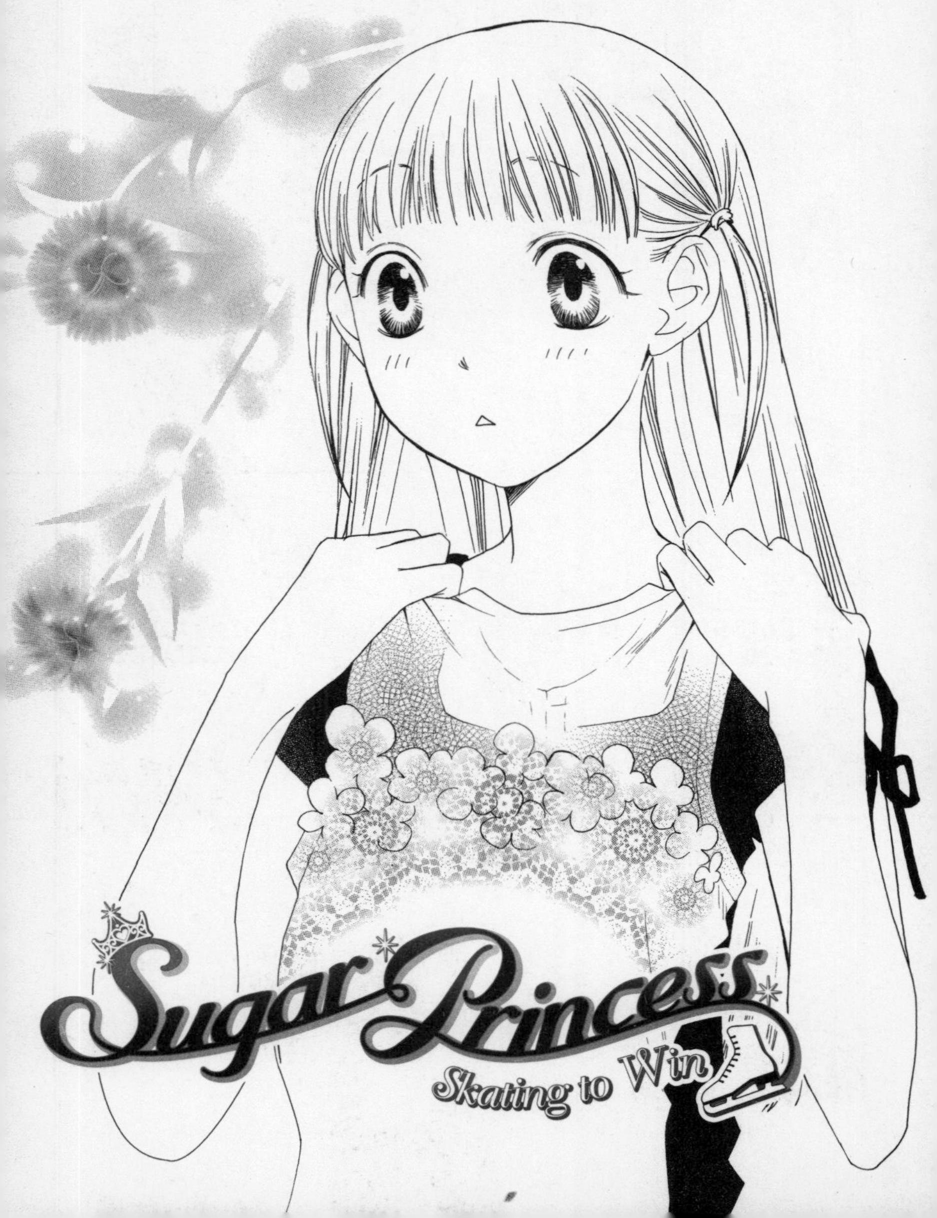
Sugar Princess
Skating to Win

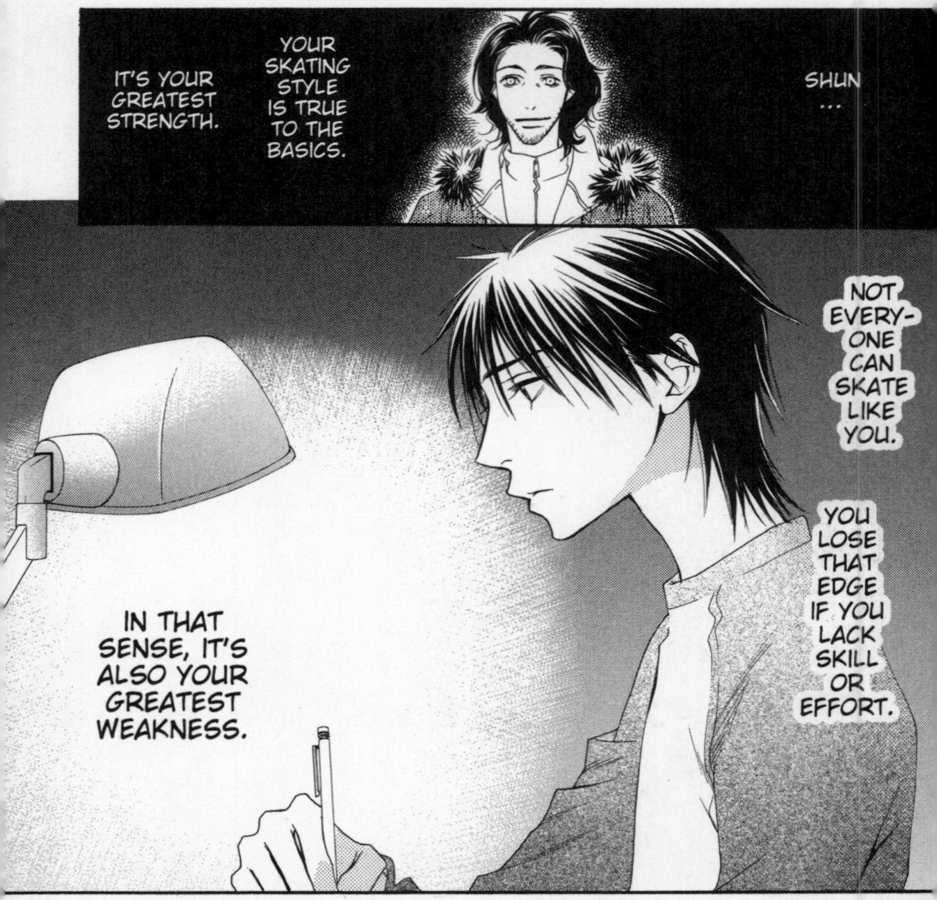
SHUN ...
YOUR SKATING STYLE IS TRUE TO THE BASICS.
IT'S YOUR GREATEST STRENGTH.
NOT EVERY-ONE CAN SKATE LIKE YOU.
YOU LOSE THAT EDGE IF YOU LACK SKILL OR EFFORT.
IN THAT SENSE, IT'S ALSO YOUR GREATEST WEAKNESS.

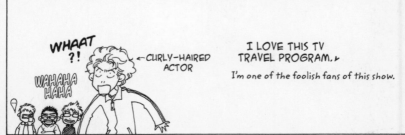

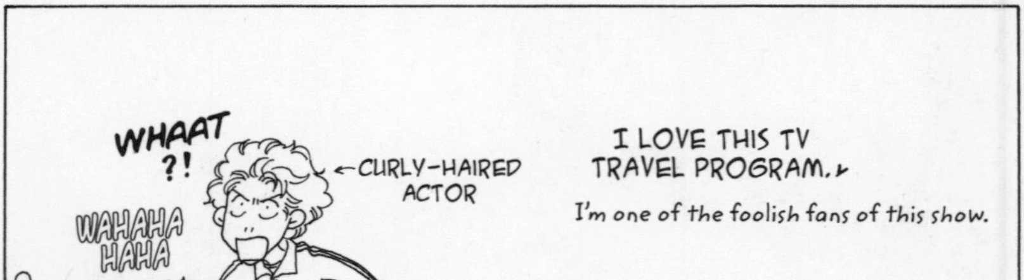
I LOVE THIS TV TRAVEL PROGRAM.
I'm one of the foolish fans of this show.
WHAAT ?!
←CURLY-HAIRED ACTOR
WAHAHA HAHA
...

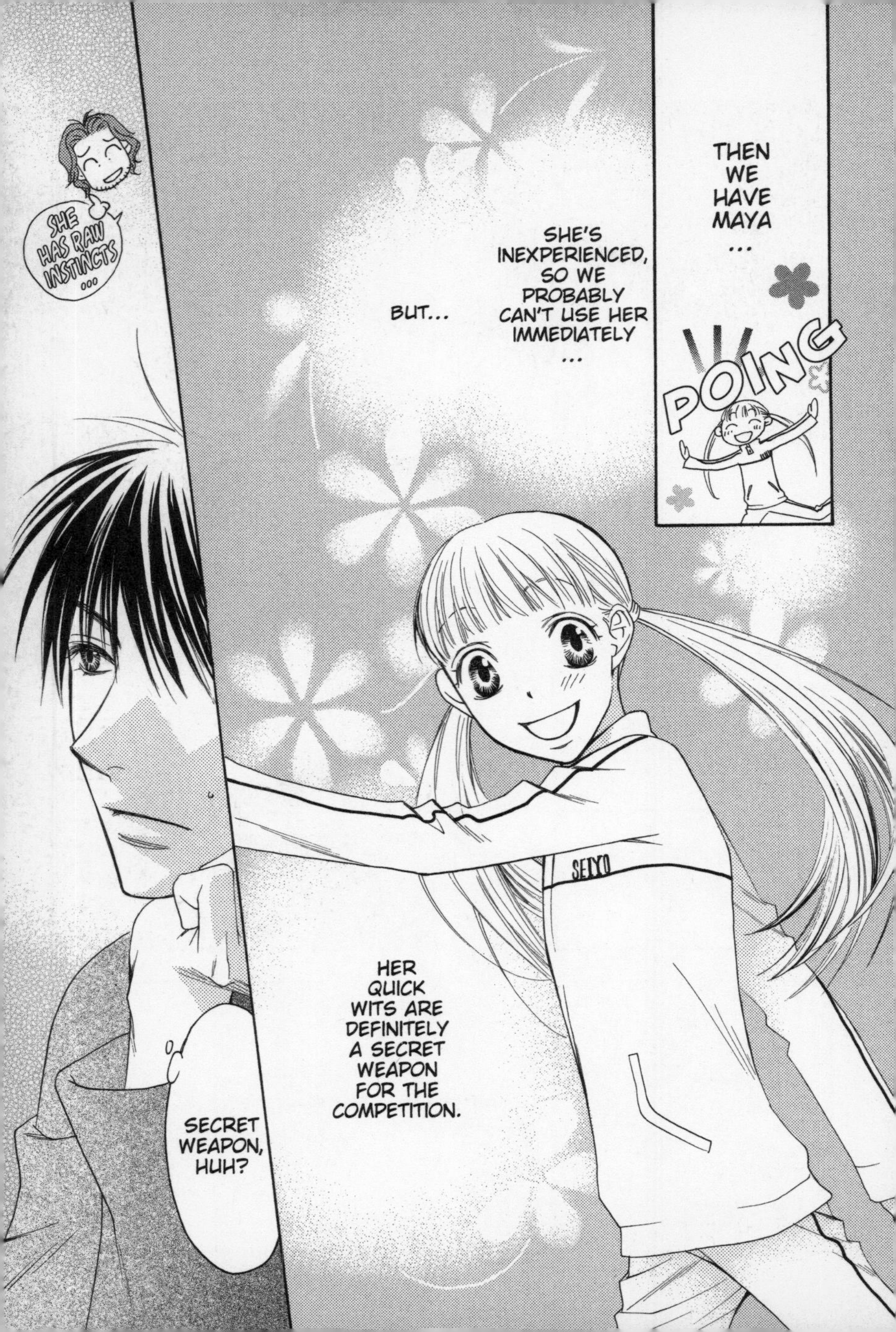
THEN WE HAVE MAYA ...
POING
SHE'S INEXPERIENCED, SO WE PROBABLY CAN'T USE HER IMMEDIATELY ...
BUT...
SHE HAS RAW INSTINCTS ...
HER QUICK WITS ARE DEFINITELY A SECRET WEAPON FOR THE COMPETITION.
SECRET WEAPON, HUH?
SEIYO

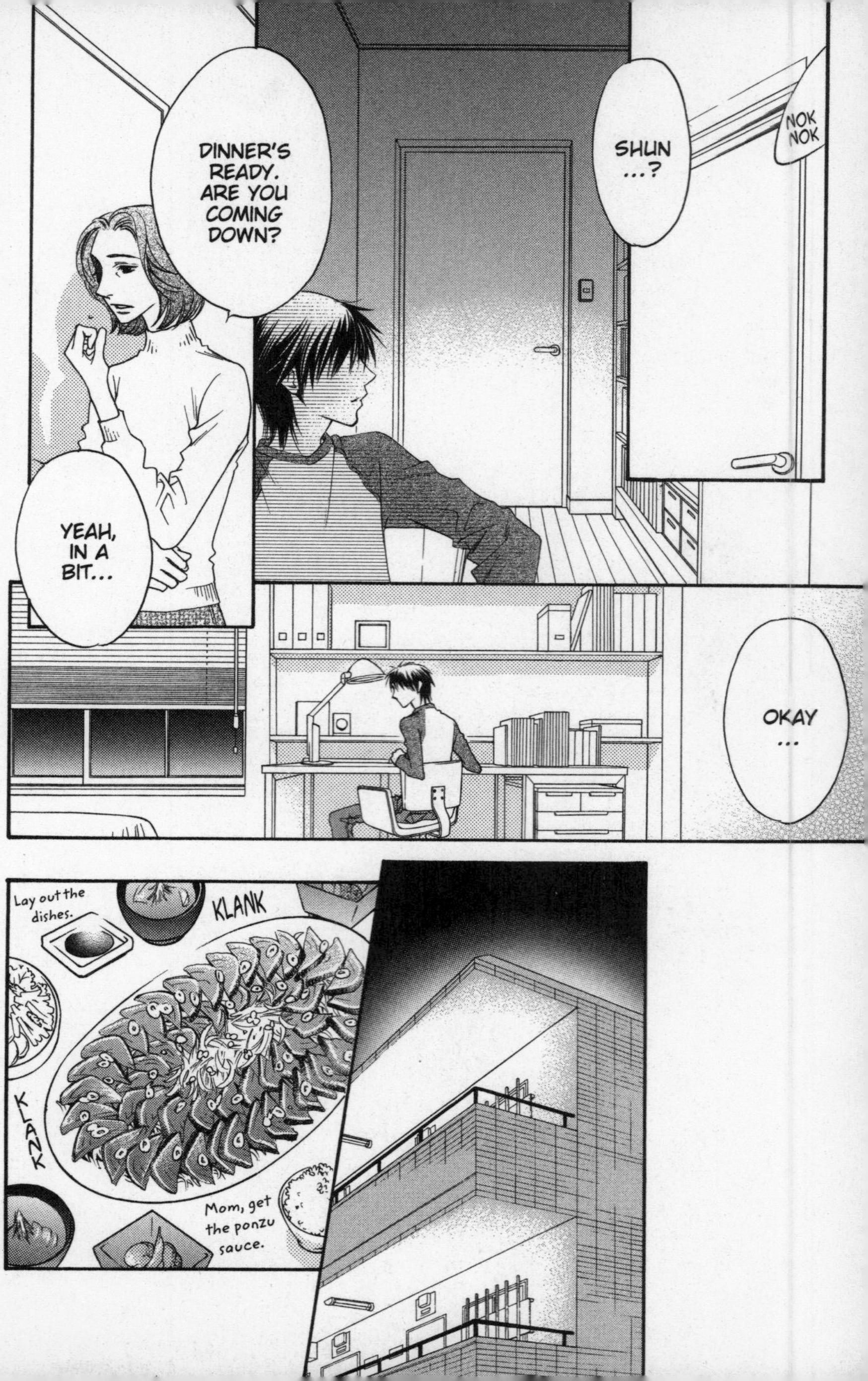
NOK NOK
SHUN ...?
DINNER'S READY. ARE YOU COMING DOWN?
YEAH, IN A BIT...
OKAY ...
KLANK
Lay out the dishes.
KLANK
Mom, get the ponzu sauce.

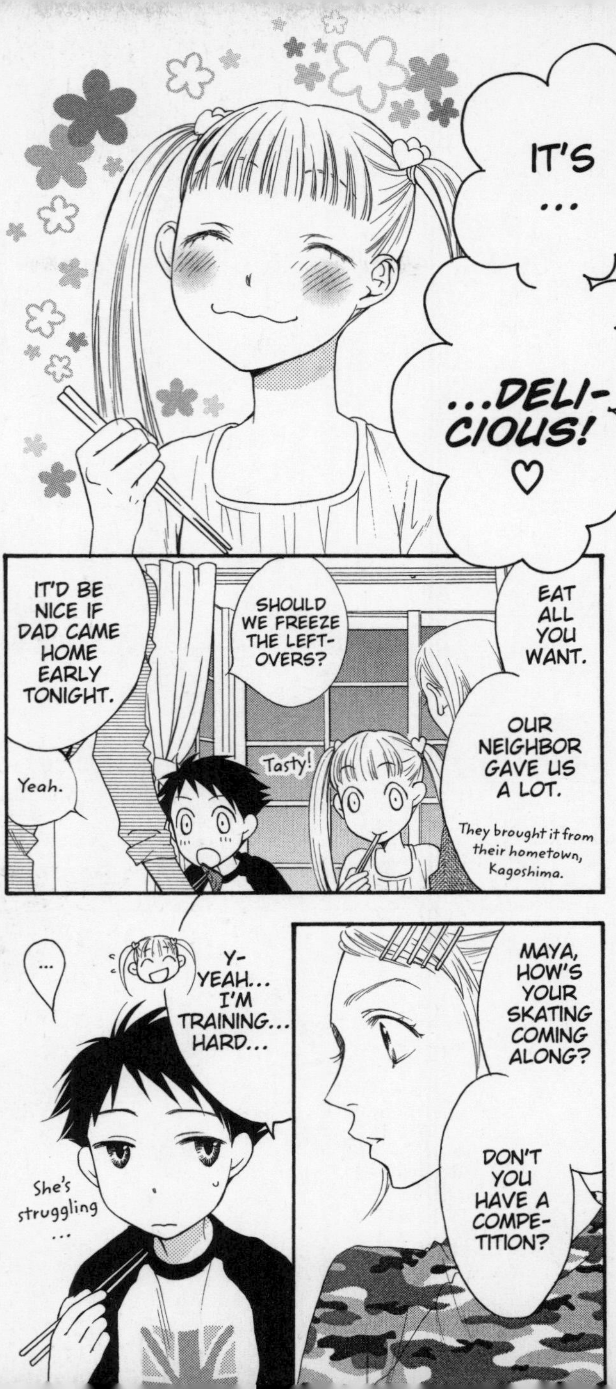
IT'S ...
...DELI-CIOUS! ♡
EAT ALL YOU WANT.
OUR NEIGHBOR GAVE US A LOT.
They brought it from their hometown, Kagoshima.
SHOULD WE FREEZE THE LEFT-OVERS?
Tasty!
IT'D BE NICE IF DAD CAME HOME EARLY TONIGHT.
Yeah.
MAYA, HOW'S YOUR SKATING COMING ALONG?
DON'T YOU HAVE A COMPETITION?
Y-YEAH... I'M TRAINING... HARD...
...
She's struggling ...

THE PERSON WHO NAMED HIM SHUN...

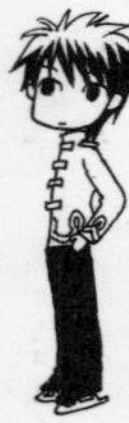

...WAS MY PREVIOUS EDITOR.

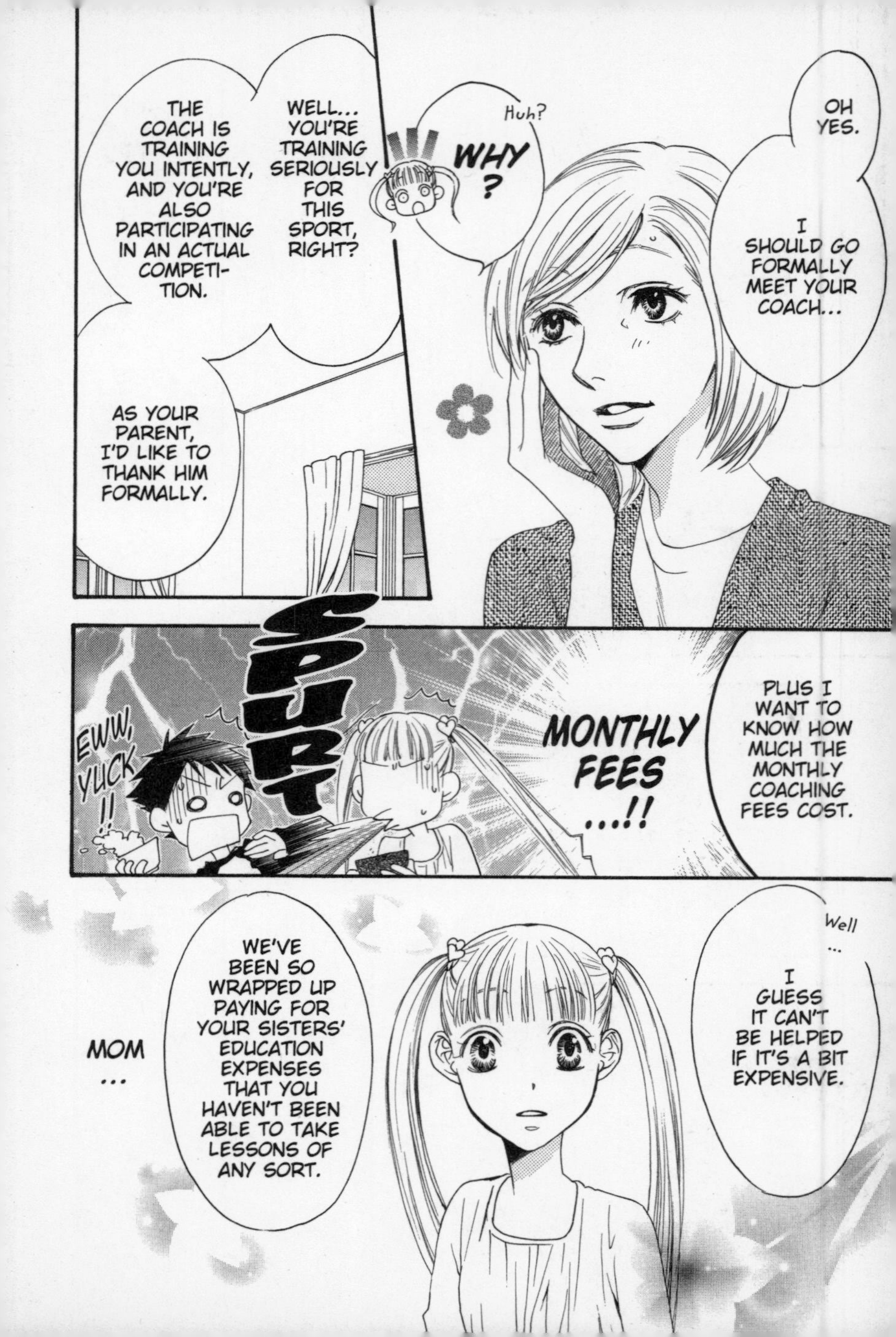
OH YES.
I SHOULD GO FORMALLY MEET YOUR COACH...
Huh?
WHY?
WELL... YOU'RE TRAINING SERIOUSLY FOR THIS SPORT, RIGHT?
THE COACH IS TRAINING YOU INTENTLY, AND YOU'RE ALSO PARTICIPATING IN AN ACTUAL COMPETITION.
AS YOUR PARENT, I'D LIKE TO THANK HIM FORMALLY.
PLUS I WANT TO KNOW HOW MUCH THE MONTHLY COACHING FEES COST.
MONTHLY FEES ...!!
SPURT
EWW, YUCK !!
Well...
I GUESS IT CAN'T BE HELPED IF IT'S A BIT EXPENSIVE.
WE'VE BEEN SO WRAPPED UP PAYING FOR YOUR SISTERS' EDUCATION EXPENSES THAT YOU HAVEN'T BEEN ABLE TO TAKE LESSONS OF ANY SORT.
MOM...

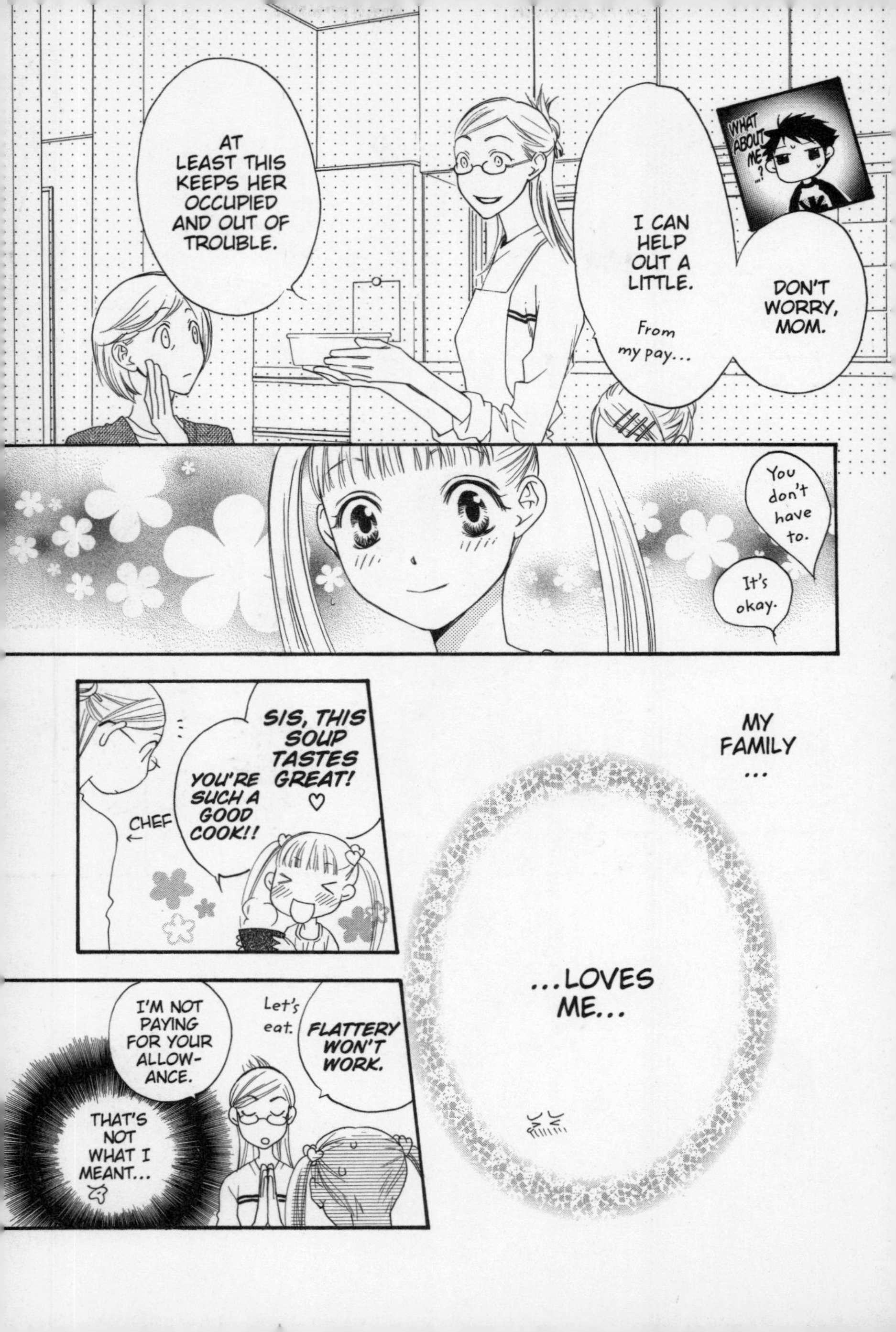
WHAT ABOUT ME...?
DON'T WORRY, MOM.
I CAN HELP OUT A LITTLE.
From my pay...
AT LEAST THIS KEEPS HER OCCUPIED AND OUT OF TROUBLE.
You don't have to.
It's okay.
MY FAMILY...
...LOVES ME...
SIS, THIS SOUP TASTES GREAT! ♡
YOU'RE SUCH A GOOD COOK!!
CHEF
FLATTERY WON'T WORK.
Let's eat.
I'M NOT PAYING FOR YOUR ALLOWANCE.
THAT'S NOT WHAT I MEANT...

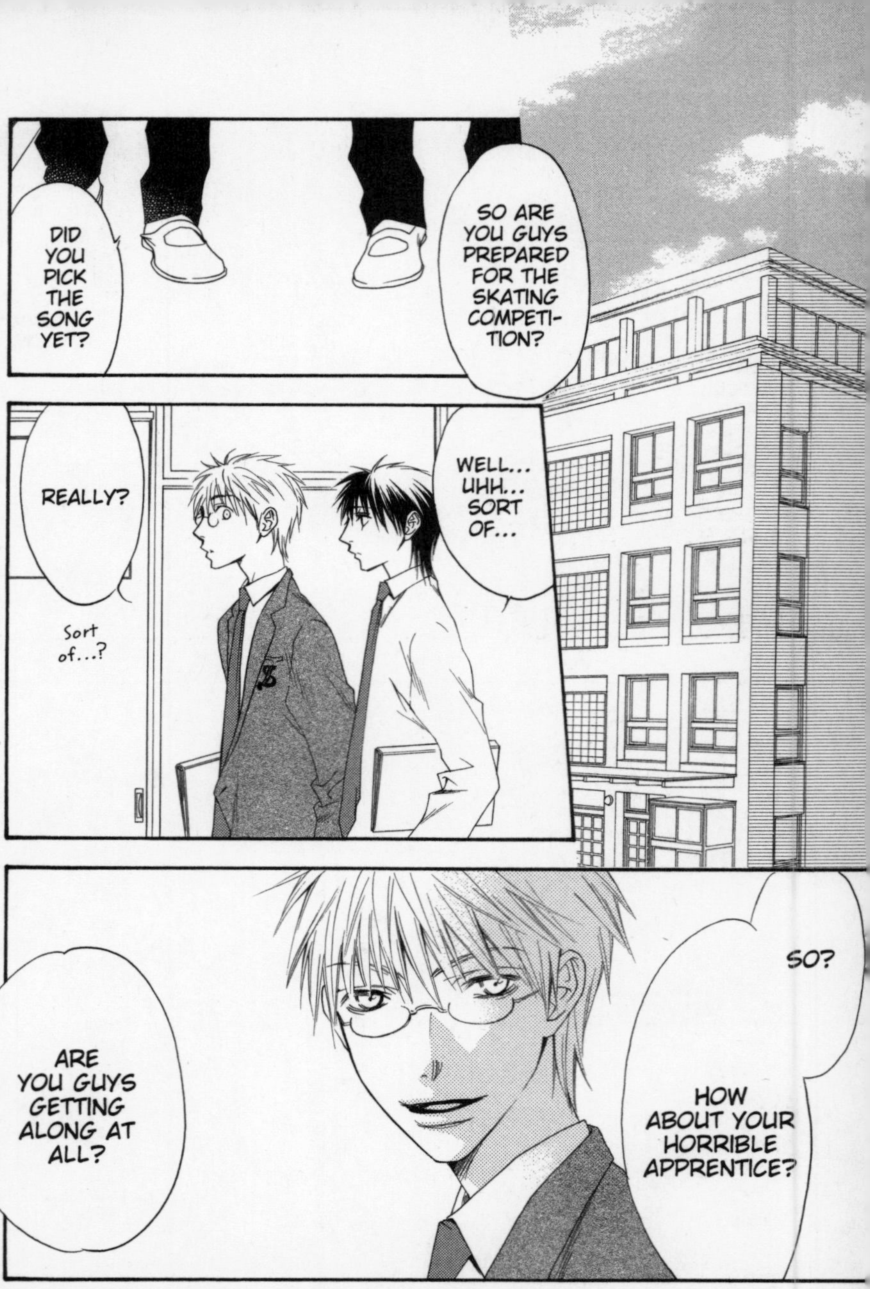
SO ARE YOU GUYS PREPARED FOR THE SKATING COMPETITION?
DID YOU PICK THE SONG YET?
WELL... UHH... SORT OF...
REALLY?
Sort of...?
SO?
HOW ABOUT YOUR HORRIBLE APPRENTICE?
ARE YOU GUYS GETTING ALONG AT ALL?

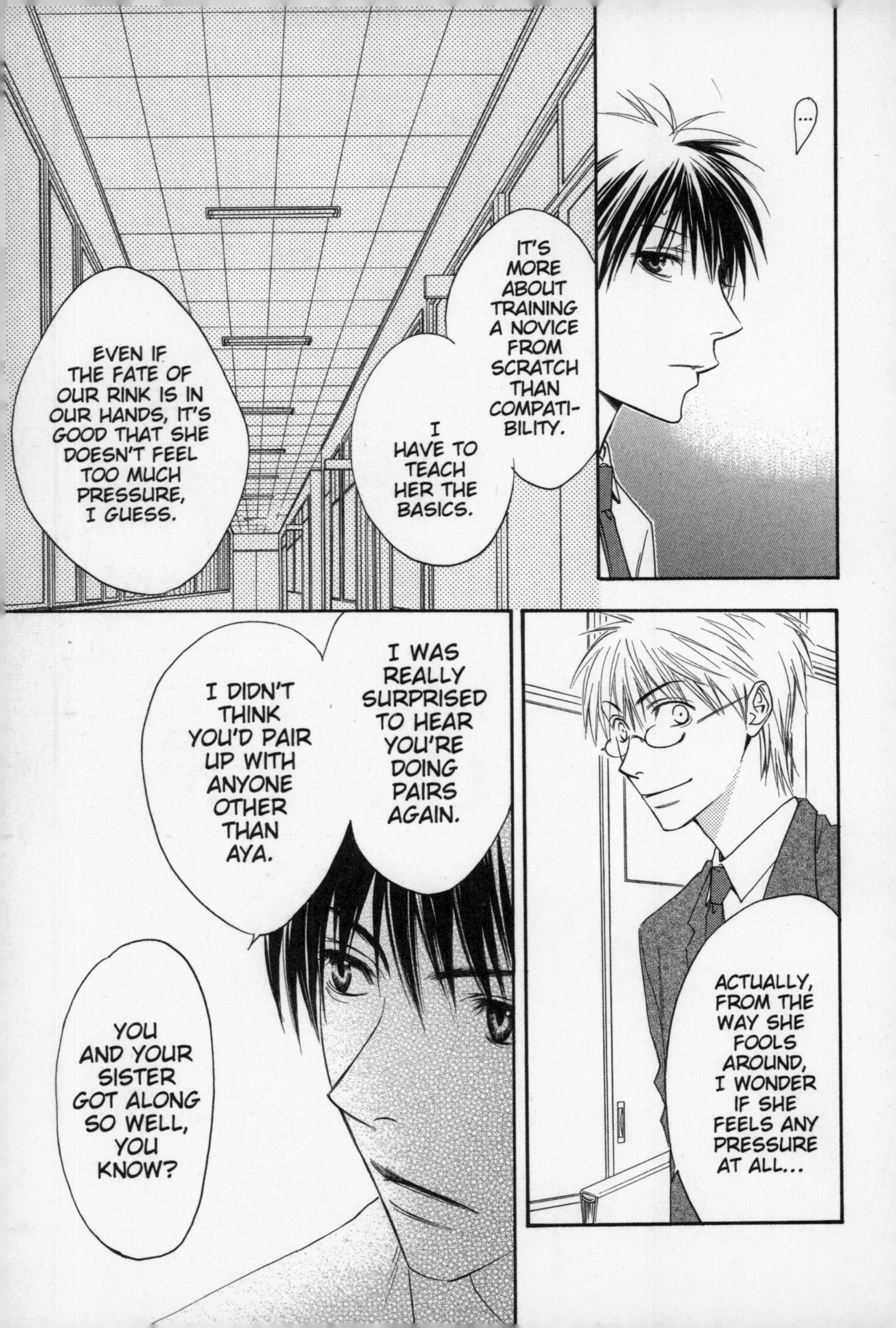
...
IT'S MORE ABOUT TRAINING A NOVICE FROM SCRATCH THAN COMPATI-BILITY.
I HAVE TO TEACH HER THE BASICS.
EVEN IF THE FATE OF OUR RINK IS IN OUR HANDS, IT'S GOOD THAT SHE DOESN'T FEEL TOO MUCH PRESSURE, I GUESS.
ACTUALLY, FROM THE WAY SHE FOOLS AROUND, I WONDER IF SHE FEELS ANY PRESSURE AT ALL...
I WAS REALLY SURPRISED TO HEAR YOU'RE DOING PAIRS AGAIN.
I DIDN'T THINK YOU'D PAIR UP WITH ANYONE OTHER THAN AYA.
YOU AND YOUR SISTER GOT ALONG SO WELL, YOU KNOW?

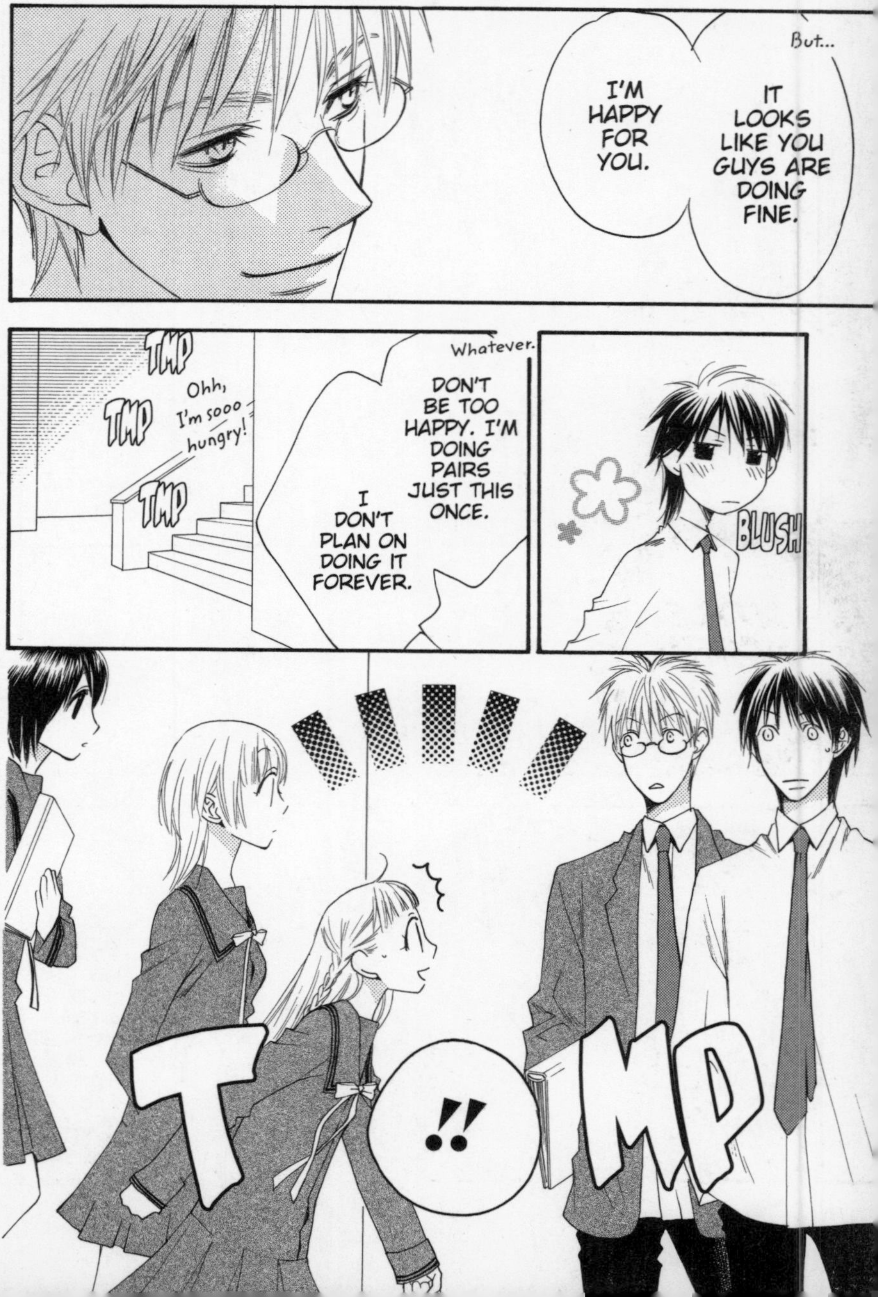
But...
IT LOOKS LIKE YOU GUYS ARE DOING FINE.
I'M HAPPY FOR YOU.
BLUSH
Whatever.
DON'T BE TOO HAPPY. I'M DOING PAIRS JUST THIS ONCE.
I DON'T PLAN ON DOING IT FOREVER.
TMP
Ohh, I'm sooo hungry!
TMP
TMP
TOMP!!

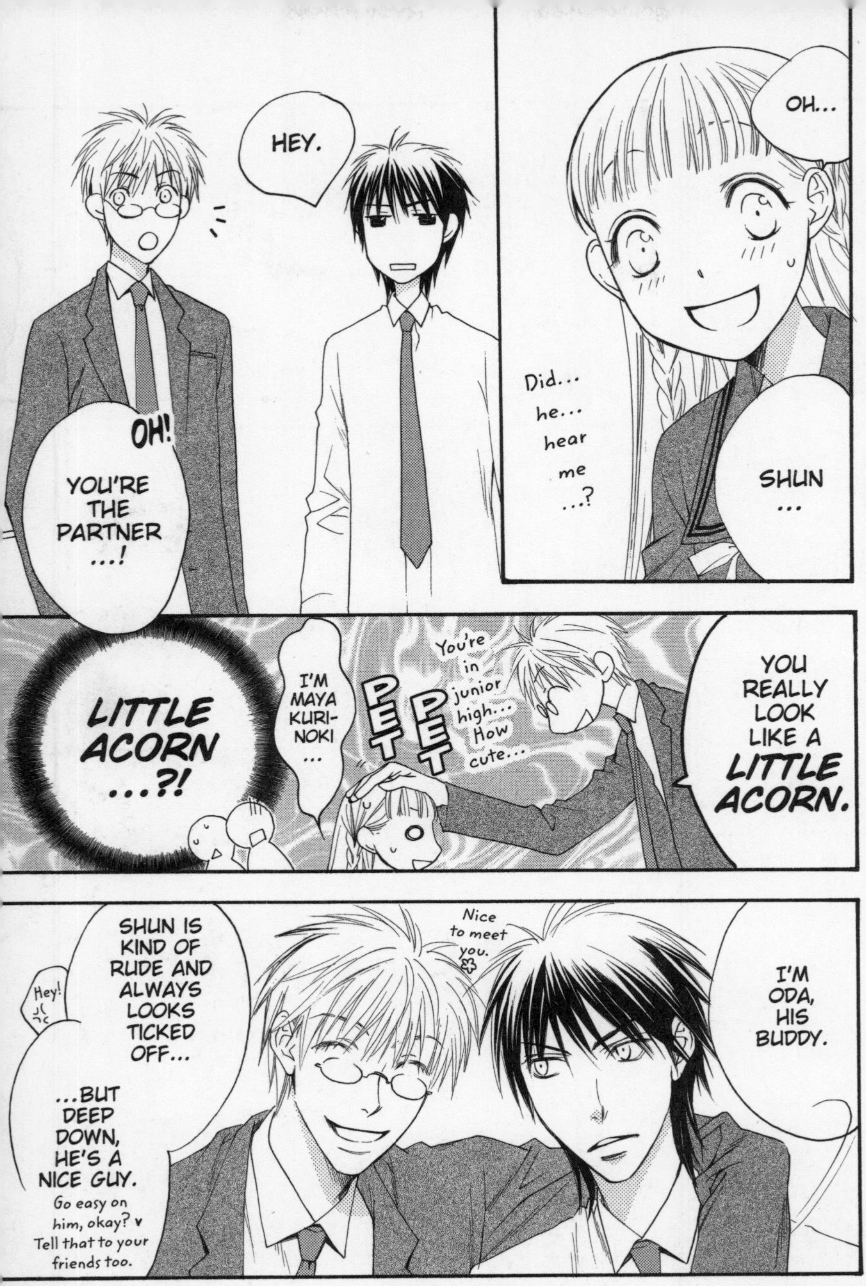
OH...
SHUN ...
Did... he... hear me ...?
HEY.
OH!
YOU'RE THE PARTNER ...!
YOU REALLY LOOK LIKE A LITTLE ACORN.
You're in junior high... How cute...
PET PET
I'M MAYA KURI-NOKI ...
LITTLE ACORN ...?!
I'M ODA, HIS BUDDY.
Nice to meet you.
SHUN IS KIND OF RUDE AND ALWAYS LOOKS TICKED OFF...
...BUT DEEP DOWN, HE'S A NICE GUY.
Go easy on him, okay? Tell that to your friends too.
Hey!

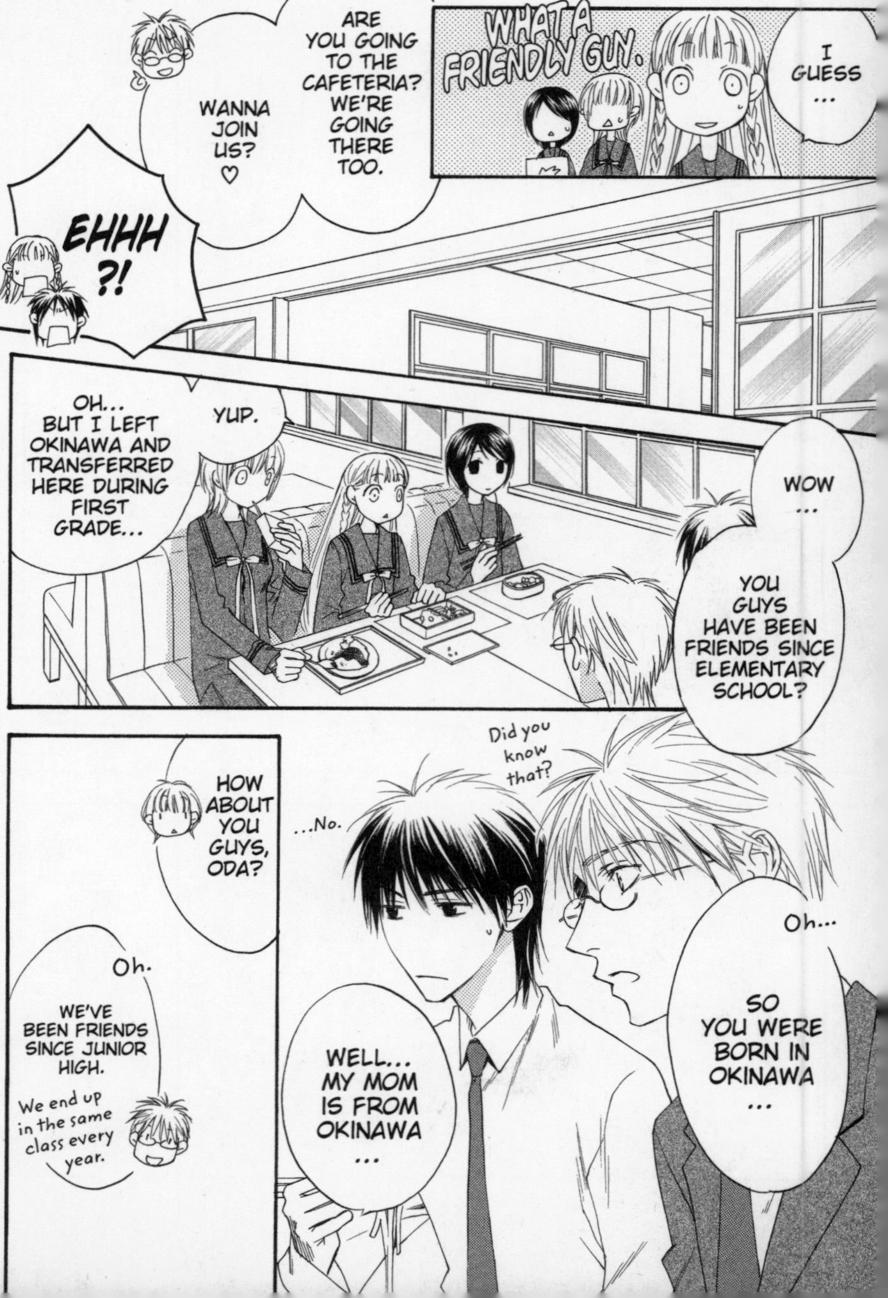
I GUESS...
WHAT A FRIENDLY GUY.
ARE YOU GOING TO THE CAFETERIA? WE'RE GOING THERE TOO.
WANNA JOIN US? ♡
EHHH?!
WOW... YOU GUYS HAVE BEEN FRIENDS SINCE ELEMENTARY SCHOOL?
YUP.
OH... BUT I LEFT OKINAWA AND TRANSFERRED HERE DURING FIRST GRADE...
Did you know that?
...No.
Oh...
SO YOU WERE BORN IN OKINAWA...
WELL... MY MOM IS FROM OKINAWA...
HOW ABOUT YOU GUYS, ODA?
Oh.
WE'VE BEEN FRIENDS SINCE JUNIOR HIGH.
We end up in the same class every year.

Chapter 11

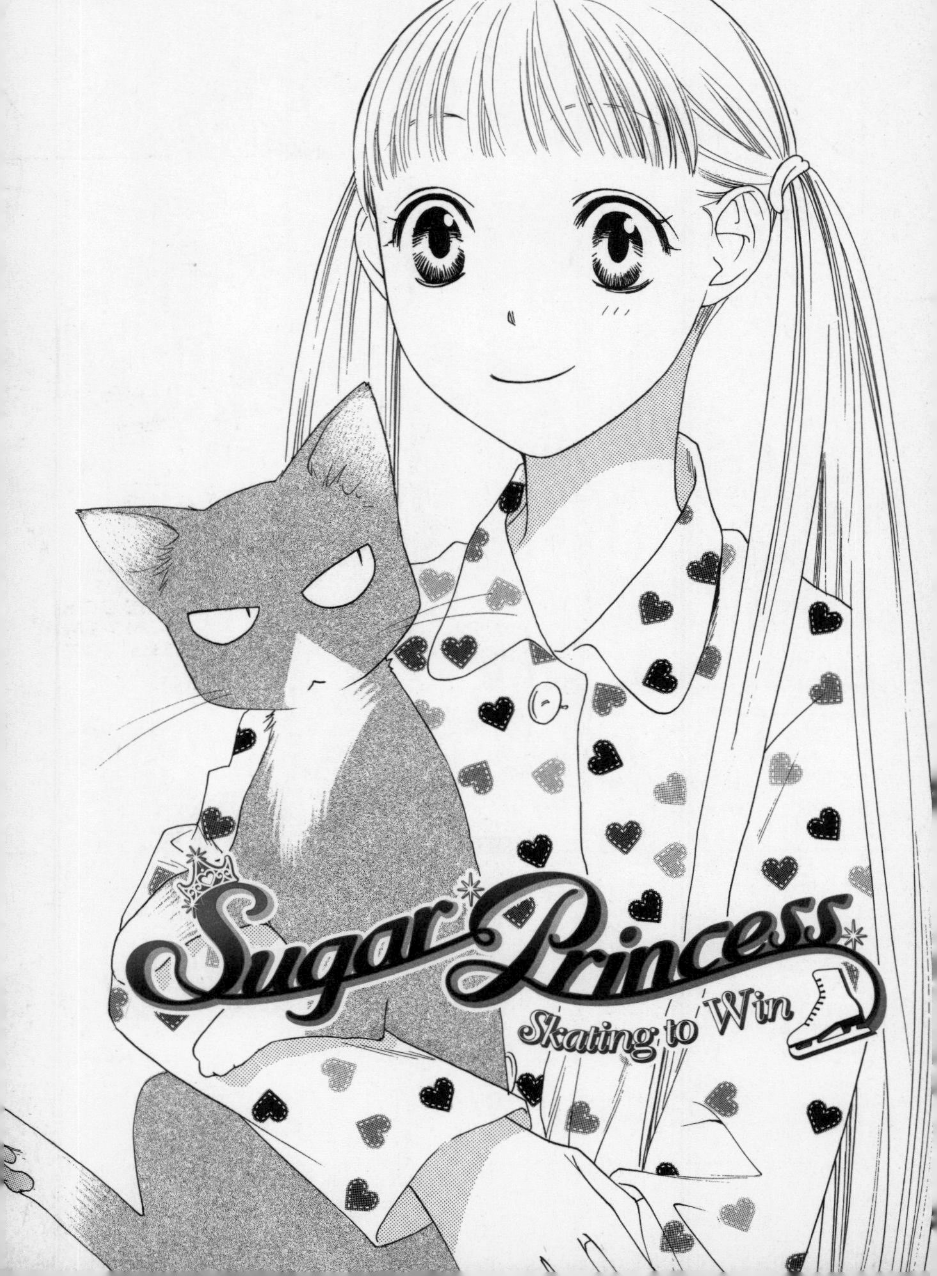
Sugar Princess
Skating to Win

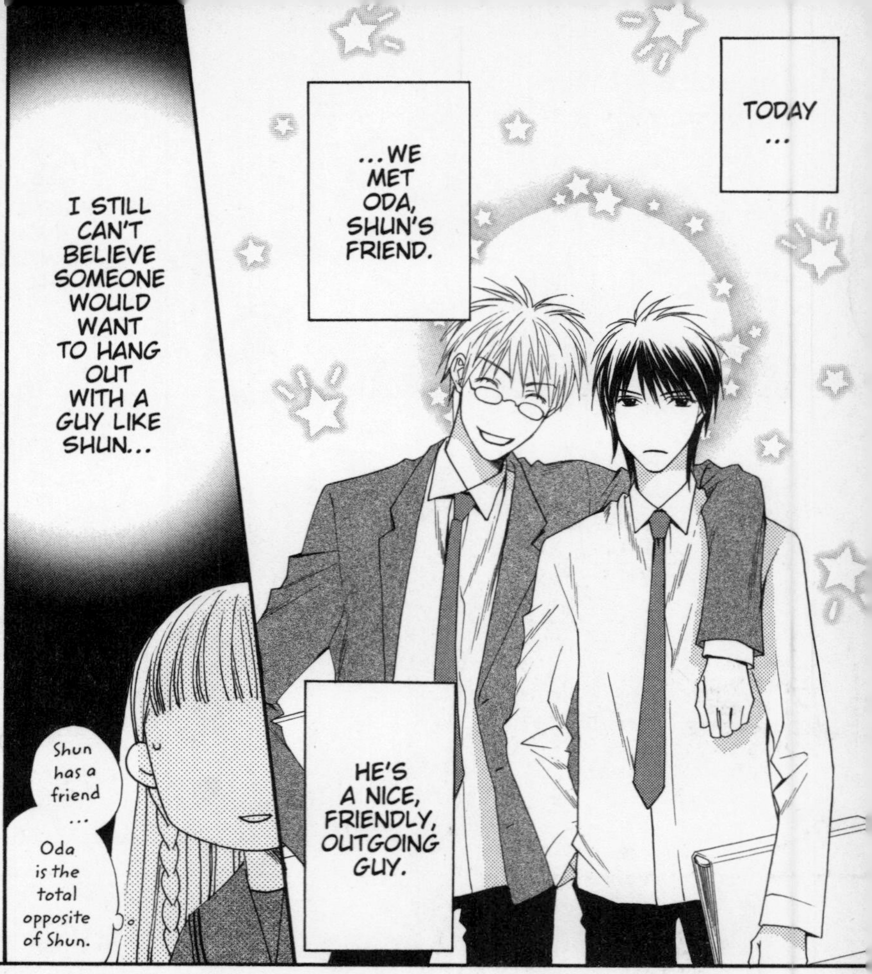
TODAY...
...WE MET ODA, SHUN'S FRIEND.
I STILL CAN'T BELIEVE SOMEONE WOULD WANT TO HANG OUT WITH A GUY LIKE SHUN...
HE'S A NICE, FRIENDLY, OUTGOING GUY.
Shun has a friend... Oda is the total opposite of Shun.

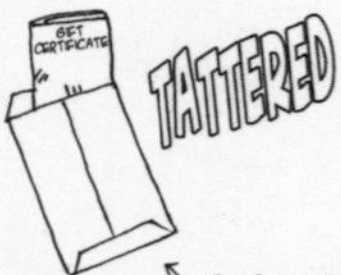
GIFT CERTIFICATE
TATTERED

WHEN I WAS A CHILD, ONE OF MY RELATIVES USED TO GIVE ME TATTERED GIFT CERTIFICATES TO BUY BOOKS* FOR NEW YEAR'S...

In fact, I received them for two or three years in a row...

*Adults usually give cash gifts to children on New Year's.

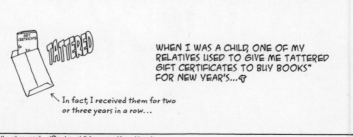

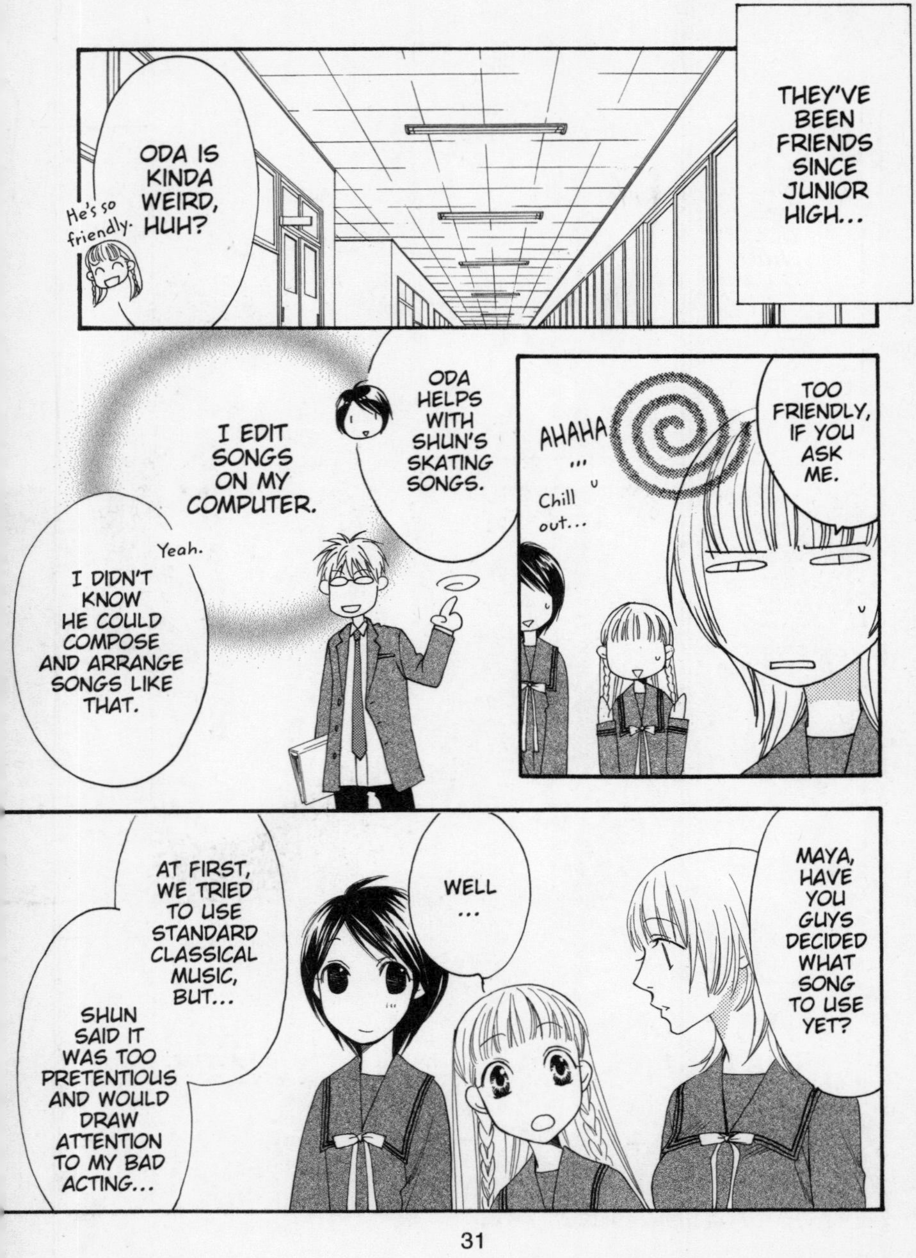
THEY'VE BEEN FRIENDS SINCE JUNIOR HIGH...
ODA IS KINDA WEIRD, HUH?
He's so friendly.
TOO FRIENDLY, IF YOU ASK ME.
AHAHA ...
Chill out...
ODA HELPS WITH SHUN'S SKATING SONGS.
I EDIT SONGS ON MY COMPUTER.
Yeah.
I DIDN'T KNOW HE COULD COMPOSE AND ARRANGE SONGS LIKE THAT.
MAYA, HAVE YOU GUYS DECIDED WHAT SONG TO USE YET?
WELL ...
AT FIRST, WE TRIED TO USE STANDARD CLASSICAL MUSIC, BUT...
SHUN SAID IT WAS TOO PRETENTIOUS AND WOULD DRAW ATTENTION TO MY BAD ACTING...

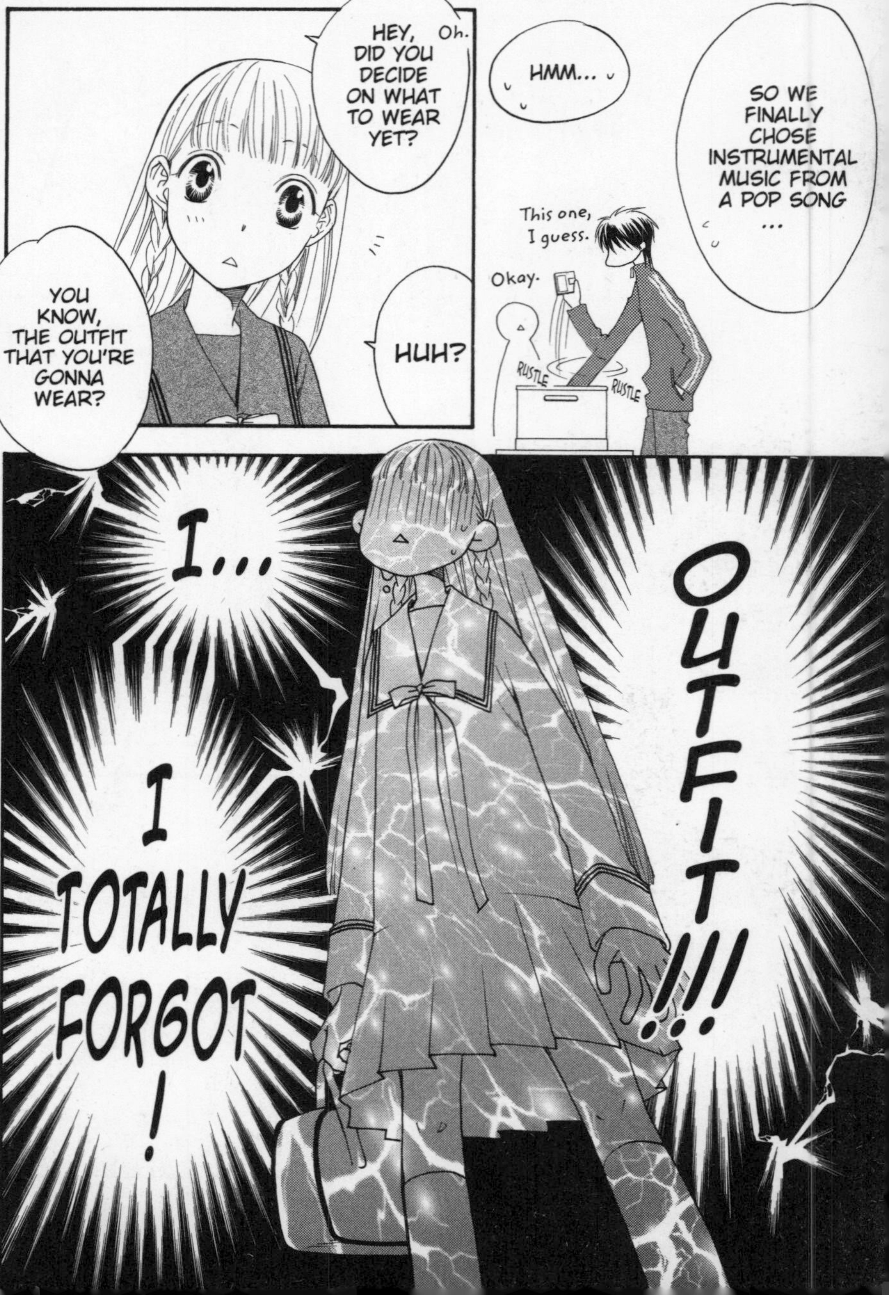
SO WE FINALLY CHOSE INSTRUMENTAL MUSIC FROM A POP SONG ...
HMM...
This one, I guess.
Okay.
RUSTLE
RUSTLE
HEY, DID YOU DECIDE ON WHAT TO WEAR YET?
Oh.
HUH?
YOU KNOW, THE OUTFIT THAT YOU'RE GONNA WEAR?
OUTFIT!!!
I...
I TOTALLY FORGOT!

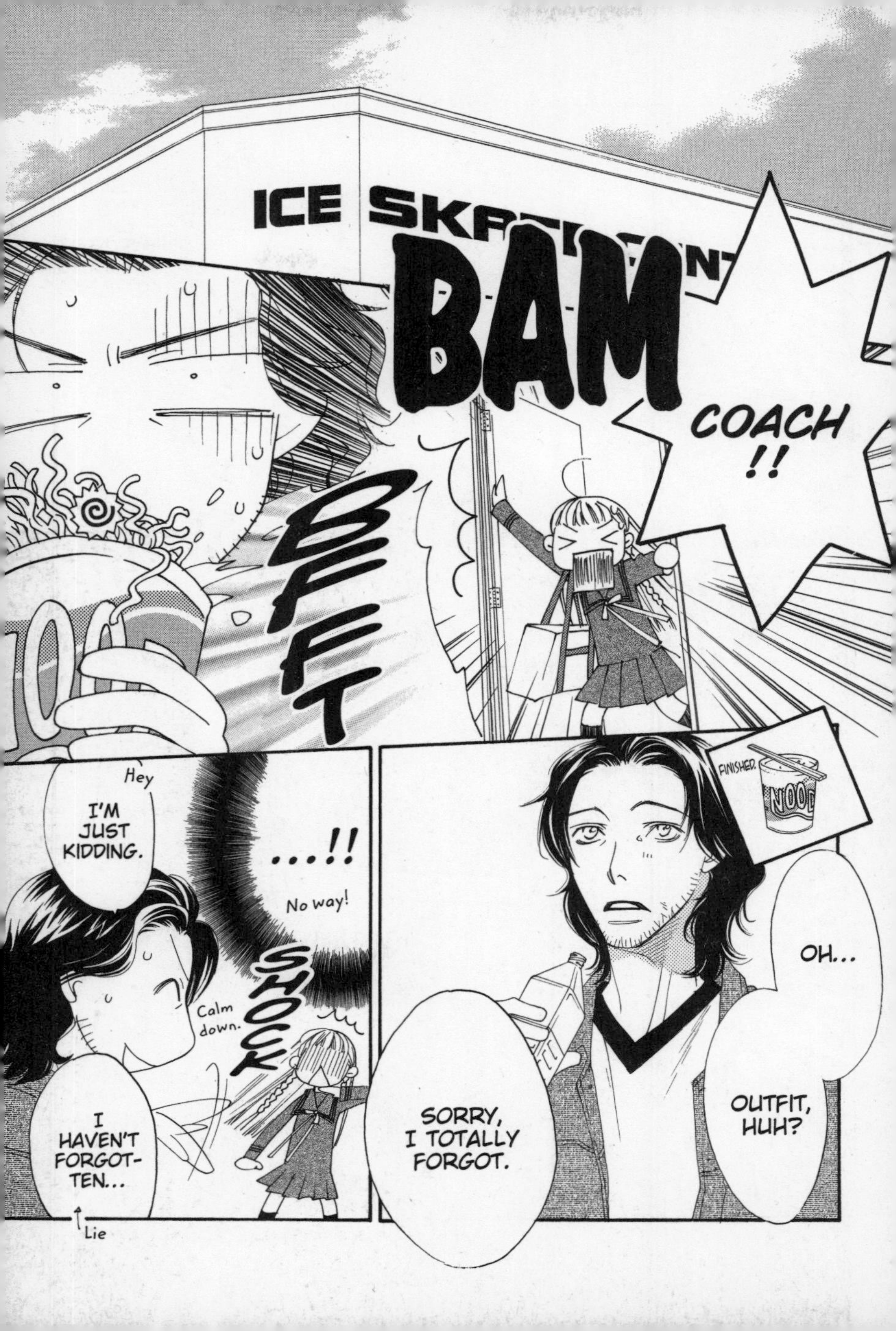

ICE
BAM
COACH !!
BFFT
FINISHED.
OH...
OUTFIT, HUH?
SORRY, I TOTALLY FORGOT.
...!!
No way!
SHOCK
Hey
I'M JUST KIDDING.
Calm down.
I HAVEN'T FORGOT-TEN...
Lie

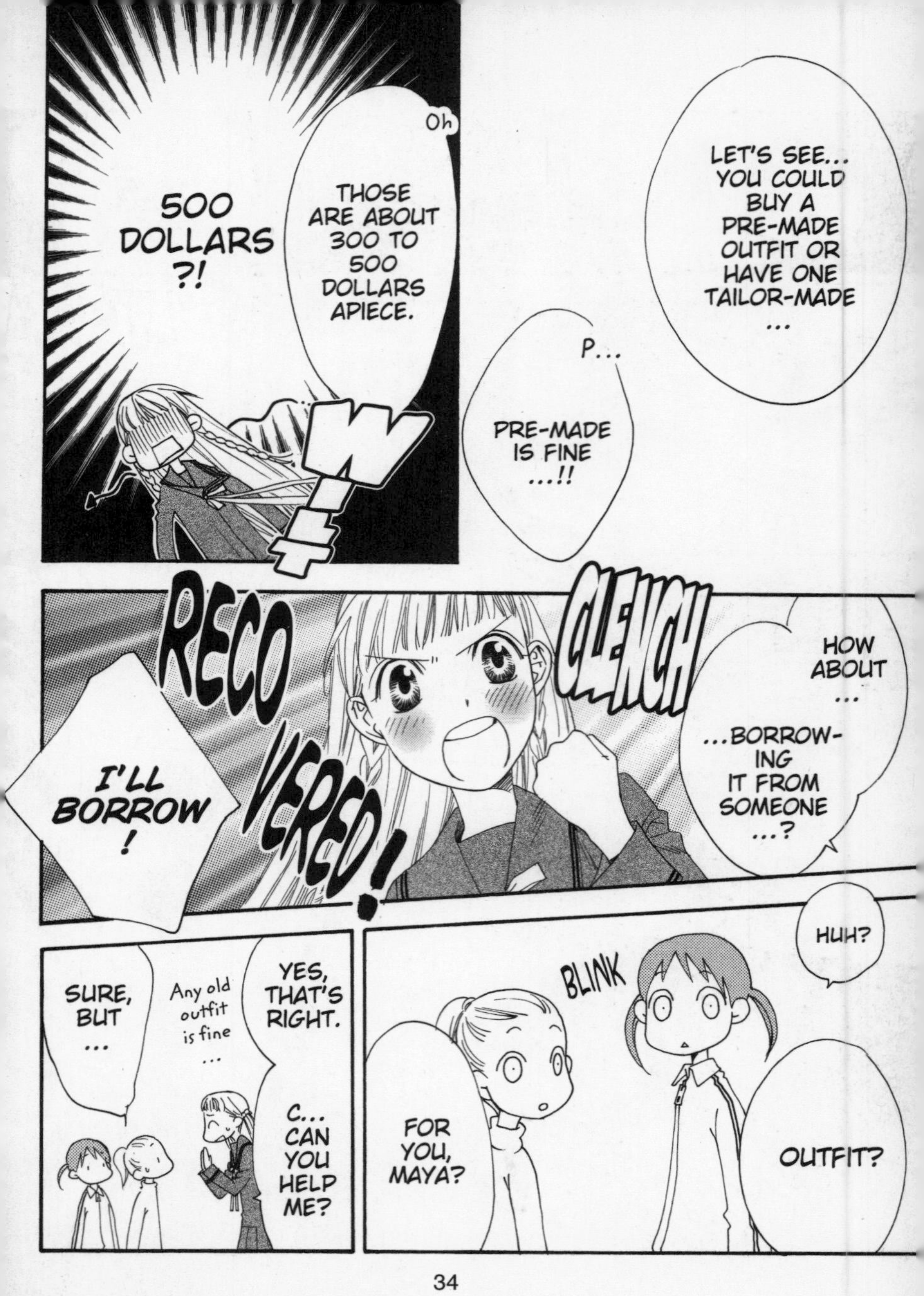
LET'S SEE... YOU COULD BUY A PRE-MADE OUTFIT OR HAVE ONE TAILOR-MADE ...
P...
PRE-MADE IS FINE ...!!
Oh
THOSE ARE ABOUT 300 TO 500 DOLLARS APIECE.
500 DOLLARS ?!
WILT
HOW ABOUT ...
...BORROW-ING IT FROM SOMEONE ...?
CLENCH
RECOVERED!
I'LL BORROW !
HUH?
BLINK
OUTFIT?
FOR YOU, MAYA?
YES, THAT'S RIGHT.
C... CAN YOU HELP ME?
Any old outfit is fine ...
SURE, BUT ...

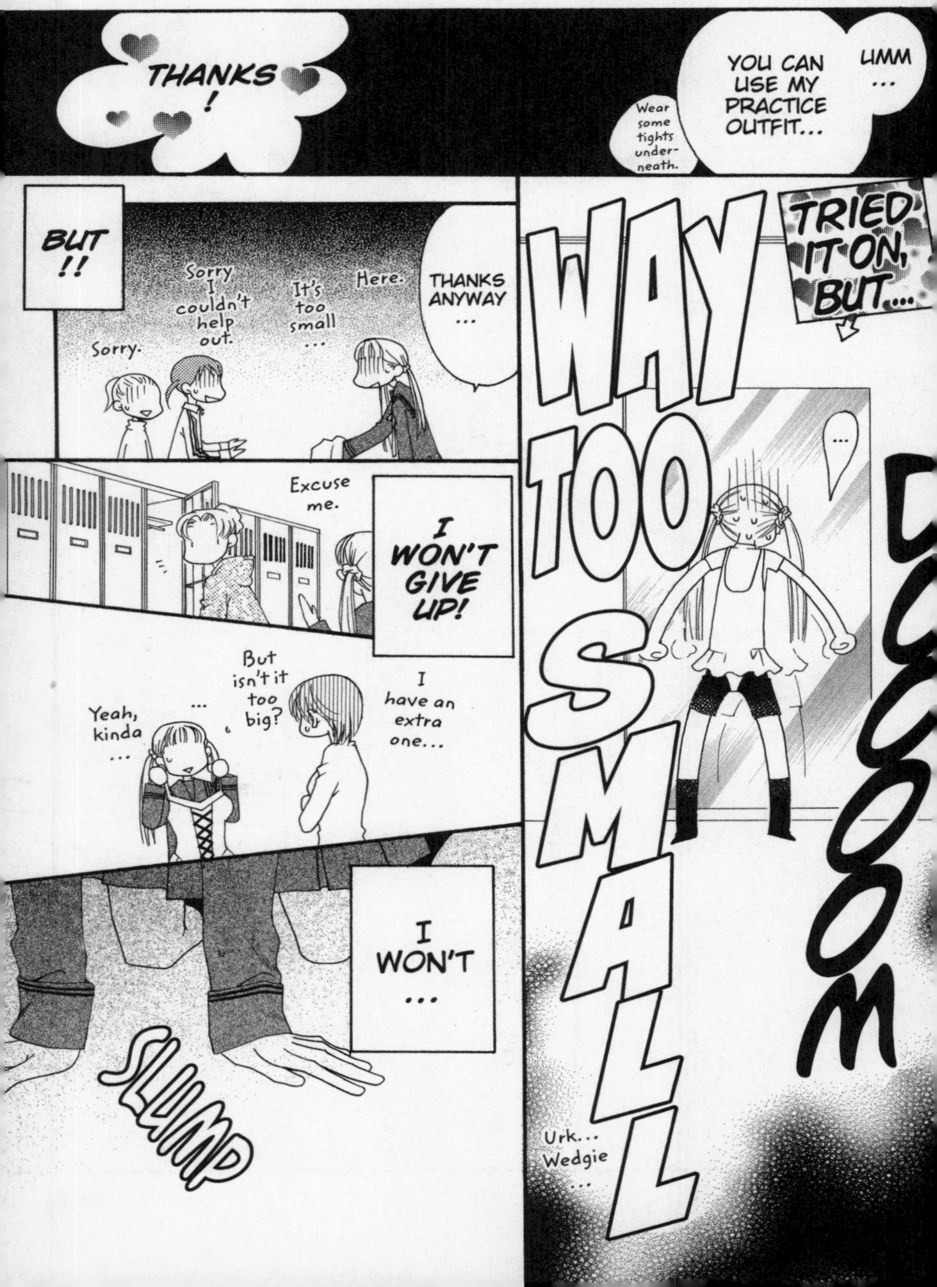
UMM ...
YOU CAN USE MY PRACTICE OUTFIT...
Wear some tights underneath.
THANKS!
TRIED IT ON, BUT...
WAY TOO SMALL
...
DOOOOOM
Urk... Wedgie ...
THANKS ANYWAY ...
Here.
It's too small ...
Sorry I couldn't help out.
Sorry.
BUT!!
I WON'T GIVE UP!
Excuse me.
I have an extra one...
But isn't it too big?
...
Yeah, kinda ...
I WON'T ...
SLUMP

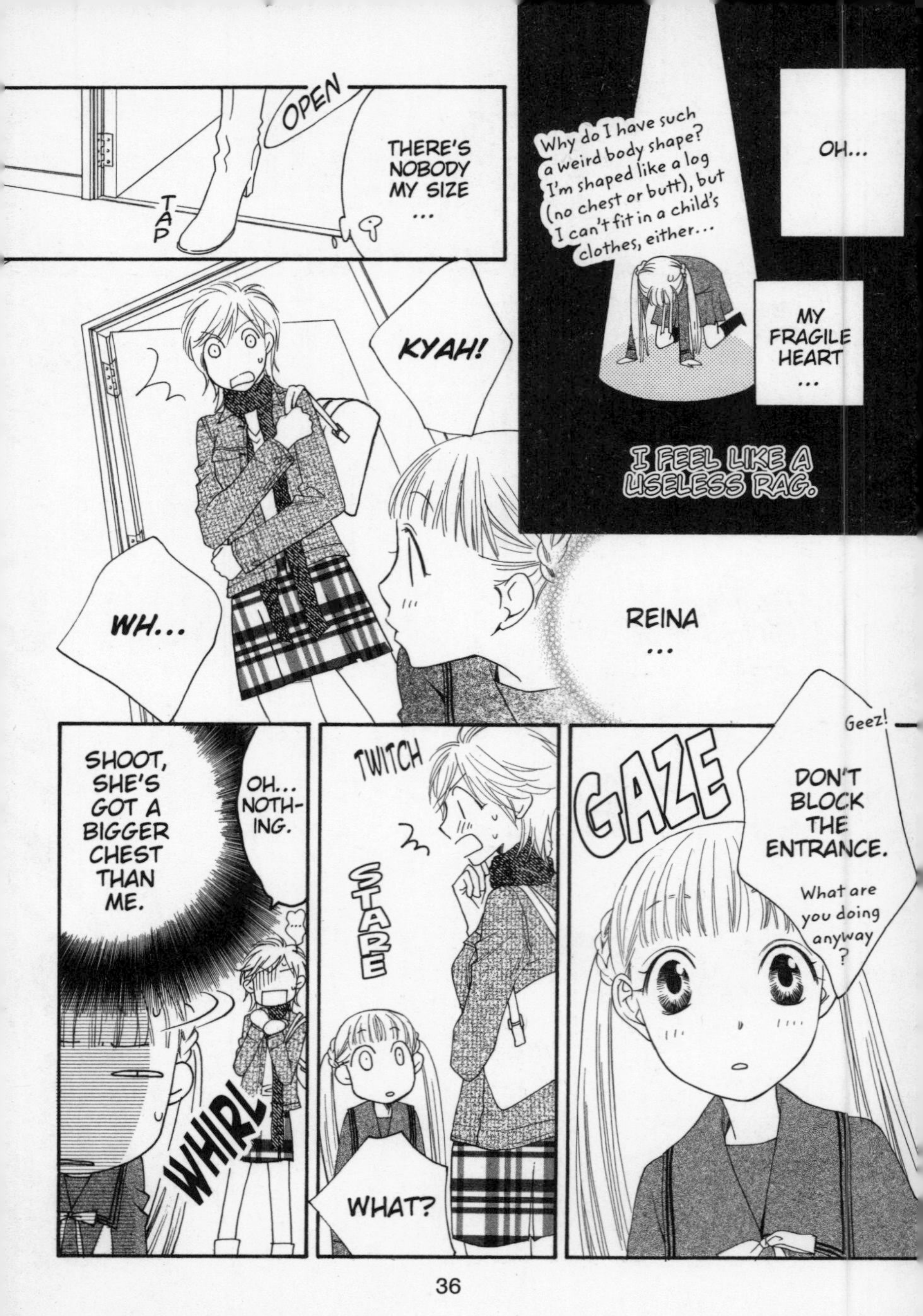
Why do I have such a weird body shape? I'm shaped like a log (no chest or butt), but I can't fit in a child's clothes, either...
OH...
MY FRAGILE HEART ...
I FEEL LIKE A USELESS RAG.
OPEN
THERE'S NOBODY MY SIZE ...
TAP
KYAH!
REINA ...
WH...
GAZE
Geez!
DON'T BLOCK THE ENTRANCE.
What are you doing anyway?
TWITCH
STARE
WHAT?
OH... NOTH-ING.
SHOOT, SHE'S GOT A BIGGER CHEST THAN ME.
WHIRL

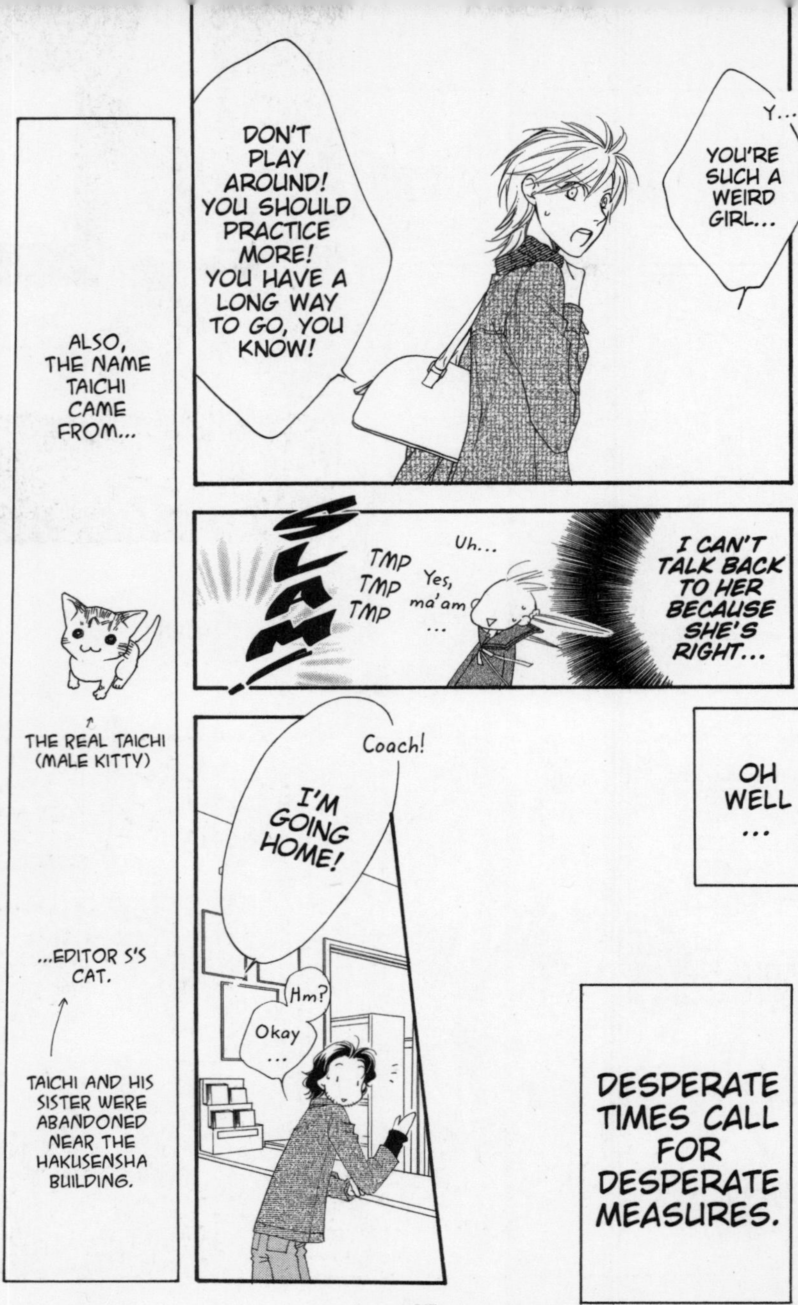
Y...
YOU'RE SUCH A WEIRD GIRL...
DON'T PLAY AROUND! YOU SHOULD PRACTICE MORE! YOU HAVE A LONG WAY TO GO, YOU KNOW!
I CAN'T TALK BACK TO HER BECAUSE SHE'S RIGHT...
Uh...
Yes, ma'am...
TMP TMP TMP
SLAM!
OH WELL...
DESPERATE TIMES CALL FOR DESPERATE MEASURES.
Coach!
I'M GOING HOME!
Hm?
Okay...
ALSO, THE NAME TAICHI CAME FROM...
THE REAL TAICHI (MALE KITTY)
...EDITOR S'S CAT.
TAICHI AND HIS SISTER WERE ABANDONED NEAR THE HAKUSENSHA BUILDING.

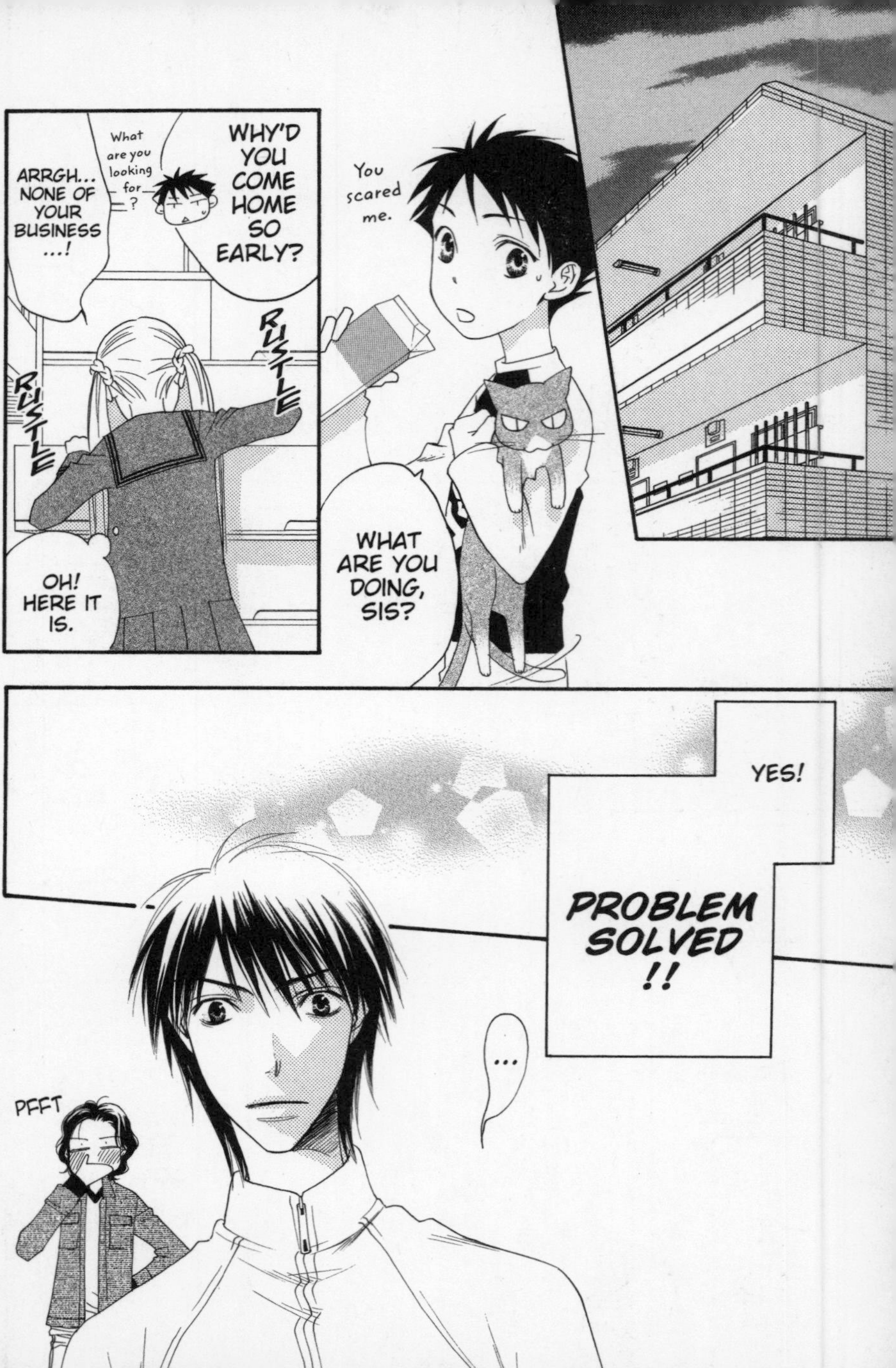
You scared me.
WHAT ARE YOU DOING, SIS?
WHY'D YOU COME HOME SO EARLY?
What are you looking for—?
ARRGH... NONE OF YOUR BUSINESS...!
RUSTLE
RUSTLE
OH! HERE IT IS.
YES!
PROBLEM SOLVED!!
...
PFFT

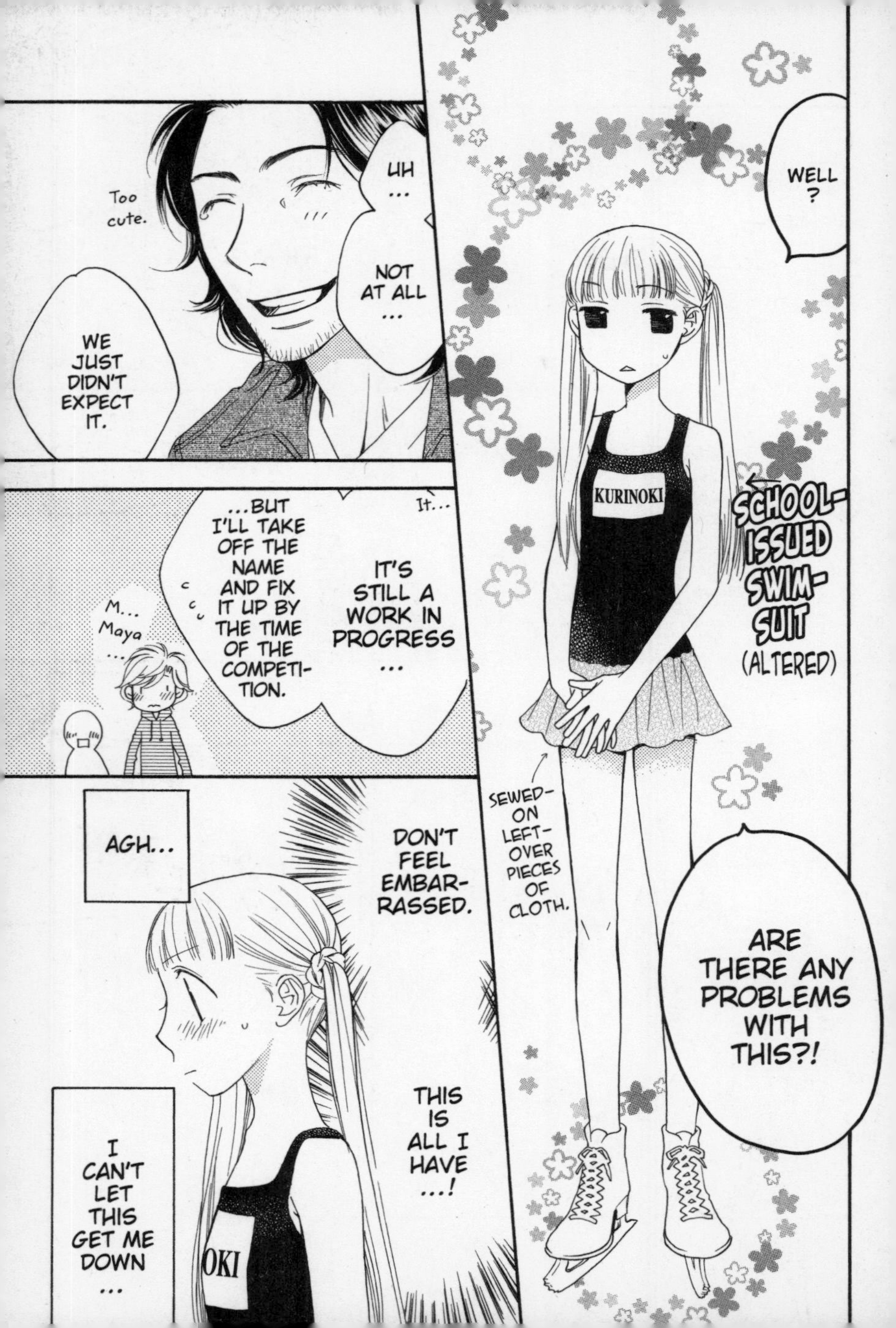
WELL?
KURINOKI
SCHOOL-ISSUED SWIM-SUIT (ALTERED)
SEWED-ON LEFT-OVER PIECES OF CLOTH.
ARE THERE ANY PROBLEMS WITH THIS?!
UH... NOT AT ALL...
Too cute.
WE JUST DIDN'T EXPECT IT.
It...
IT'S STILL A WORK IN PROGRESS...
...BUT I'LL TAKE OFF THE NAME AND FIX IT UP BY THE TIME OF THE COMPETITION.
M... Maya...
DON'T FEEL EMBARRASSED.
AGH...
THIS IS ALL I HAVE...!
I CAN'T LET THIS GET ME DOWN...
OKI

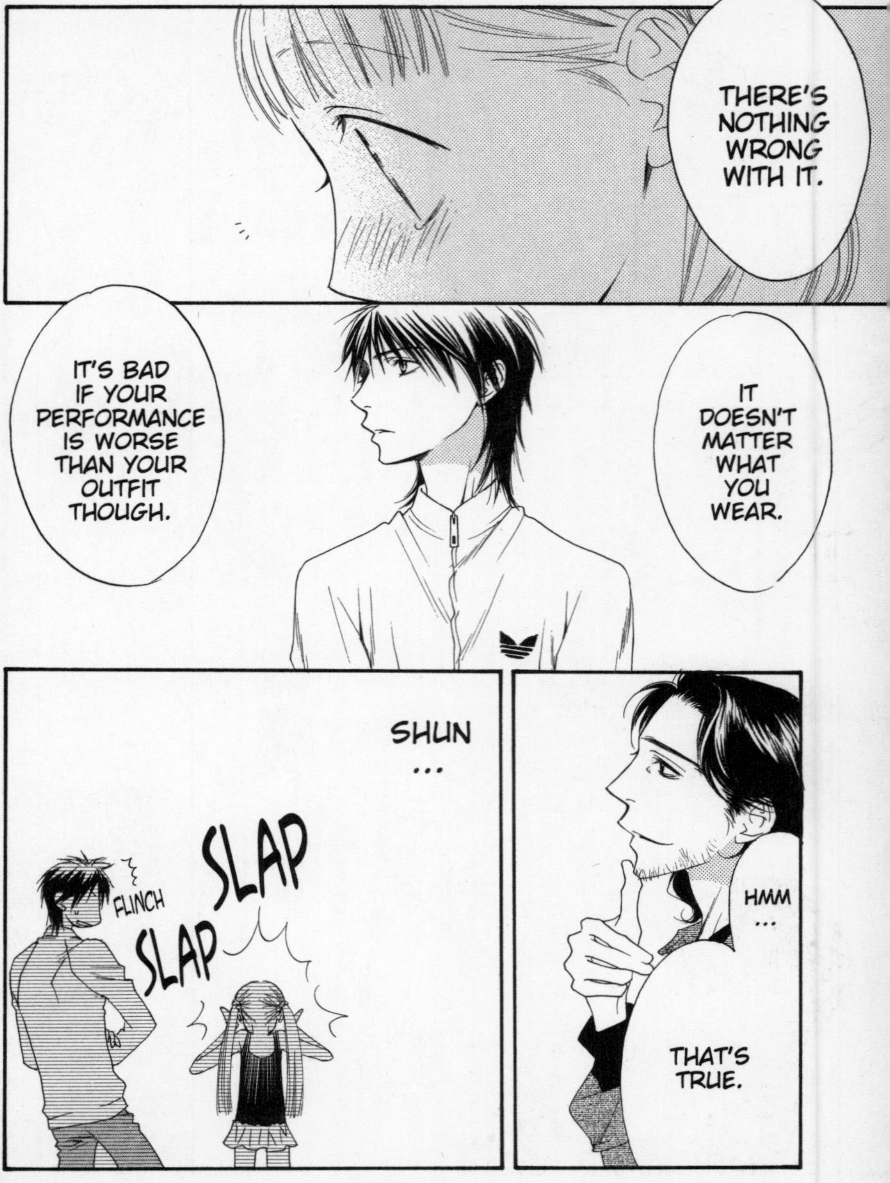
THERE'S NOTHING WRONG WITH IT.
IT DOESN'T MATTER WHAT YOU WEAR.
IT'S BAD IF YOUR PERFORMANCE IS WORSE THAN YOUR OUTFIT THOUGH.
HMM ...
THAT'S TRUE.
SHUN ...
SLAP
SLAP
FLINCH

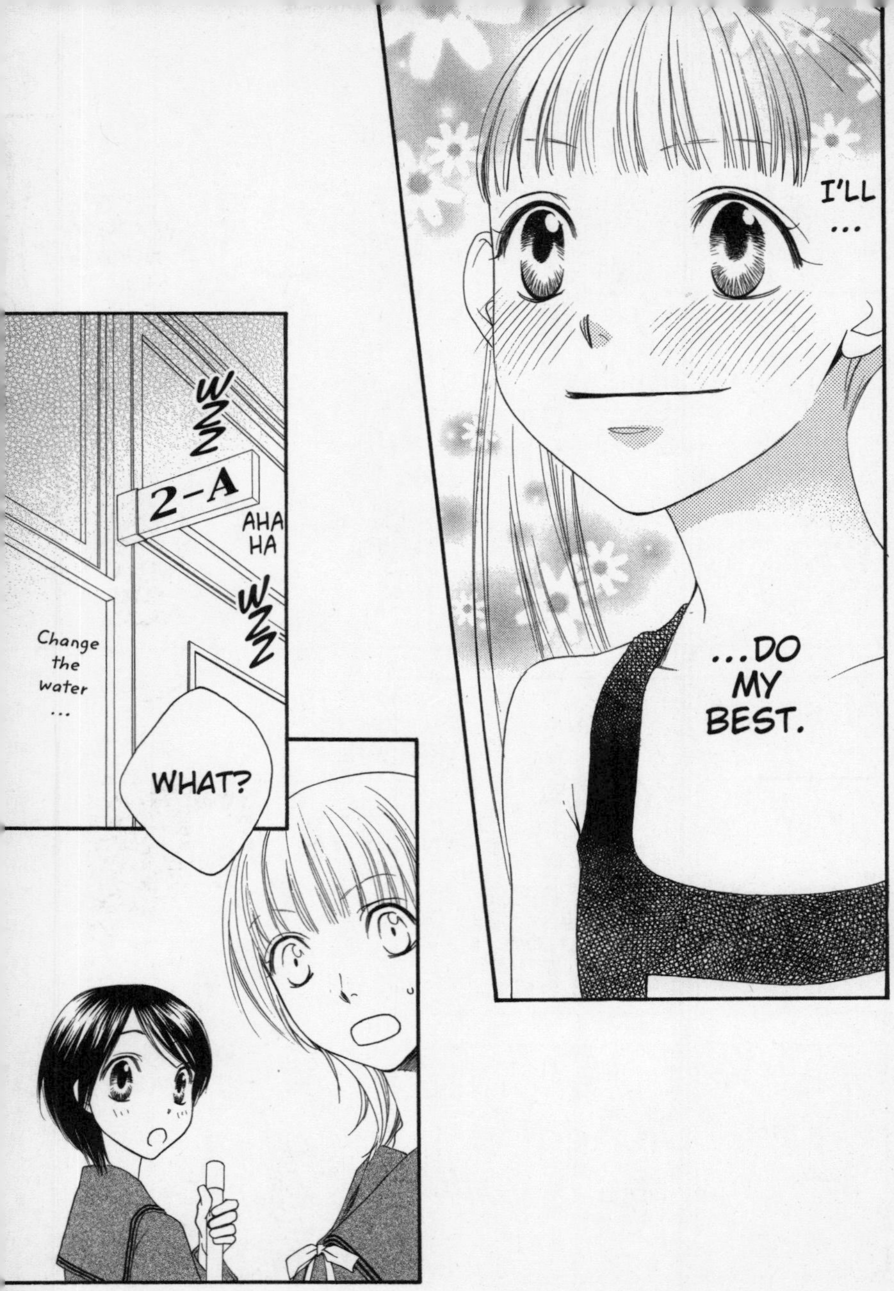

I'LL ...
...DO MY BEST.
WZZ
2-A
AHA HA
WZZ
Change the water ...
WHAT?

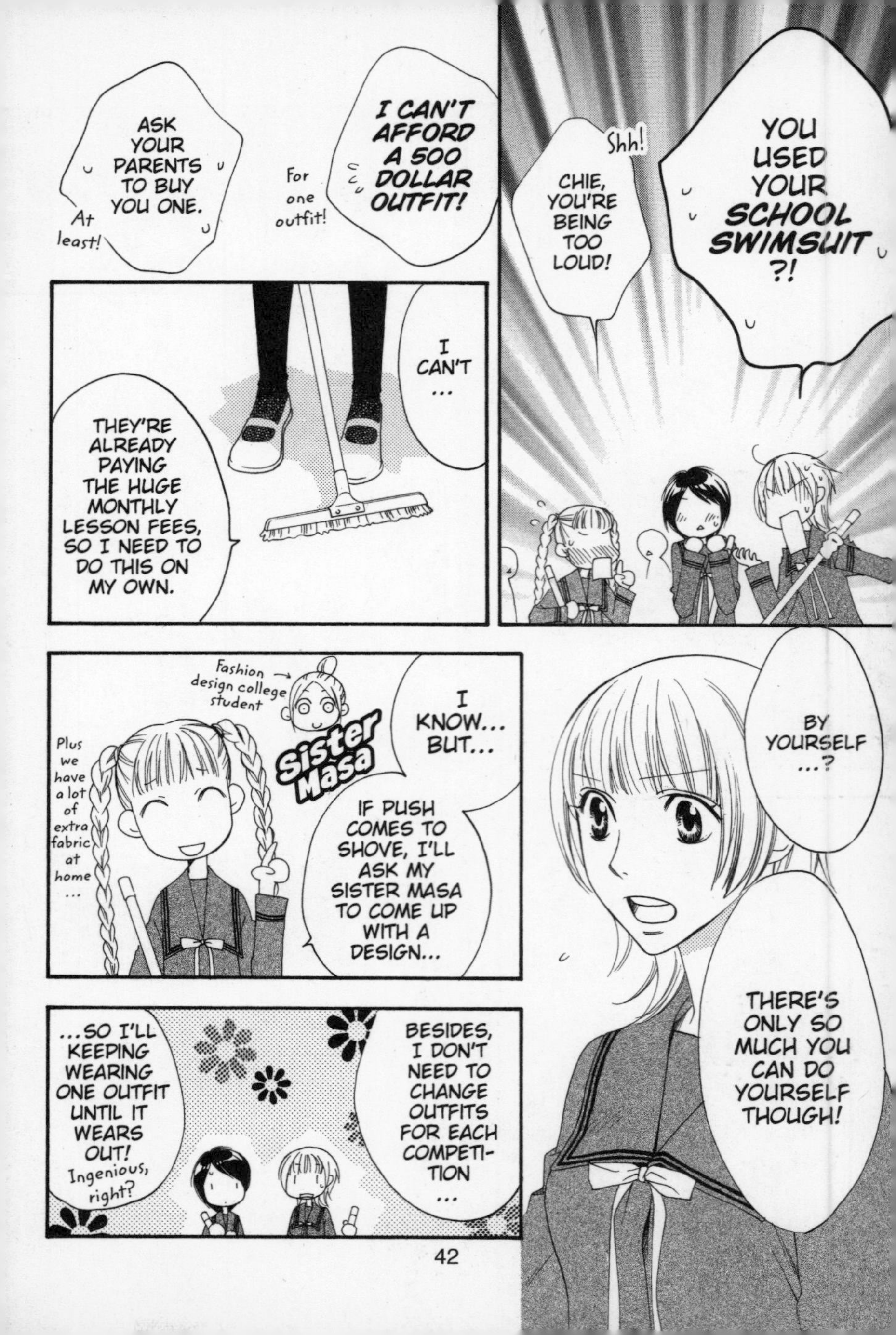
YOU USED YOUR SCHOOL SWIMSUIT ?!
Shh!
CHIE, YOU'RE BEING TOO LOUD!
I CAN'T AFFORD A 500 DOLLAR OUTFIT!
For one outfit!
ASK YOUR PARENTS TO BUY YOU ONE.
At least!
I CAN'T ...
THEY'RE ALREADY PAYING THE HUGE MONTHLY LESSON FEES, SO I NEED TO DO THIS ON MY OWN.
BY YOURSELF ...?
THERE'S ONLY SO MUCH YOU CAN DO YOURSELF THOUGH!
I KNOW... BUT...
IF PUSH COMES TO SHOVE, I'LL ASK MY SISTER MASA TO COME UP WITH A DESIGN...
Sister Masa
Fashion design college student
Plus we have a lot of extra fabric at home ...
BESIDES, I DON'T NEED TO CHANGE OUTFITS FOR EACH COMPETITION ...
...SO I'LL KEEPING WEARING ONE OUTFIT UNTIL IT WEARS OUT!
Ingenious, right?

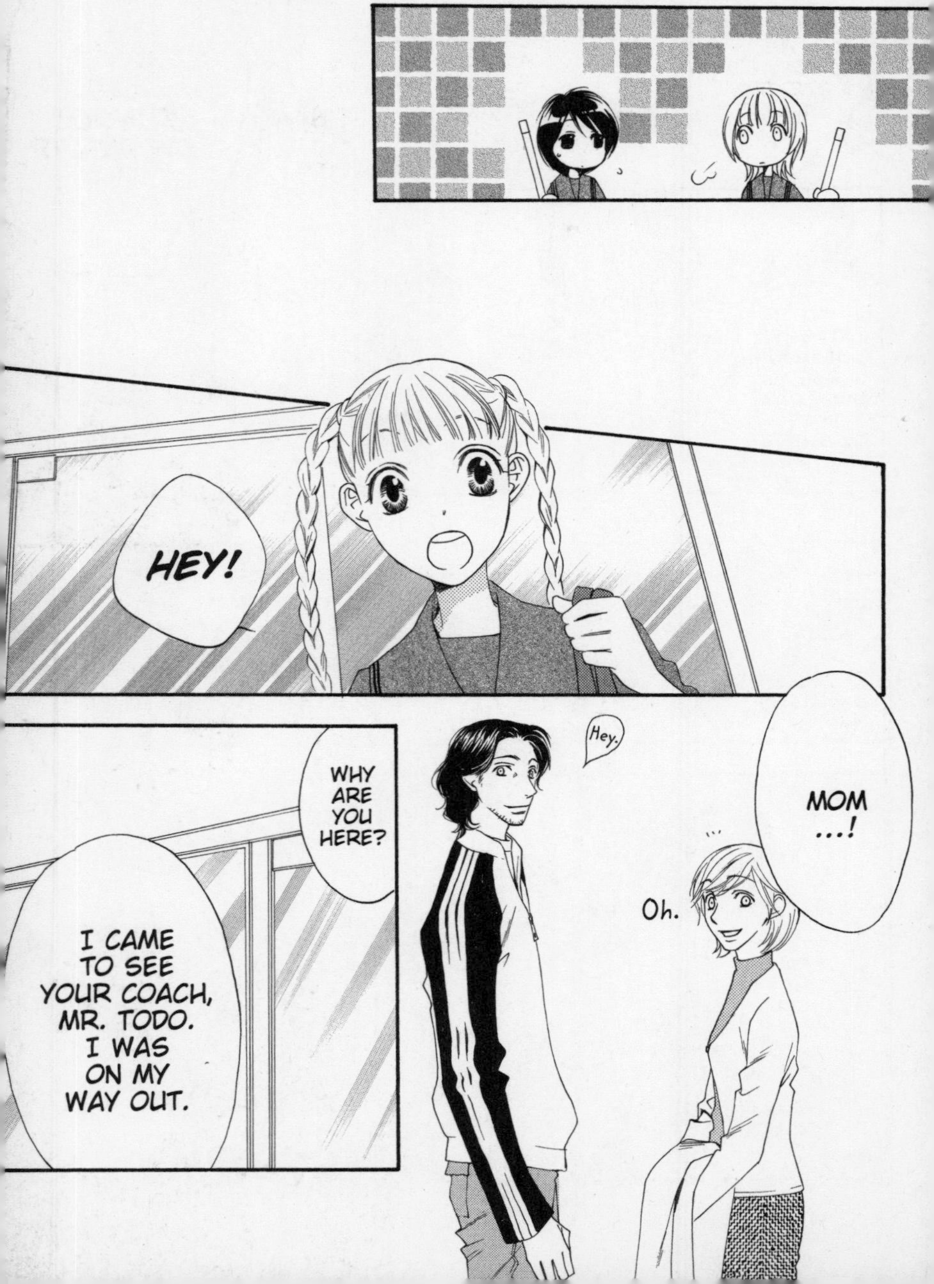
HEY!
MOM ...!
Oh.
...
Hey.
WHY ARE YOU HERE?
I CAME TO SEE YOUR COACH, MR. TODO. I WAS ON MY WAY OUT.

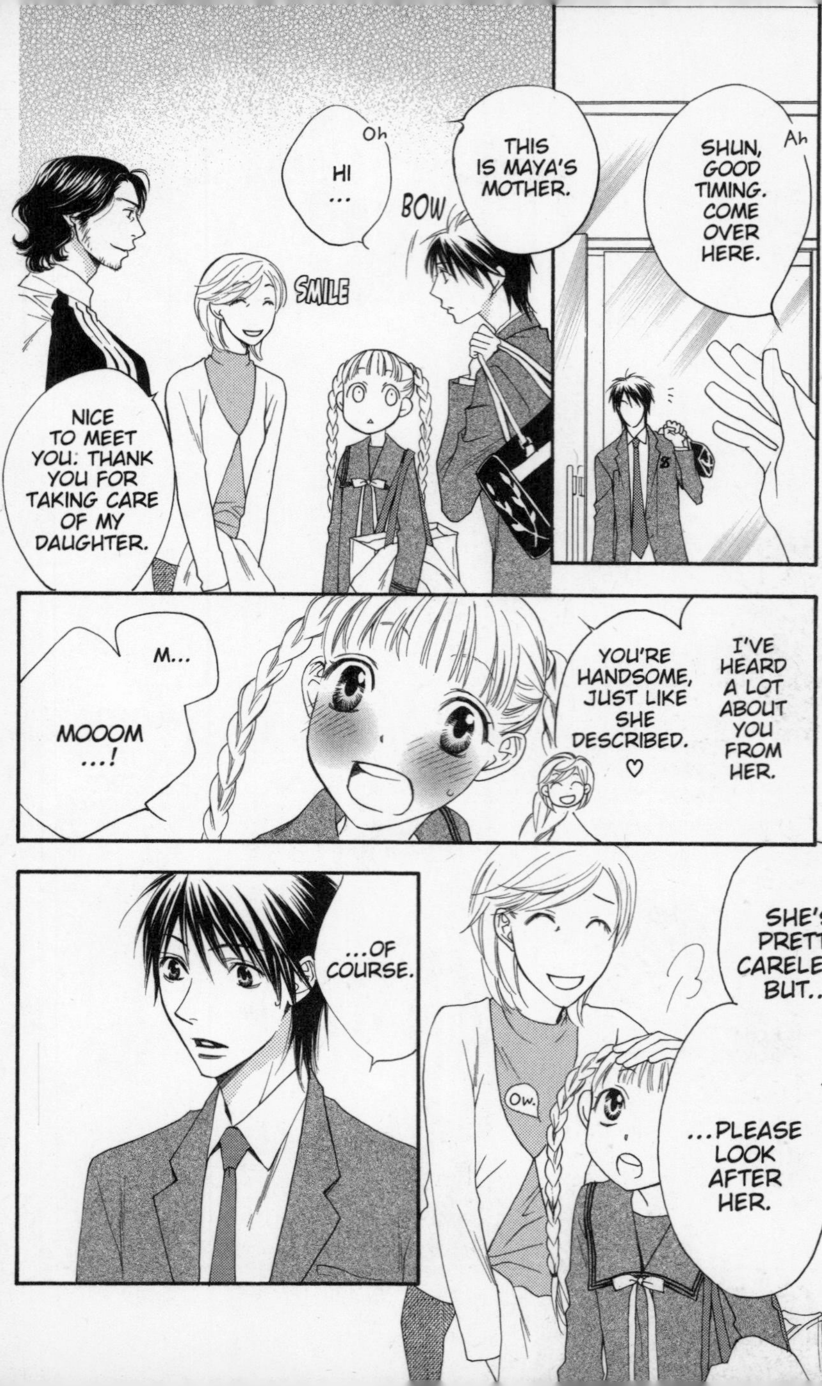
Ah
SHUN, GOOD TIMING. COME OVER HERE.
THIS IS MAYA'S MOTHER.
BOW
Oh
HI ...
SMILE
NICE TO MEET YOU. THANK YOU FOR TAKING CARE OF MY DAUGHTER.
I'VE HEARD A LOT ABOUT YOU FROM HER.
YOU'RE HANDSOME, JUST LIKE SHE DESCRIBED. ♡
M...
MOOOM ...!
SHE'S PRETTY CARELESS, BUT...
...PLEASE LOOK AFTER HER.
Ow.
...OF COURSE.

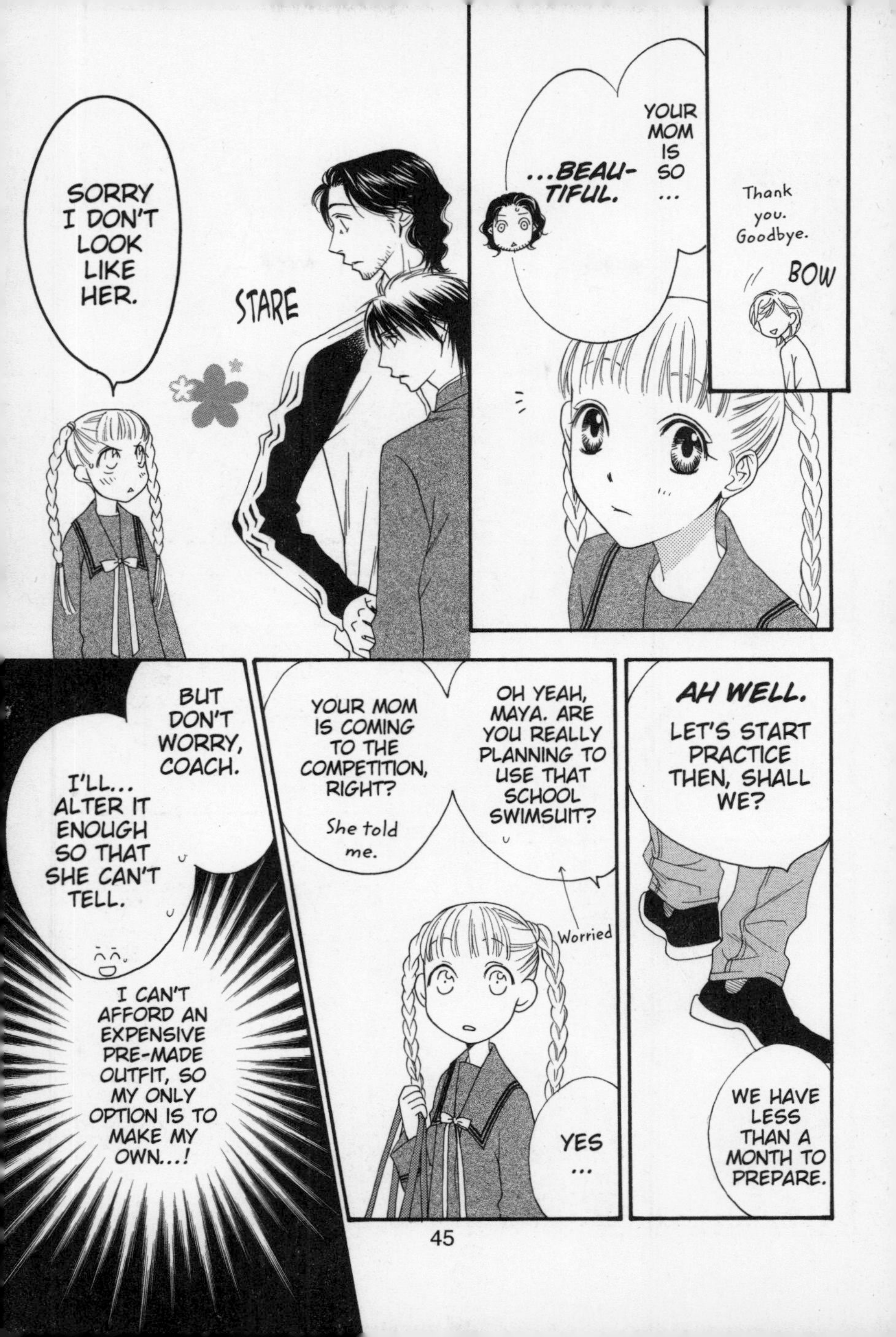

Thank you. Goodbye.
BOW
YOUR MOM IS SO ...
...BEAU-TIFUL.
SORRY I DON'T LOOK LIKE HER.
STARE
AH WELL.
LET'S START PRACTICE THEN, SHALL WE?
WE HAVE LESS THAN A MONTH TO PREPARE.
OH YEAH, MAYA. ARE YOU REALLY PLANNING TO USE THAT SCHOOL SWIMSUIT?
YOUR MOM IS COMING TO THE COMPETITION, RIGHT?
She told me.
Worried
YES ...
BUT DON'T WORRY, COACH.
I'LL... ALTER IT ENOUGH SO THAT SHE CAN'T TELL.
I CAN'T AFFORD AN EXPENSIVE PRE-MADE OUTFIT, SO MY ONLY OPTION IS TO MAKE MY OWN...!

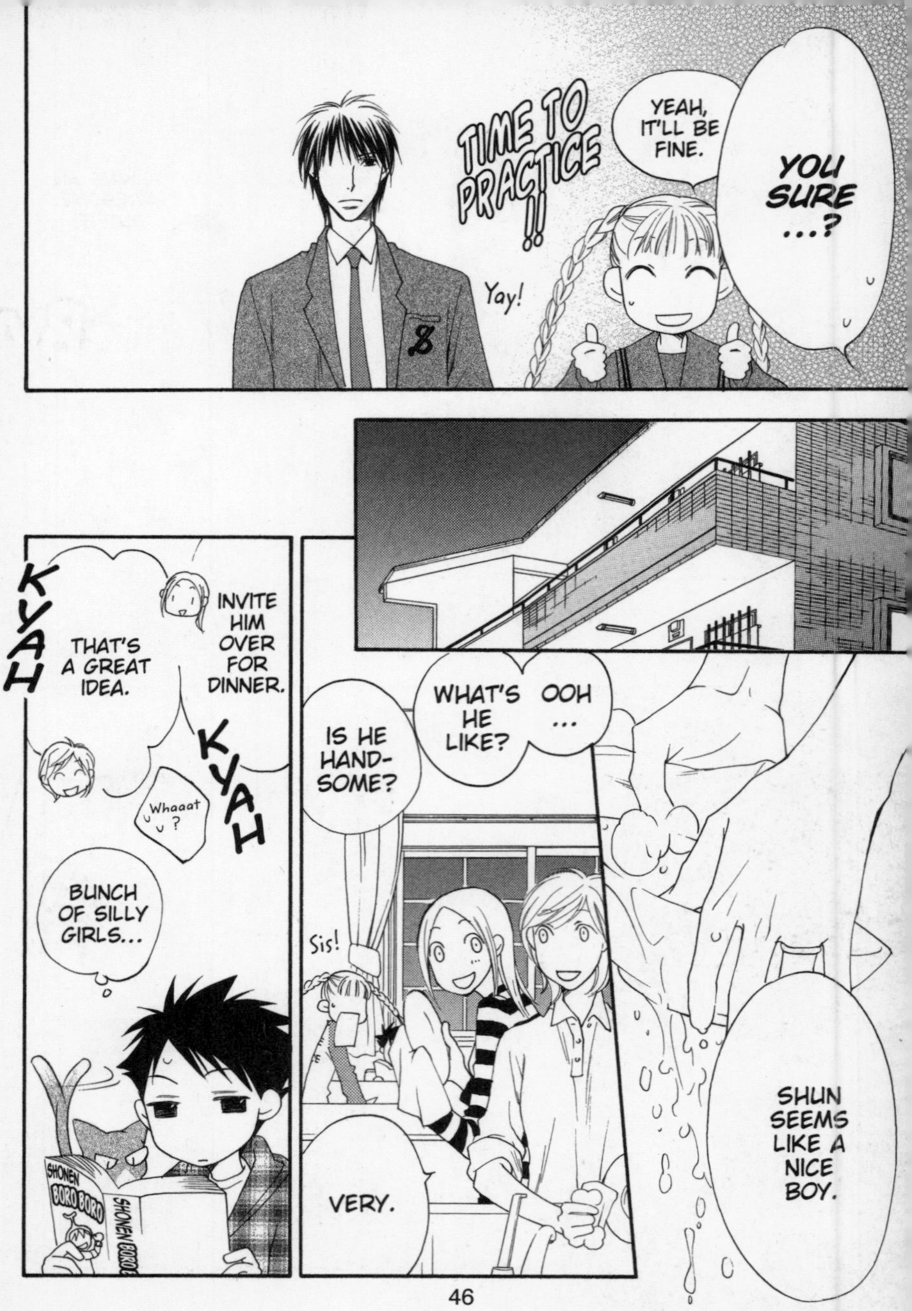
YOU SURE ...?
YEAH, IT'LL BE FINE.
TIME TO PRACTICE !!
Yay!
SHUN SEEMS LIKE A NICE BOY.
OOH ...
WHAT'S HE LIKE?
IS HE HANDSOME?
VERY.
Sis!
INVITE HIM OVER FOR DINNER.
THAT'S A GREAT IDEA.
KYAH
KYAH
Whaaat?
BUNCH OF SILLY GIRLS...
SHONEN BORO BORO
SHONEN BORO B

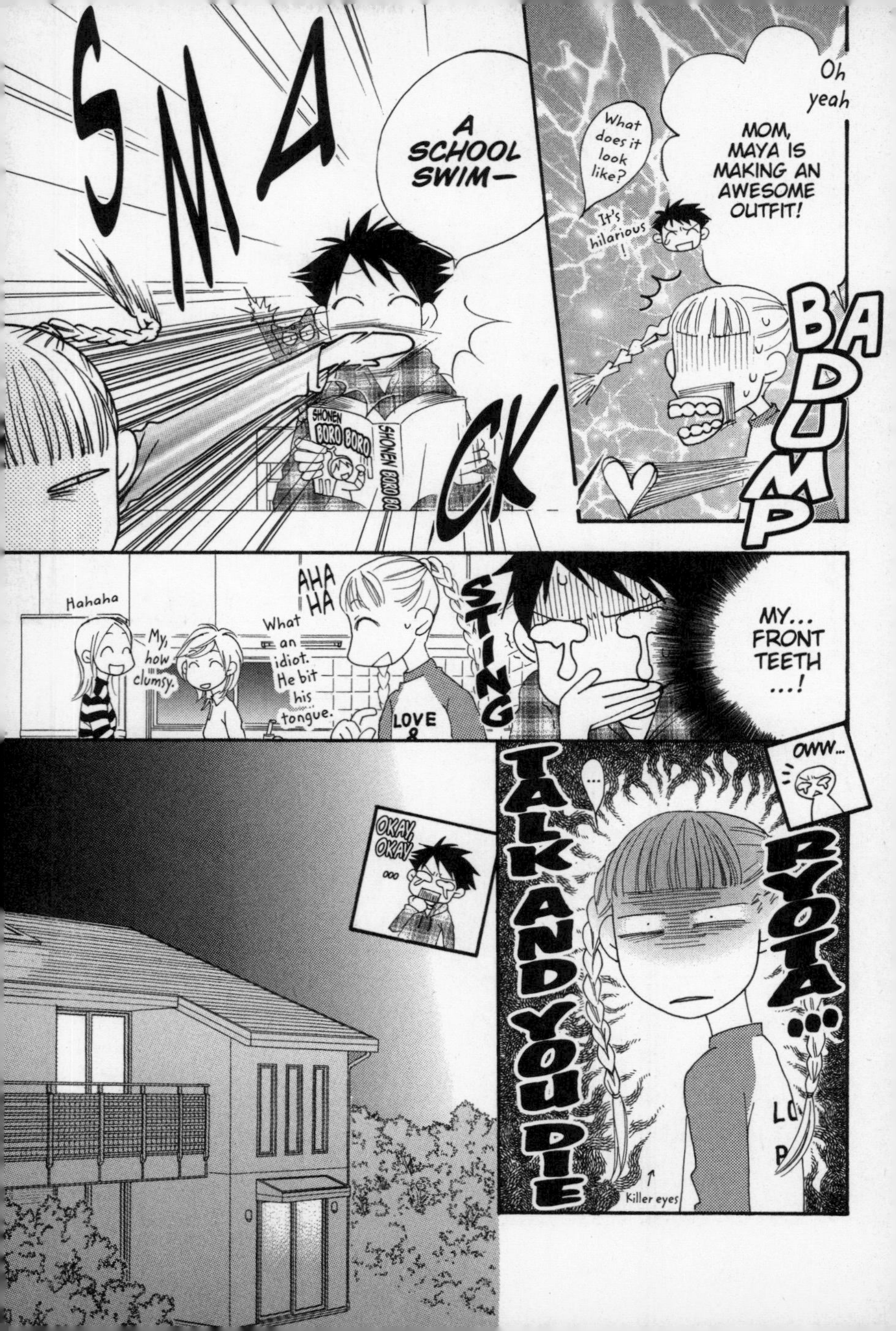
Oh yeah
MOM, MAYA IS MAKING AN AWESOME OUTFIT!
What does it look like?
It's hilarious!
BADUMP
A SCHOOL SWIM—
SMACK
SHONEN BORO BORO
MY... FRONT TEETH ...!
STING
AHA HA
What an idiot. He bit his tongue.
My, how clumsy.
Hahaha
OWW...
RYOTA...
TALK AND YOU DIE
...
Killer eyes
OKAY, OKAY ...

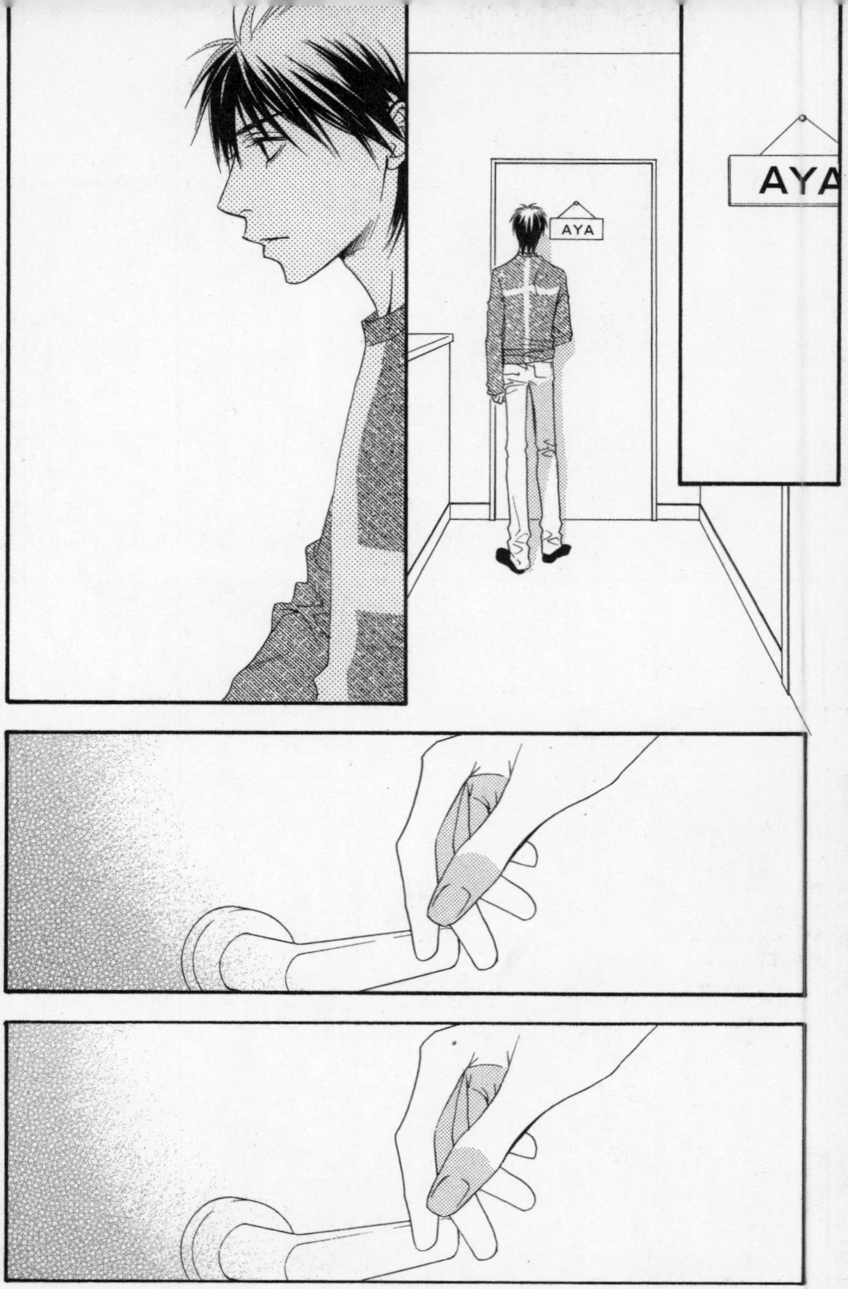
AYA
AYA

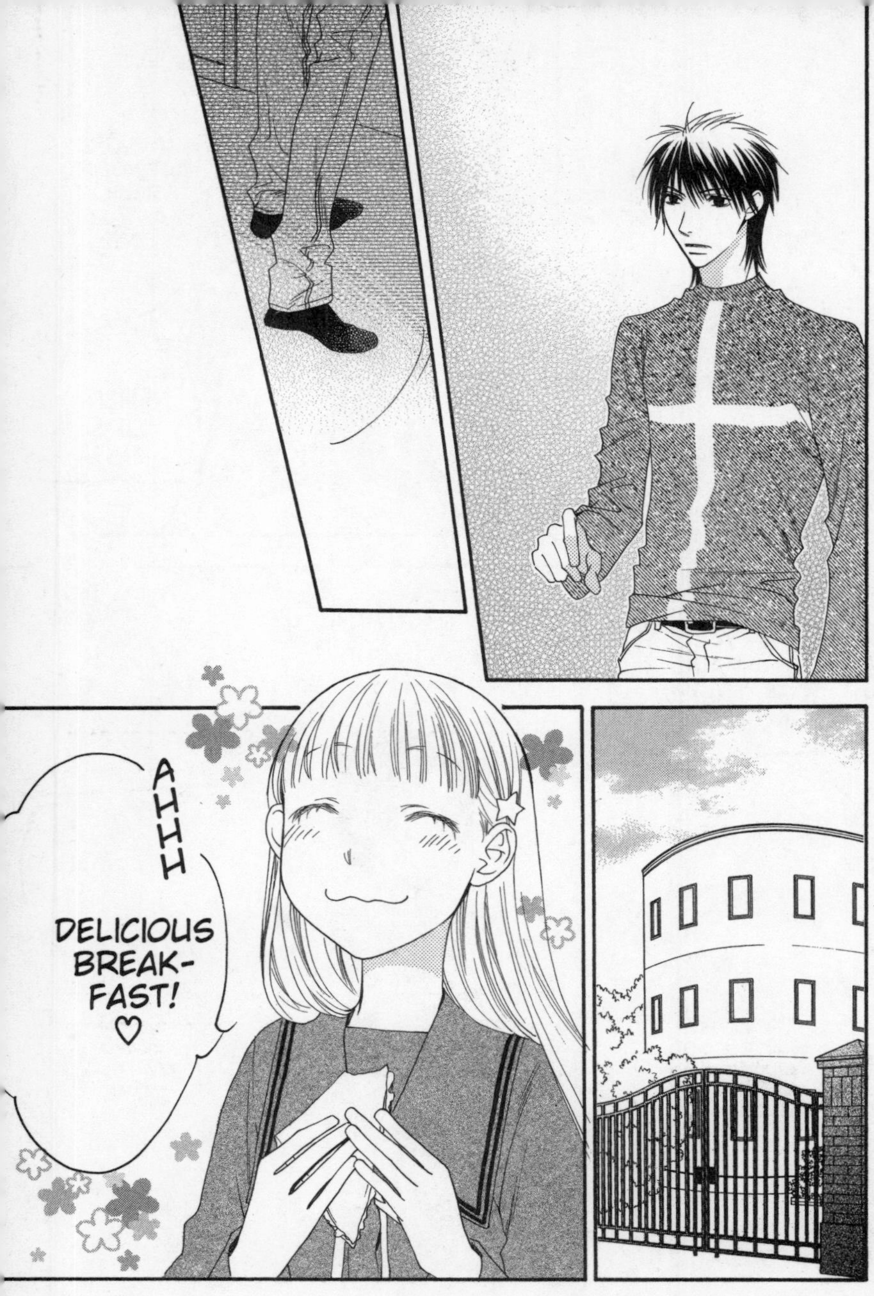
AHHH
DELICIOUS BREAK-FAST! ♡

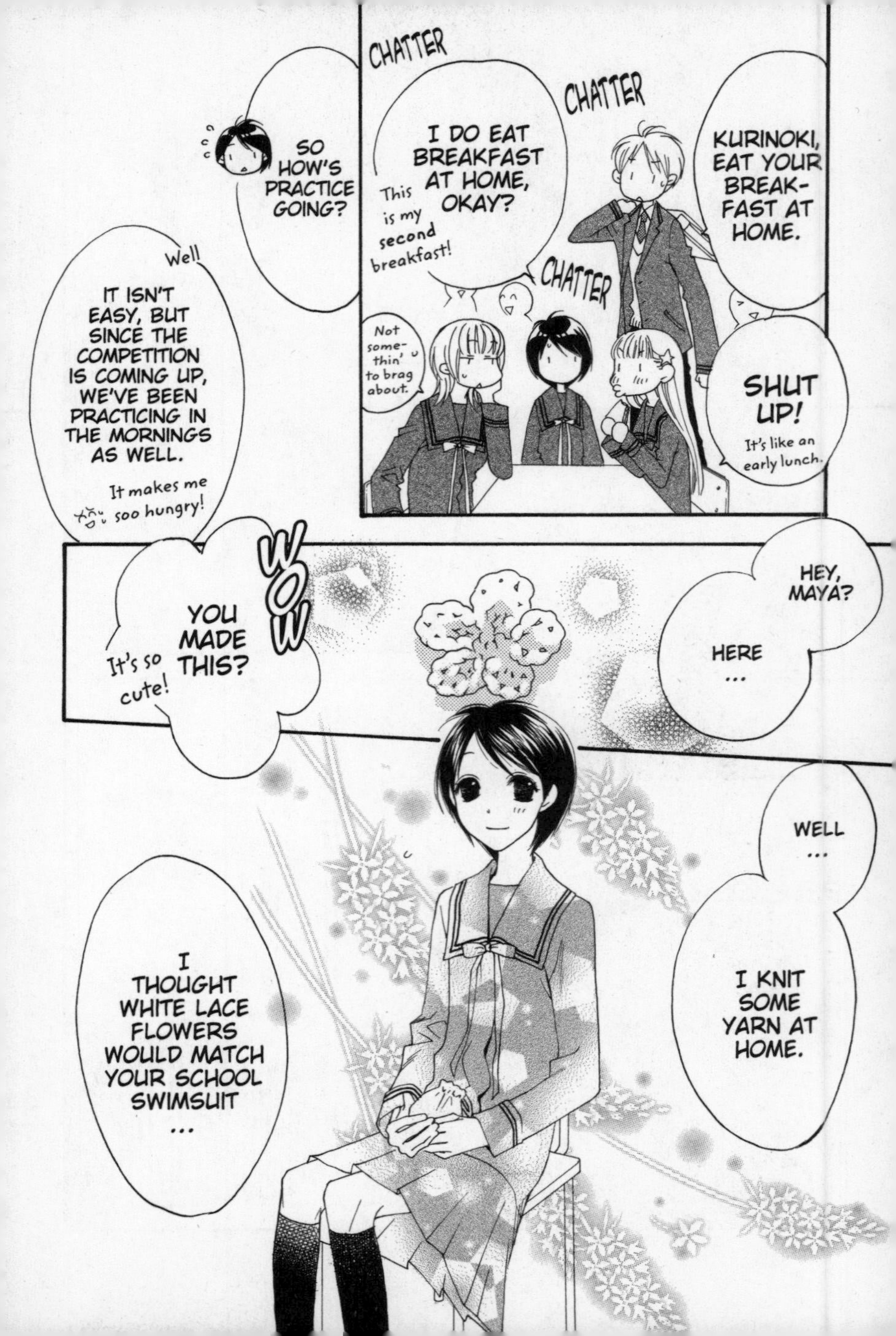
CHATTER
KURINOKI, EAT YOUR BREAK-FAST AT HOME.
CHATTER
I DO EAT BREAKFAST AT HOME, OKAY? This is my second breakfast!
CHATTER
SHUT UP! It's like an early lunch.
Not somethin' to brag about.
SO HOW'S PRACTICE GOING?
Well
IT ISN'T EASY, BUT SINCE THE COMPETITION IS COMING UP, WE'VE BEEN PRACTICING IN THE MORNINGS AS WELL.
It makes me soo hungry!
HEY, MAYA?
HERE...
WOW
YOU MADE THIS?
It's so cute!
WELL...
I KNIT SOME YARN AT HOME.
I THOUGHT WHITE LACE FLOWERS WOULD MATCH YOUR SCHOOL SWIMSUIT...

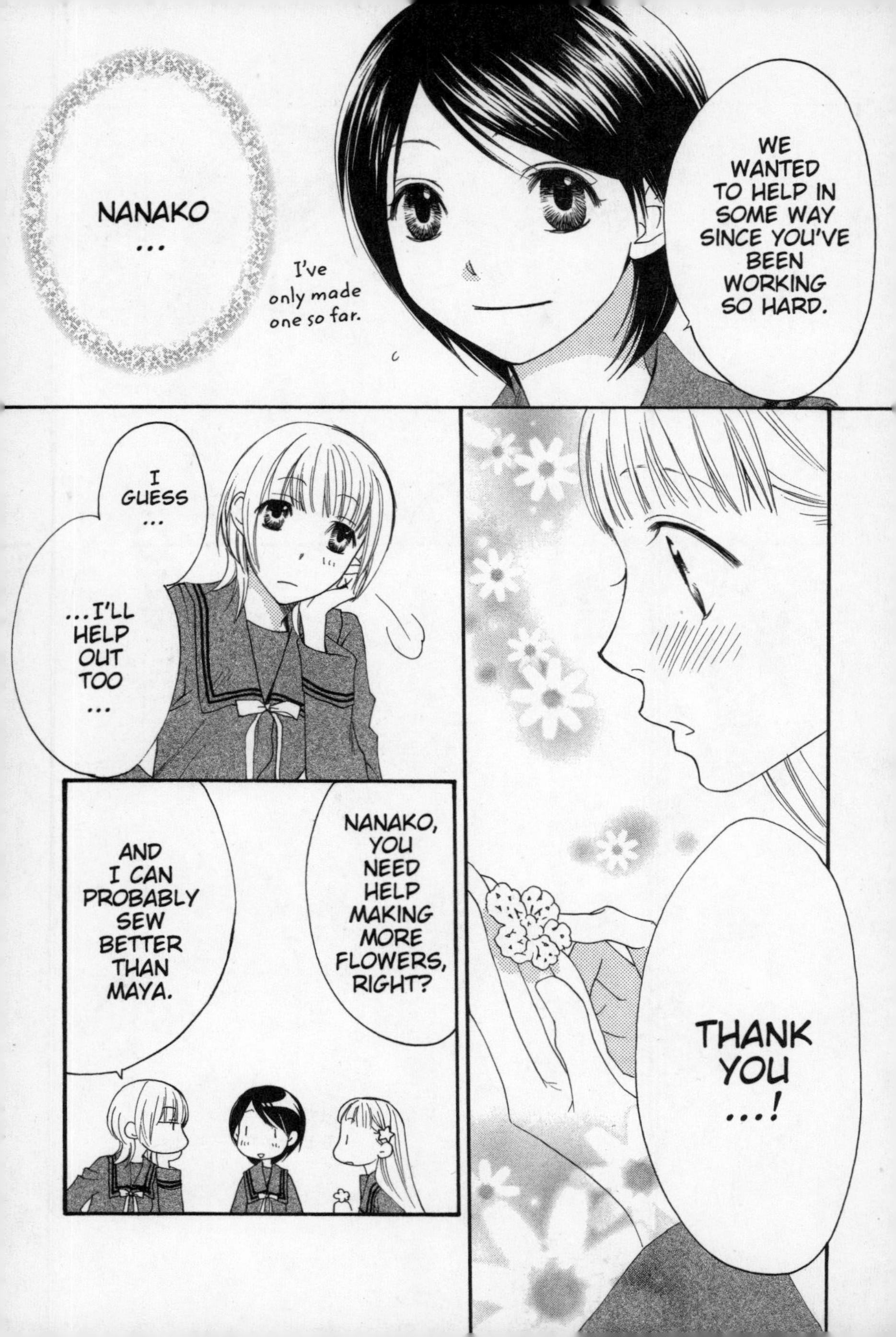
WE WANTED TO HELP IN SOME WAY SINCE YOU'VE BEEN WORKING SO HARD.
I've only made one so far.
NANAKO ...
THANK YOU ...!
I GUESS ...
...I'LL HELP OUT TOO ...
NANAKO, YOU NEED HELP MAKING MORE FLOWERS, RIGHT?
AND I CAN PROBABLY SEW BETTER THAN MAYA.

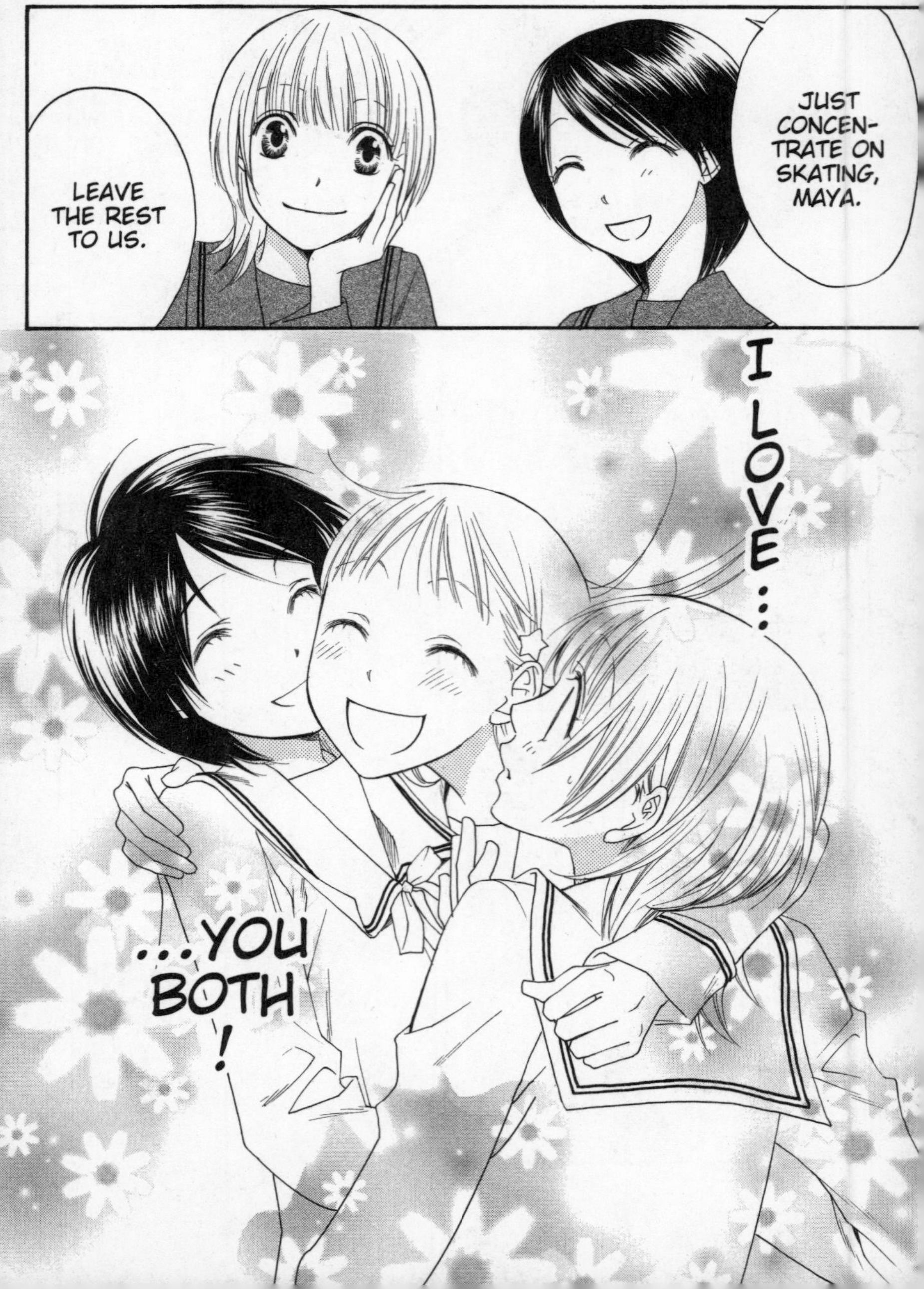
JUST CONCENTRATE ON SKATING, MAYA.
LEAVE THE REST TO US.
I LOVE...
...YOU BOTH!

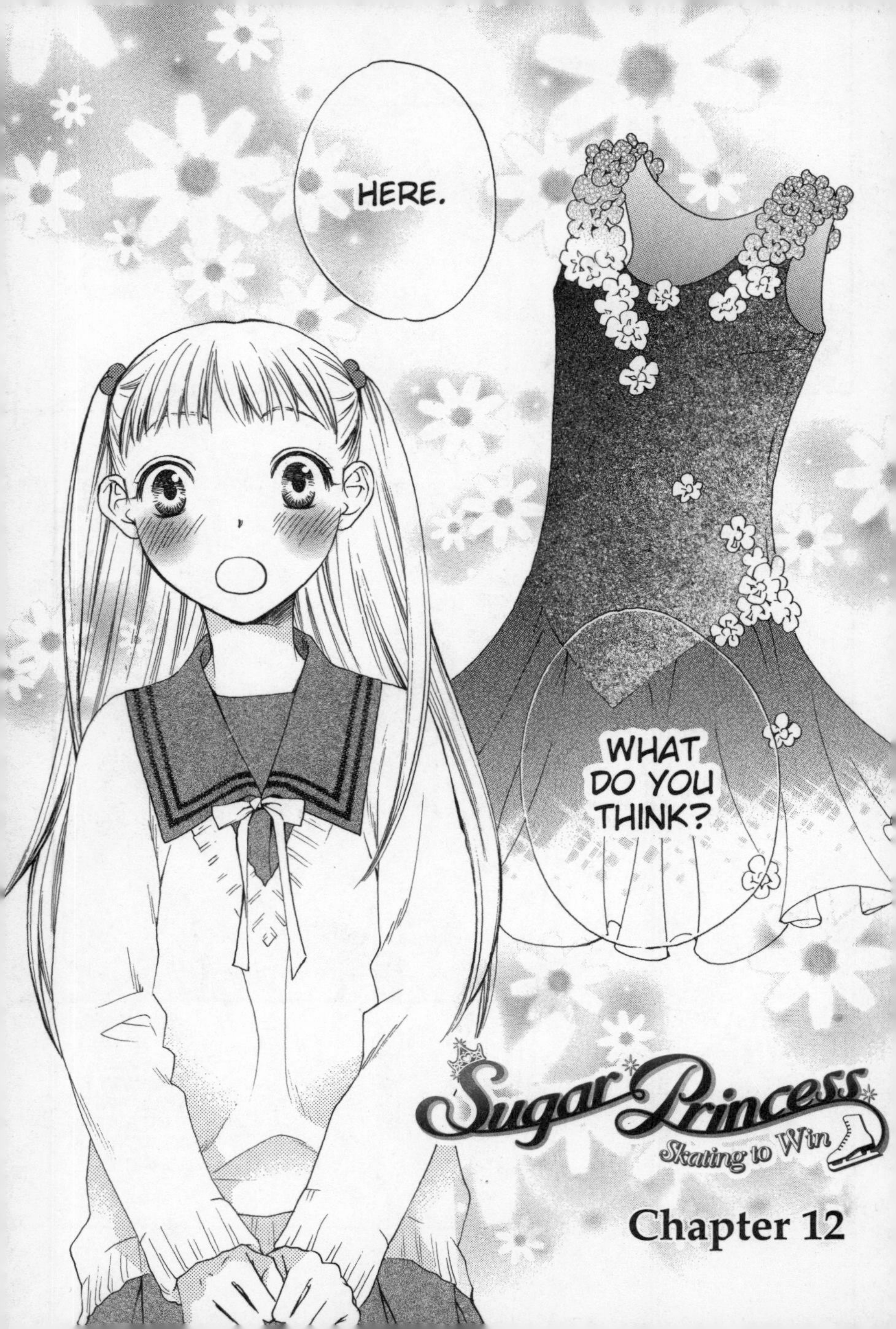
HERE.
WHAT DO YOU THINK?
Sugar Princess
Skating to Win
Chapter 12

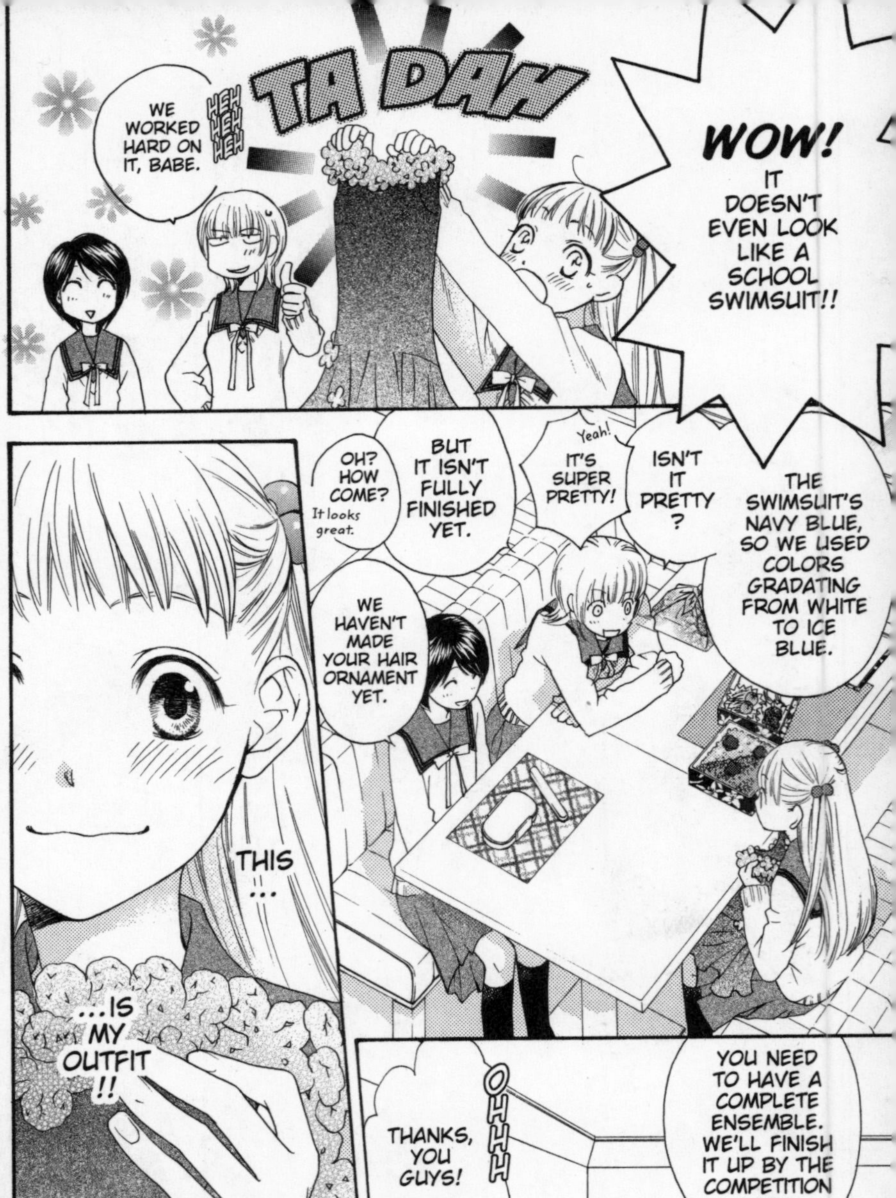
WOW! IT DOESN'T EVEN LOOK LIKE A SCHOOL SWIMSUIT!!
TIA DAH
HEH HEH HEH
WE WORKED HARD ON IT, BABE.
ISN'T IT PRETTY?
THE SWIMSUIT'S NAVY BLUE, SO WE USED COLORS GRADATING FROM WHITE TO ICE BLUE.
Yeah!
IT'S SUPER PRETTY!
BUT IT ISN'T FULLY FINISHED YET.
OH? HOW COME?
It looks great.
WE HAVEN'T MADE YOUR HAIR ORNAMENT YET.
YOU NEED TO HAVE A COMPLETE ENSEMBLE. WE'LL FINISH IT UP BY THE COMPETITION DATE.
OHHHH
THANKS, YOU GUYS!
THIS!! ...
...IS MY OUTFIT!!

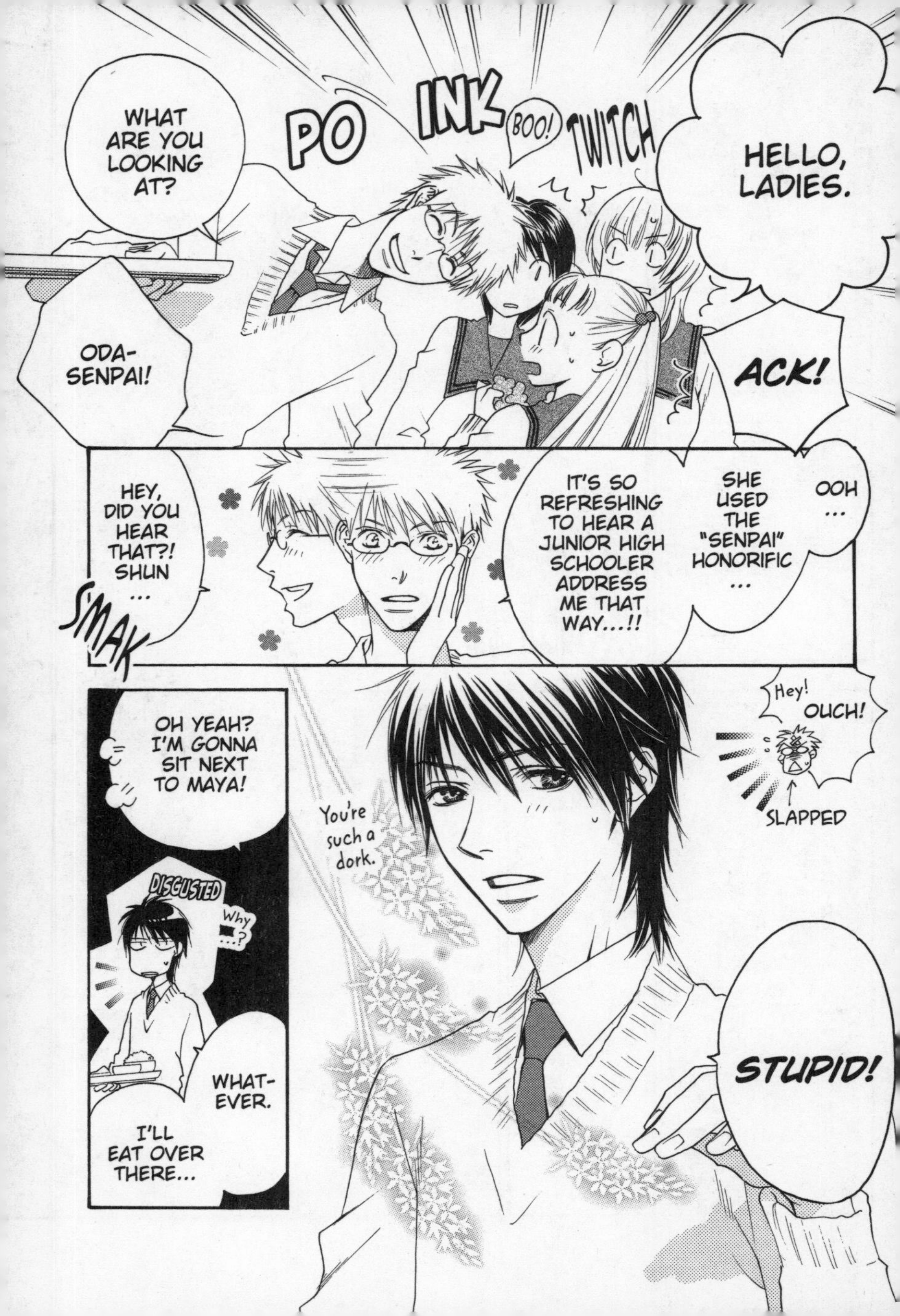
HELLO, LADIES.
TWITCH
BOO!
PO INK
WHAT ARE YOU LOOKING AT?
ACK!
ODA-SENPAI!
OOH ...
SHE USED THE "SENPAI" HONORIFIC ...
IT'S SO REFRESHING TO HEAR A JUNIOR HIGH SCHOOLER ADDRESS ME THAT WAY...!!
HEY, DID YOU HEAR THAT?! SHUN ...
SMAK
Hey!
OUCH!
SLAPPED
STUPID!
You're such a dork.
OH YEAH? I'M GONNA SIT NEXT TO MAYA!
DISGUSTED
Why ...?
WHAT-EVER.
I'LL EAT OVER THERE...

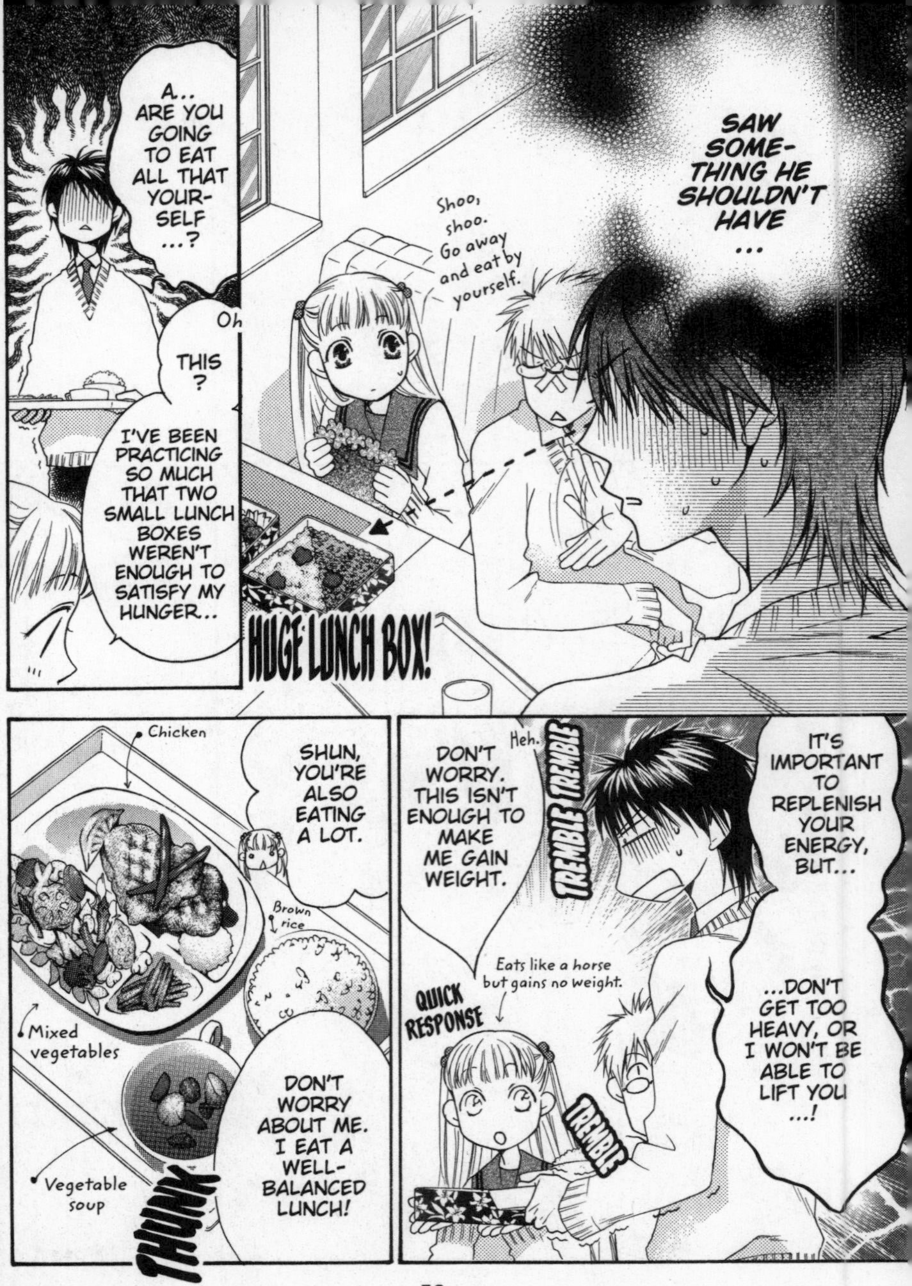
SAW SOME-THING HE SHOULDN'T HAVE ...
Shoo, shoo. Go away and eat by yourself.
A... ARE YOU GOING TO EAT ALL THAT YOUR-SELF ...?
Oh THIS ?
I'VE BEEN PRACTICING SO MUCH THAT TWO SMALL LUNCH BOXES WEREN'T ENOUGH TO SATISFY MY HUNGER...
HUGE LUNCH BOX!
IT'S IMPORTANT TO REPLENISH YOUR ENERGY, BUT...
Heh.
TREMBLE TREMBLE
DON'T WORRY. THIS ISN'T ENOUGH TO MAKE ME GAIN WEIGHT.
...DON'T GET TOO HEAVY, OR I WON'T BE ABLE TO LIFT YOU ...!
Eats like a horse but gains no weight.
QUICK RESPONSE
TREMBLE
SHUN, YOU'RE ALSO EATING A LOT.
Chicken
Brown rice
Mixed vegetables
Vegetable soup
DON'T WORRY ABOUT ME. I EAT A WELL-BALANCED LUNCH!
THUNK

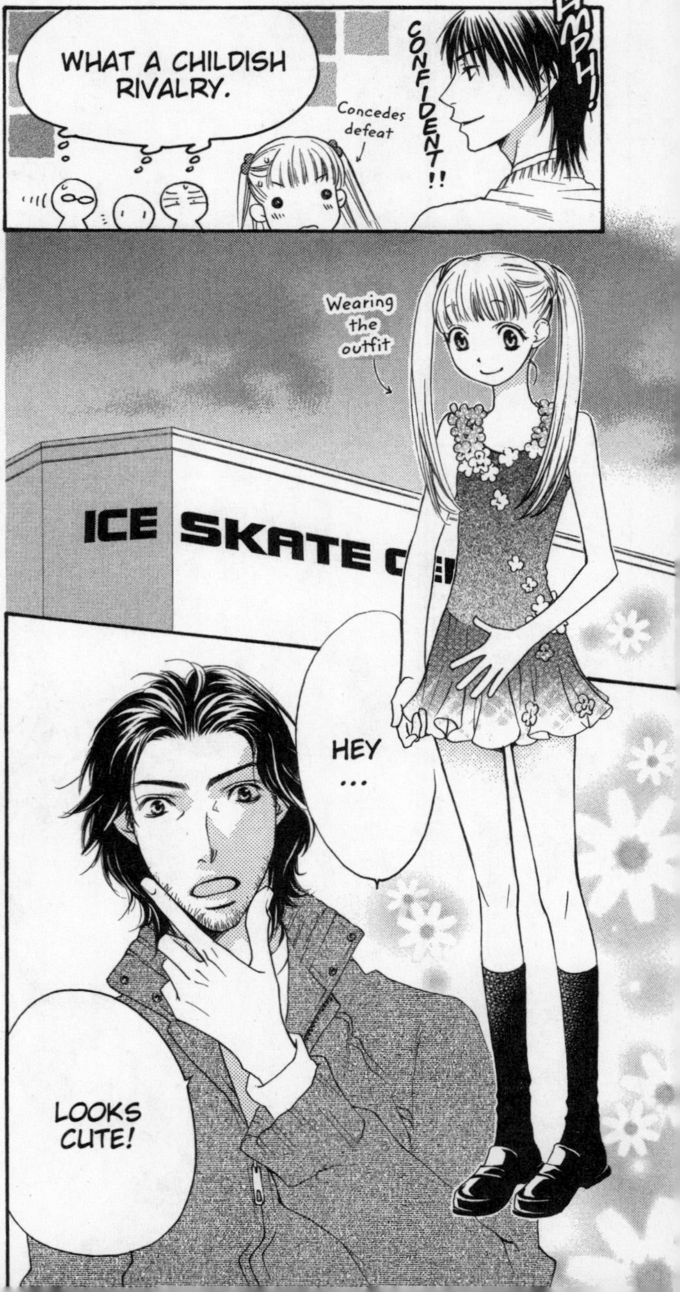
HMPH!
CONFIDENT!!
Concedes defeat
WHAT A CHILDISH RIVALRY.
Wearing the outfit
ICE SKATE
HEY ...
LOOKS CUTE!

I SAW SKATING OUTFITS (FOR KIDS) AT THE SKATING RINK SHOP.

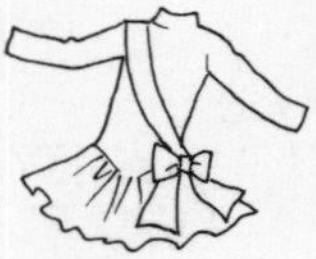

THERE WAS A WIDE VARIETY OF OUTFITS. I ALMOST BOUGHT THEM, THEY WERE SO ADORABLE.

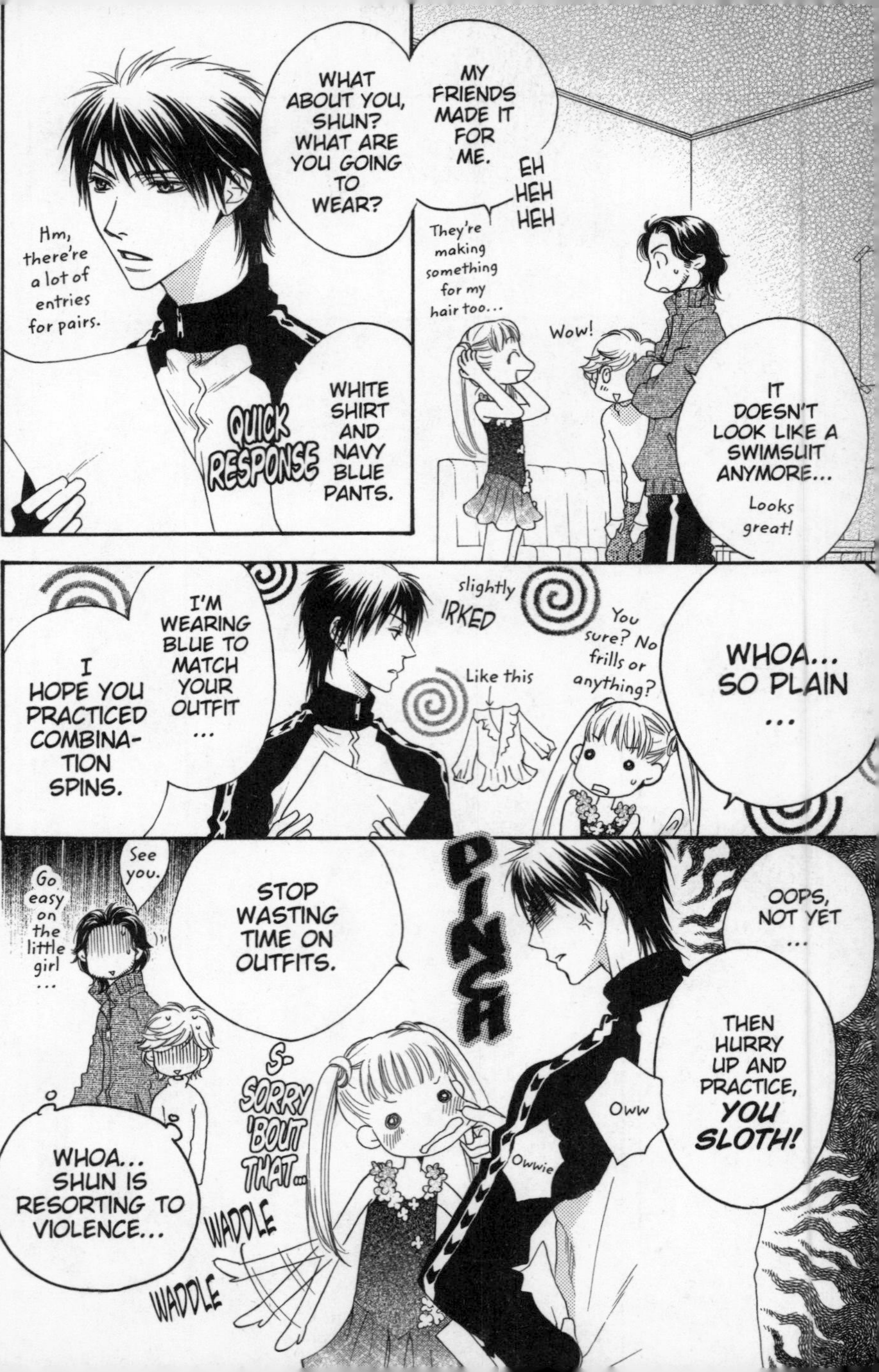

MY FRIENDS MADE IT FOR ME.
EH HEH HEH
They're making something for my hair too...
IT DOESN'T LOOK LIKE A SWIMSUIT ANYMORE...
Looks great!
Wow!
WHAT ABOUT YOU, SHUN? WHAT ARE YOU GOING TO WEAR?
Hm, there're a lot of entries for pairs.
WHITE SHIRT AND NAVY BLUE PANTS.
QUICK RESPONSE
WHOA... SO PLAIN ...
You sure? No frills or anything?
Like this
slightly IRKED
I'M WEARING BLUE TO MATCH YOUR OUTFIT ...
I HOPE YOU PRACTICED COMBINATION SPINS.
OOPS, NOT YET ...
PINCH
THEN HURRY UP AND PRACTICE, YOU SLOTH!
Oww
Owwie
STOP WASTING TIME ON OUTFITS.
See you.
Go easy on the little girl ...
S-SORRY 'BOUT THAT...
WHOA... SHUN IS RESORTING TO VIOLENCE...
WADDLE
WADDLE

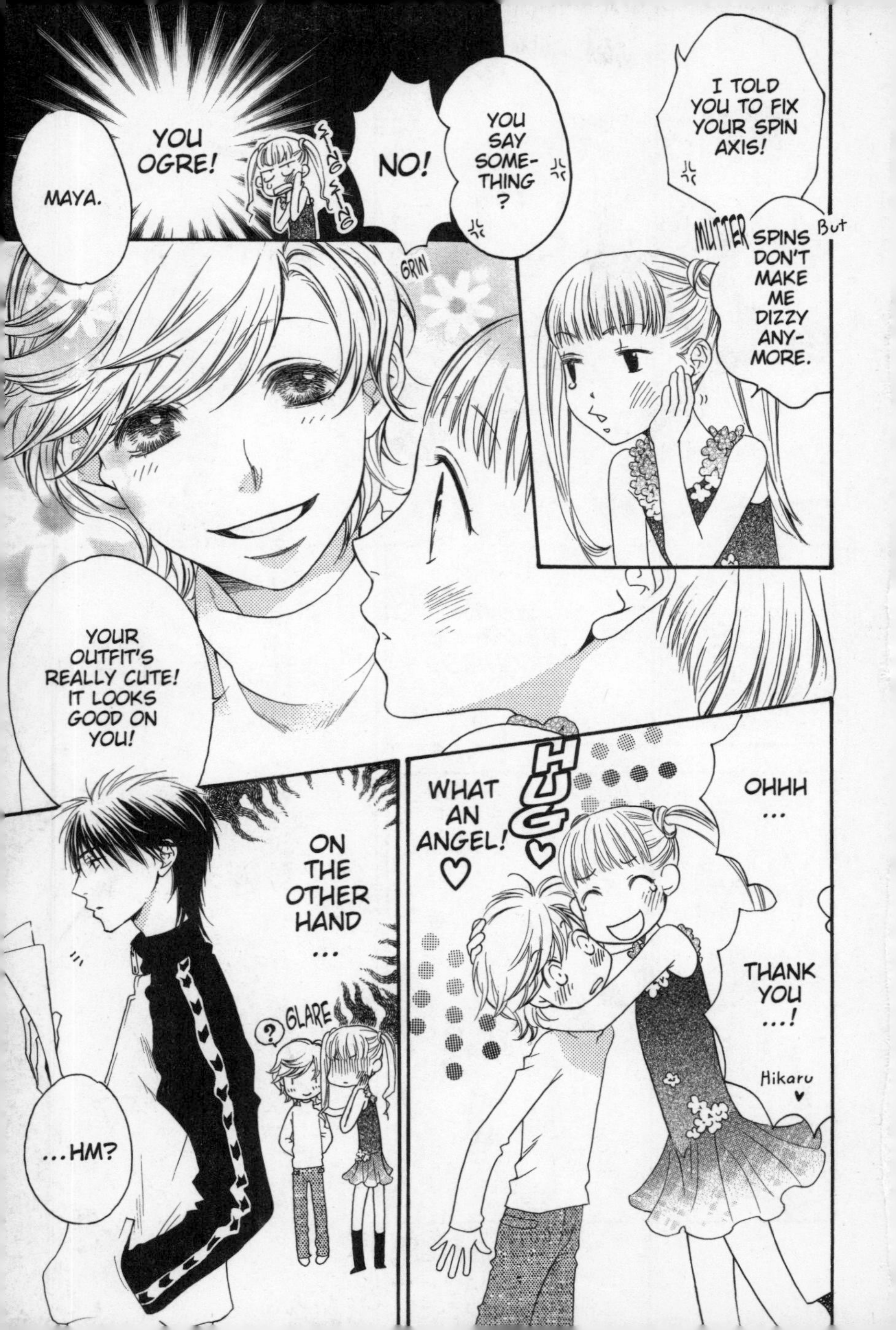
I TOLD YOU TO FIX YOUR SPIN AXIS!
YOU SAY SOME-THING?
NO!
STING STING
YOU OGRE!
MAYA.
But SPINS DON'T MAKE ME DIZZY ANY-MORE.
MUTTER
GRIN
YOUR OUTFIT'S REALLY CUTE! IT LOOKS GOOD ON YOU!
OHHH ...
HUG
WHAT AN ANGEL!
THANK YOU ...!
Hikaru
ON THE OTHER HAND ...
GLARE
...HM?

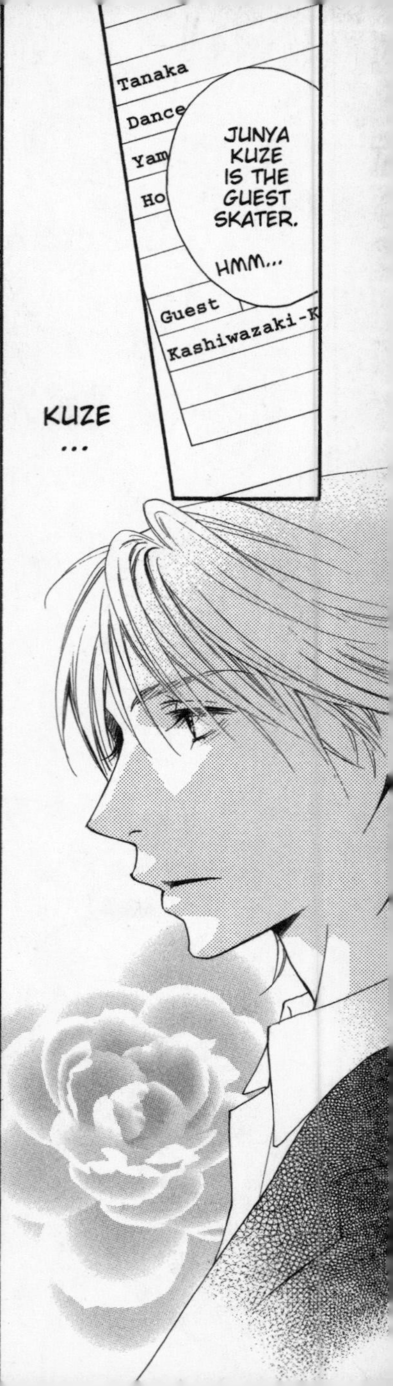
Tanaka
Dance
Yam
Ho
Guest
Kashiwazaki-K
JUNYA KUZE IS THE GUEST SKATER.
HMM...
KUZE ...

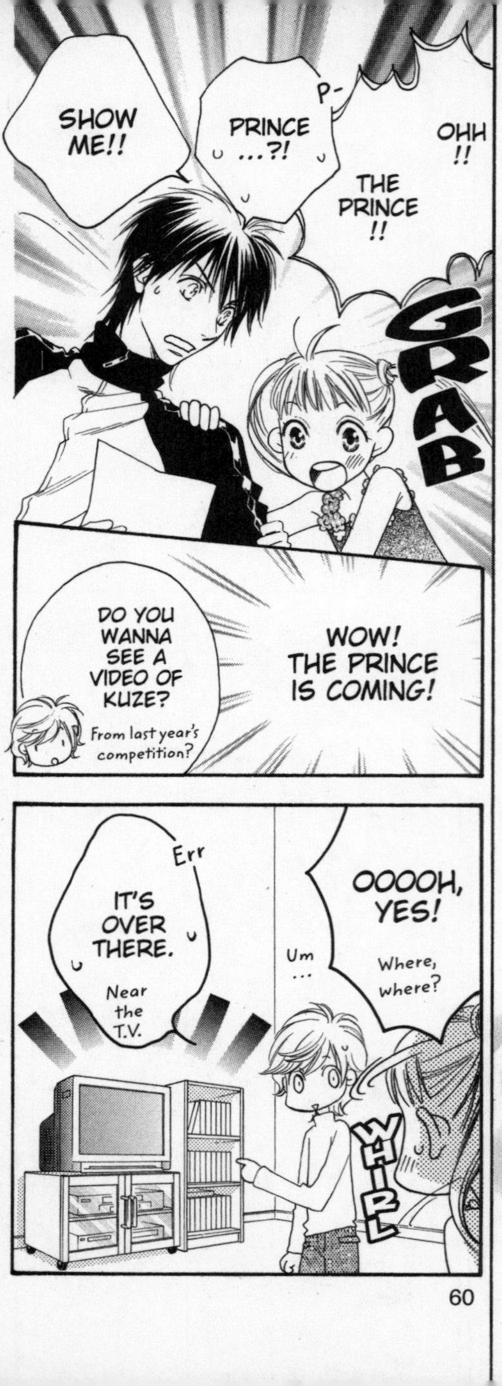
OHH !!
P-
PRINCE ...?!
THE PRINCE !!
GRAB
SHOW ME!!
WOW! THE PRINCE IS COMING!
DO YOU WANNA SEE A VIDEO OF KUZE?
From last year's competition?
OOOOH, YES!
Where, where?
Um ...
WHIRL
Err
IT'S OVER THERE.
Near the T.V.

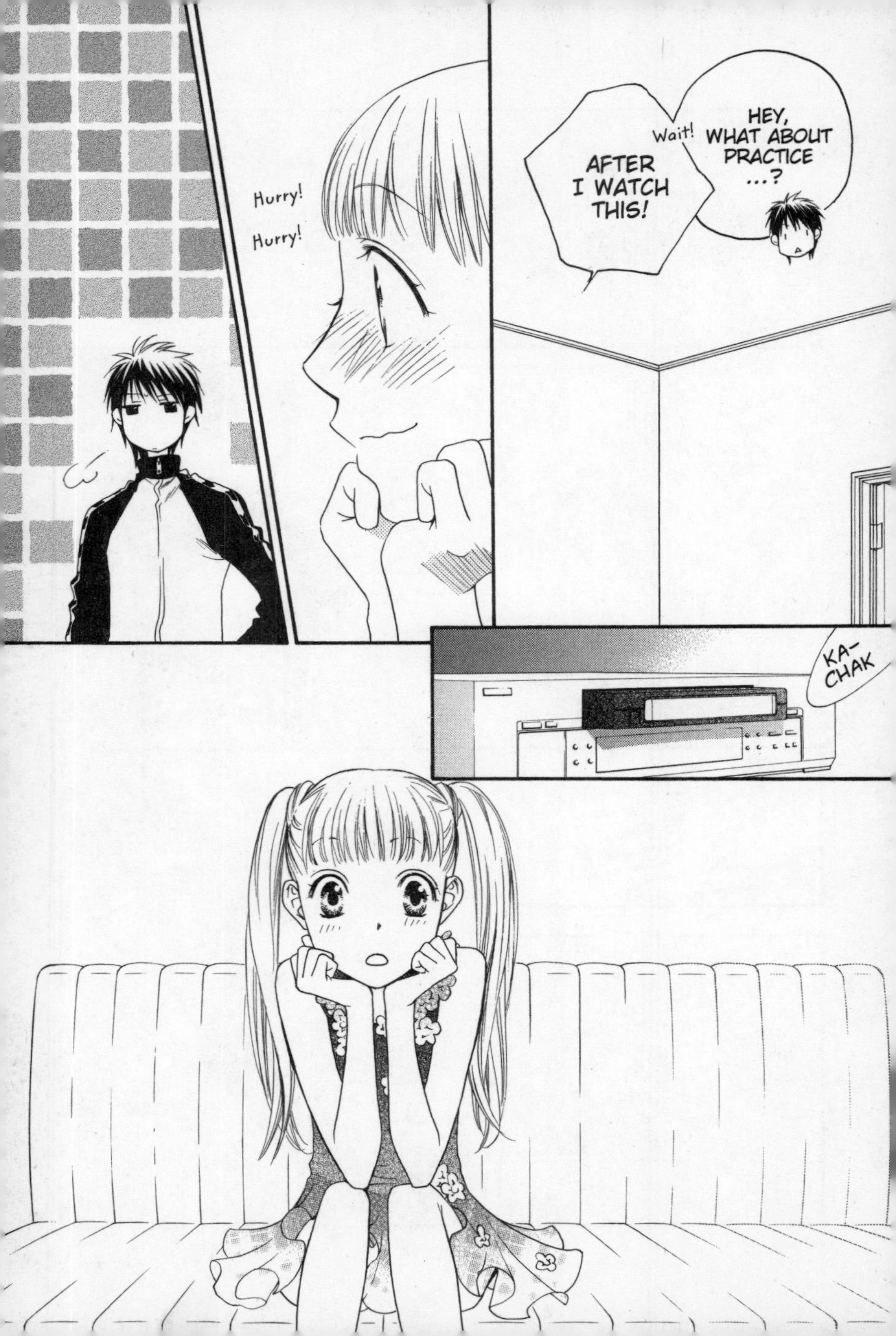
HEY, WHAT ABOUT PRACTICE ...?
Wait!
AFTER I WATCH THIS!
Hurry!
Hurry!
KA-CHAK

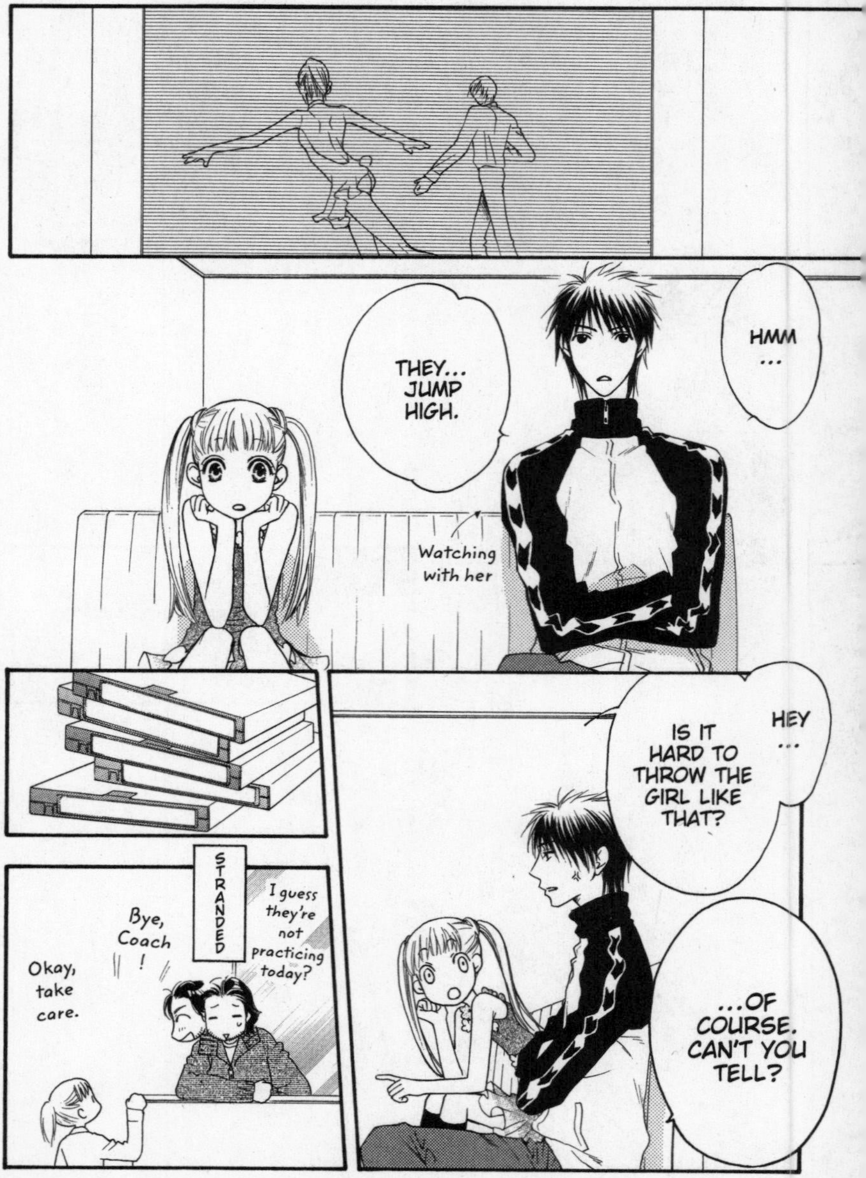
HMM...
THEY... JUMP HIGH.
Watching with her
HEY...
IS IT HARD TO THROW THE GIRL LIKE THAT?
...OF COURSE. CAN'T YOU TELL?
STRANDED
I guess they're not practicing today?
Bye, Coach!
Okay, take care.

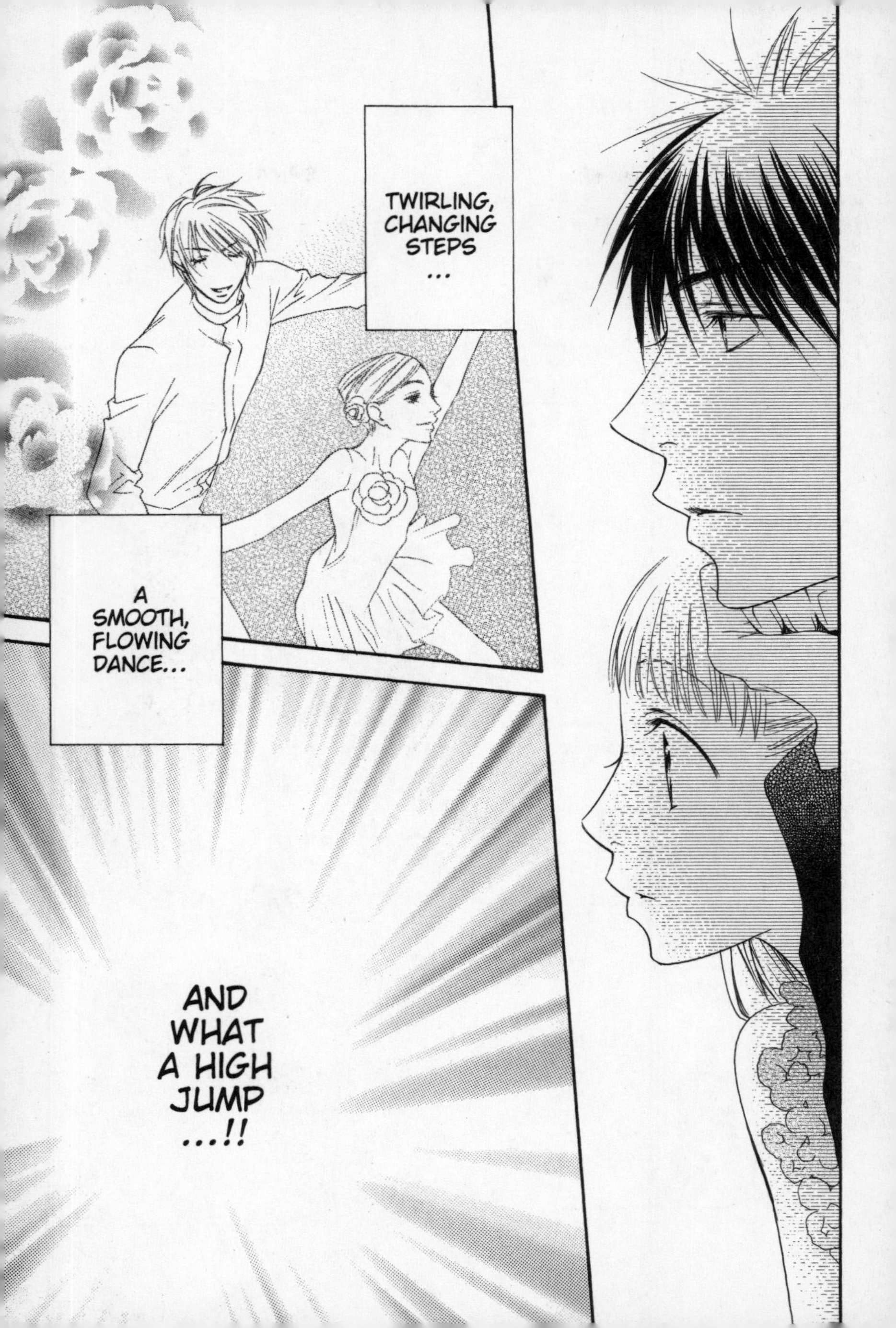
TWIRLING, CHANGING STEPS ...
A SMOOTH, FLOWING DANCE...
AND WHAT A HIGH JUMP ...!!

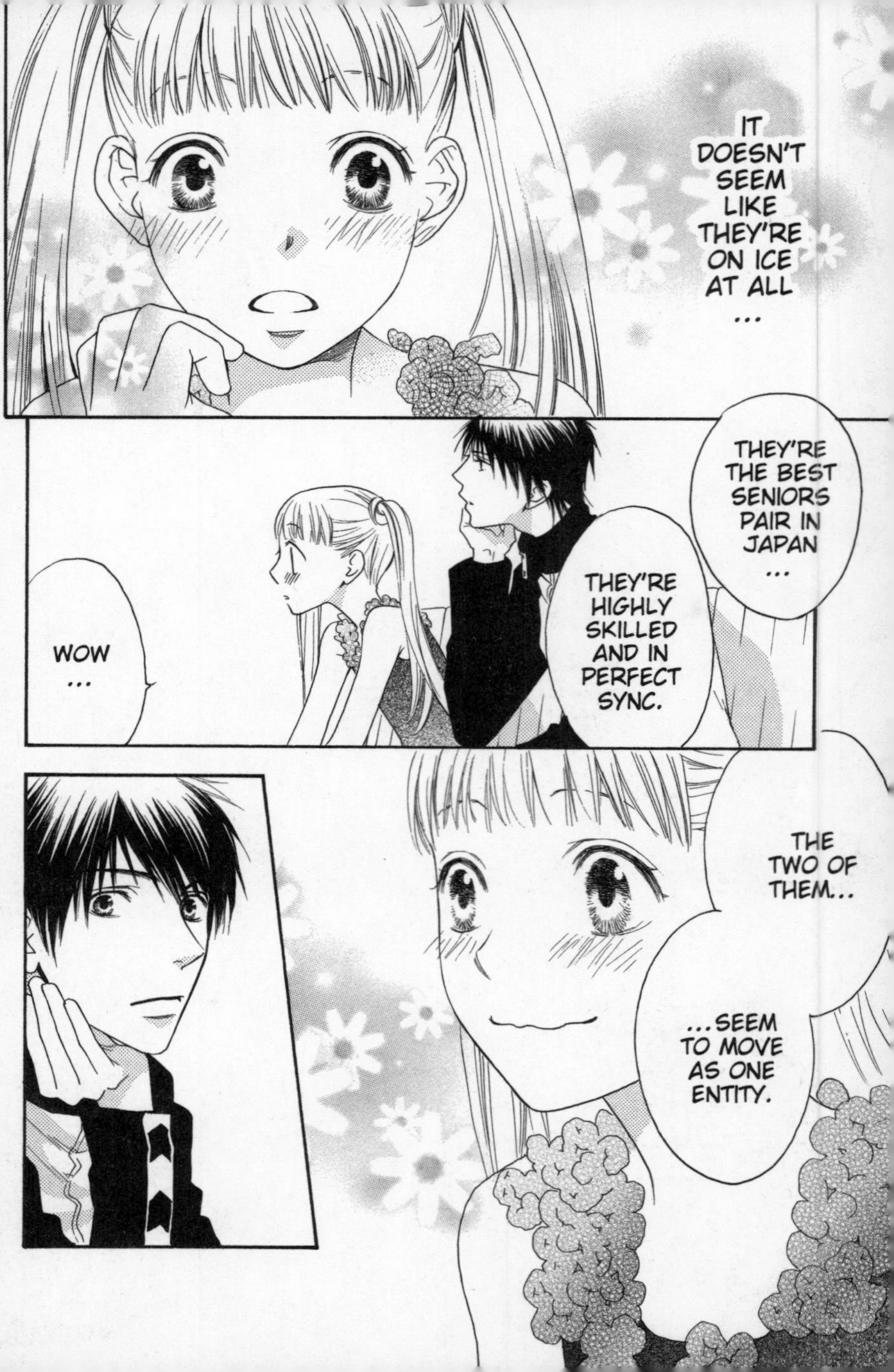
IT DOESN'T SEEM LIKE THEY'RE ON ICE AT ALL ...
THEY'RE THE BEST SENIORS PAIR IN JAPAN ...
THEY'RE HIGHLY SKILLED AND IN PERFECT SYNC.
WOW ...
THE TWO OF THEM...
...SEEM TO MOVE AS ONE ENTITY.

Chapter 13

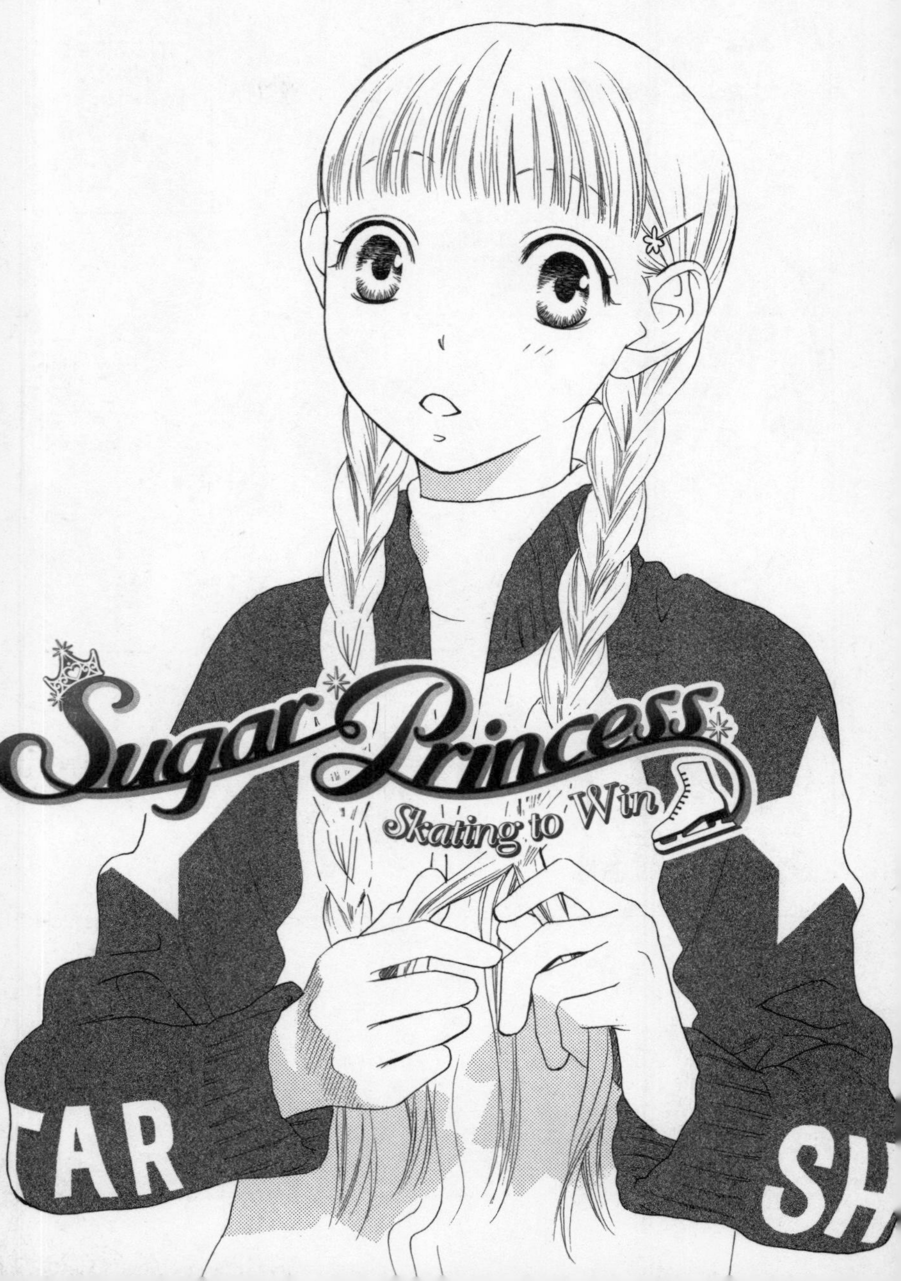
Sugar Princess
Skating to Win
TAR
SH

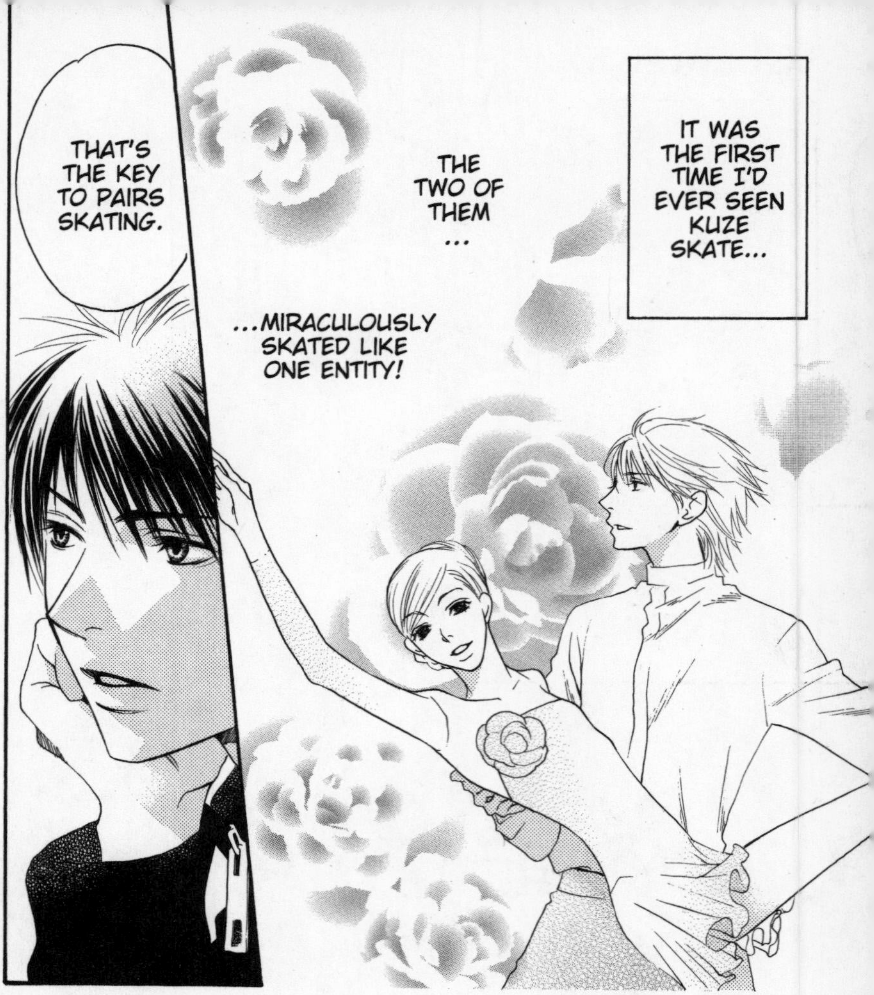
IT WAS THE FIRST TIME I'D EVER SEEN KUZE SKATE...
THE TWO OF THEM ...
...MIRACULOUSLY SKATED LIKE ONE ENTITY!
THAT'S THE KEY TO PAIRS SKATING.

I LOVE THE WHITE FROST THAT FORMS ON ICE CUBES...✧

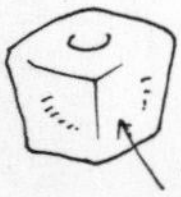
This part. It's soft and slushy.

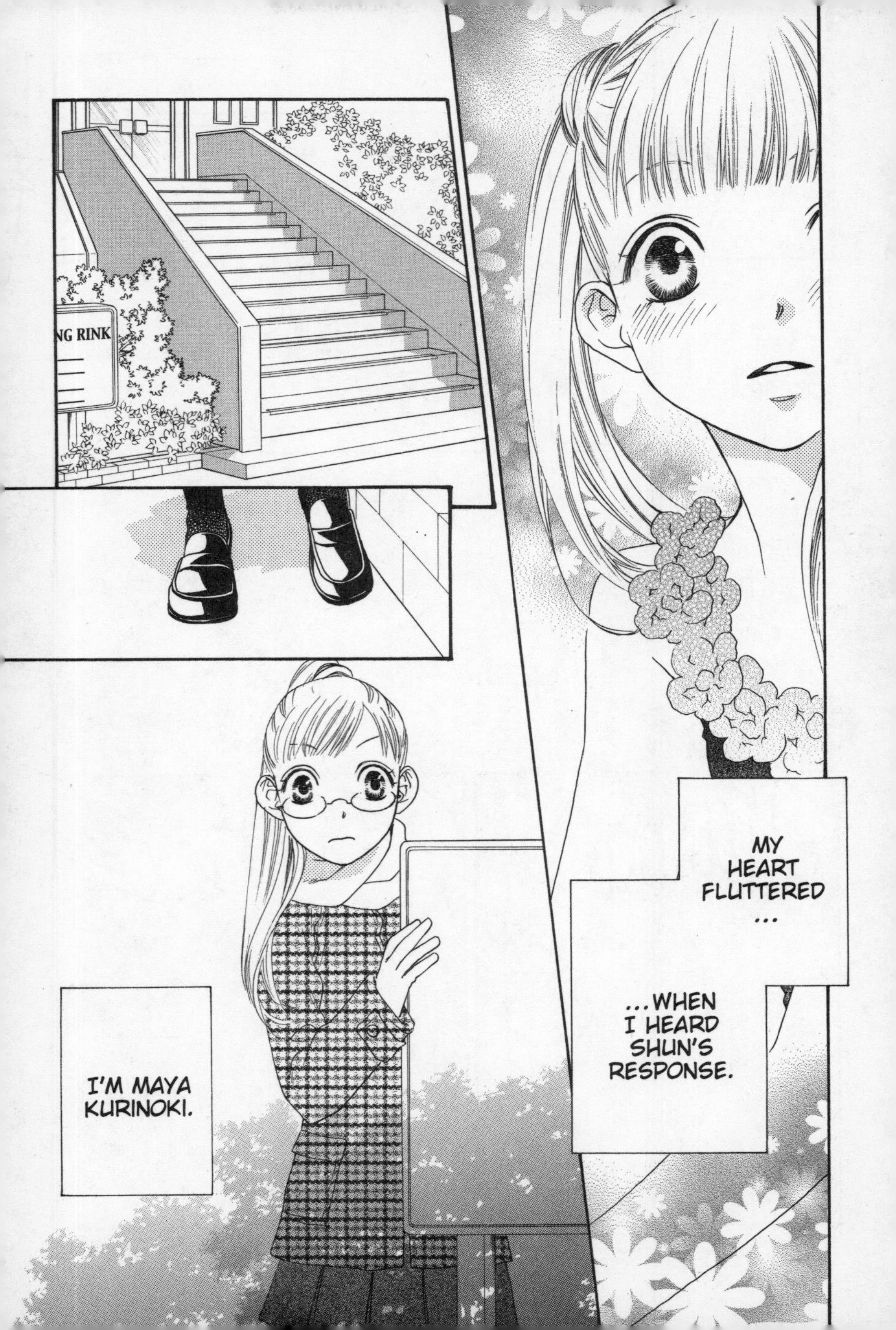
MY HEART FLUTTERED ...
...WHEN I HEARD SHUN'S RESPONSE.
NG RINK
I'M MAYA KURINOKI.

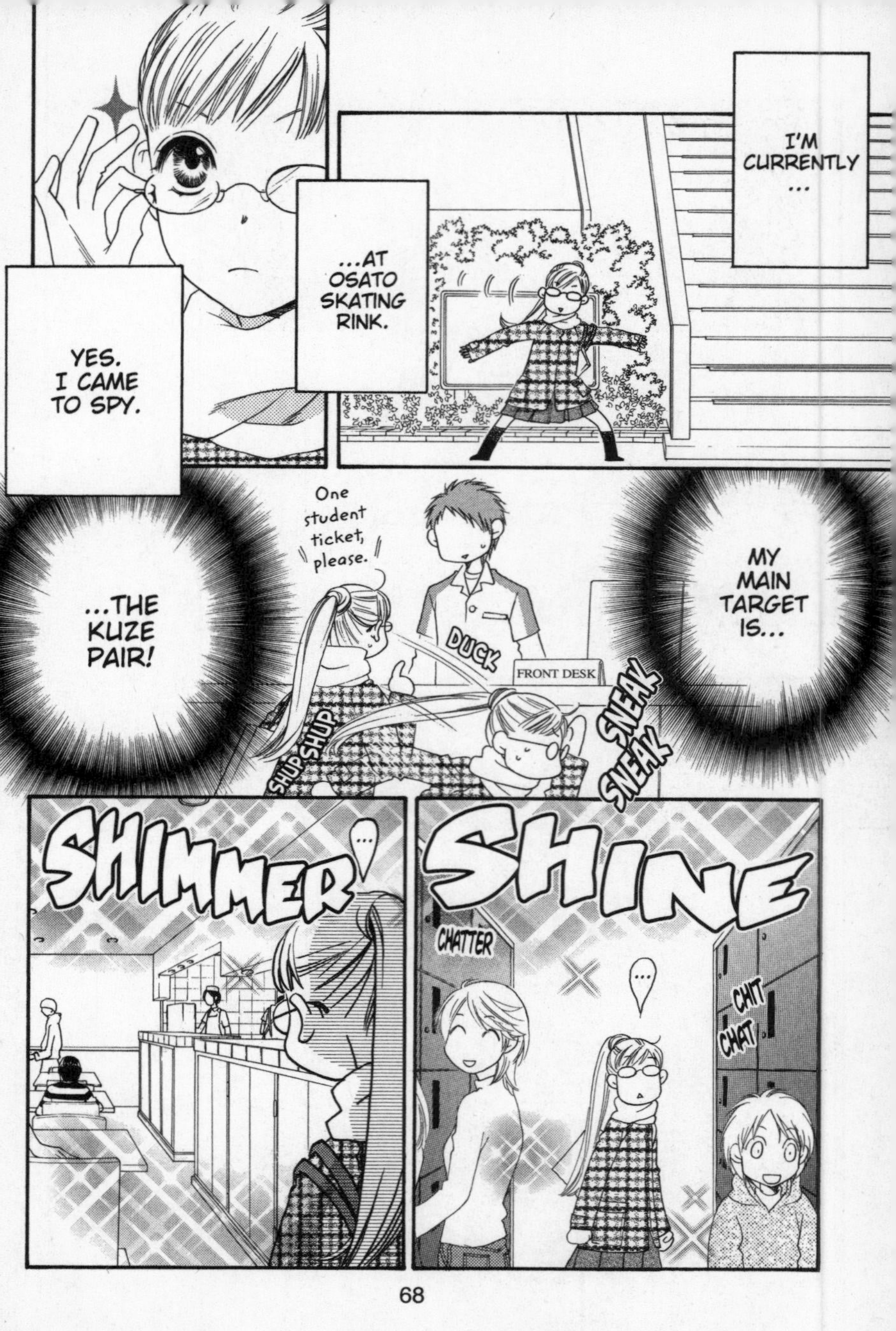
I'M CURRENTLY ...
...AT OSATO SKATING RINK.
YES. I CAME TO SPY.
MY MAIN TARGET IS...
One student ticket, please.
DUCK
FRONT DESK
SNEAK SNEAK
SHUP SHUP
...THE KUZE PAIR!
SHINE
CHATTER
...
CHIT CHAT
SHIMMER
...

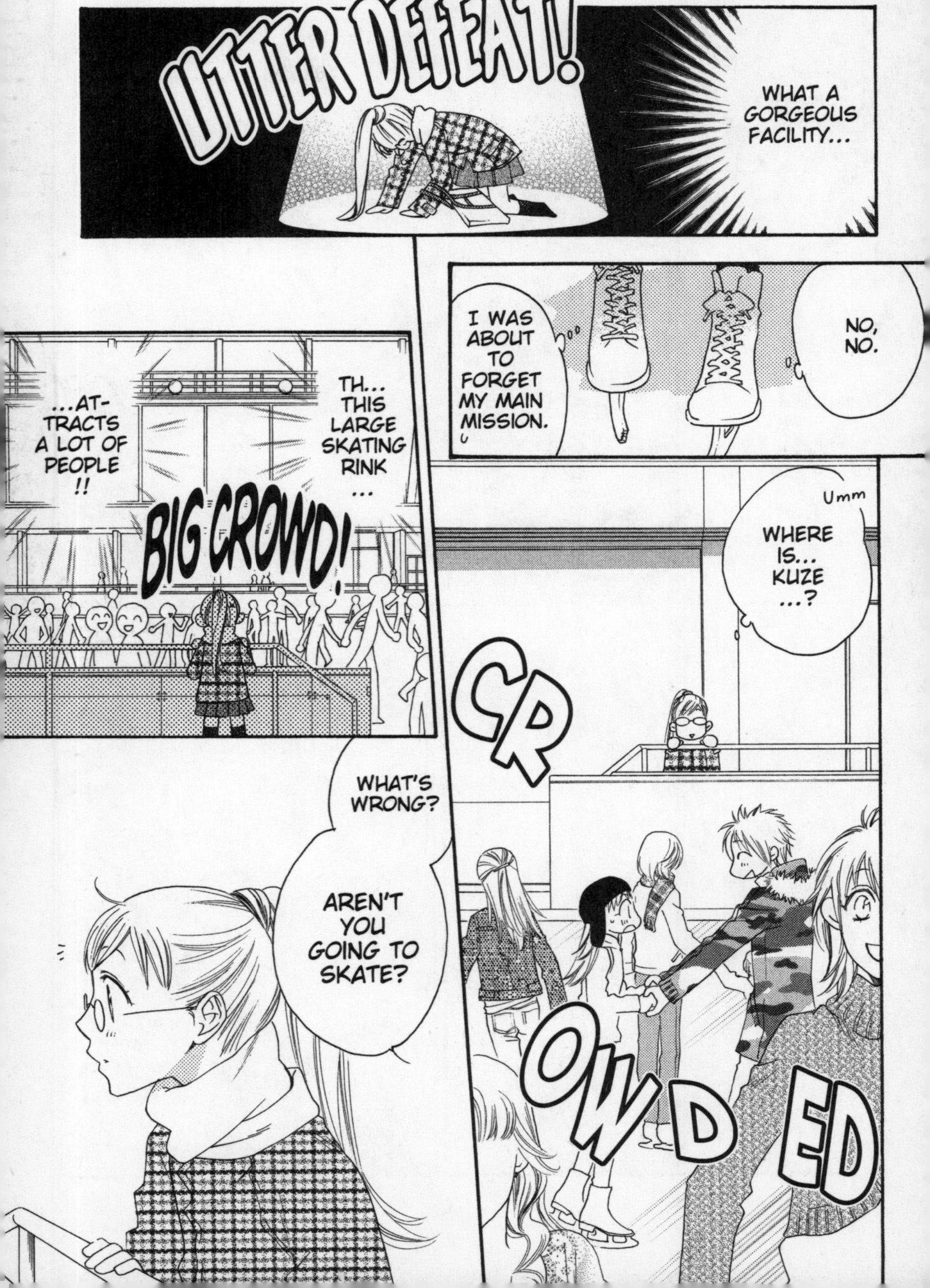
WHAT A GORGEOUS FACILITY...
UTTER DEFEAT!
NO, NO.
I WAS ABOUT TO FORGET MY MAIN MISSION.
TH... THIS LARGE SKATING RINK ...
...AT-TRACTS A LOT OF PEOPLE !!
BIG CROWD!
Umm
WHERE IS... KUZE ...?
CROWDED
WHAT'S WRONG?
AREN'T YOU GOING TO SKATE?

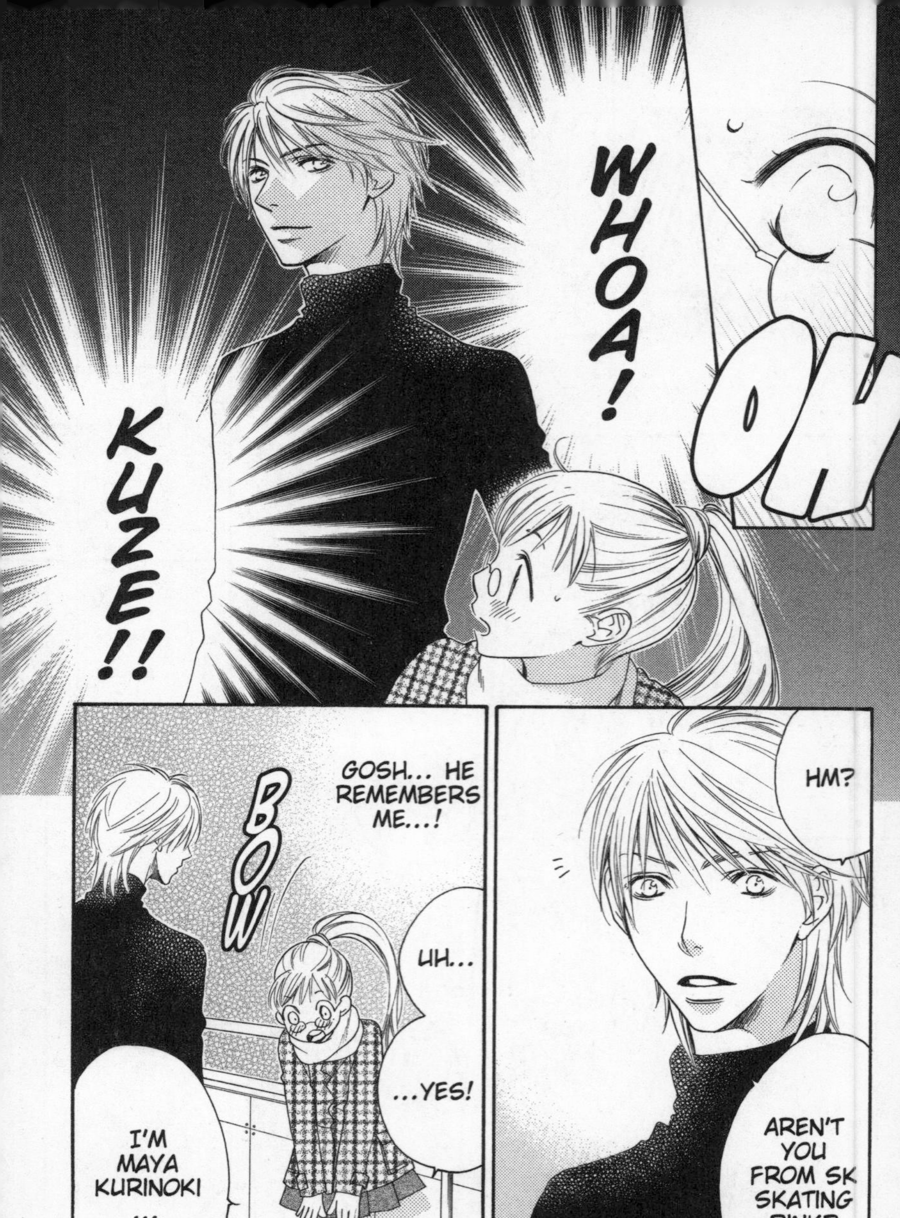
OH
WHOA!
KUZE!!
HM?
AREN'T YOU FROM SK SKATING RINK?
GOSH... HE REMEMBERS ME...!
BOW
UH...
...YES!
I'M MAYA KURINOKI ...

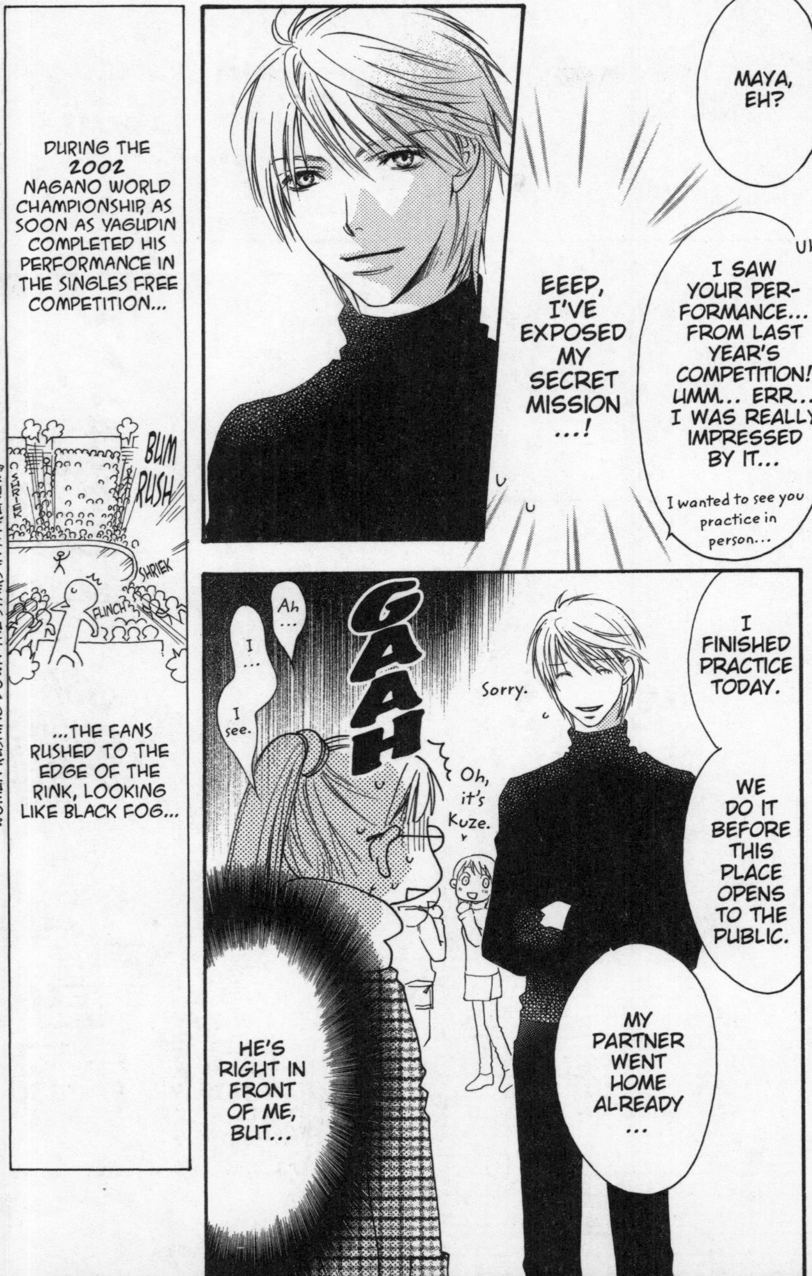
MAYA, EH?
Uh
I SAW YOUR PER-FORMANCE... FROM LAST YEAR'S COMPETITION! UMM... ERR... I WAS REALLY IMPRESSED BY IT...
I wanted to see you practice in person...
EEEP, I'VE EXPOSED MY SECRET MISSION ...!
I FINISHED PRACTICE TODAY.
WE DO IT BEFORE THIS PLACE OPENS TO THE PUBLIC.
Sorry.
MY PARTNER WENT HOME ALREADY ...
Oh, it's Kuze.
GAAH
Ah ...
I ...
I see.
HE'S RIGHT IN FRONT OF ME, BUT...
DURING THE 2002 NAGANO WORLD CHAMPIONSHIP, AS SOON AS YAGUDIN COMPLETED HIS PERFORMANCE IN THE SINGLES FREE COMPETITION...
BUM RUSH
SHRIEK
FLINCH
...THE FANS RUSHED TO THE EDGE OF THE RINK, LOOKING LIKE BLACK FOG...
WOMEN RUSHING DOWN THE STAIRS IN A FRENZY.

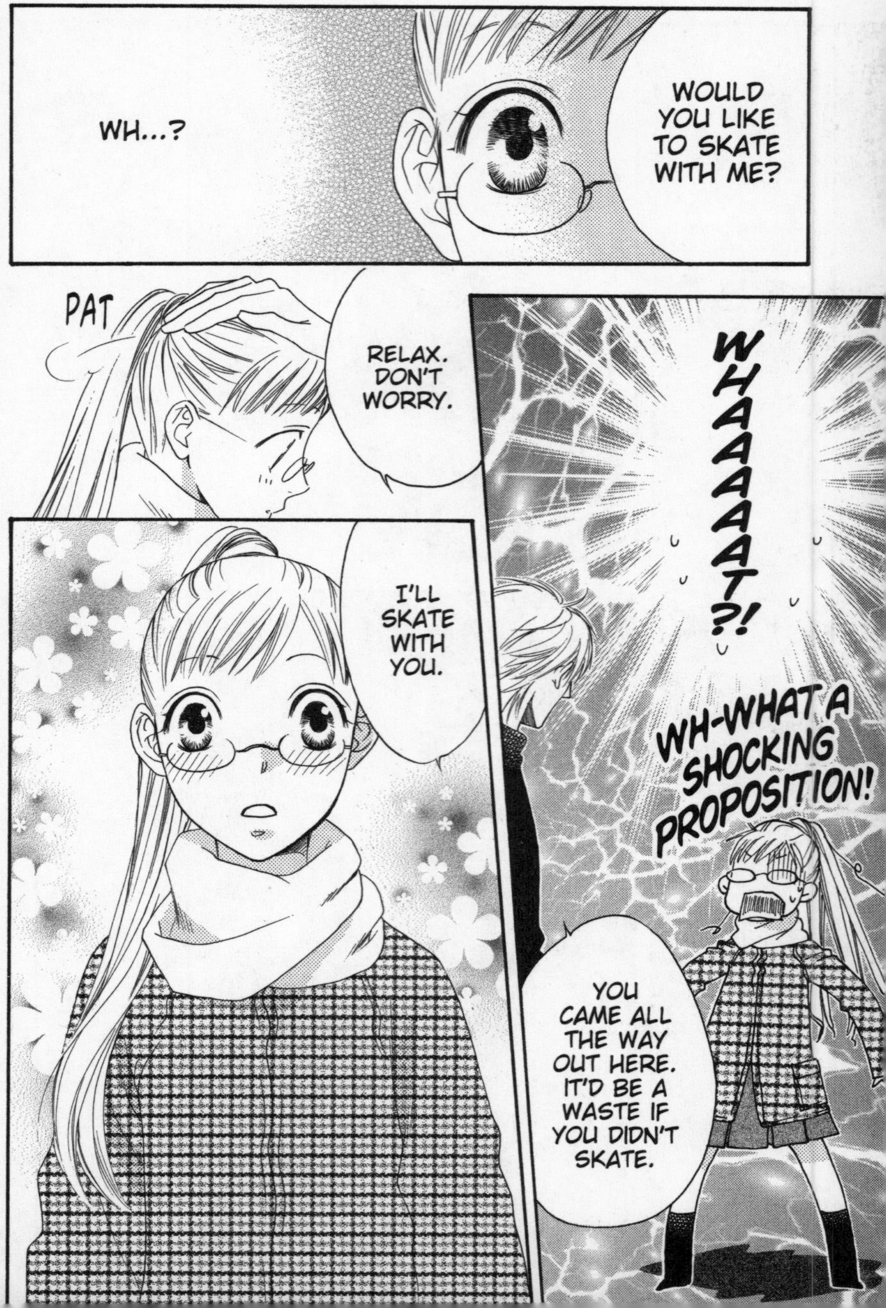
WOULD YOU LIKE TO SKATE WITH ME?
WH...?
WHAAAAAAT?!
WH-WHAT A SHOCKING PROPOSITION!
YOU CAME ALL THE WAY OUT HERE. IT'D BE A WASTE IF YOU DIDN'T SKATE.
PAT
RELAX. DON'T WORRY.
I'LL SKATE WITH YOU.

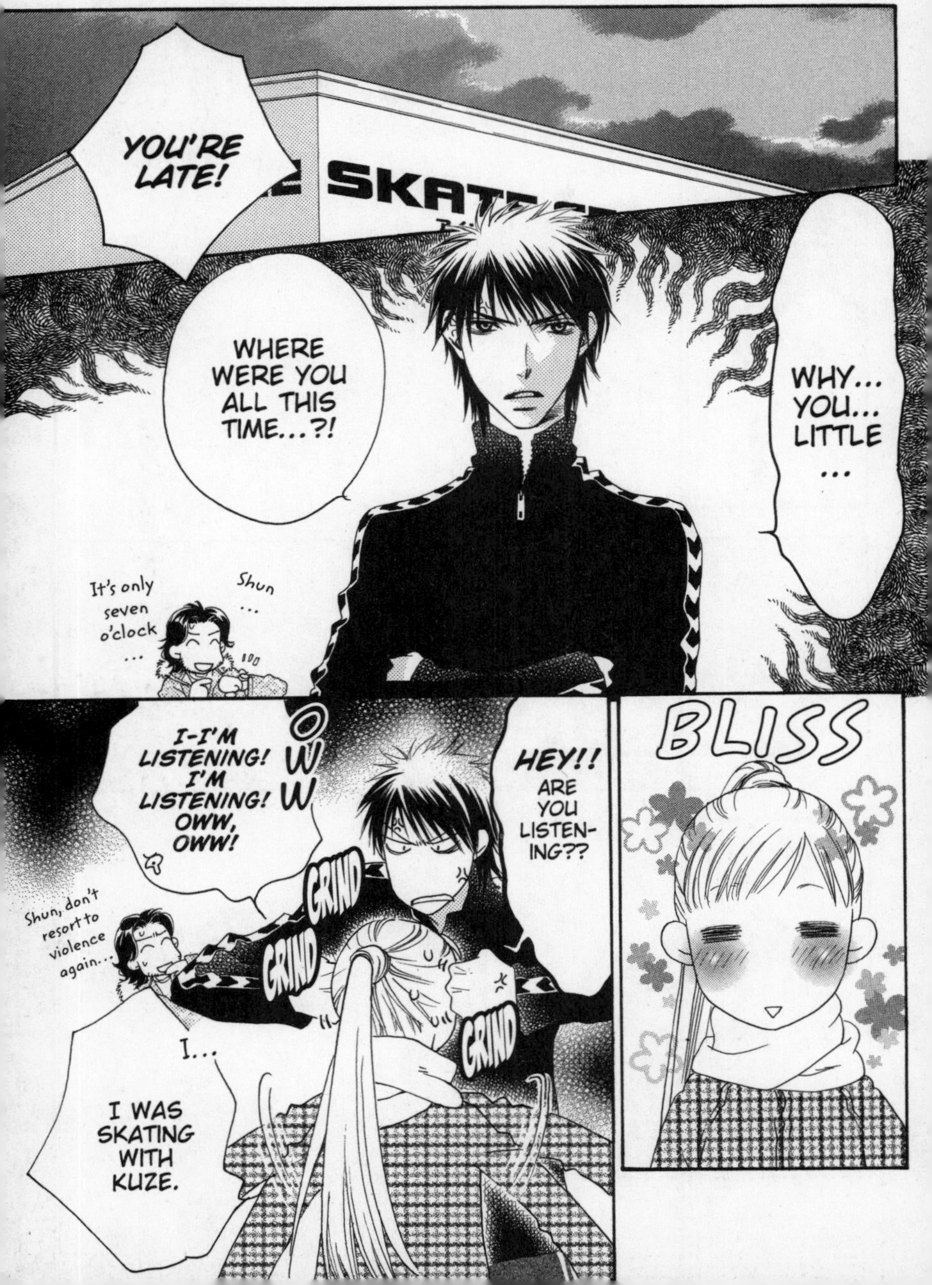
YOU'RE LATE!
SKATE
WHY... YOU... LITTLE ...
WHERE WERE YOU ALL THIS TIME...?!
Shun ...
It's only seven o'clock ...
BLISS
HEY!! ARE YOU LISTENING??
OWW
I-I'M LISTENING! I'M LISTENING! OWW, OWW!
GRIND
GRIND
GRIND
Shun, don't resort to violence again...
I...
I WAS SKATING WITH KUZE.

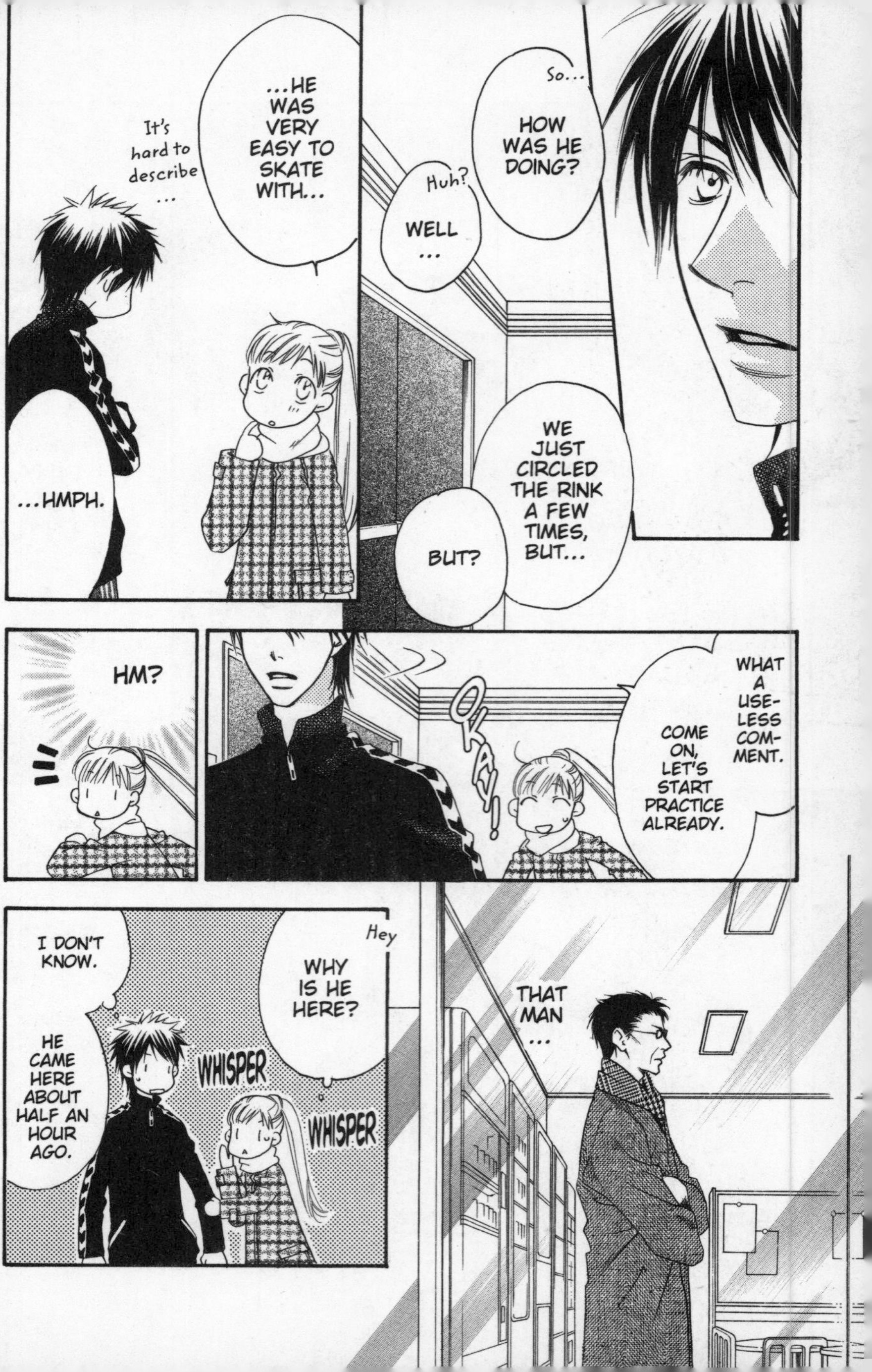
So...
HOW WAS HE DOING?
Huh?
WELL ...
WE JUST CIRCLED THE RINK A FEW TIMES, BUT...
BUT?
...HE WAS VERY EASY TO SKATE WITH...
It's hard to describe ...
...HMPH.
WHAT A USE-LESS COM-MENT.
COME ON, LET'S START PRACTICE ALREADY.
OKAY!
HM?
THAT MAN ...
Hey
WHY IS HE HERE?
WHISPER
WHISPER
I DON'T KNOW.
HE CAME HERE ABOUT HALF AN HOUR AGO.

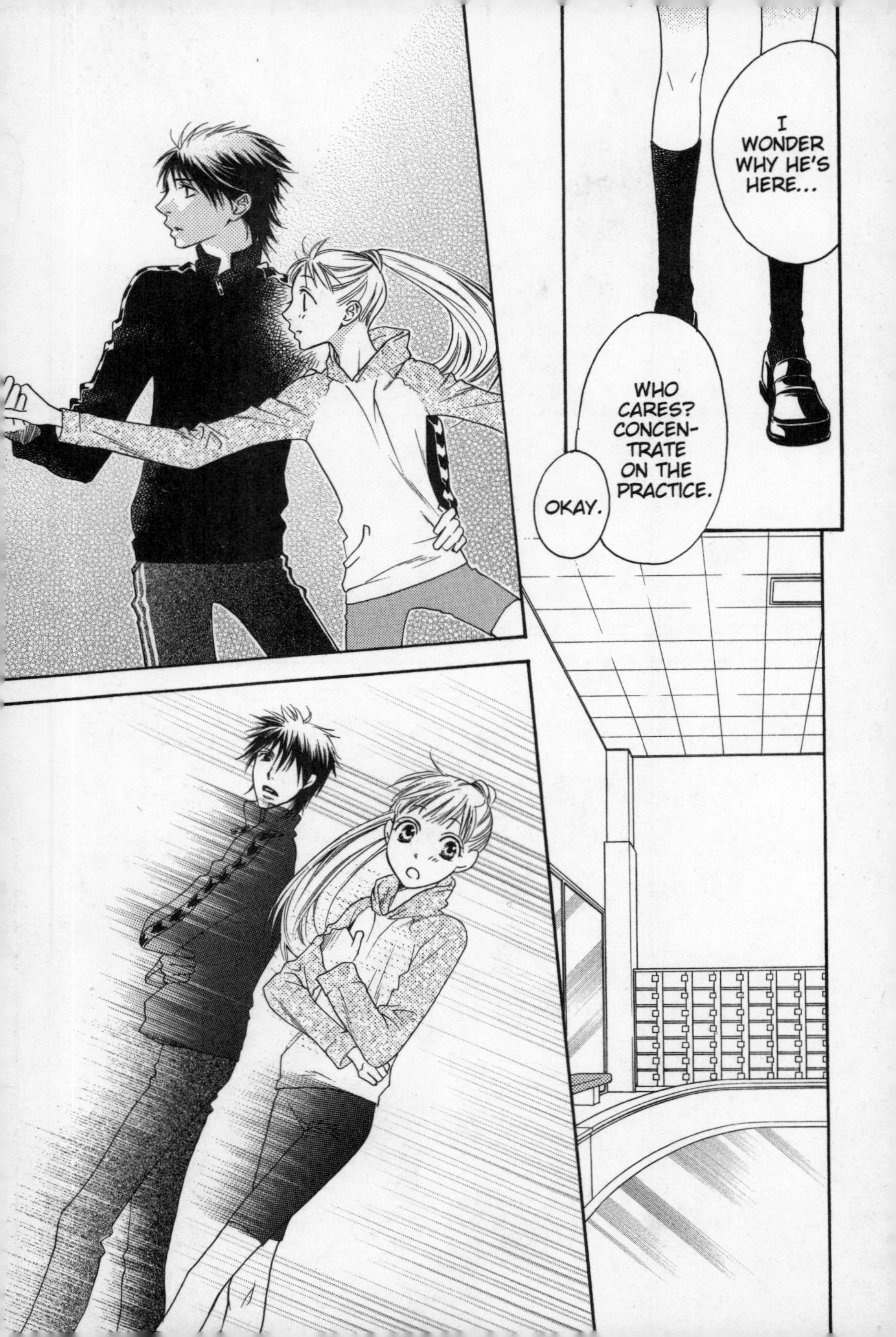
I WONDER WHY HE'S HERE...
WHO CARES? CONCENTRATE ON THE PRACTICE.
OKAY.

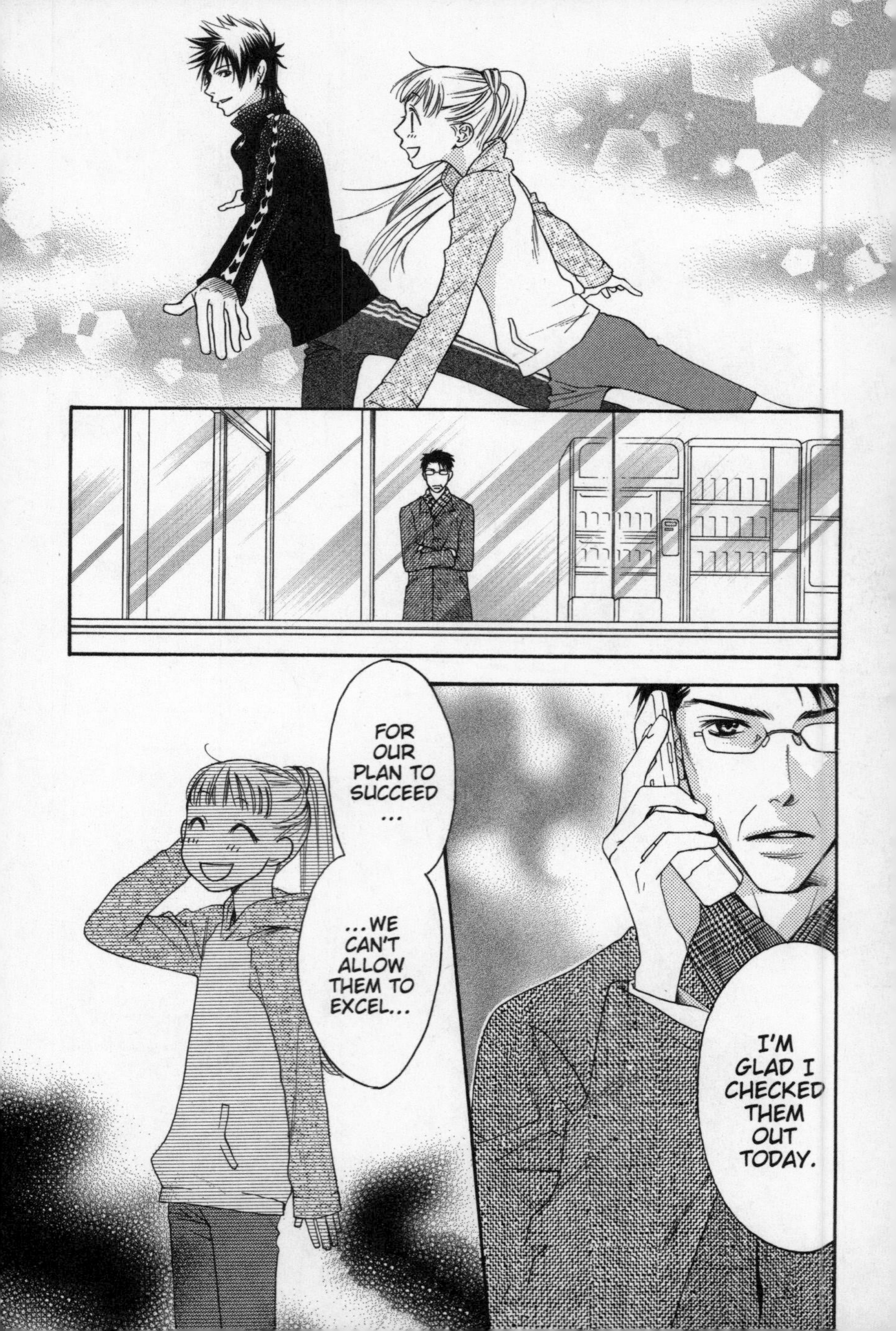
I'M GLAD I CHECKED THEM OUT TODAY.
FOR OUR PLAN TO SUCCEED...
...WE CAN'T ALLOW THEM TO EXCEL...

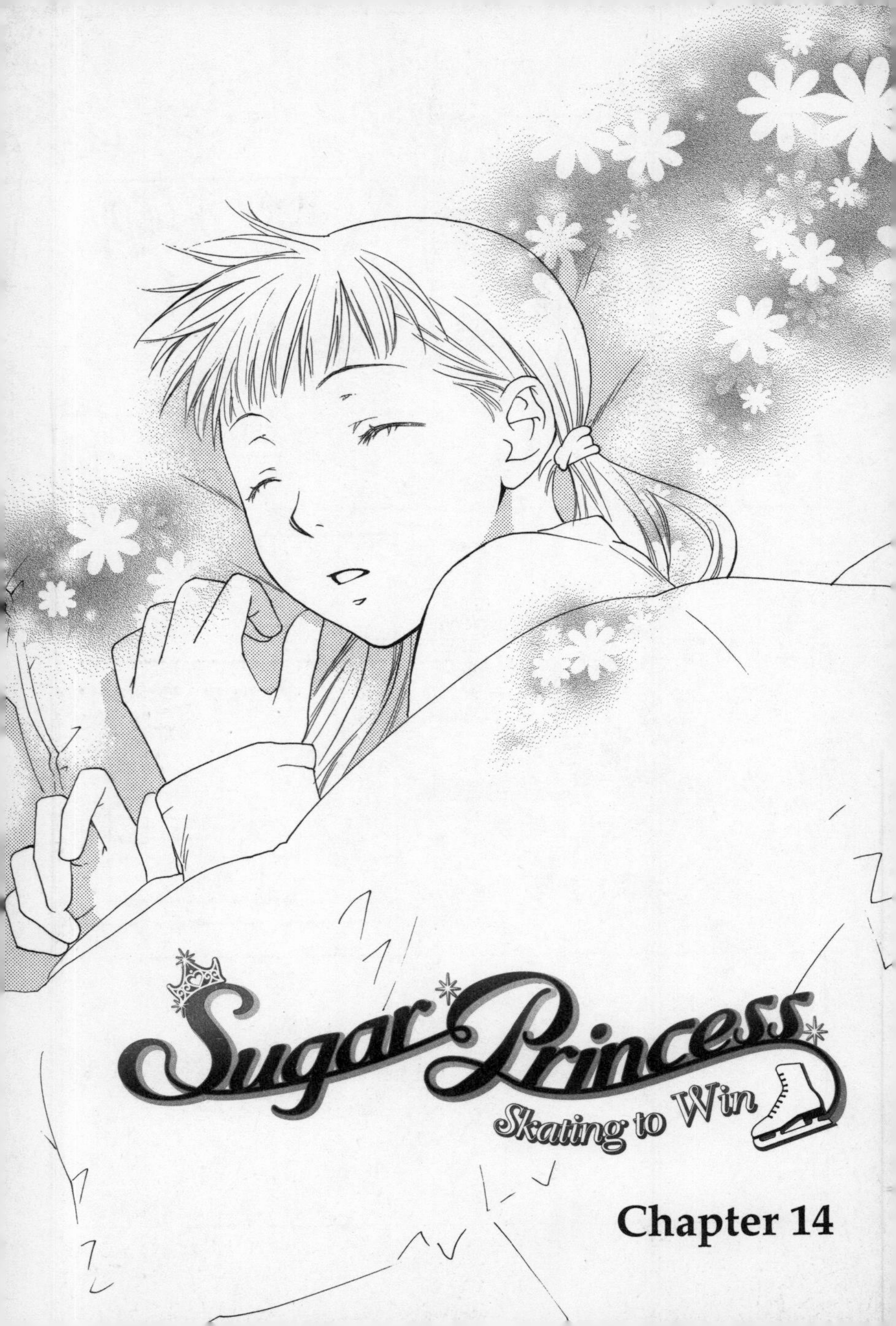
Sugar Princess
Skating to Win
Chapter 14

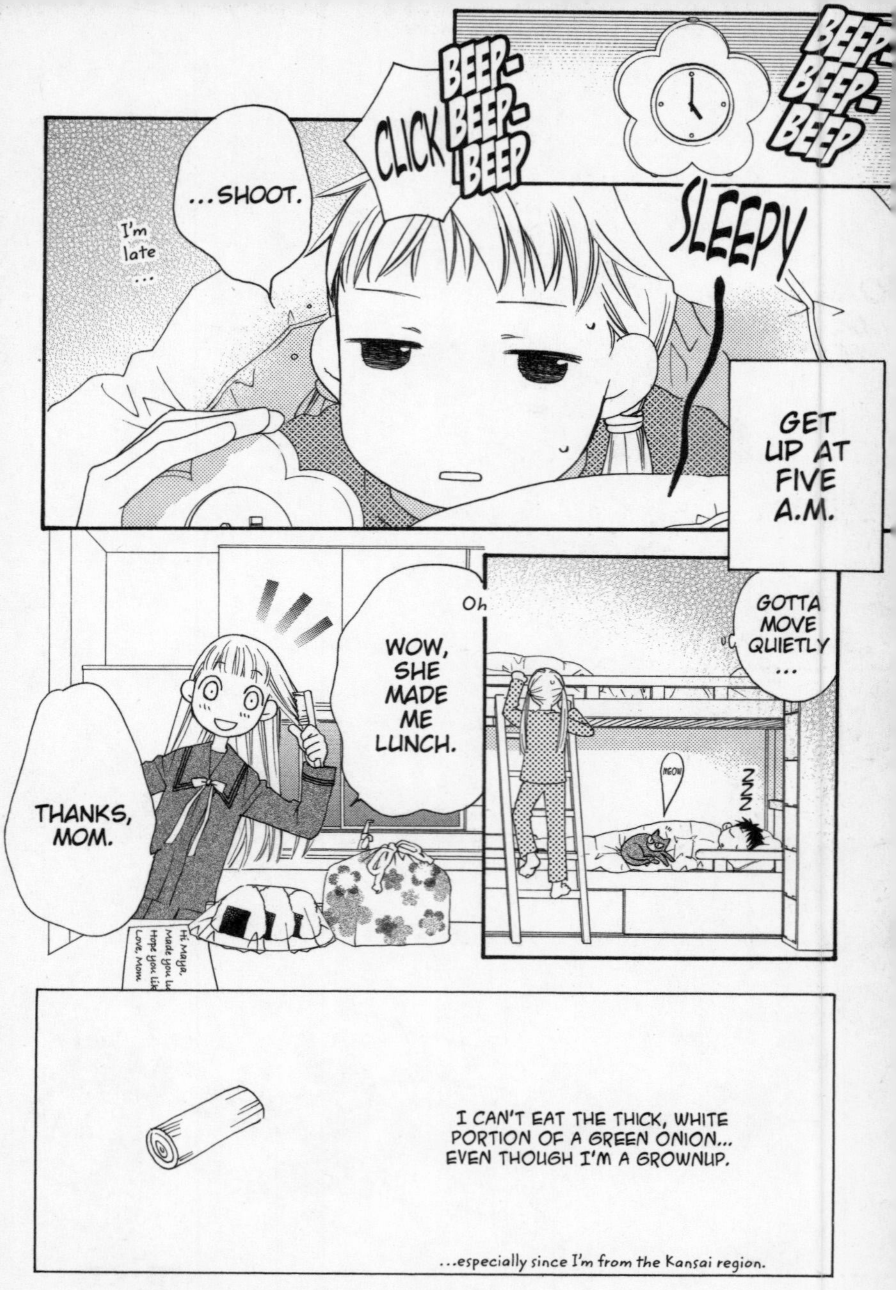
BEEP-BEEP-BEEP
CLICK BEEP-BEEP-BEEP
SLEEPY
...SHOOT.
I'm late ...
GET UP AT FIVE A.M.
GOTTA MOVE QUIETLY ...
MEOW
ZZZ
Oh
WOW, SHE MADE ME LUNCH.
THANKS, MOM.
Hi Maya.
Love, Mom
I CAN'T EAT THE THICK, WHITE PORTION OF A GREEN ONION... EVEN THOUGH I'M A GROWNUP.
...especially since I'm from the Kansai region.

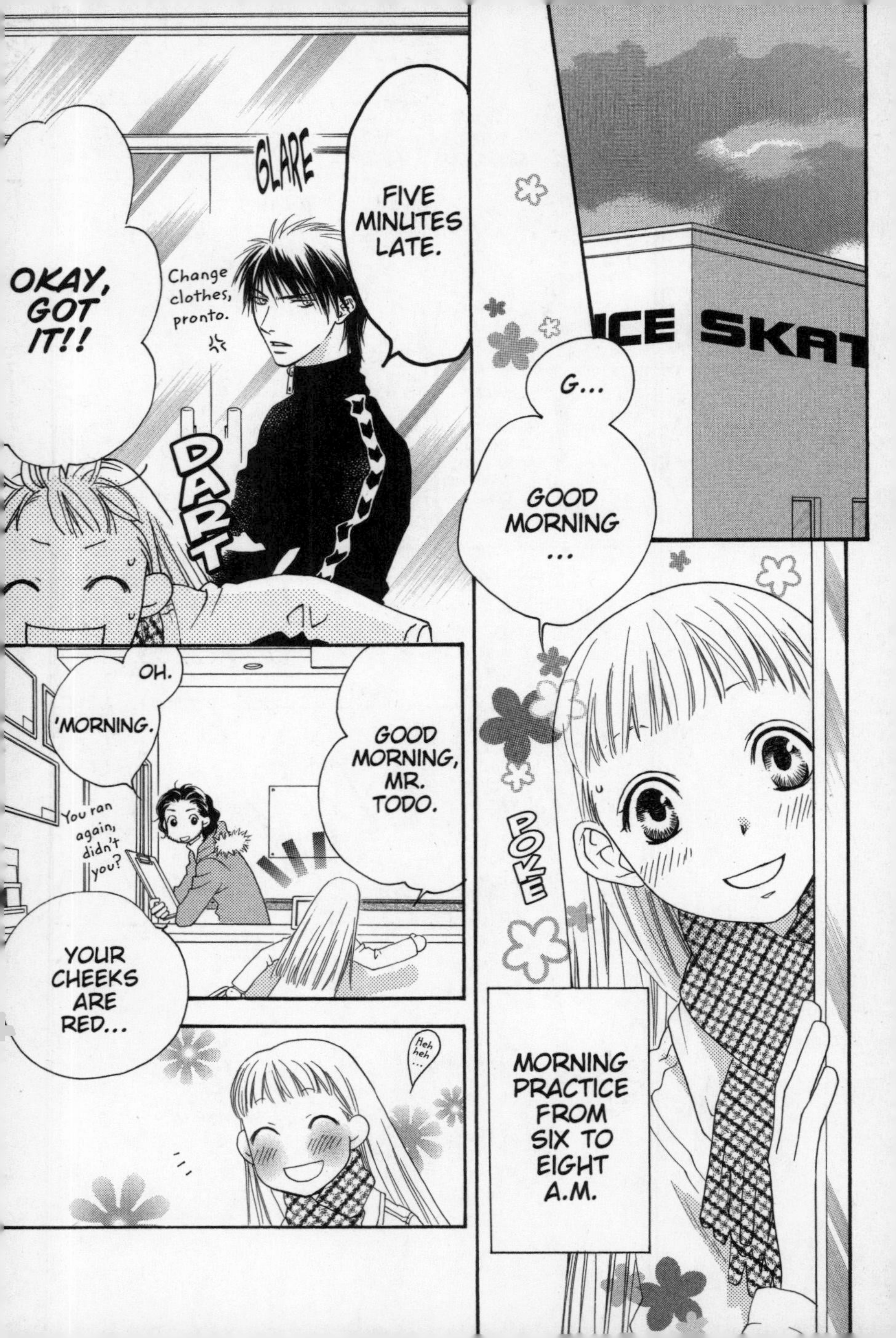
ICE SKAT
G...
GOOD MORNING ...
POKE
MORNING PRACTICE FROM SIX TO EIGHT A.M.
FIVE MINUTES LATE.
GLARE
Change clothes, pronto.
OKAY, GOT IT!!
DART
GOOD MORNING, MR. TODO.
OH.
'MORNING.
You ran again, didn't you?
YOUR CHEEKS ARE RED...
Heh heh ...

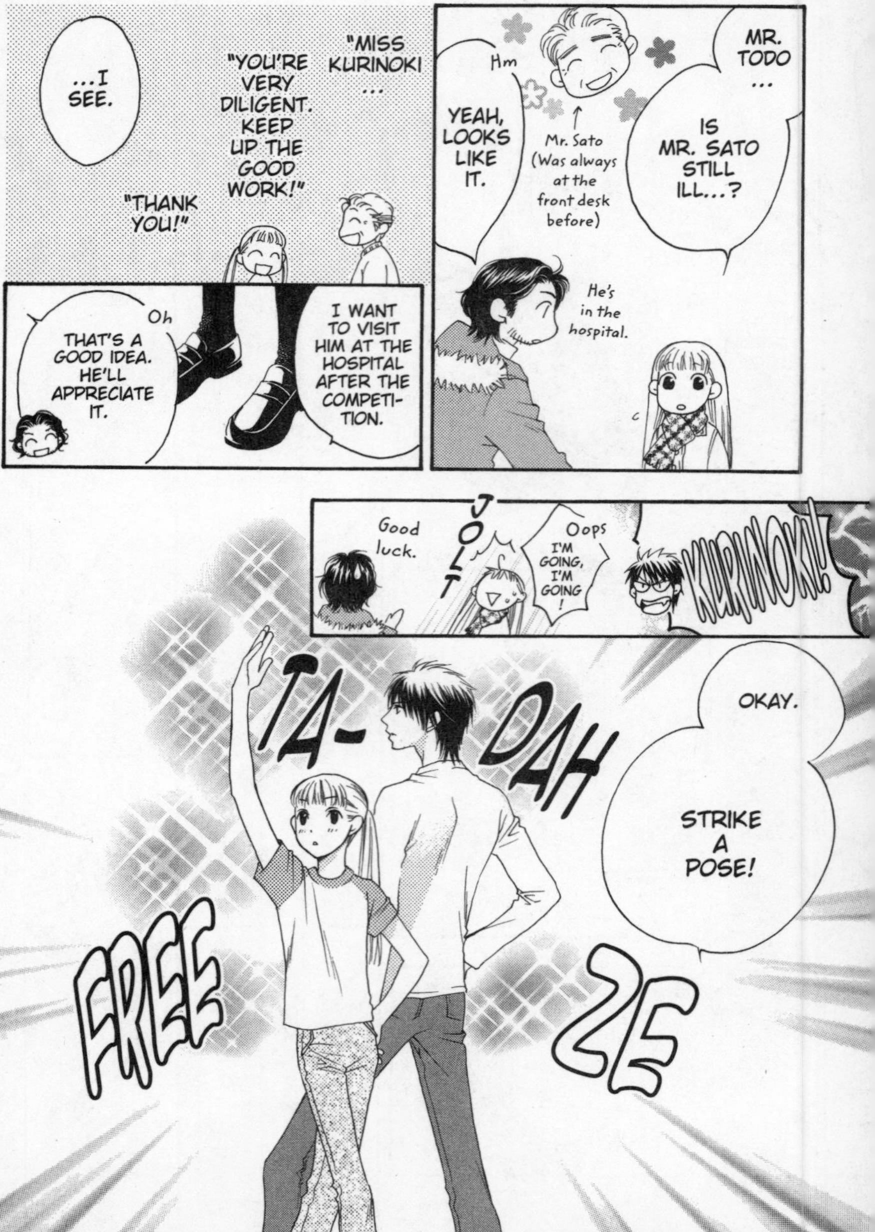
MR. TODO ...
IS MR. SATO STILL ILL...?
Hm
YEAH, LOOKS LIKE IT.
Mr. Sato (Was always at the front desk before)
He's in the hospital.
"MISS KURINOKI ...
"YOU'RE VERY DILIGENT. KEEP UP THE GOOD WORK!"
"THANK YOU!"
...I SEE.
I WANT TO VISIT HIM AT THE HOSPITAL AFTER THE COMPETITION.
Oh
THAT'S A GOOD IDEA. HE'LL APPRECIATE IT.
KURINOKI!!
Oops
I'M GOING, I'M GOING!
JOLT
Good luck.
OKAY.
STRIKE A POSE!
TA-DAH
FREEZE

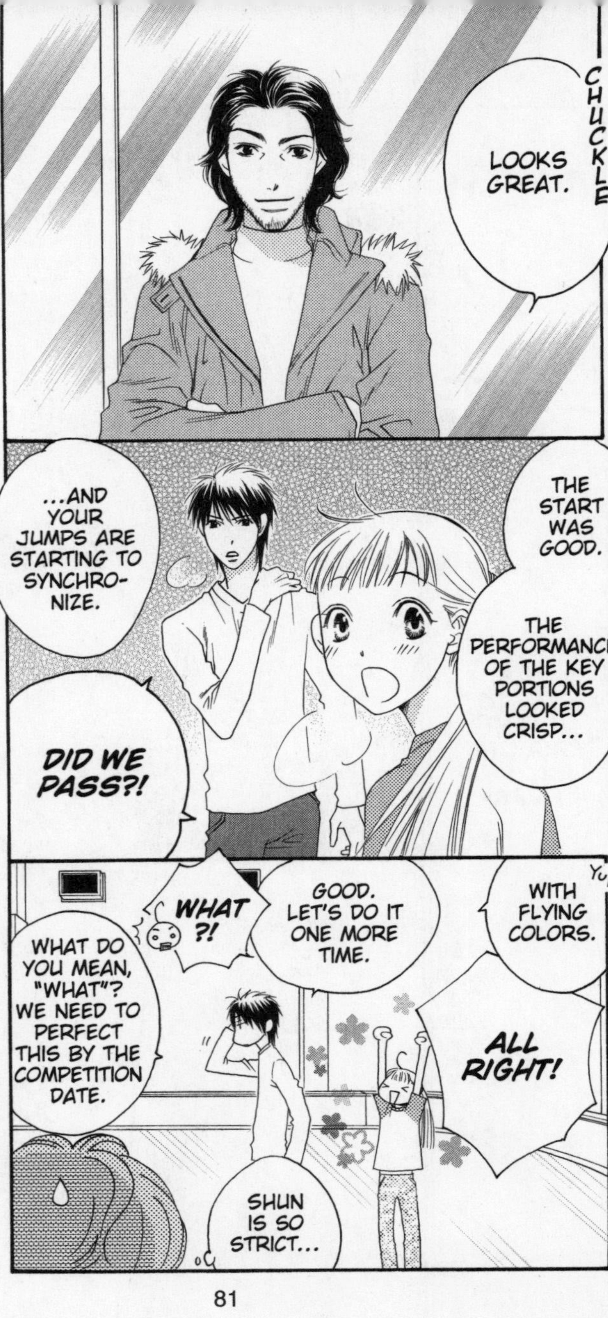
CHUCKLE
LOOKS GREAT.
THE START WAS GOOD.
THE PERFORMANCE OF THE KEY PORTIONS LOOKED CRISP...
...AND YOUR JUMPS ARE STARTING TO SYNCHRO-NIZE.
DID WE PASS?!
Yup
WITH FLYING COLORS.
ALL RIGHT!
GOOD. LET'S DO IT ONE MORE TIME.
WHAT?!
WHAT DO YOU MEAN, "WHAT"? WE NEED TO PERFECT THIS BY THE COMPETITION DATE.
SHUN IS SO STRICT...

MY FORMER EDITOR S AND I WENT TO AN ICE SHOW. AT THE END OF THE EVENT, THE SKATERS THREW SIGNED BALLS INTO THE CROWD. OF COURSE, THE FANS RUSHED TO THE EDGE OF THE RINK, SEPARATING THE TWO OF US. WHEN EDITOR S FOUND ME...

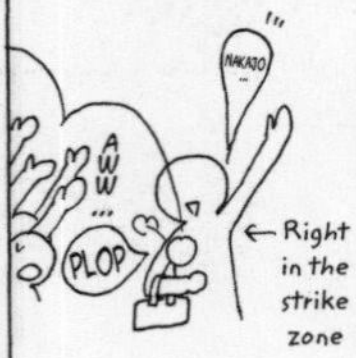
NAKAJO...
AWW...
PLOP
← Right in the strike zone

...A SIGNED BALL LANDED IN MY OLD EDITOR'S ARMS. TALK ABOUT LUCK!

THE BALL HAPPENED TO BE SIGNED BY THE MOST POPULAR SKATER, JOHNNY WEIR. THE FEMALE FANS STARED AT US WITH JEALOUSY...

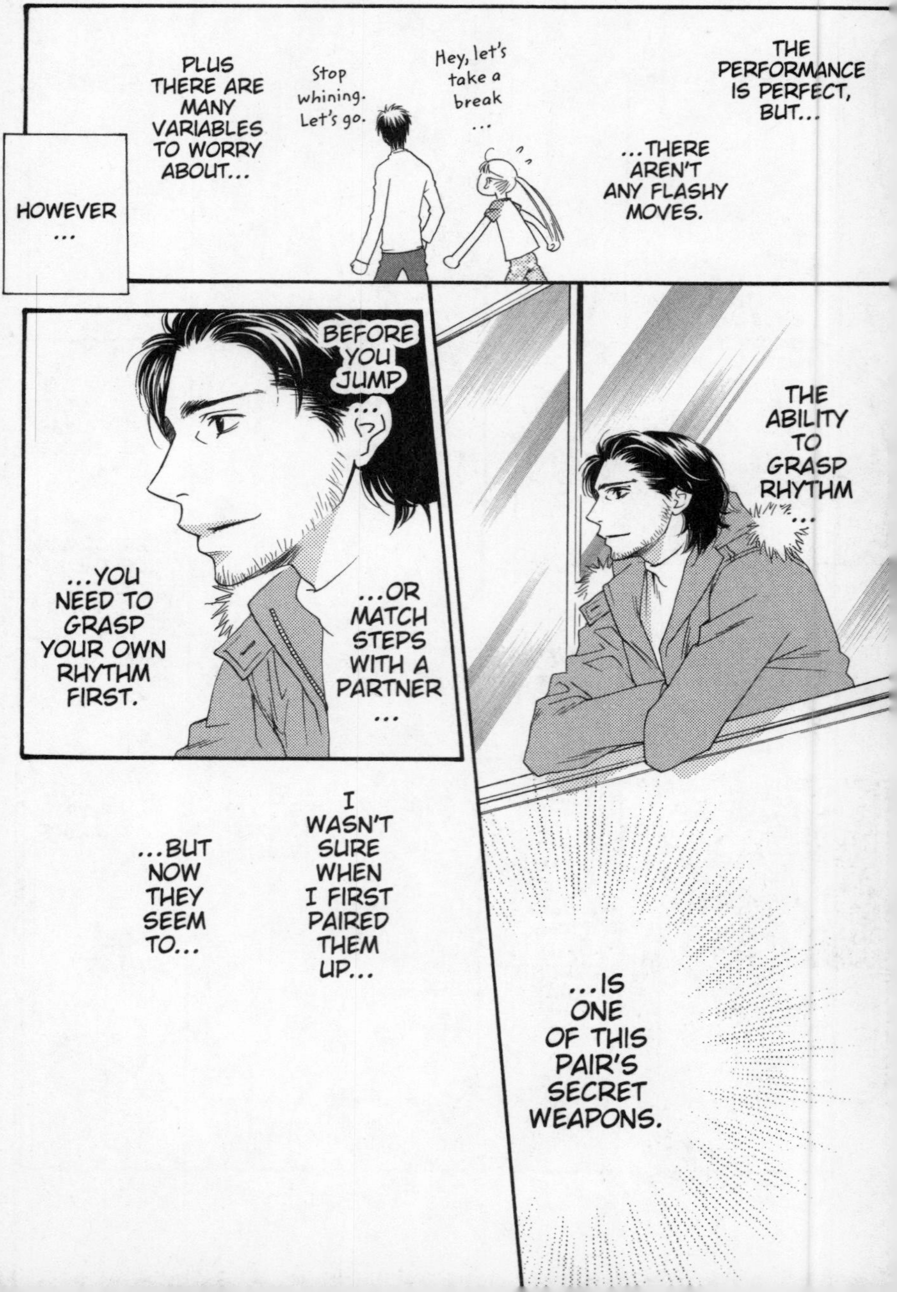
THE PERFORMANCE IS PERFECT, BUT...
...THERE AREN'T ANY FLASHY MOVES.
Hey, let's take a break ...
Stop whining. Let's go.
PLUS THERE ARE MANY VARIABLES TO WORRY ABOUT...
HOWEVER ...
THE ABILITY TO GRASP RHYTHM ...
...IS ONE OF THIS PAIR'S SECRET WEAPONS.
BEFORE YOU JUMP ...
...OR MATCH STEPS WITH A PARTNER ...
...YOU NEED TO GRASP YOUR OWN RHYTHM FIRST.
I WASN'T SURE WHEN I FIRST PAIRED THEM UP...
...BUT NOW THEY SEEM TO...

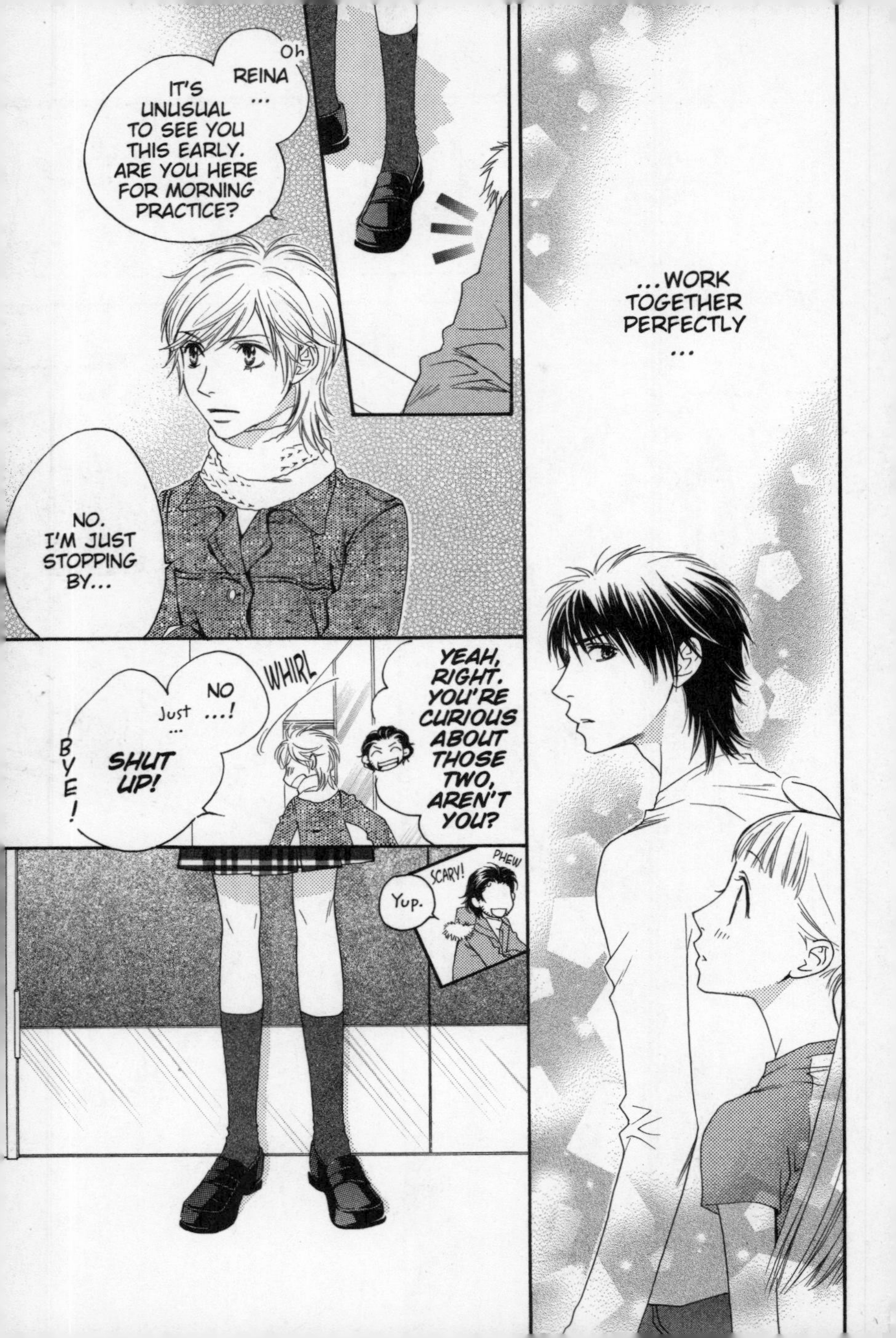

...WORK TOGETHER PERFECTLY ...
Oh
REINA ... IT'S UNUSUAL TO SEE YOU THIS EARLY. ARE YOU HERE FOR MORNING PRACTICE?
NO. I'M JUST STOPPING BY...
YEAH, RIGHT. YOU'RE CURIOUS ABOUT THOSE TWO, AREN'T YOU?
WHIRL
NO ...! Just ... SHUT UP!
BYE!
PHEW
SCARY!
Yup.

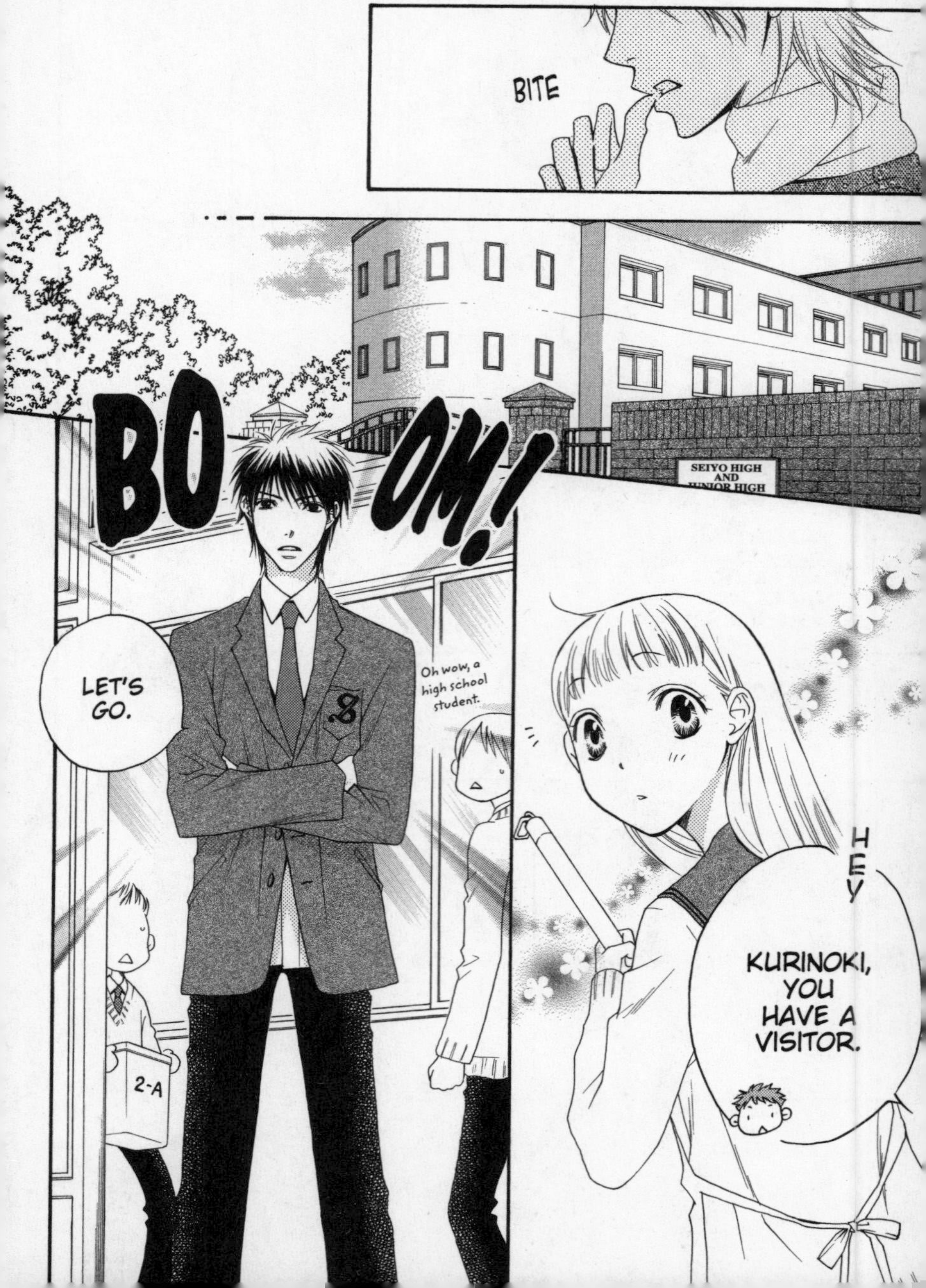
BITE
SEIYO HIGH AND JUNIOR HIGH
HEY
KURINOKI, YOU HAVE A VISITOR.
BO-OM!
LET'S GO.
Oh wow, a high school student.
2-A

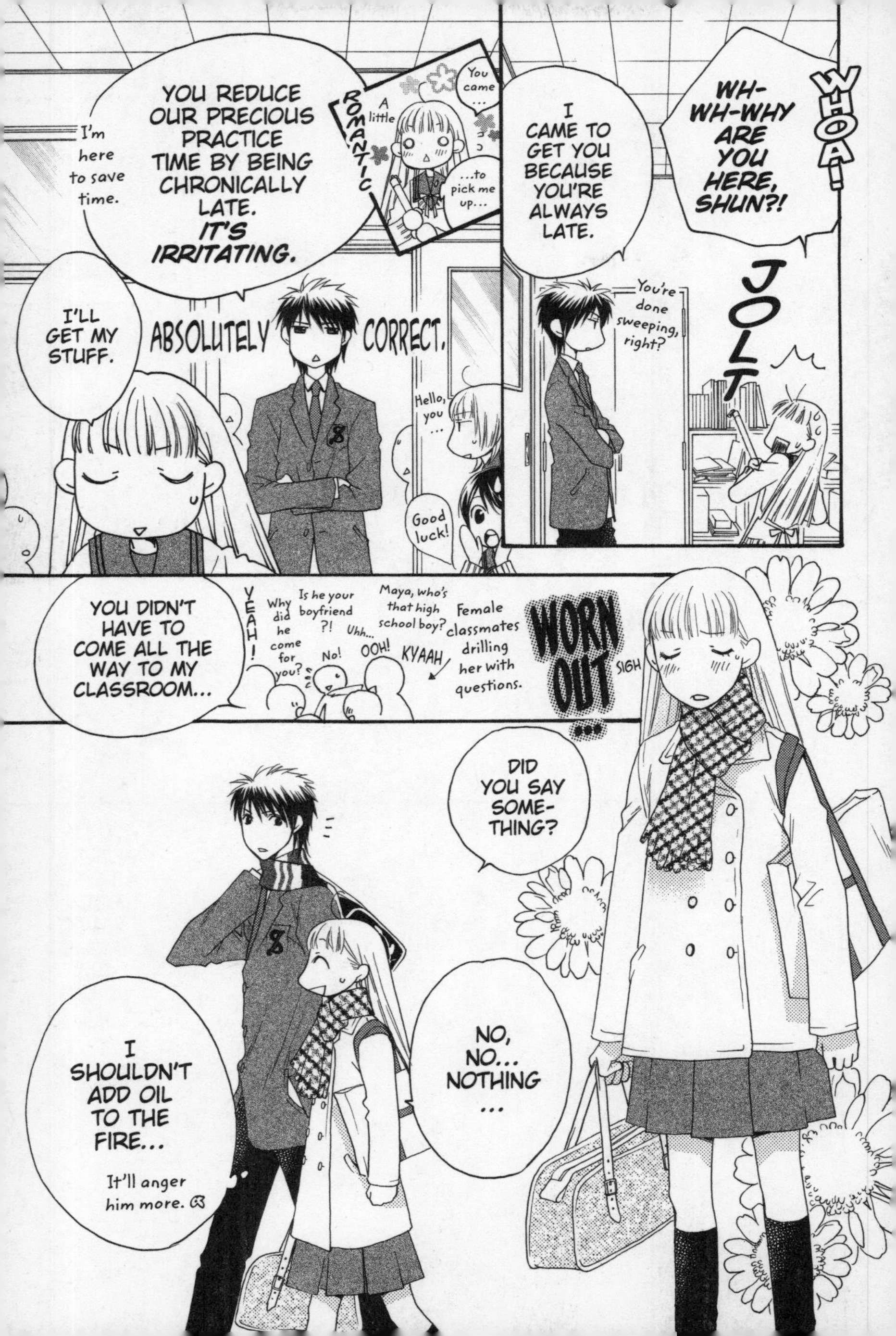
WHOA!
WH-WH-WHY ARE YOU HERE, SHUN?!
I CAME TO GET YOU BECAUSE YOU'RE ALWAYS LATE.
JOLT
You're done sweeping, right?
YOU REDUCE OUR PRECIOUS PRACTICE TIME BY BEING CHRONICALLY LATE. IT'S IRRITATING.
I'm here to save time.
ROMANTIC
A little
You came...
...to pick me up...
ABSOLUTELY CORRECT.
I'LL GET MY STUFF.
Hello, you...
Good luck!
WORN OUT
SIGH
Female classmates drilling her with questions.
Maya, who's that high school boy?
KYAAH
OOH!
Is he your boyfriend?!
Uhh...
No!
Why did he come for you?
YEAH!
YOU DIDN'T HAVE TO COME ALL THE WAY TO MY CLASSROOM...
DID YOU SAY SOMETHING?
NO, NO... NOTHING...
I SHOULDN'T ADD OIL TO THE FIRE...
It'll anger him more.

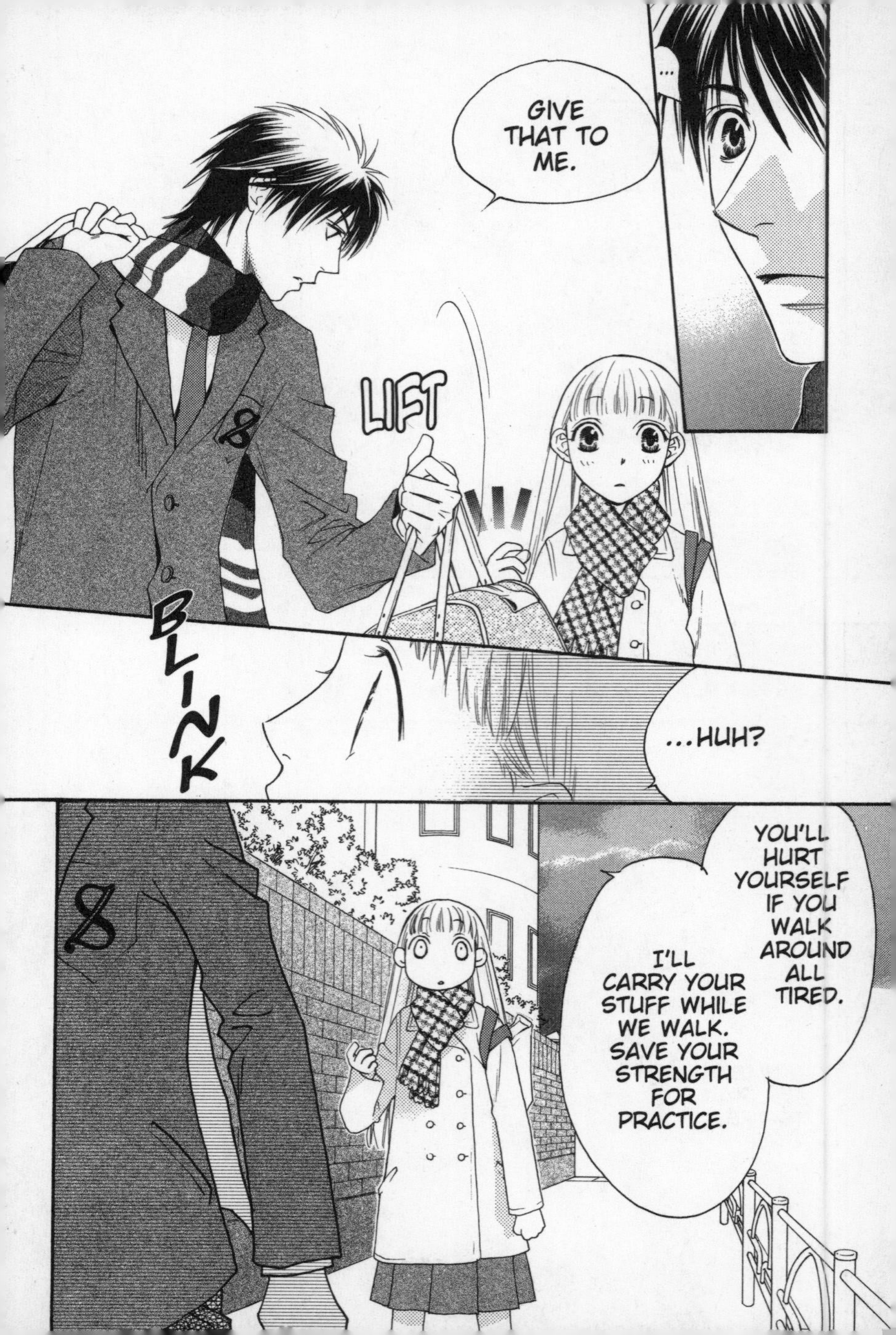
...
GIVE THAT TO ME.
LIFT
...HUH?
BLINK
YOU'LL HURT YOURSELF IF YOU WALK AROUND ALL TIRED.
I'LL CARRY YOUR STUFF WHILE WE WALK. SAVE YOUR STRENGTH FOR PRACTICE.

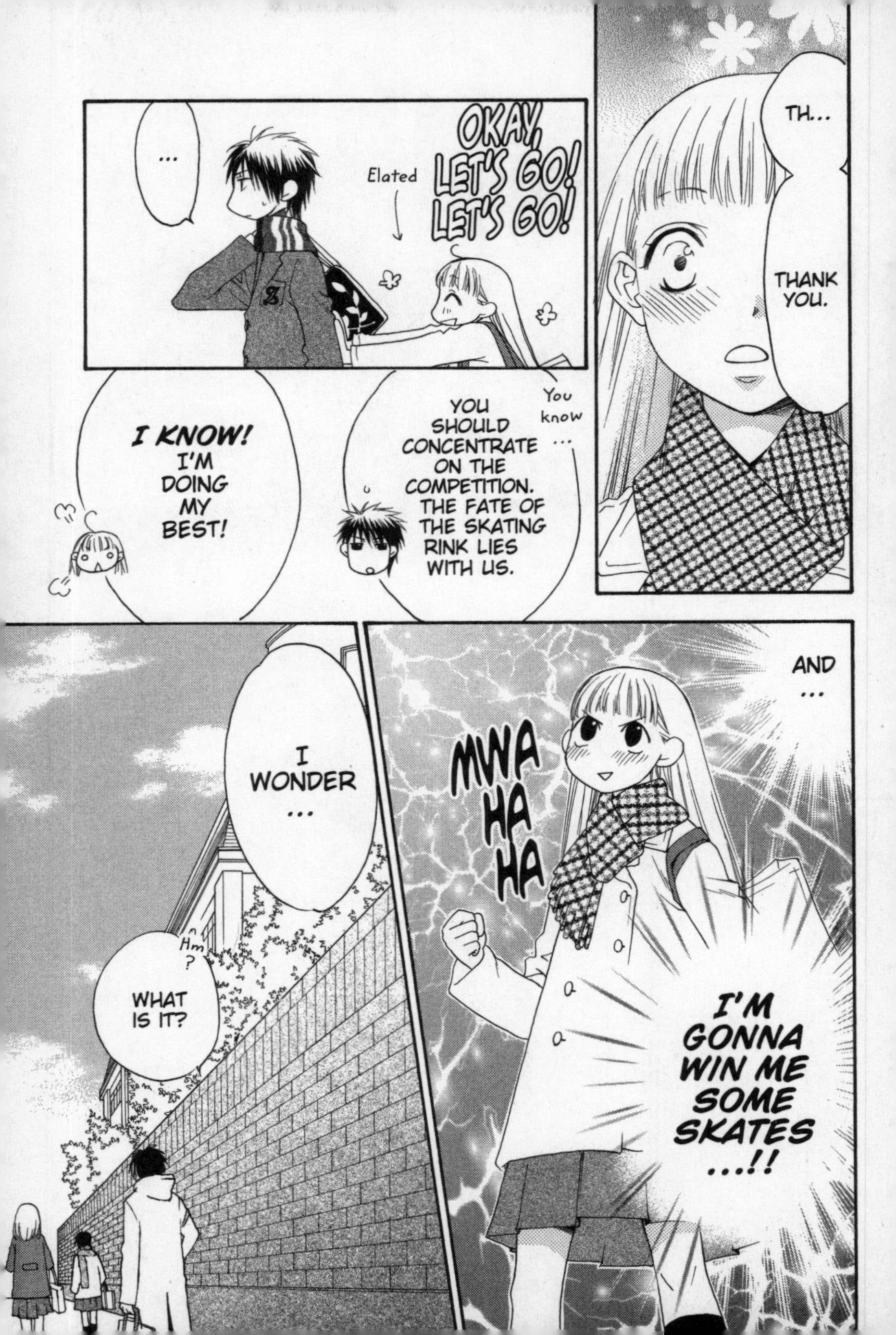
TH...
THANK YOU.
...
OKAY, LET'S GO! LET'S GO!
Elated
You know ...
YOU SHOULD CONCENTRATE ON THE COMPETITION. THE FATE OF THE SKATING RINK LIES WITH US.
I KNOW! I'M DOING MY BEST!
AND ...
MWA HA HA
I'M GONNA WIN ME SOME SKATES ...!!
I WONDER ...
Hm?
WHAT IS IT?

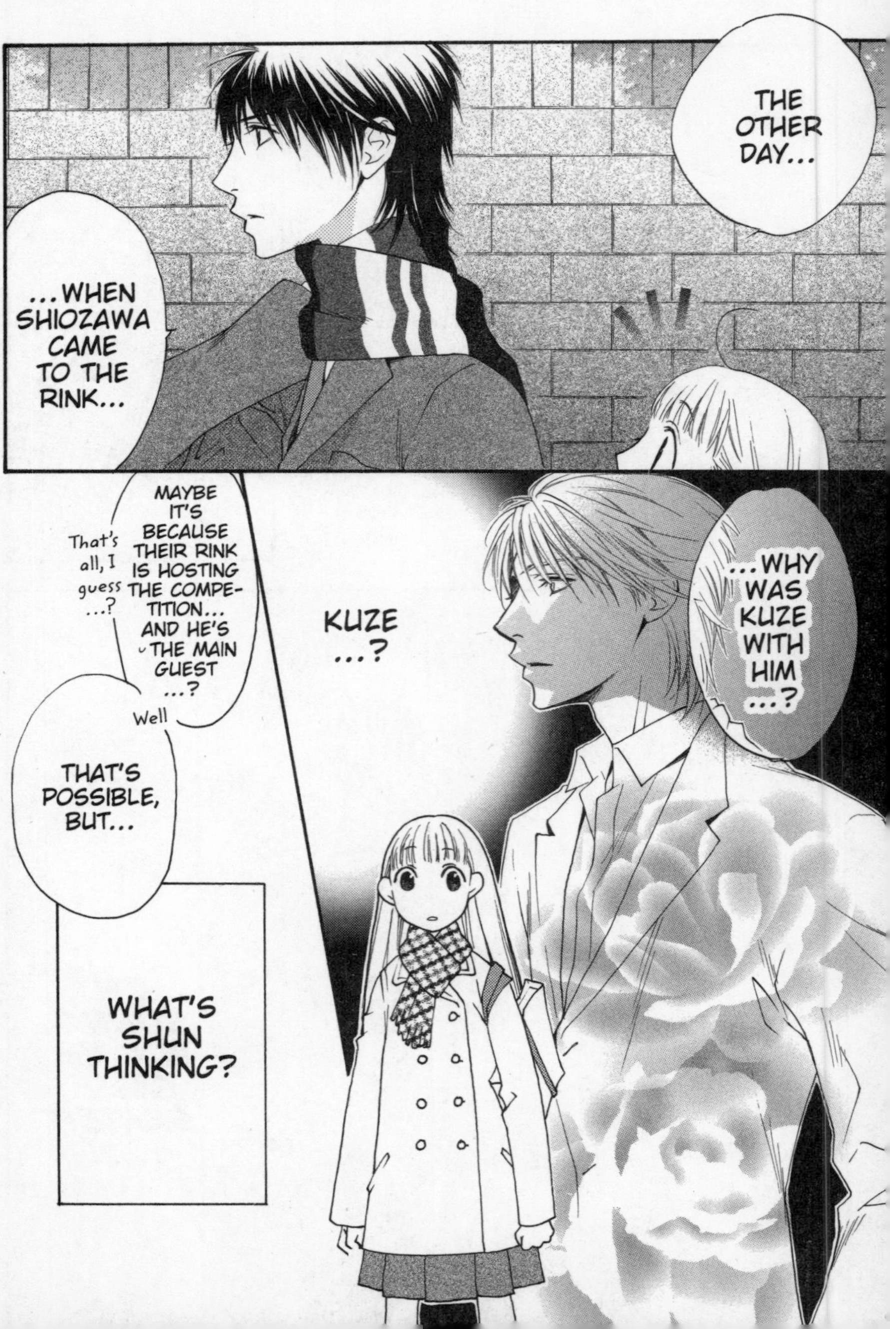
THE OTHER DAY...
...WHEN SHIOZAWA CAME TO THE RINK...
...WHY WAS KUZE WITH HIM...?
KUZE ...?
MAYBE IT'S BECAUSE THEIR RINK IS HOSTING THE COMPETITION... AND HE'S THE MAIN GUEST ...?
That's all, I guess ...?
Well
THAT'S POSSIBLE, BUT...
WHAT'S SHUN THINKING?

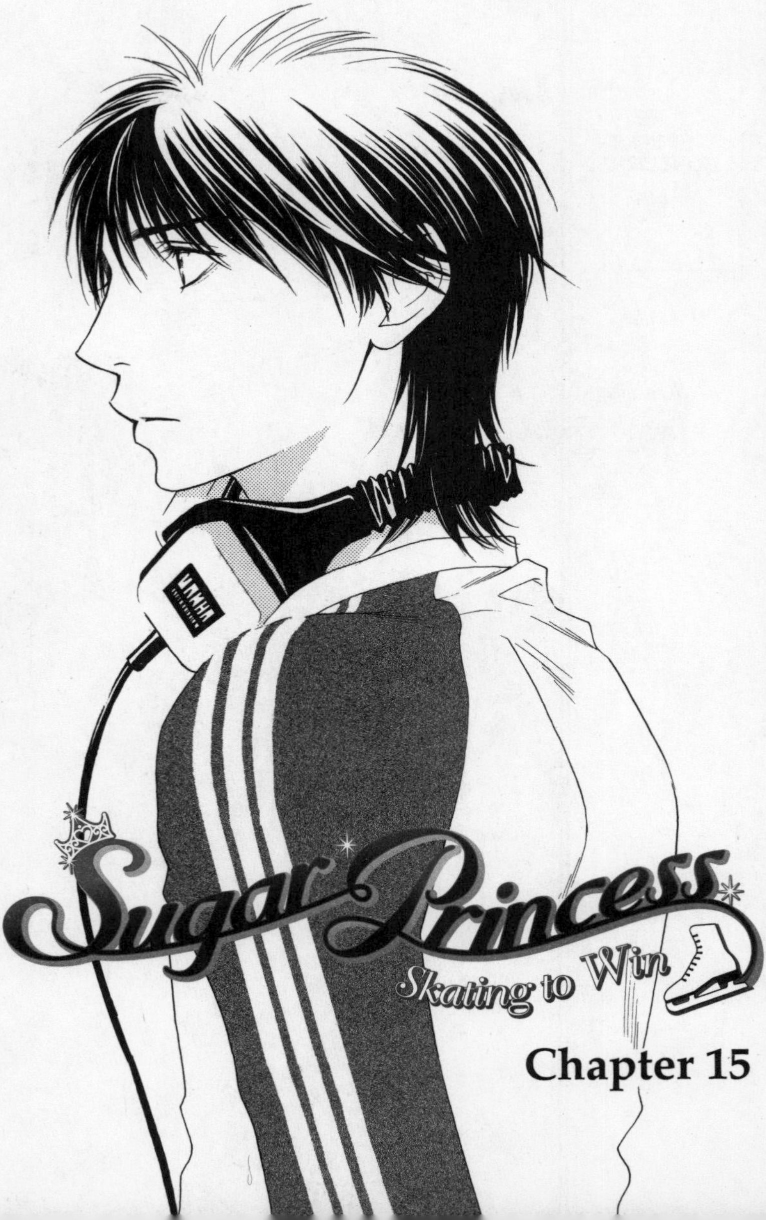
Sugar Princess
Skating to Win

Chapter 15

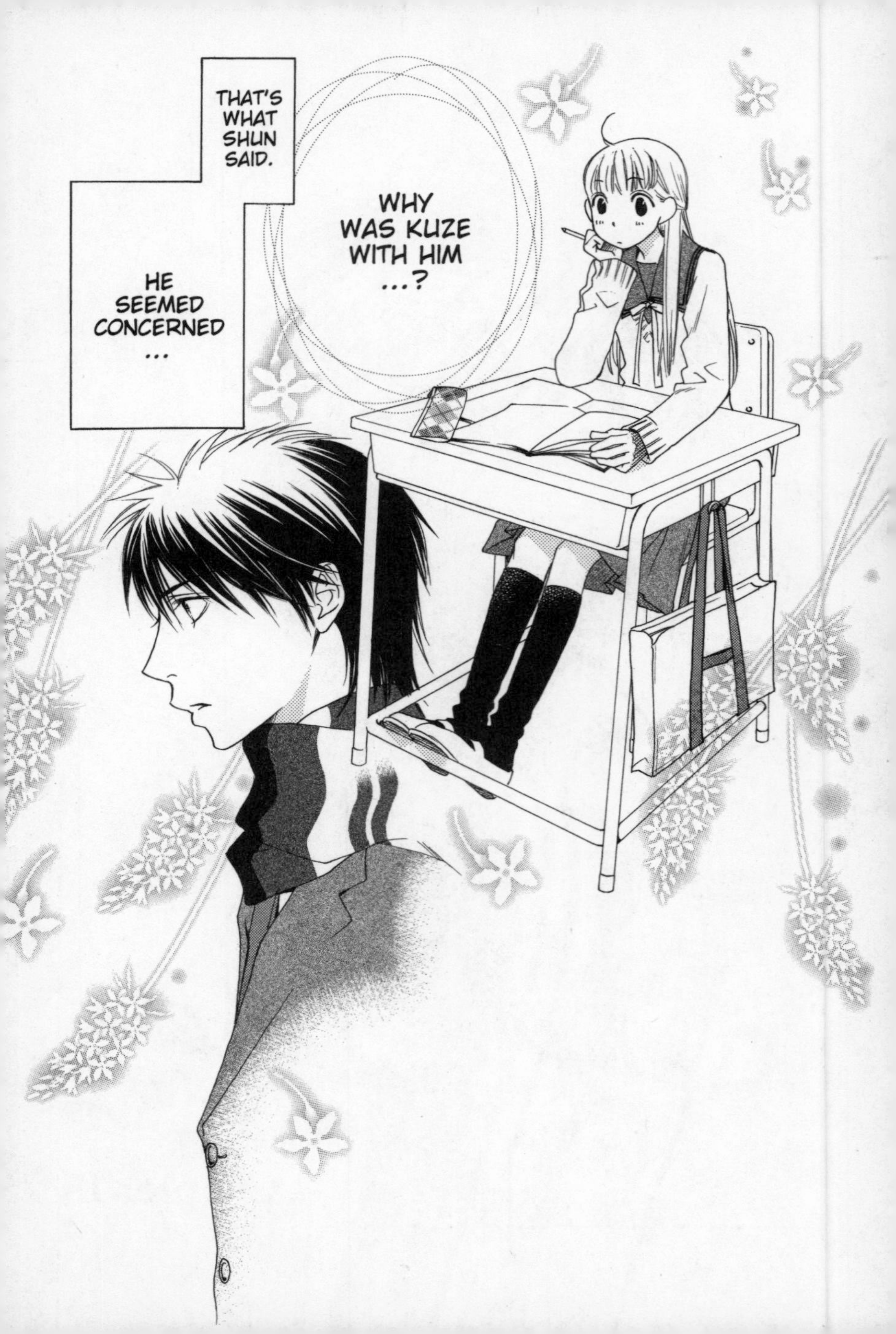
WHY WAS KUZE WITH HIM ...?
THAT'S WHAT SHUN SAID.
HE SEEMED CONCERNED ...

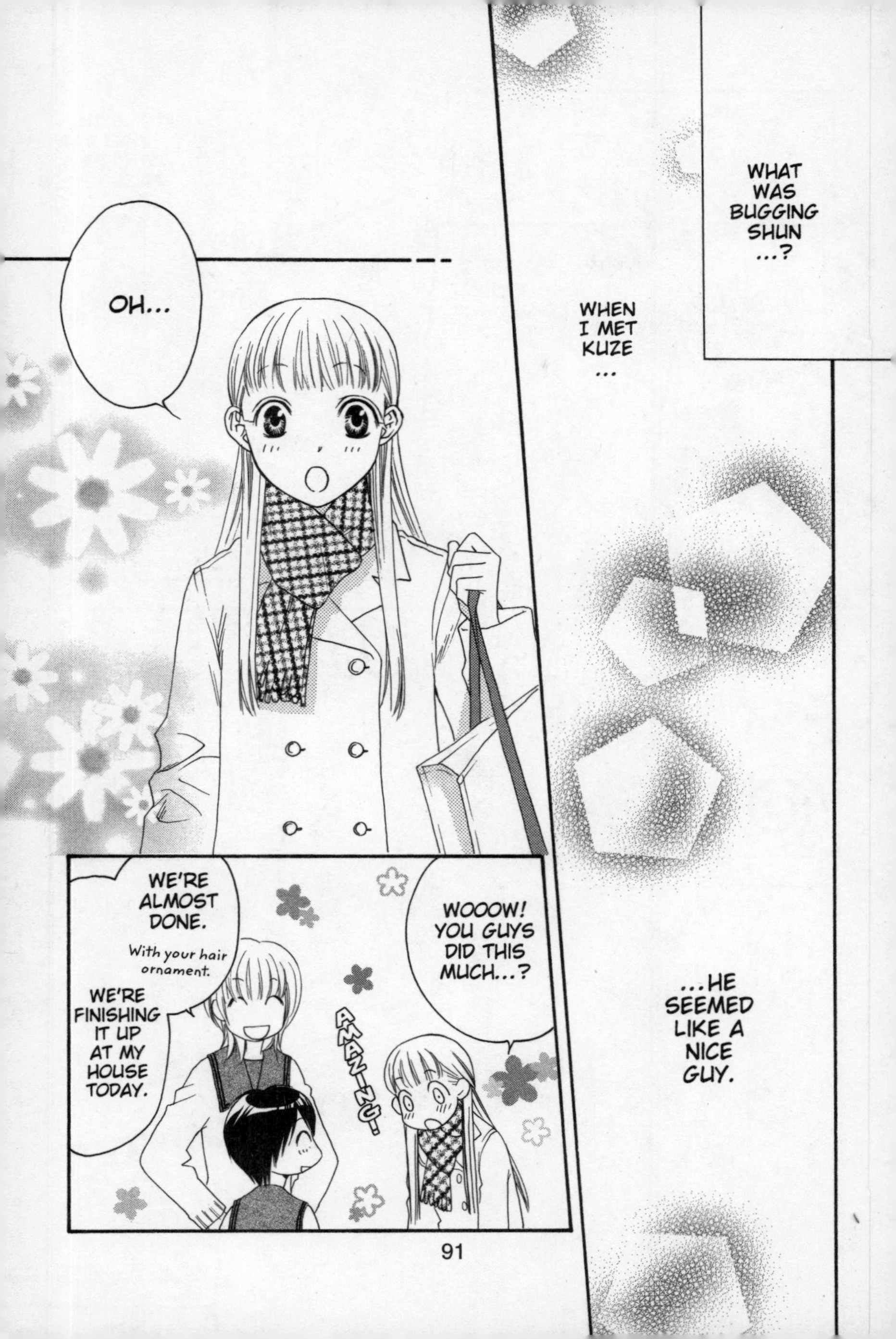
WHAT WAS BUGGING SHUN ...?
WHEN I MET KUZE ...
...HE SEEMED LIKE A NICE GUY.
OH...
WOOOW! YOU GUYS DID THIS MUCH...?
AMAZING!
WE'RE ALMOST DONE.
With your hair ornament.
WE'RE FINISHING IT UP AT MY HOUSE TODAY.

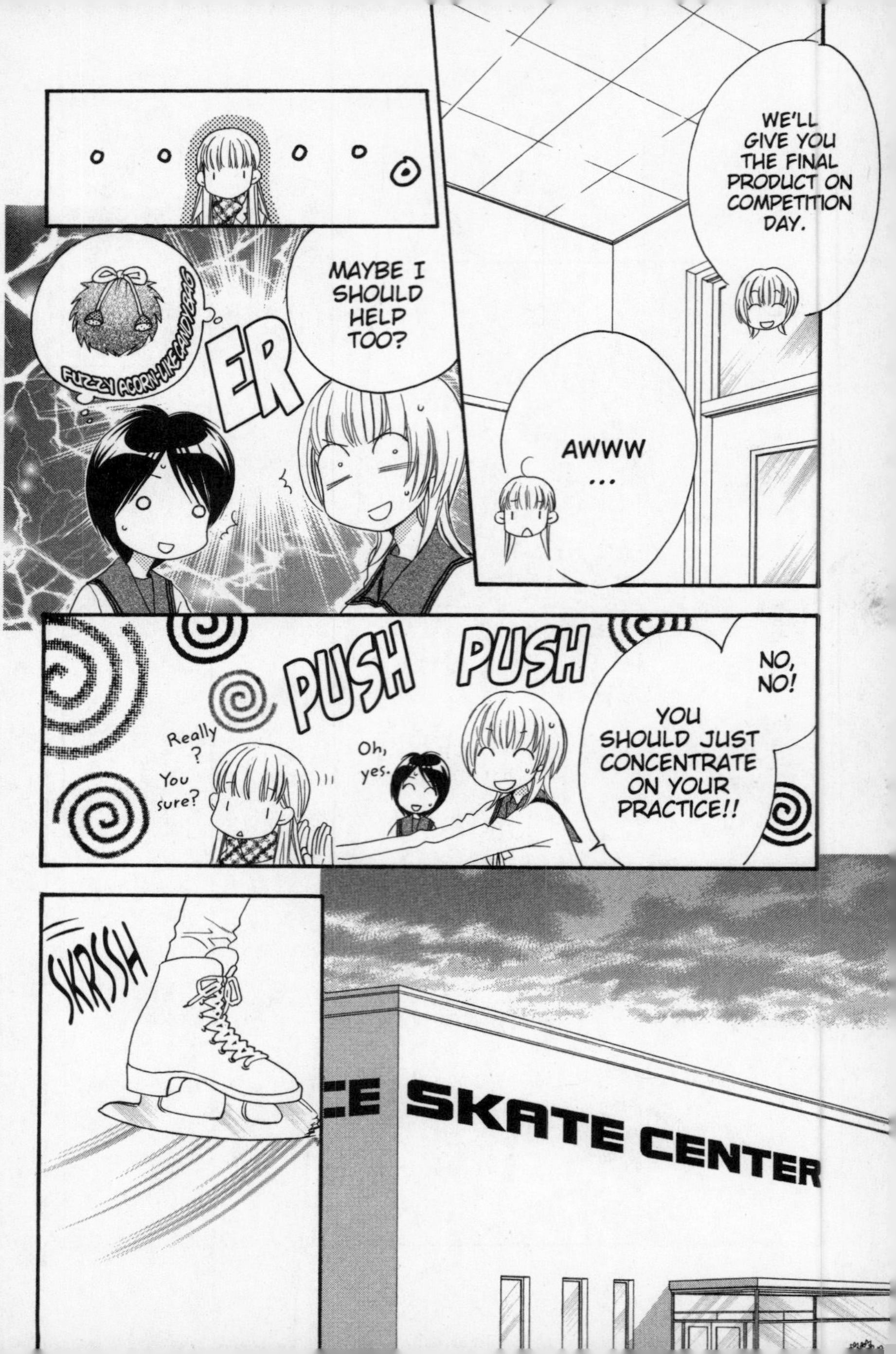
WE'LL GIVE YOU THE FINAL PRODUCT ON COMPETITION DAY.
AWWW ...
MAYBE I SHOULD HELP TOO?
ER
FUZZY ACORN-LIKE CANDY BAG
PUSH PUSH
NO, NO!
YOU SHOULD JUST CONCENTRATE ON YOUR PRACTICE!!
Oh, yes.
Really? You sure?
CE SKATE CENTER
SKRSSH

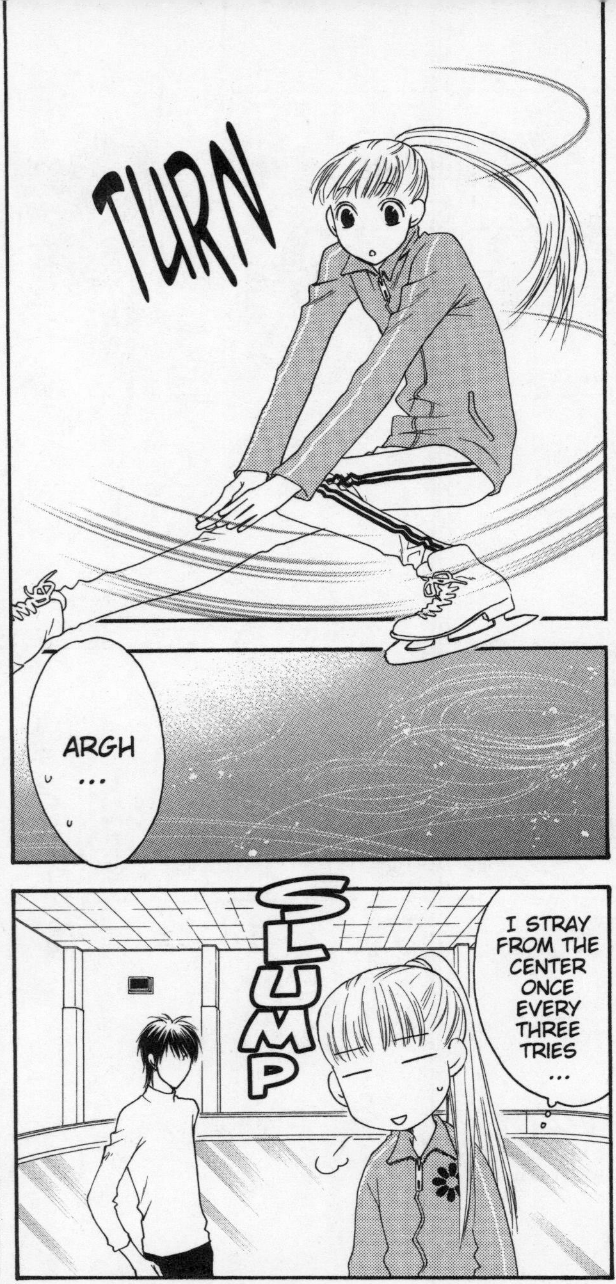
TURN
ARGH ...
I STRAY FROM THE CENTER ONCE EVERY THREE TRIES ...
SLUMP

REGARDING THE SKATING STYLES OF THE TWO BOYS...

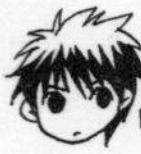

SHUN IS PLUSHENKO STYLE.

KUZE IS YAGUDIN STYLE.

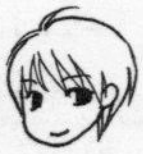

...THAT'S THE IMAGE I HAVE WHEN I DRAW THEM.

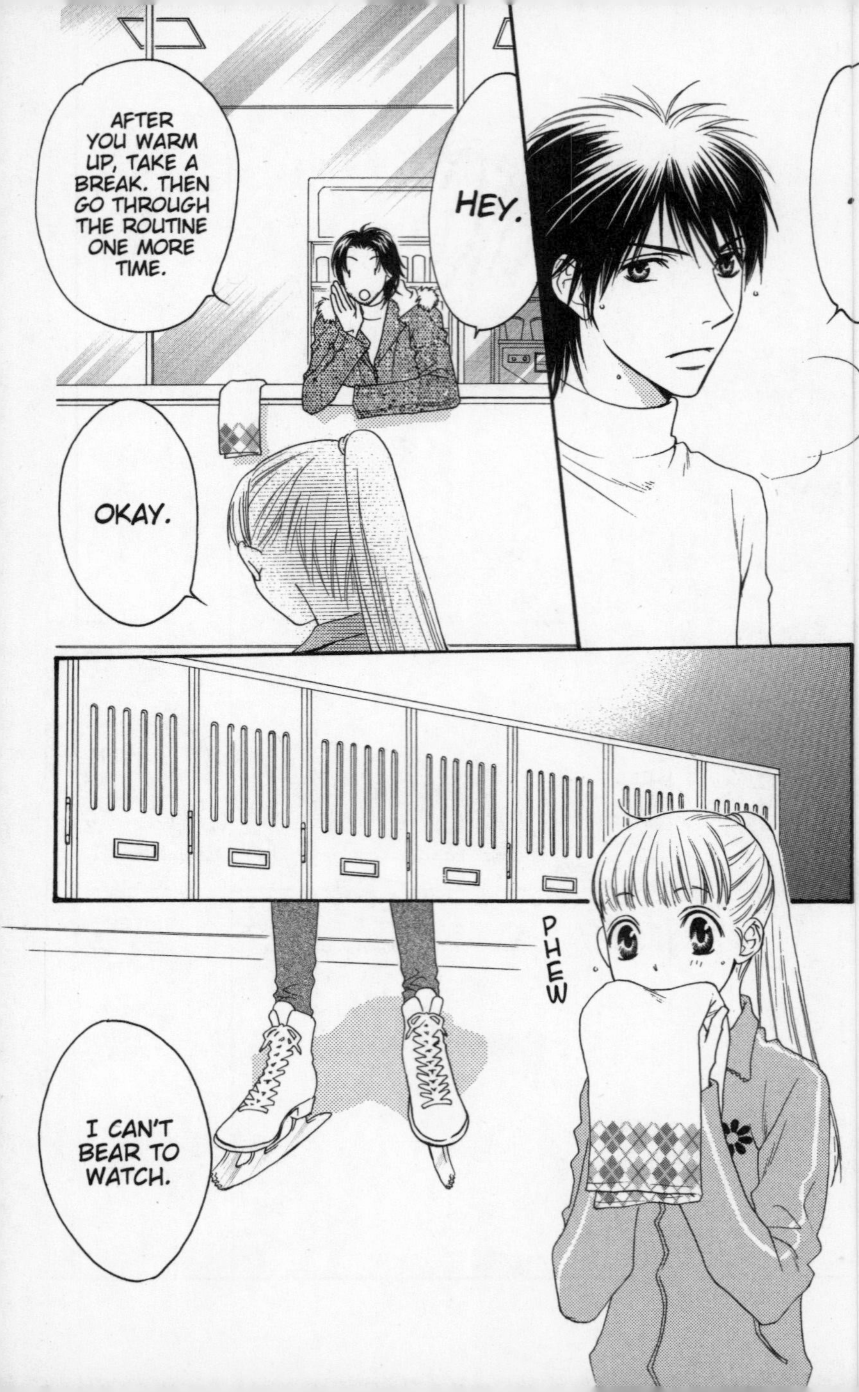
...
HEY.
AFTER YOU WARM UP, TAKE A BREAK. THEN GO THROUGH THE ROUTINE ONE MORE TIME.
OKAY.
PHEW
I CAN'T BEAR TO WATCH.

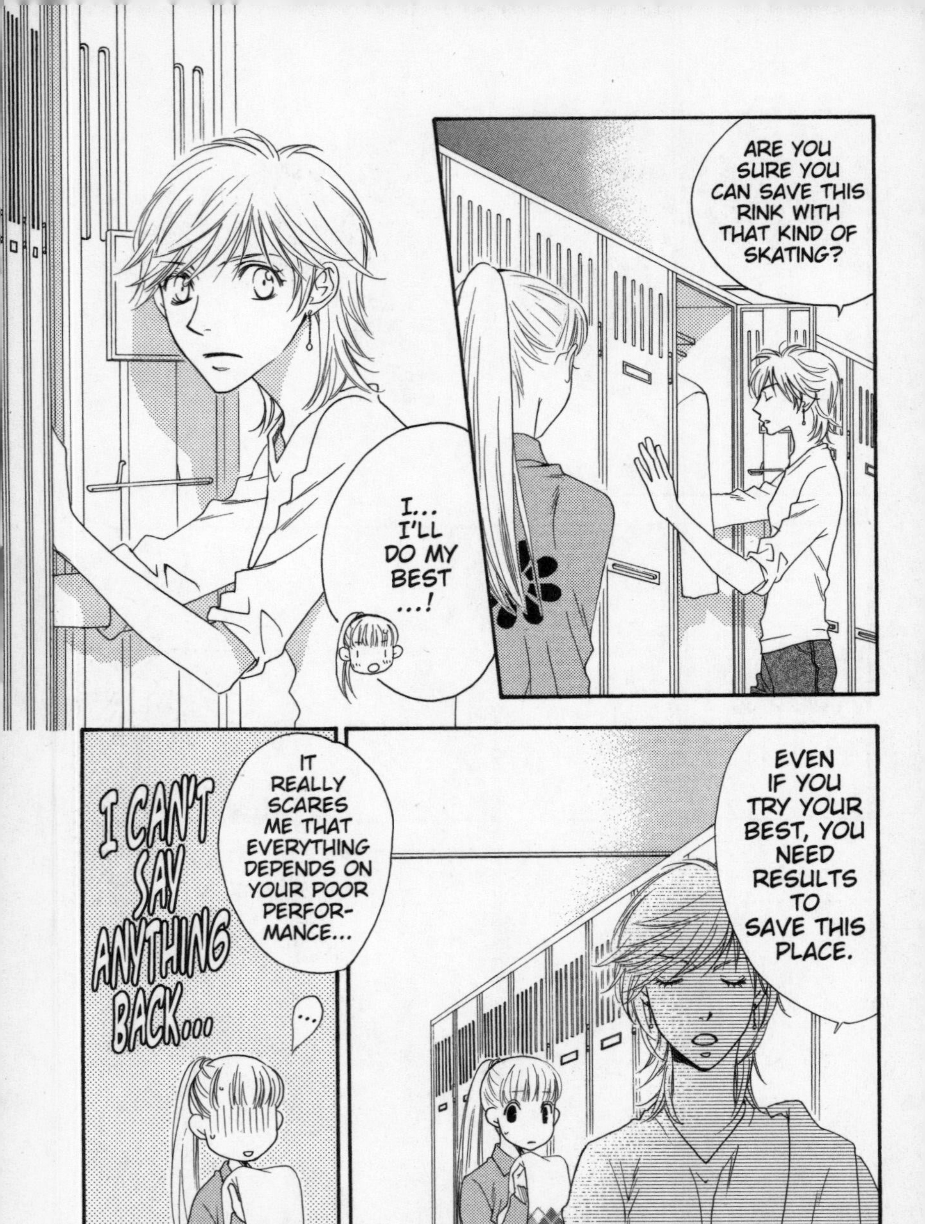
ARE YOU SURE YOU CAN SAVE THIS RINK WITH THAT KIND OF SKATING?
I... I'LL DO MY BEST ...!
EVEN IF YOU TRY YOUR BEST, YOU NEED RESULTS TO SAVE THIS PLACE.
IT REALLY SCARES ME THAT EVERYTHING DEPENDS ON YOUR POOR PERFORMANCE...
I CAN'T SAY ANYTHING BACK...
...

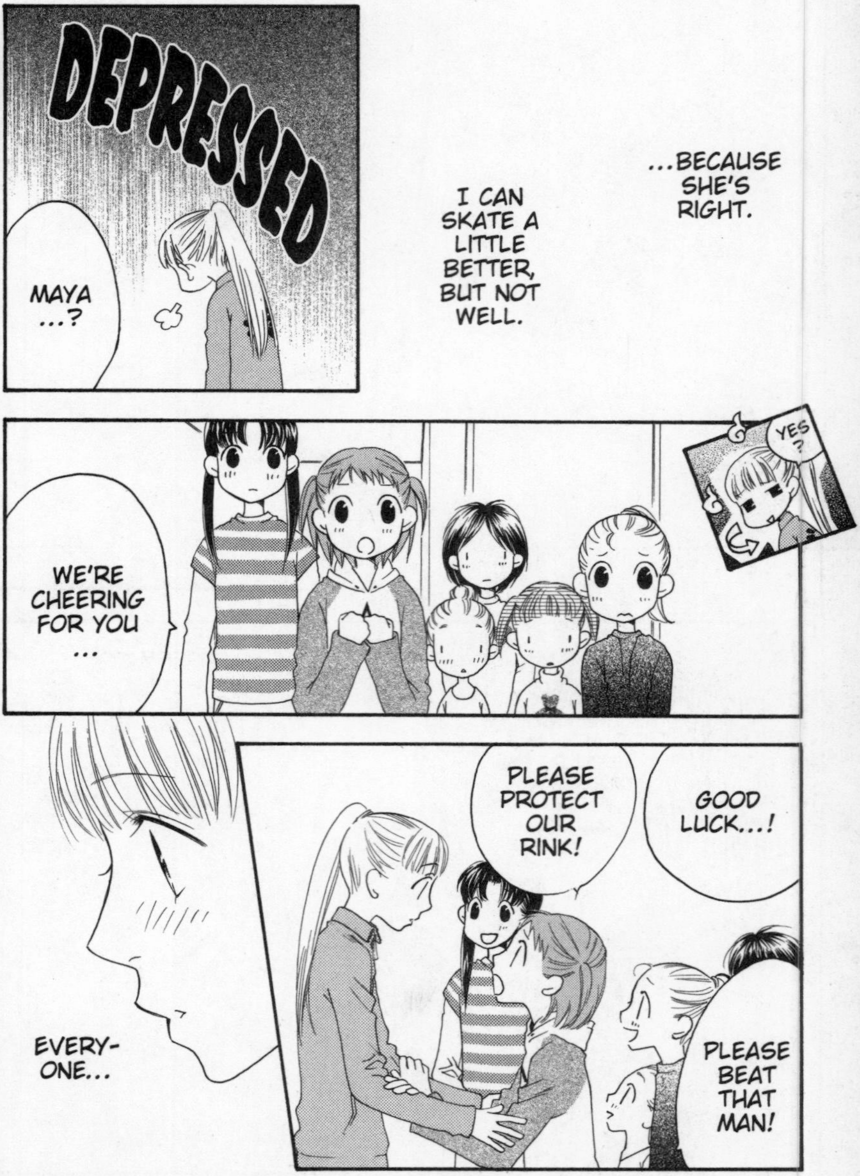
...BECAUSE SHE'S RIGHT.
I CAN SKATE A LITTLE BETTER, BUT NOT WELL.
DEPRESSED
MAYA ...?
YES ?
WE'RE CHEERING FOR YOU ...
GOOD LUCK...!
PLEASE PROTECT OUR RINK!
PLEASE BEAT THAT MAN!
EVERY-ONE...

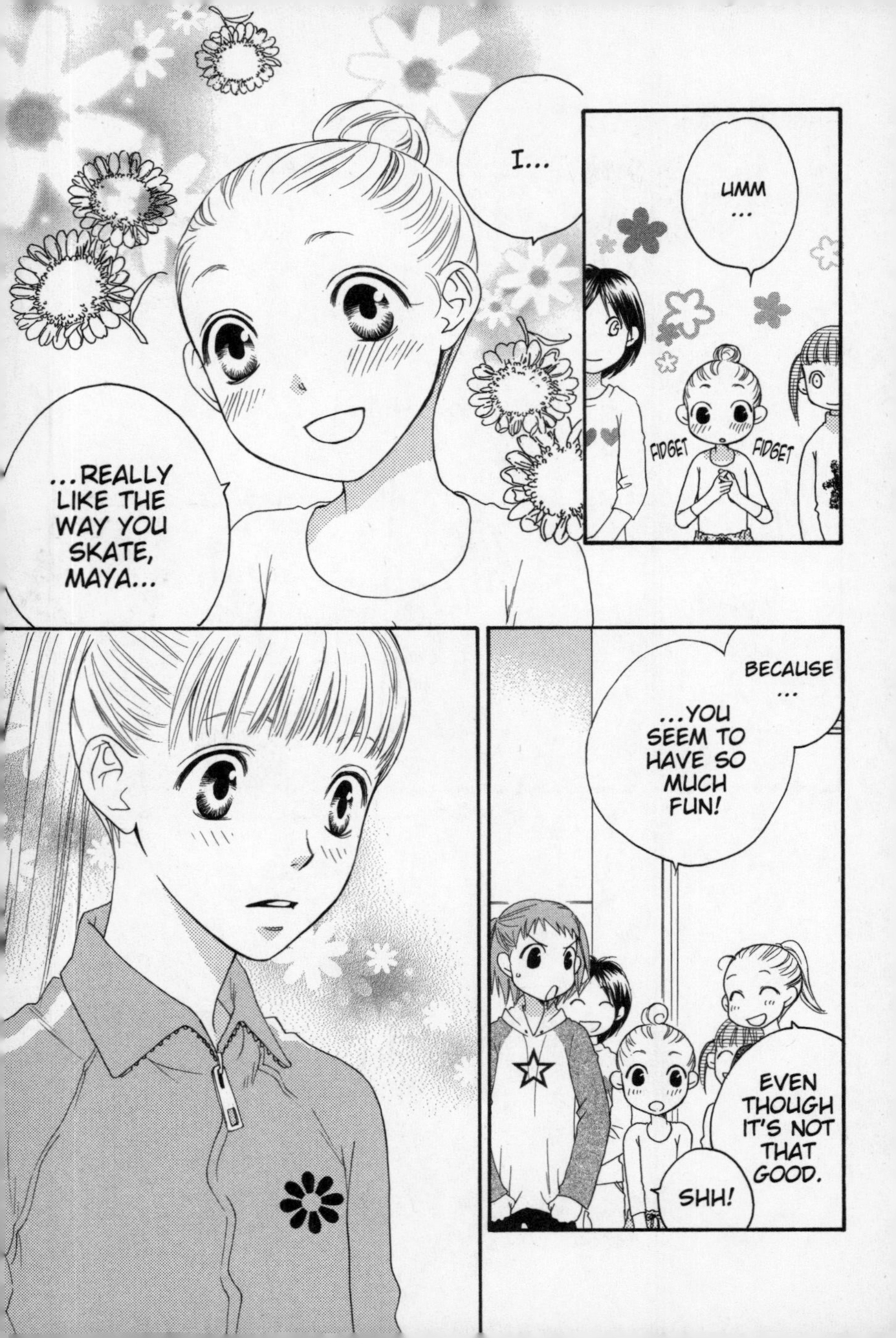
UMM ...
FIDGET
FIDGET
I...
...REALLY LIKE THE WAY YOU SKATE, MAYA...
BECAUSE ...
...YOU SEEM TO HAVE SO MUCH FUN!
EVEN THOUGH IT'S NOT THAT GOOD.
SHH!

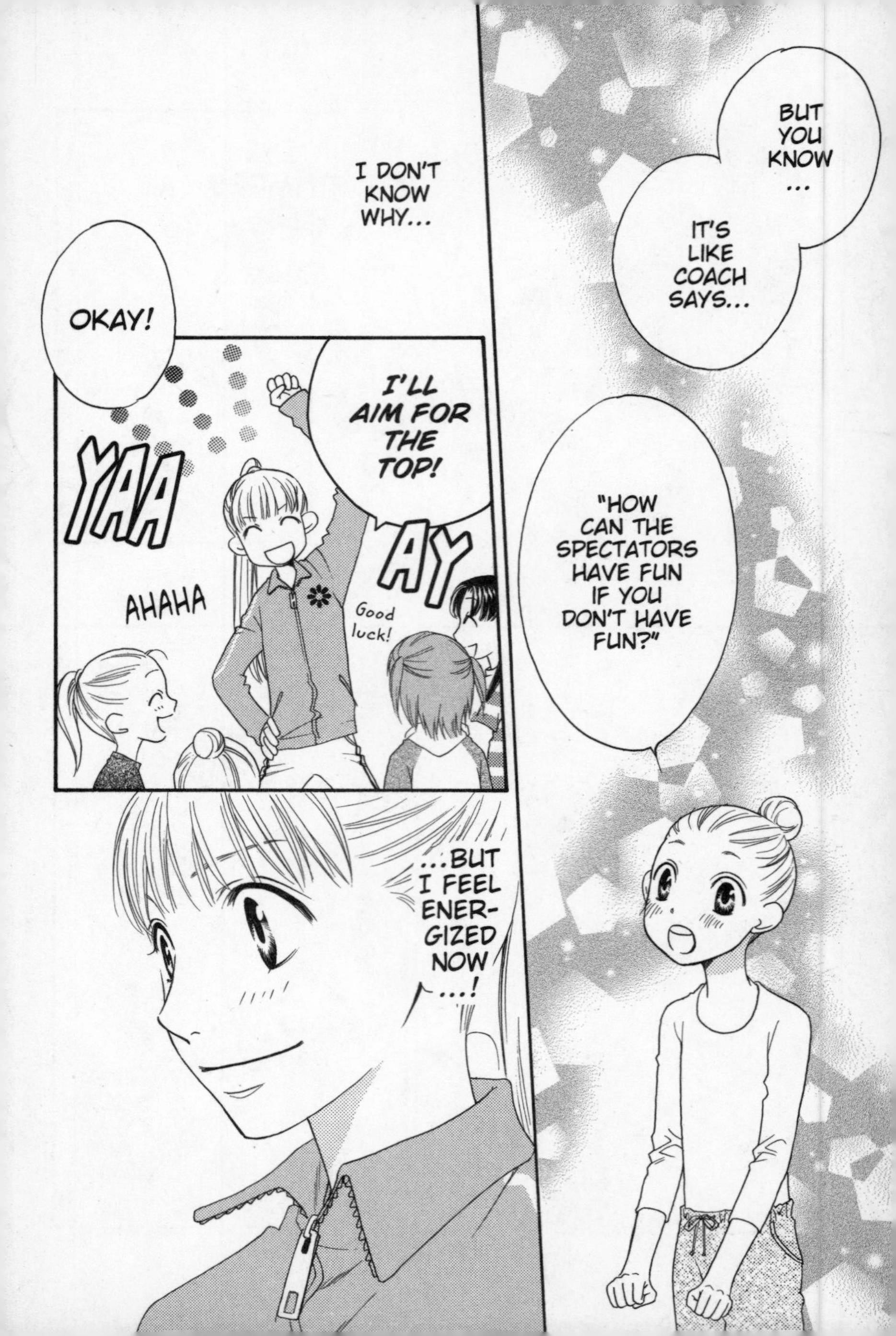
BUT YOU KNOW...
IT'S LIKE COACH SAYS...
"HOW CAN THE SPECTATORS HAVE FUN IF YOU DON'T HAVE FUN?"
I DON'T KNOW WHY...
I'LL AIM FOR THE TOP!
OKAY!
YAA AY
Good luck!
AHAHA
...BUT I FEEL ENERGIZED NOW...!

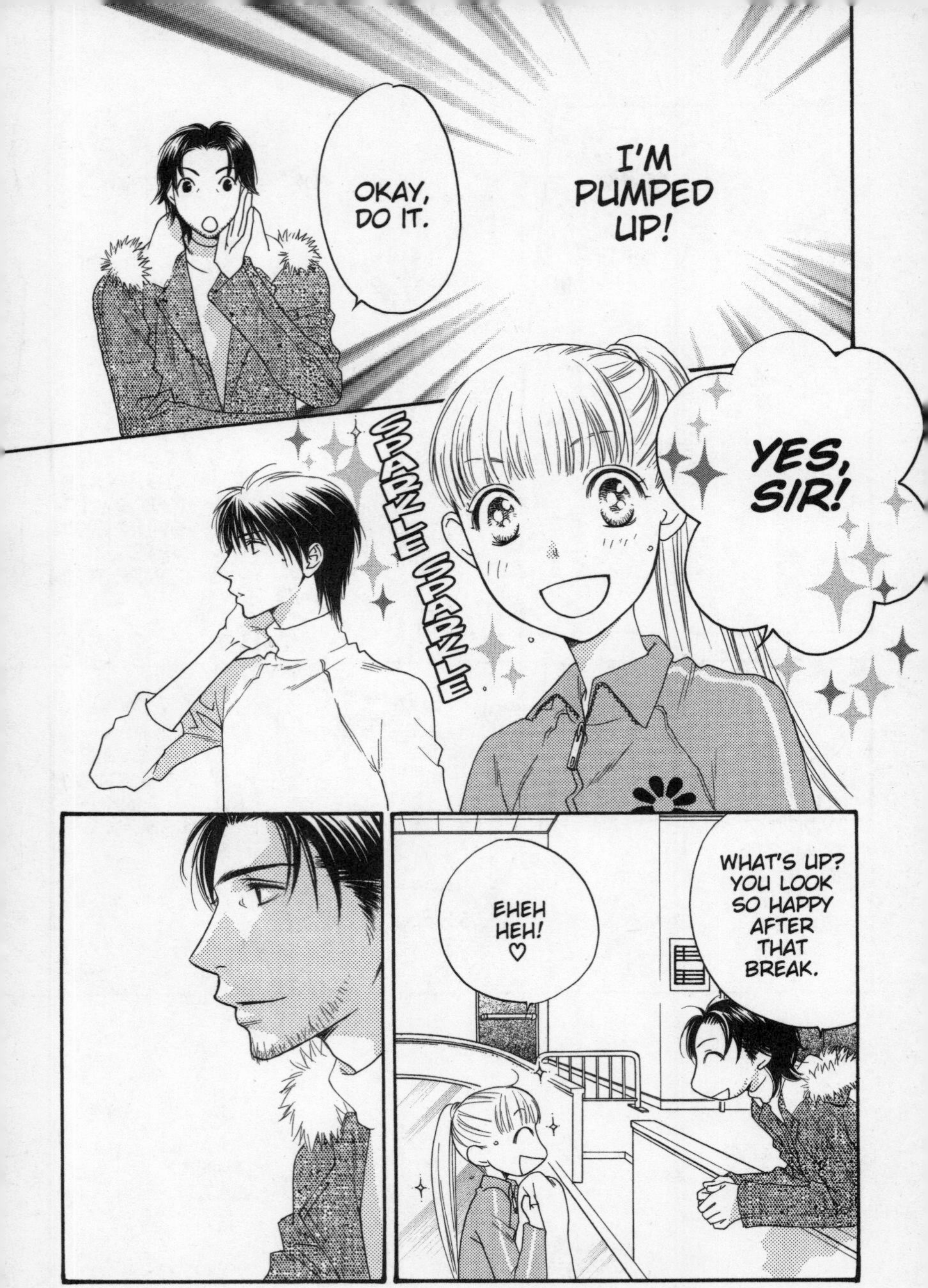
I'M PUMPED UP!
OKAY, DO IT.
YES, SIR!
SPARKLE SPARKLE
WHAT'S UP? YOU LOOK SO HAPPY AFTER THAT BREAK.
EHEH HEH! ♡

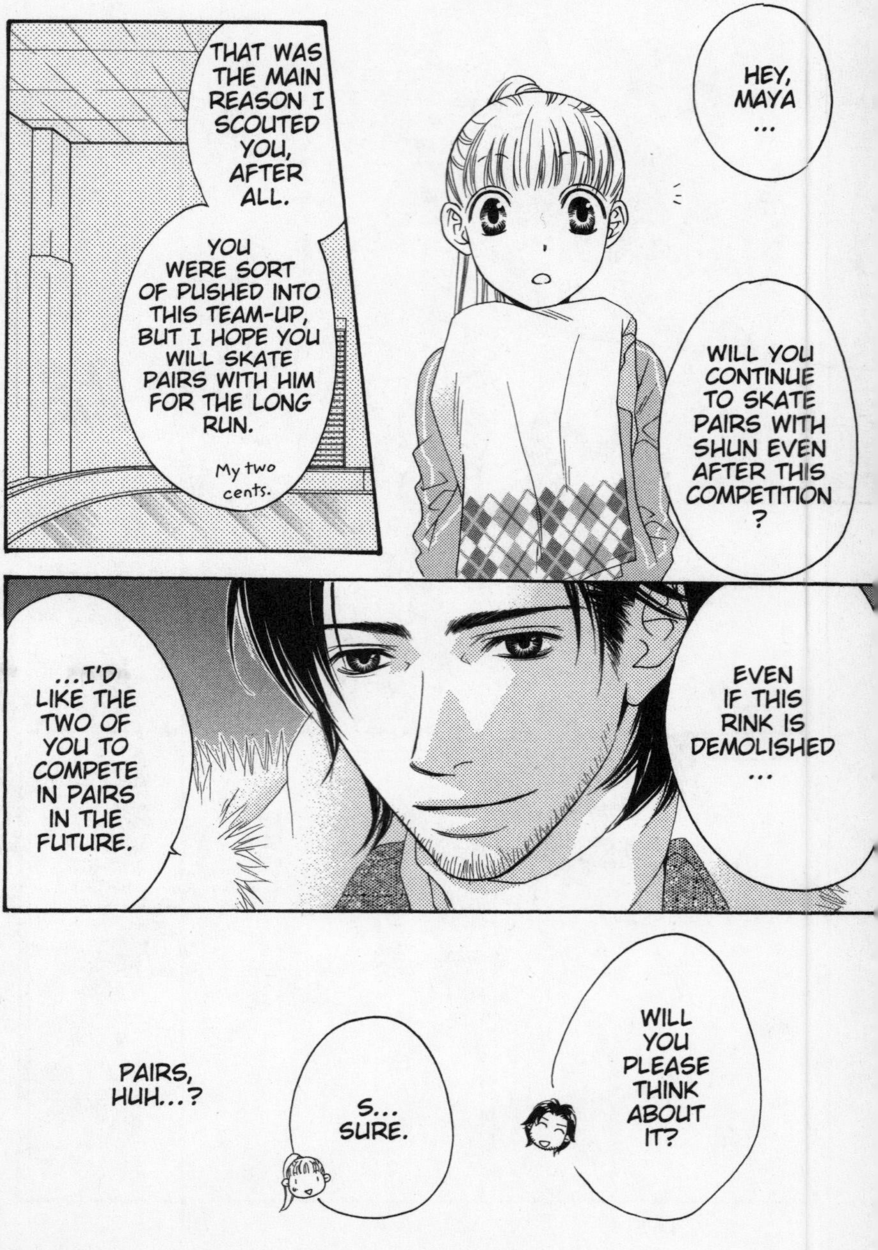
HEY, MAYA...
WILL YOU CONTINUE TO SKATE PAIRS WITH SHUN EVEN AFTER THIS COMPETITION?
THAT WAS THE MAIN REASON I SCOUTED YOU, AFTER ALL.
YOU WERE SORT OF PUSHED INTO THIS TEAM-UP, BUT I HOPE YOU WILL SKATE PAIRS WITH HIM FOR THE LONG RUN.
My two cents.
EVEN IF THIS RINK IS DEMOLISHED...
...I'D LIKE THE TWO OF YOU TO COMPETE IN PAIRS IN THE FUTURE.
WILL YOU PLEASE THINK ABOUT IT?
S... SURE.
PAIRS, HUH...?

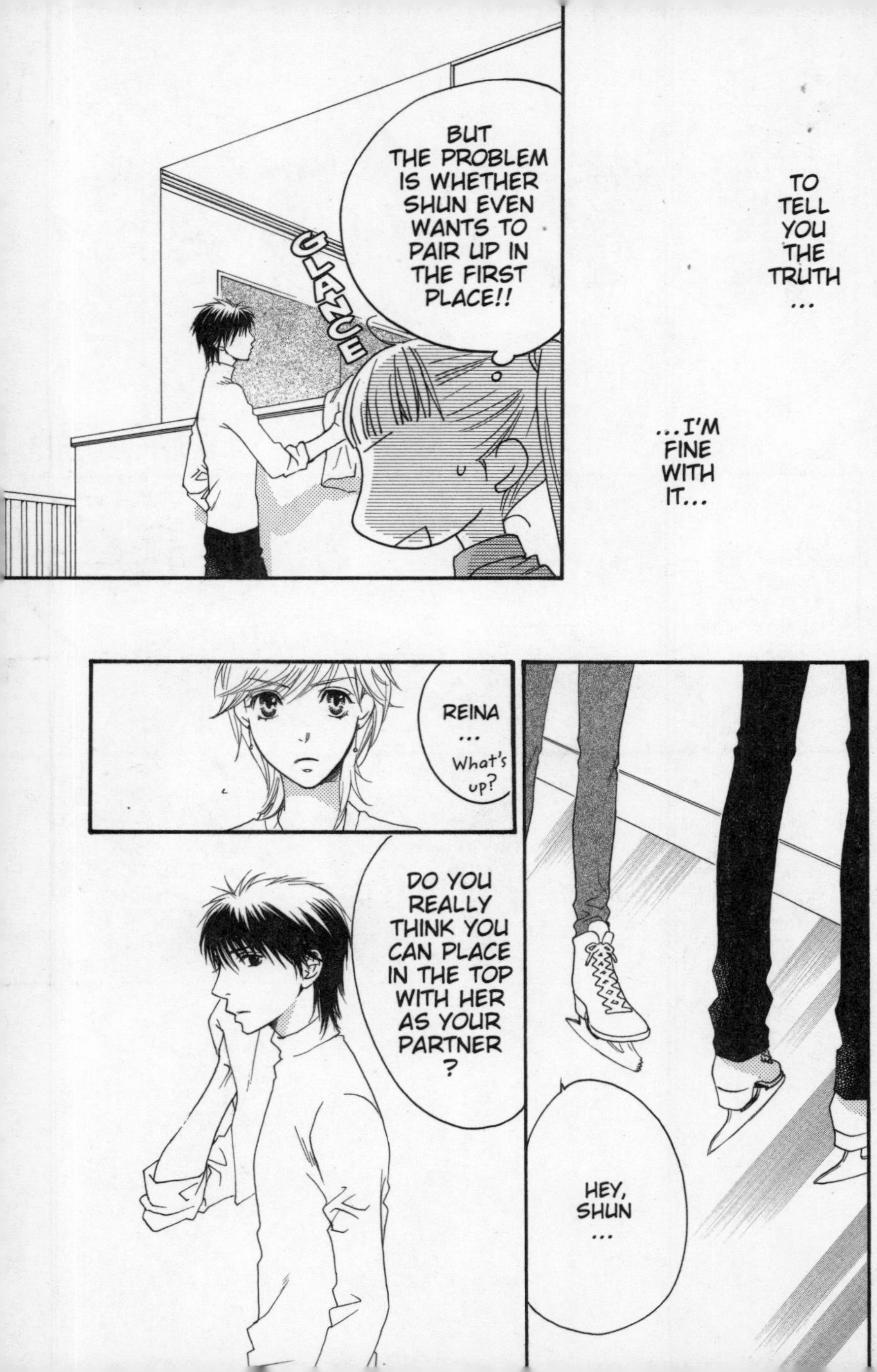
TO TELL YOU THE TRUTH...
...I'M FINE WITH IT...
BUT THE PROBLEM IS WHETHER SHUN EVEN WANTS TO PAIR UP IN THE FIRST PLACE!!
GLANCE
HEY, SHUN...
REINA...
What's up?
DO YOU REALLY THINK YOU CAN PLACE IN THE TOP WITH HER AS YOUR PARTNER?

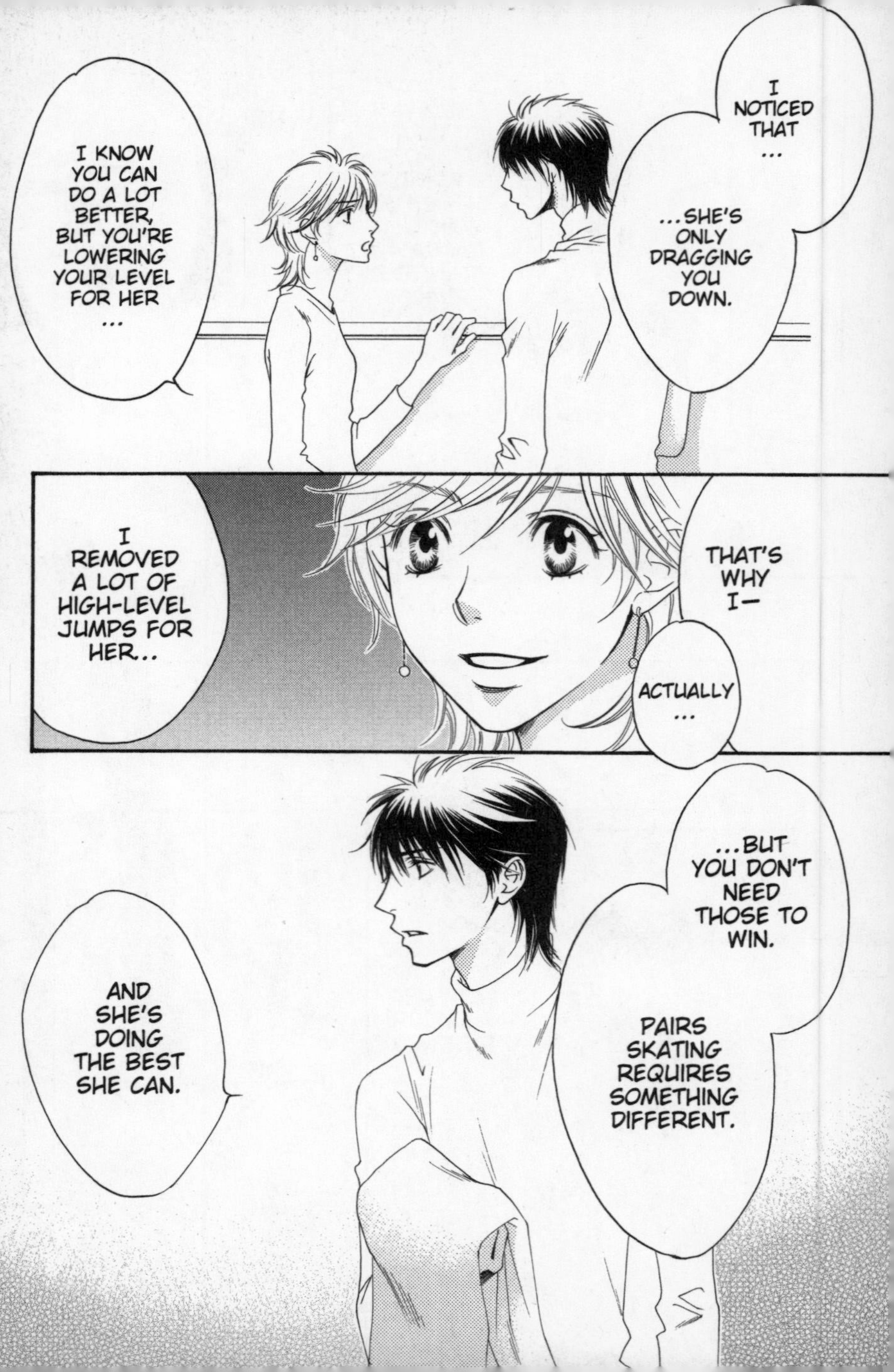
I NOTICED THAT ...
...SHE'S ONLY DRAGGING YOU DOWN.
I KNOW YOU CAN DO A LOT BETTER, BUT YOU'RE LOWERING YOUR LEVEL FOR HER ...
THAT'S WHY I—
ACTUALLY ...
I REMOVED A LOT OF HIGH-LEVEL JUMPS FOR HER...
...BUT YOU DON'T NEED THOSE TO WIN.
PAIRS SKATING REQUIRES SOMETHING DIFFERENT.
AND SHE'S DOING THE BEST SHE CAN.

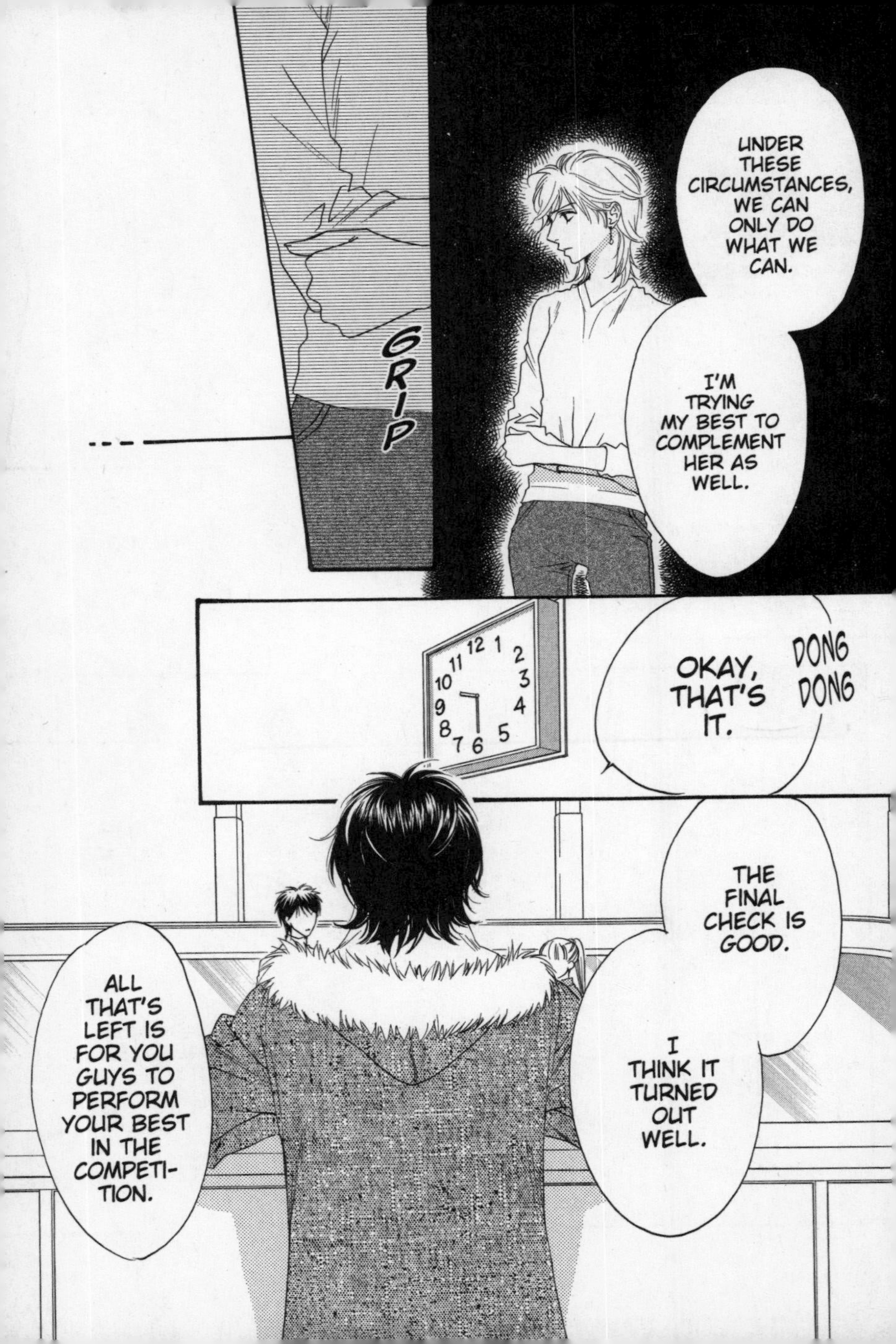
UNDER THESE CIRCUMSTANCES, WE CAN ONLY DO WHAT WE CAN.
I'M TRYING MY BEST TO COMPLEMENT HER AS WELL.
GRIP
...
OKAY, THAT'S IT.
DONG DONG
THE FINAL CHECK IS GOOD.
I THINK IT TURNED OUT WELL.
ALL THAT'S LEFT IS FOR YOU GUYS TO PERFORM YOUR BEST IN THE COMPETITION.

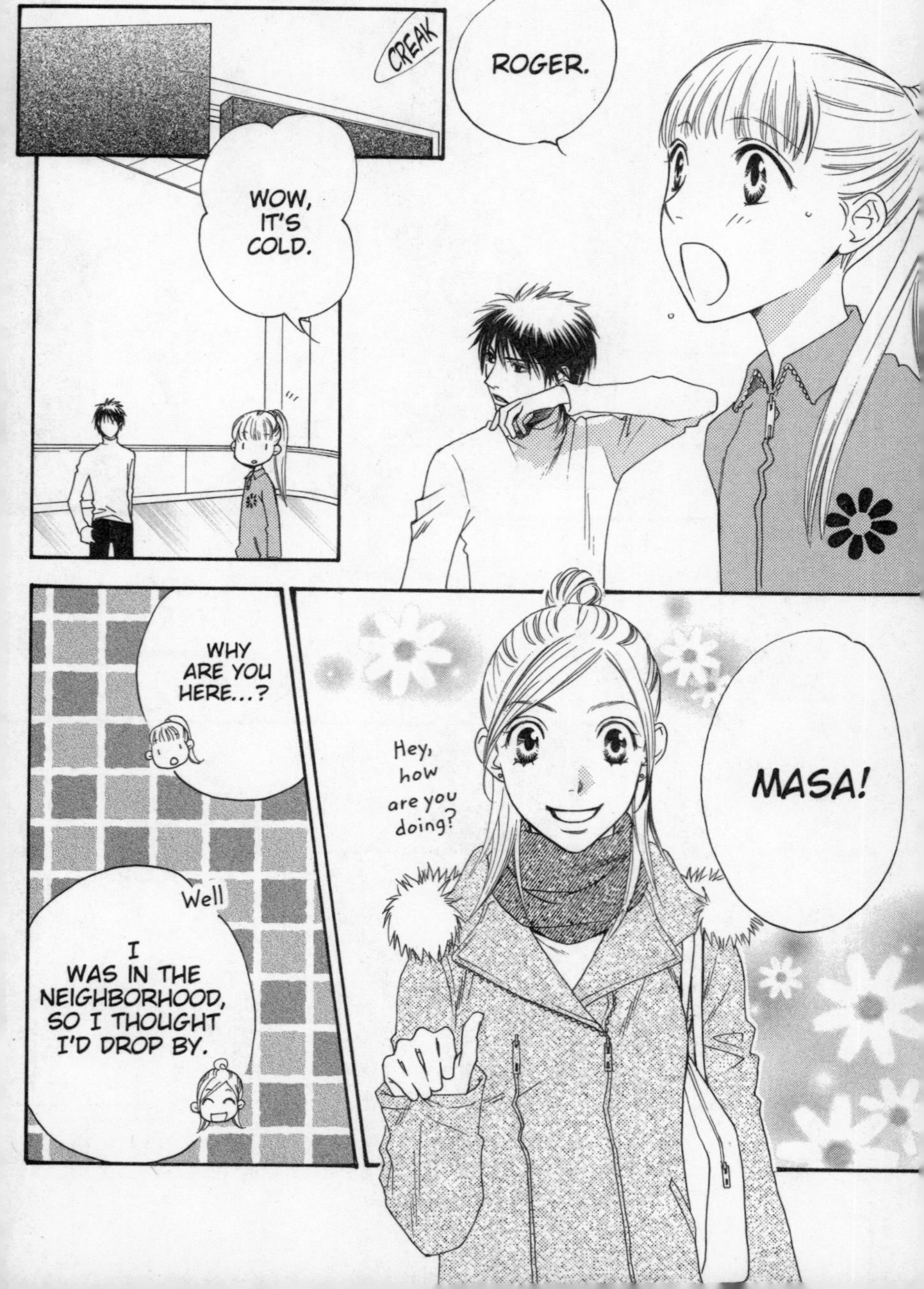
ROGER.
CREAK
WOW, IT'S COLD.
MASA!
Hey, how are you doing?
WHY ARE YOU HERE...?
Well
I WAS IN THE NEIGHBORHOOD, SO I THOUGHT I'D DROP BY.

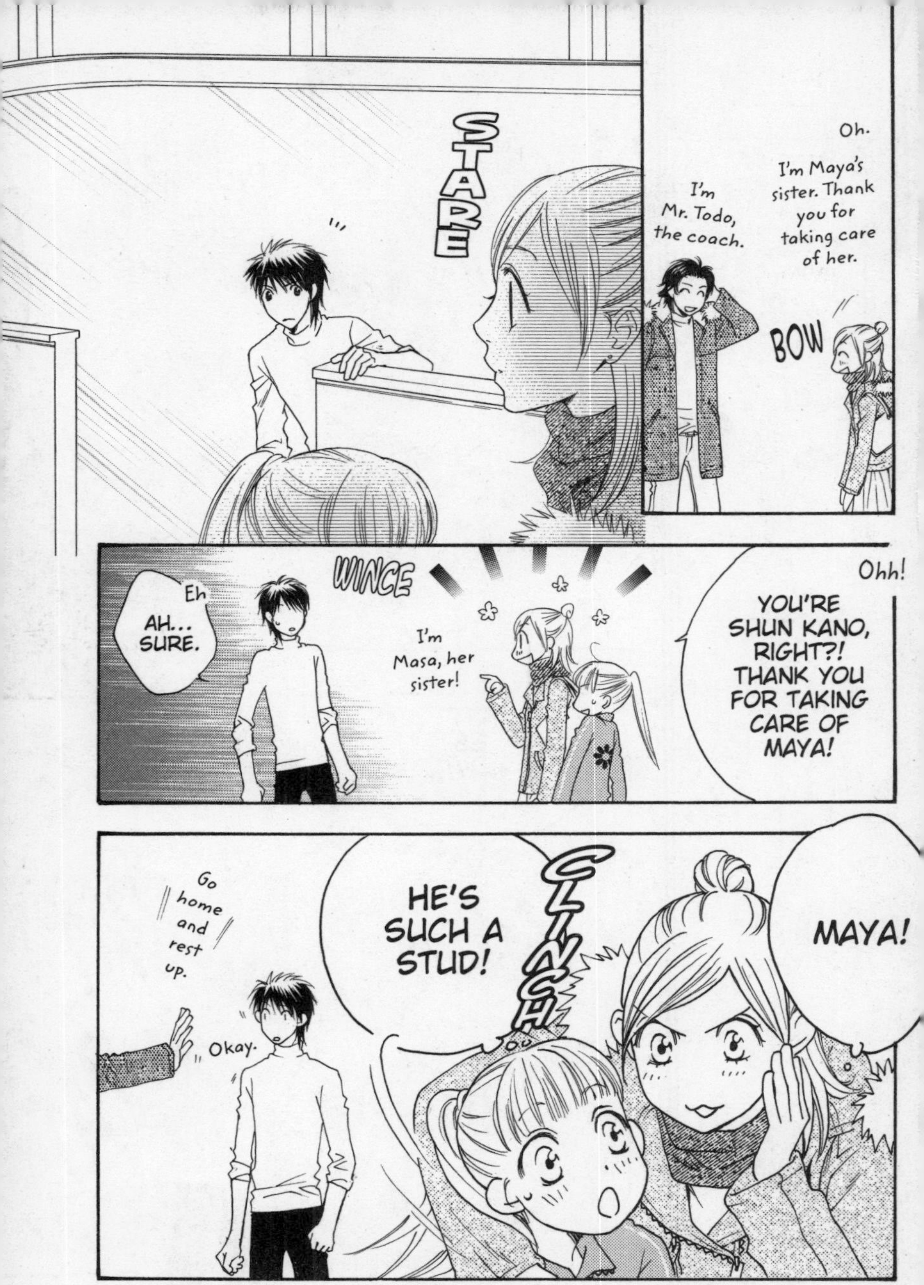

Oh.
I'm Maya's sister. Thank you for taking care of her.
I'm Mr. Todo, the coach.
BOW
STARE
Ohh!
YOU'RE SHUN KANO, RIGHT?! THANK YOU FOR TAKING CARE OF MAYA!
I'm Masa, her sister!
WINCE
Eh
AH... SURE.
MAYA!
CLINCH
HE'S SUCH A STUD!
Go home and rest up.
Okay.

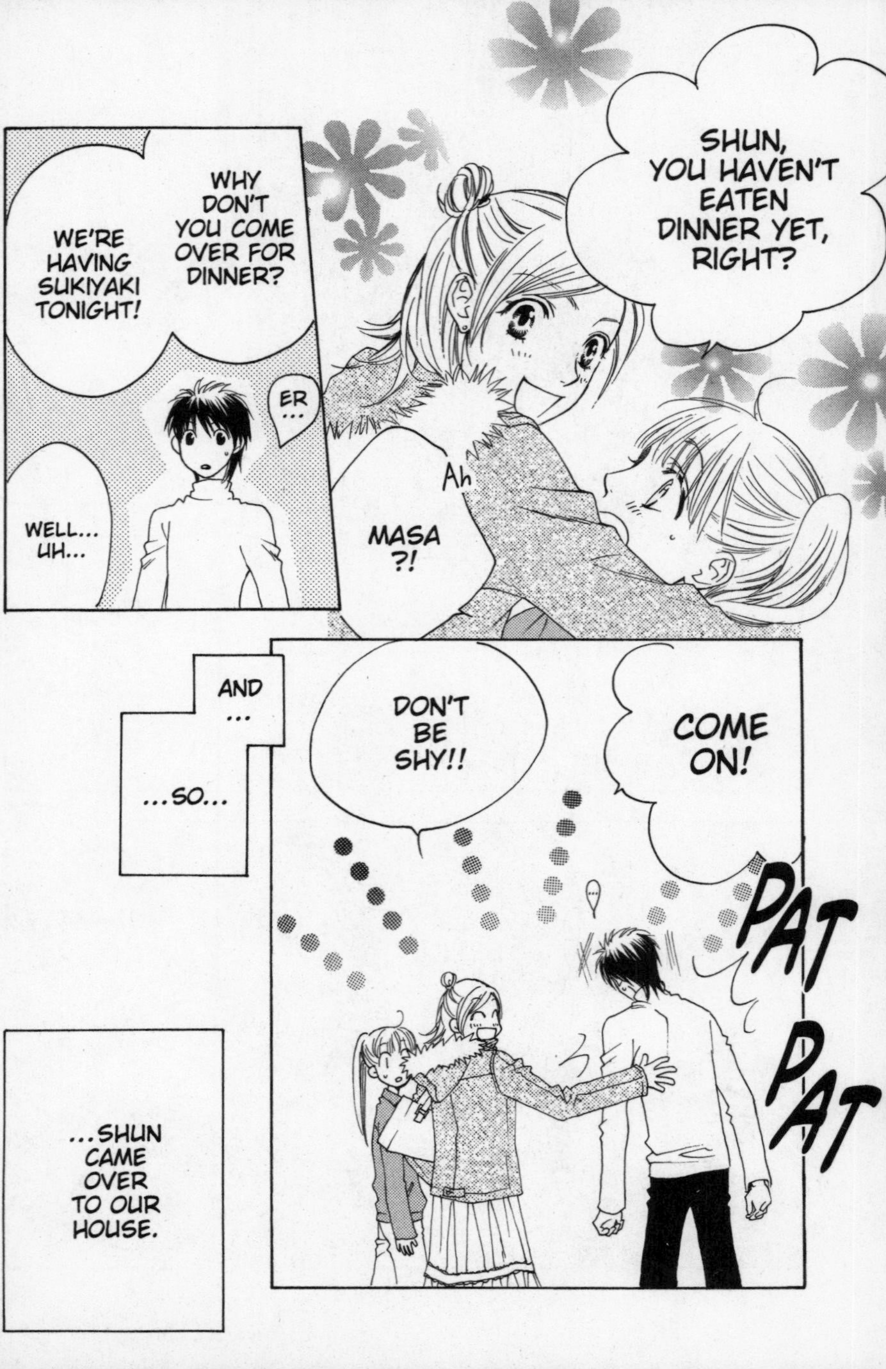
SHUN, YOU HAVEN'T EATEN DINNER YET, RIGHT?
Ah
MASA ?!
WHY DON'T YOU COME OVER FOR DINNER?
WE'RE HAVING SUKIYAKI TONIGHT!
ER...
WELL... UH...
COME ON!
DON'T BE SHY!!
PAT PAT
...
AND...
...SO...
...SHUN CAME OVER TO OUR HOUSE.

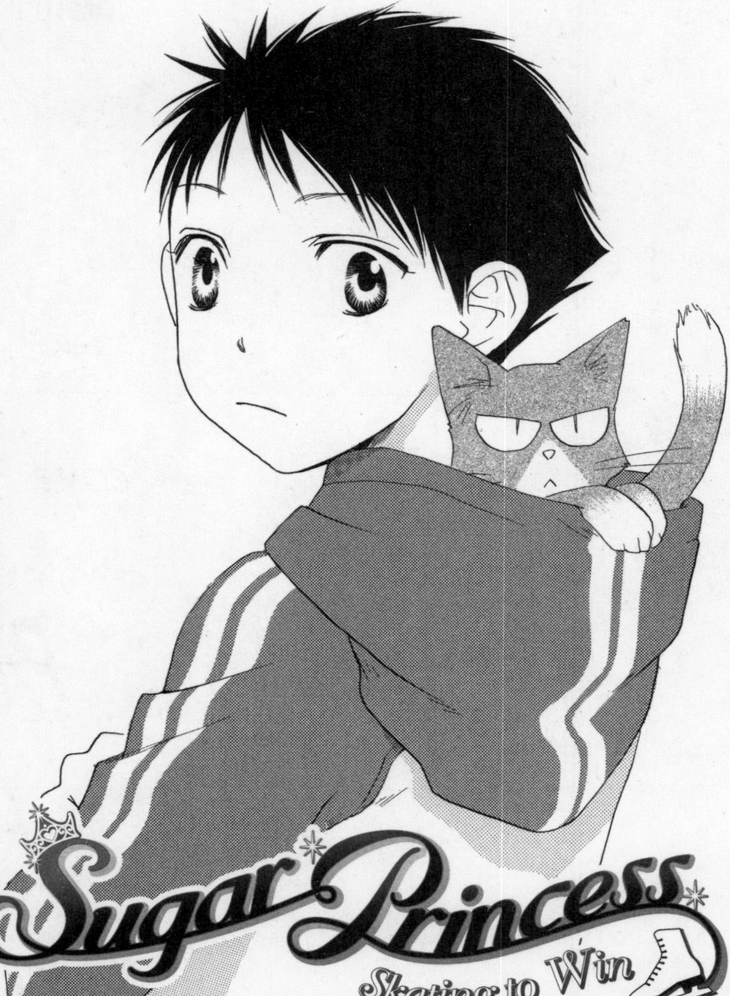
Sugar Princess
Skating to Win

Chapter 16

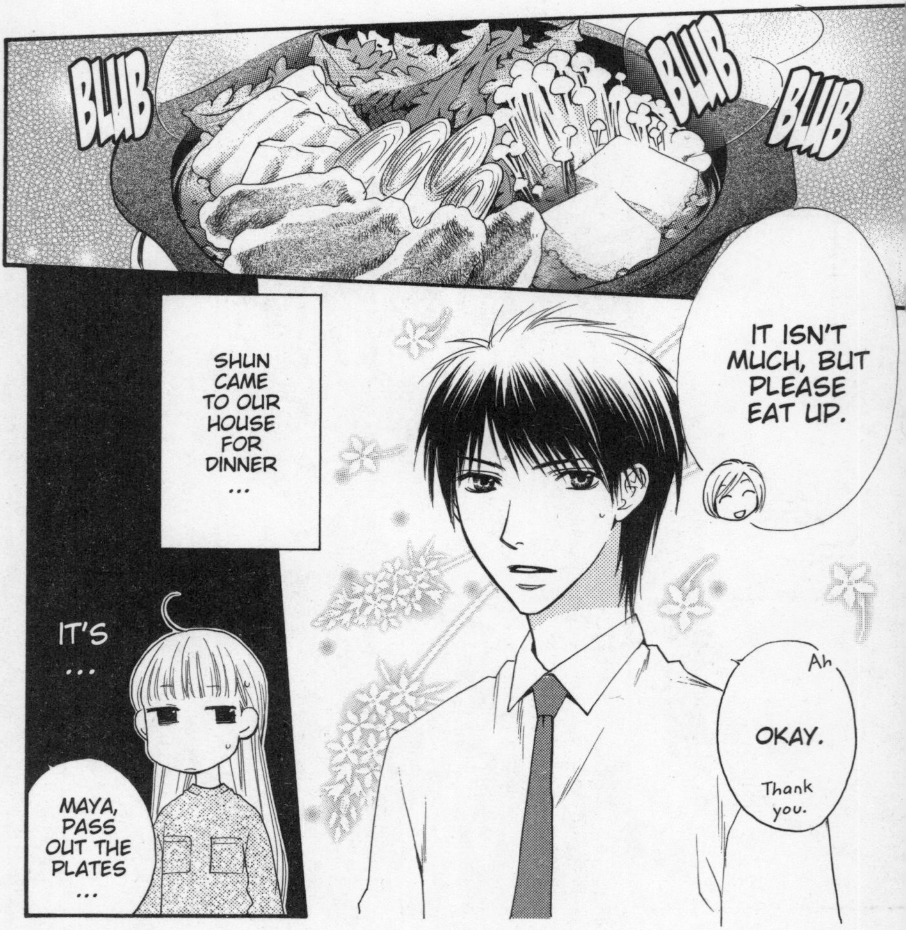
BLUB
BLUB
BLUB
IT ISN'T MUCH, BUT PLEASE EAT UP.
Ah
OKAY.
Thank you.
SHUN CAME TO OUR HOUSE FOR DINNER ...
IT'S ...
MAYA, PASS OUT THE PLATES ...

I BOUGHT A NINTENDO DS LITE. ~

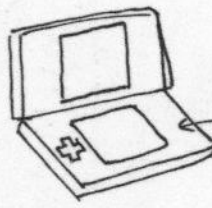

MY MOM USES IT MORE THAN ME THOUGH.

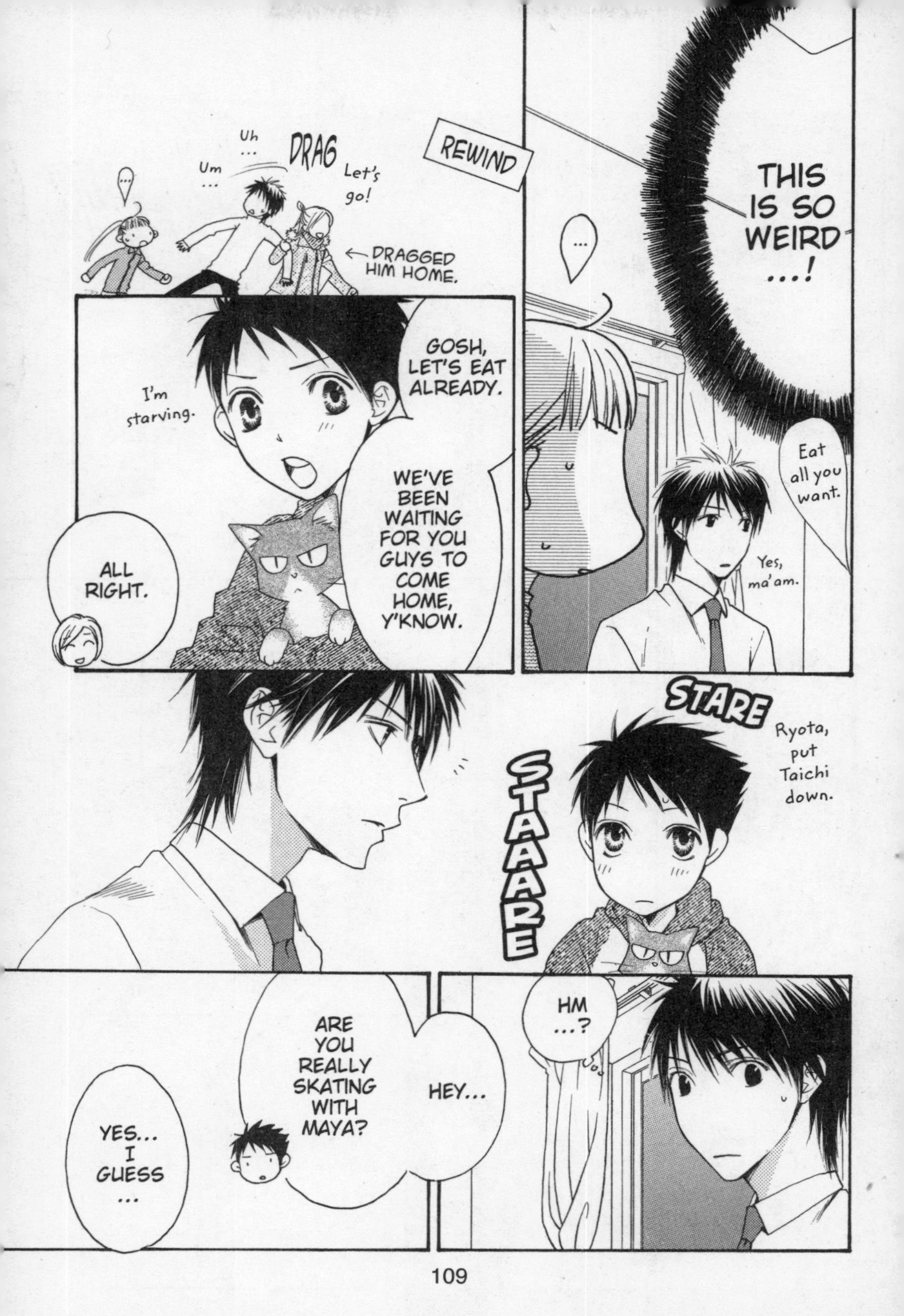
THIS IS SO WEIRD ...!
...
Eat all you want.
Yes, ma'am.
REWIND
Uh ...
DRAG
Let's go!
Um ...
...
← DRAGGED HIM HOME.
GOSH, LET'S EAT ALREADY.
I'm starving.
WE'VE BEEN WAITING FOR YOU GUYS TO COME HOME, Y'KNOW.
ALL RIGHT.
STARE
Ryota, put Taichi down.
STAAAARE
HM ...?
HEY...
ARE YOU REALLY SKATING WITH MAYA?
YES... I GUESS ...

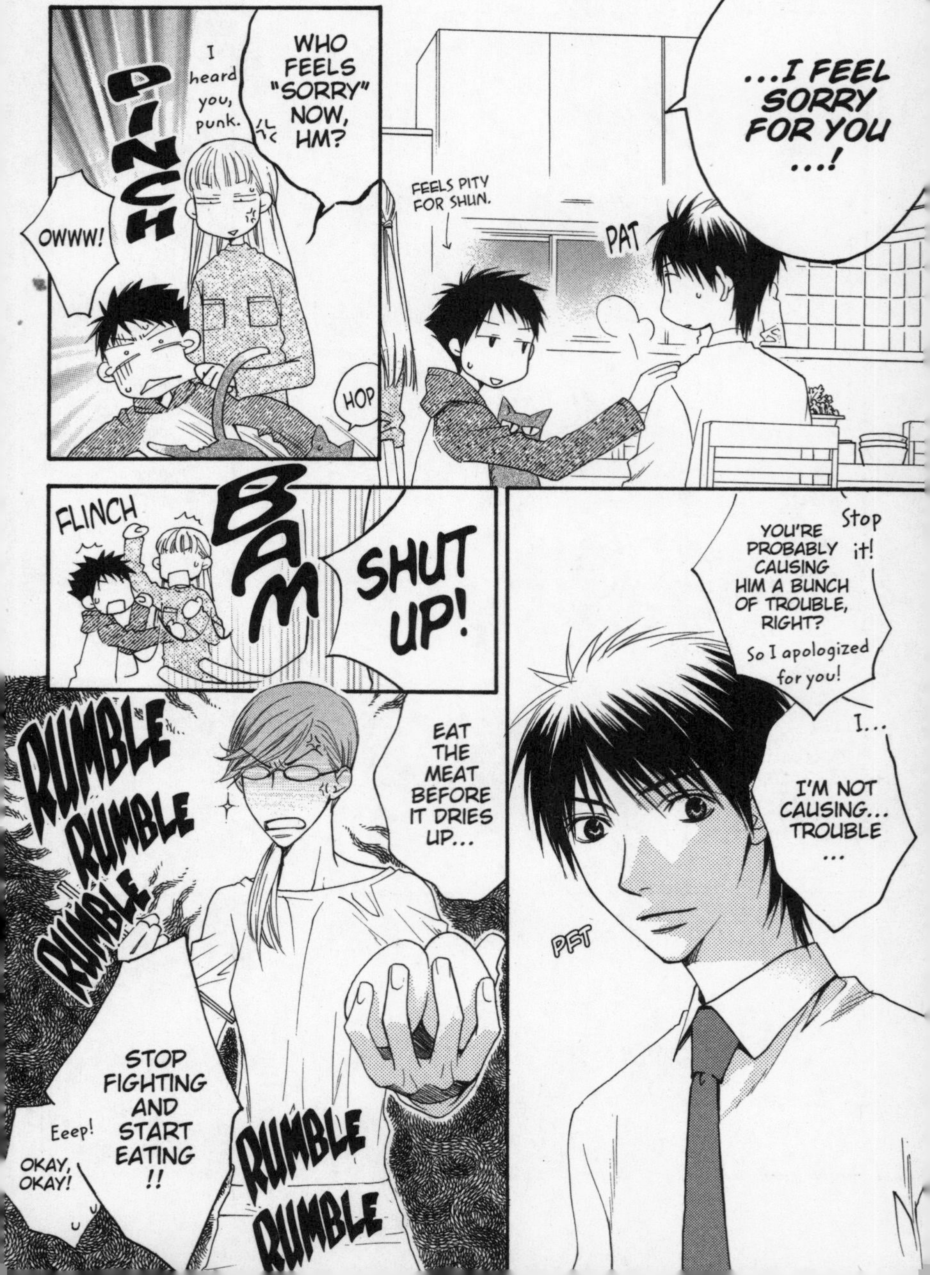
...I FEEL SORRY FOR YOU ...!
PAT
FEELS PITY FOR SHUN.
WHO FEELS "SORRY" NOW, HM?
I heard you, punk.
PINCH
OWWW!
HOP
Stop it!
YOU'RE PROBABLY CAUSING HIM A BUNCH OF TROUBLE, RIGHT?
So I apologized for you!
I...
I'M NOT CAUSING... TROUBLE ...
PFT
SHUT UP!
BAM
FLINCH
EAT THE MEAT BEFORE IT DRIES UP...
RUMBLE RUMBLE RUMBLE
STOP FIGHTING AND START EATING !!
Eeep!
OKAY, OKAY!
RUMBLE RUMBLE

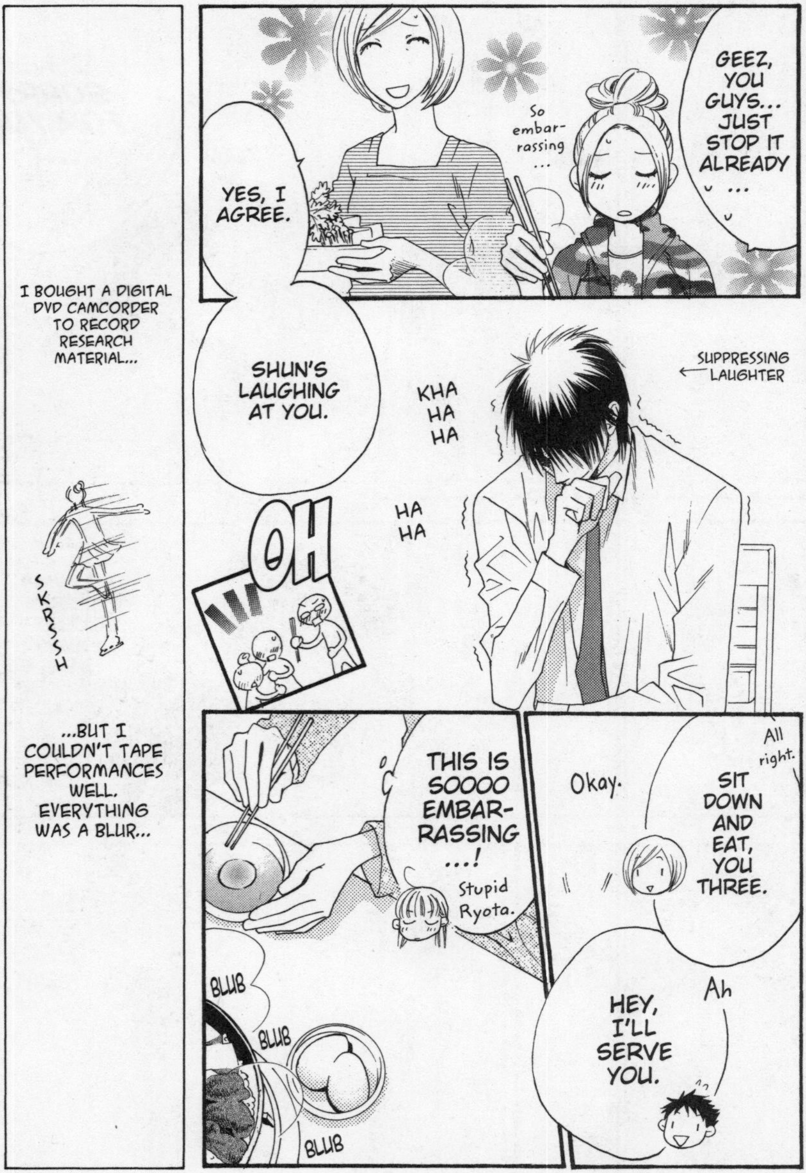
GEEZ, YOU GUYS... JUST STOP IT ALREADY ...
So embarrassing...
YES, I AGREE.
SUPPRESSING LAUGHTER
KHA HA HA
HA HA
SHUN'S LAUGHING AT YOU.
OH
All right.
SIT DOWN AND EAT, YOU THREE.
Okay.
Ah
HEY, I'LL SERVE YOU.
THIS IS SOOOO EMBARRASSING...!
Stupid Ryota.
BLUB
BLUB
BLUB
I BOUGHT A DIGITAL DVD CAMCORDER TO RECORD RESEARCH MATERIAL...
SKRSSH
...BUT I COULDN'T TAPE PERFORMANCES WELL. EVERYTHING WAS A BLUR...

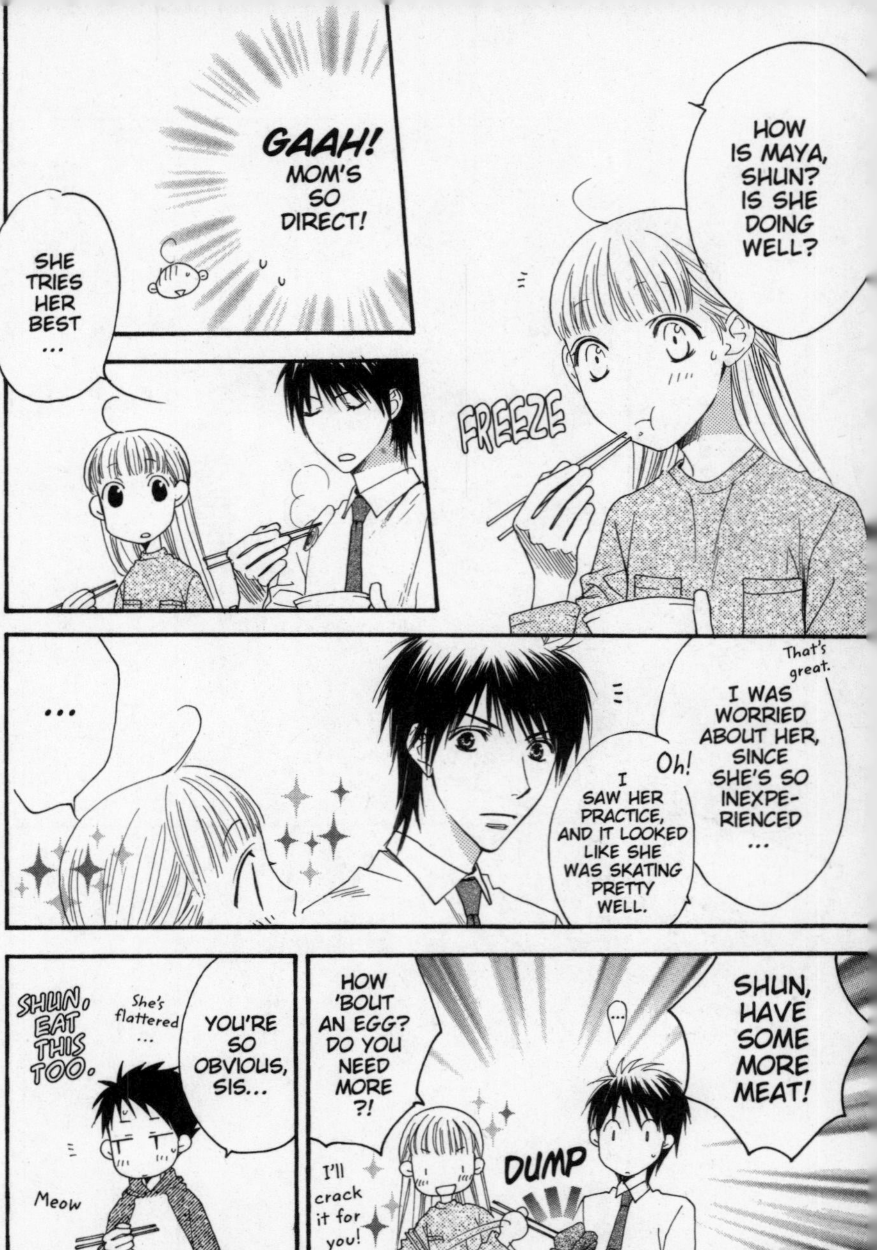
HOW IS MAYA, SHUN? IS SHE DOING WELL?
FREEZE
GAAH! MOM'S SO DIRECT!
SHE TRIES HER BEST...
That's great.
I WAS WORRIED ABOUT HER, SINCE SHE'S SO INEXPE-RIENCED...
Oh!
I SAW HER PRACTICE, AND IT LOOKED LIKE SHE WAS SKATING PRETTY WELL.
...
SHUN, HAVE SOME MORE MEAT!
...
HOW 'BOUT AN EGG? DO YOU NEED MORE?!
DUMP
I'll crack it for you!
YOU'RE SO OBVIOUS, SIS...
She's flattered...
SHUN, EAT THIS TOO.
Meow

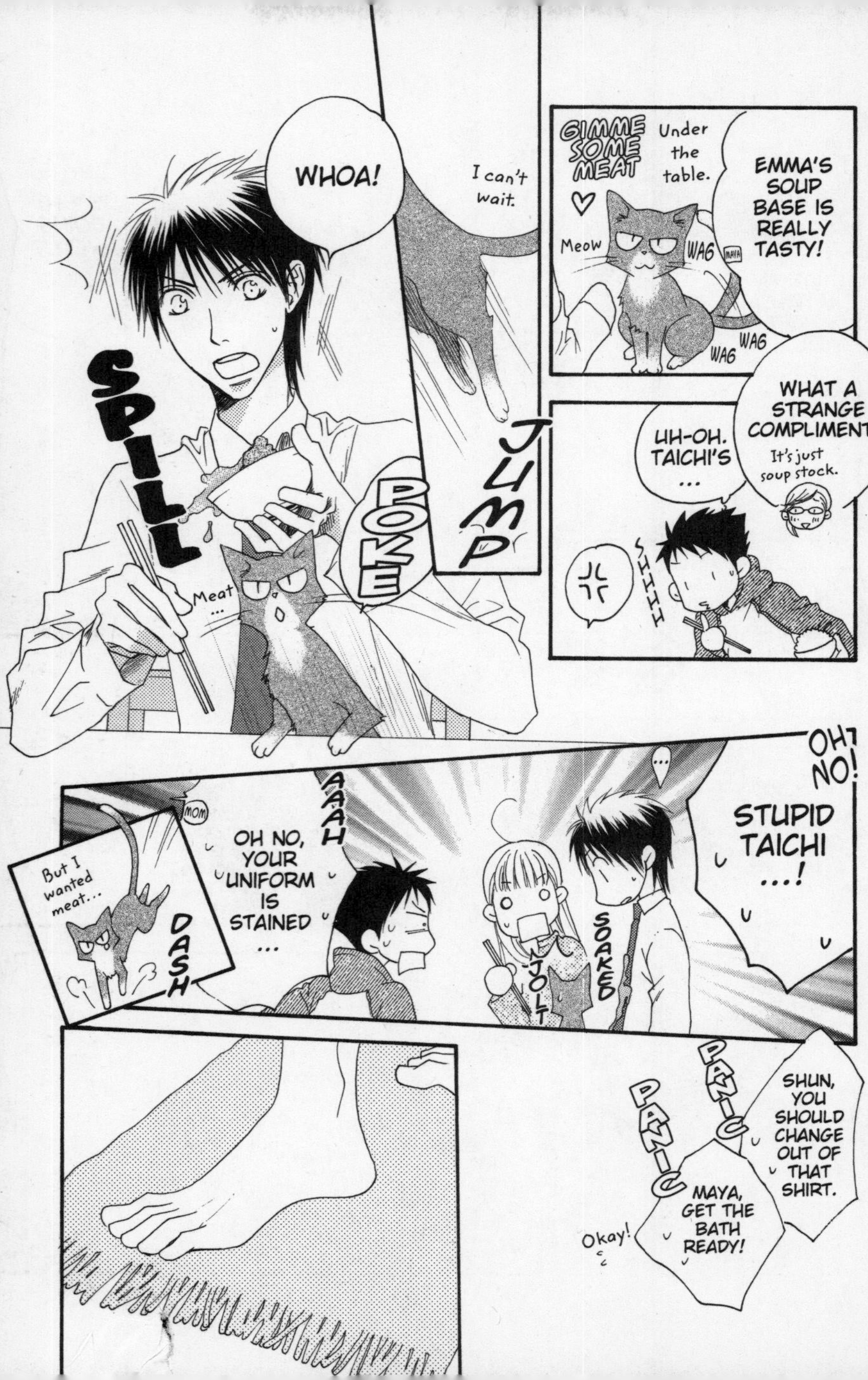
EMMA'S SOUP BASE IS REALLY TASTY!
Under the table.
GIMME SOME MEAT
Meow
WAG
MAYA
WAG WAG
WHAT A STRANGE COMPLIMENT.
It's just soup stock.
UH-OH. TAICHI'S ...
SHHHH
I can't wait.
JUMP
WHOA!
POKE
SPILL
Meat ...
OH NO!
STUPID TAICHI ...!
SOAKED
JOLT
AAAAH
OH NO, YOUR UNIFORM IS STAINED ...
MOM
DASH
But I wanted meat...
SHUN, YOU SHOULD CHANGE OUT OF THAT SHIRT.
PANIC
PANIC
MAYA, GET THE BATH READY!
Okay!

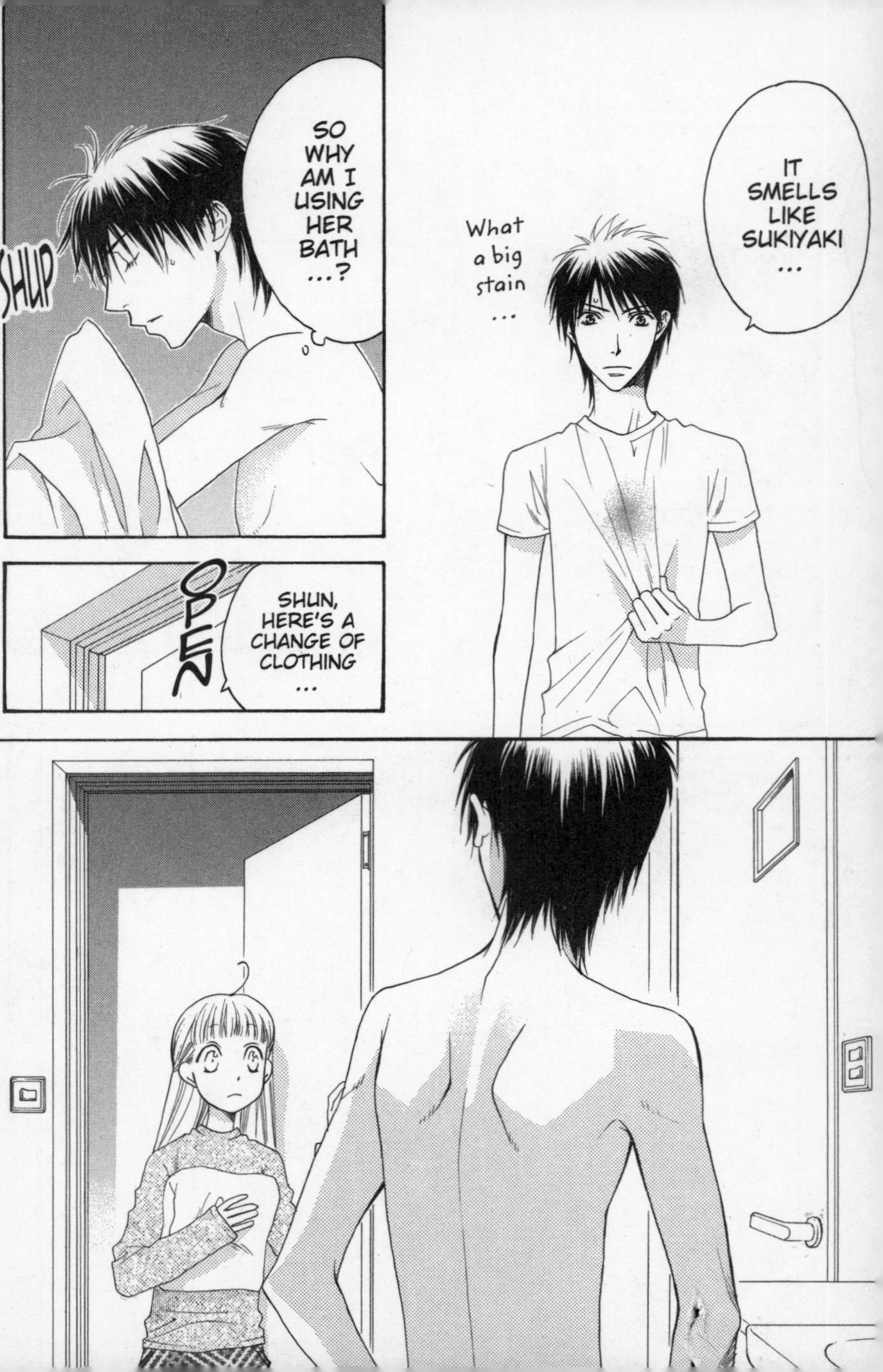
IT SMELLS LIKE SUKIYAKI ...
What a big stain ...
SO WHY AM I USING HER BATH ...?
SHUP
OPEN
SHUN, HERE'S A CHANGE OF CLOTHING ...

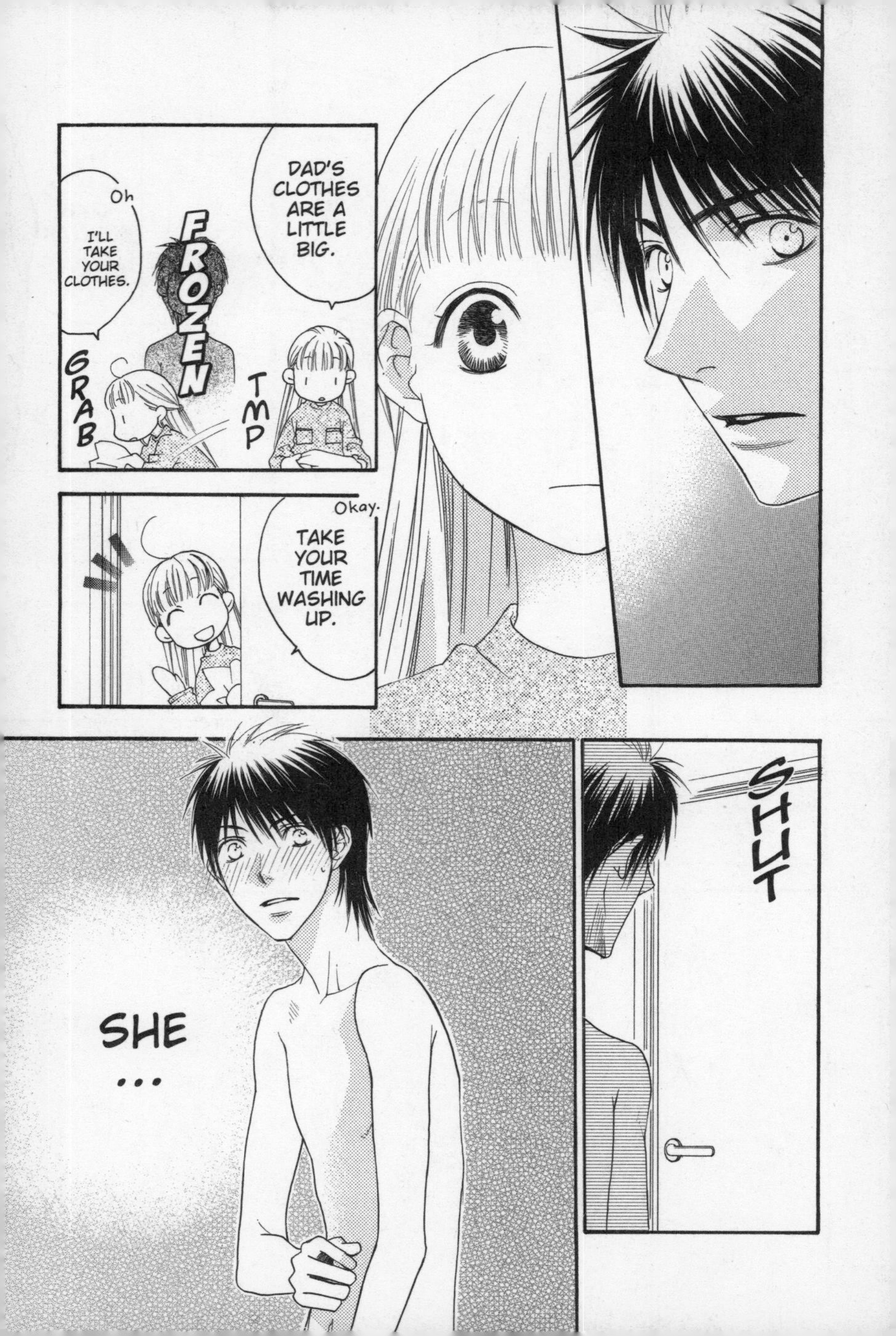
DAD'S CLOTHES ARE A LITTLE BIG.
Oh
I'LL TAKE YOUR CLOTHES.
FROZEN
TMP
GRAB
Okay.
TAKE YOUR TIME WASHING UP.
SHUT
SHE ...

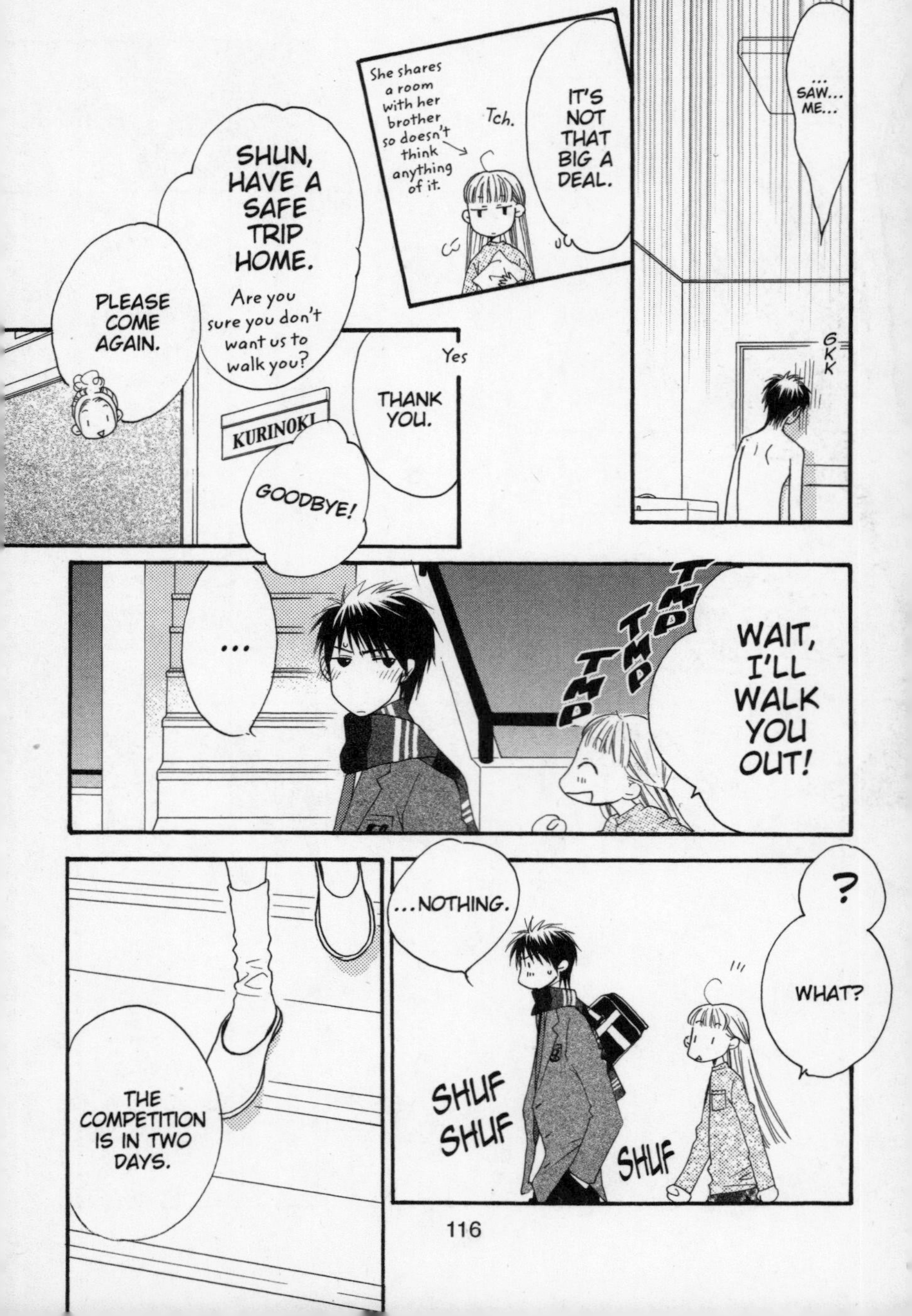
...SAW... ME...
GKK
IT'S NOT THAT BIG A DEAL.
Tch.
She shares a room with her brother so doesn't think anything of it.
SHUN, HAVE A SAFE TRIP HOME.
Are you sure you don't want us to walk you?
Yes
THANK YOU.
PLEASE COME AGAIN.
KURINOKI
GOODBYE!
WAIT, I'LL WALK YOU OUT!
TMP TMP TMP
...
?
WHAT?
...NOTHING.
SHUF SHUF
SHUF
THE COMPETITION IS IN TWO DAYS.

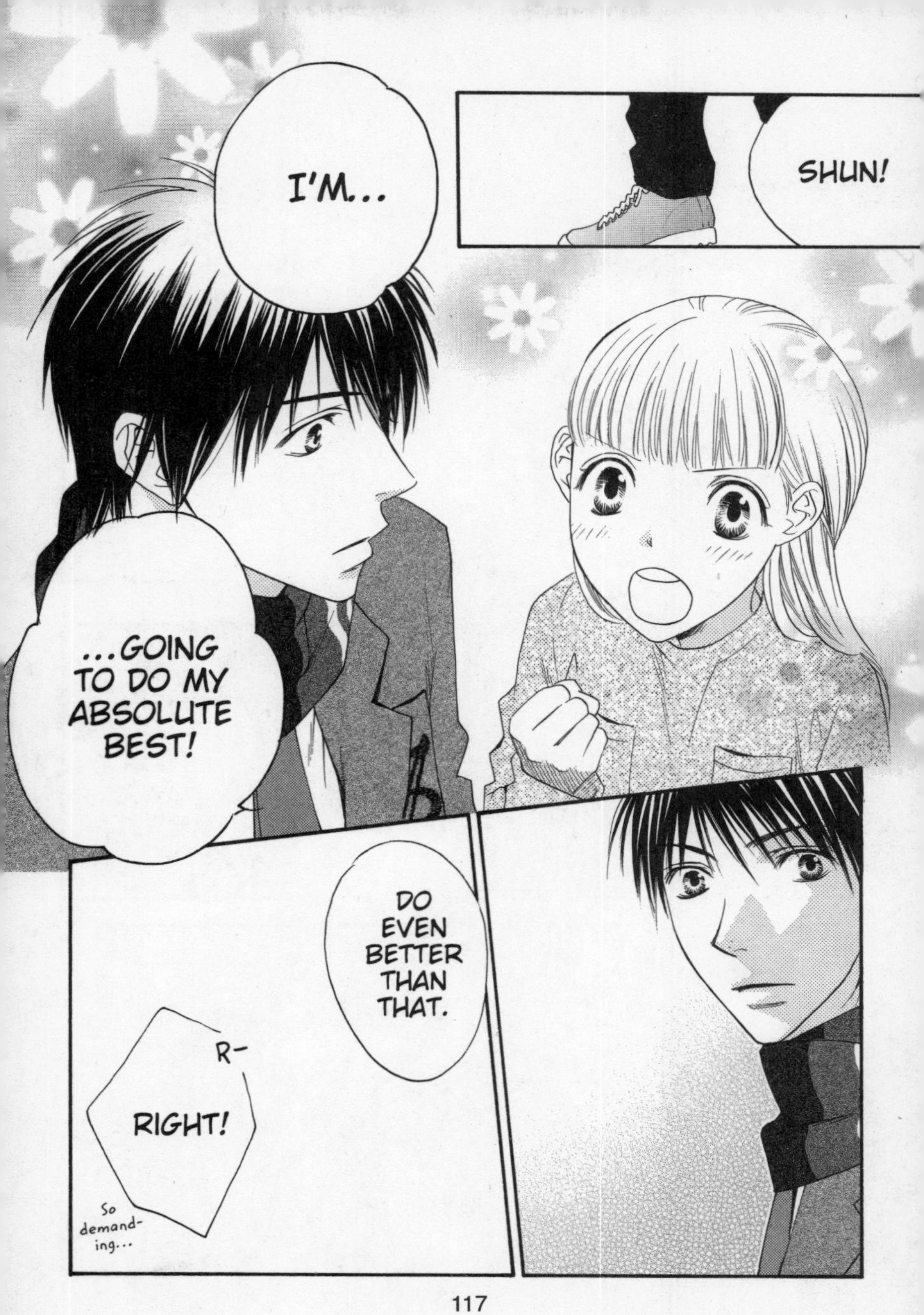
SHUN!
I'M...
...GOING TO DO MY ABSOLUTE BEST!
DO EVEN BETTER THAN THAT.
R- RIGHT!
So demand-ing...

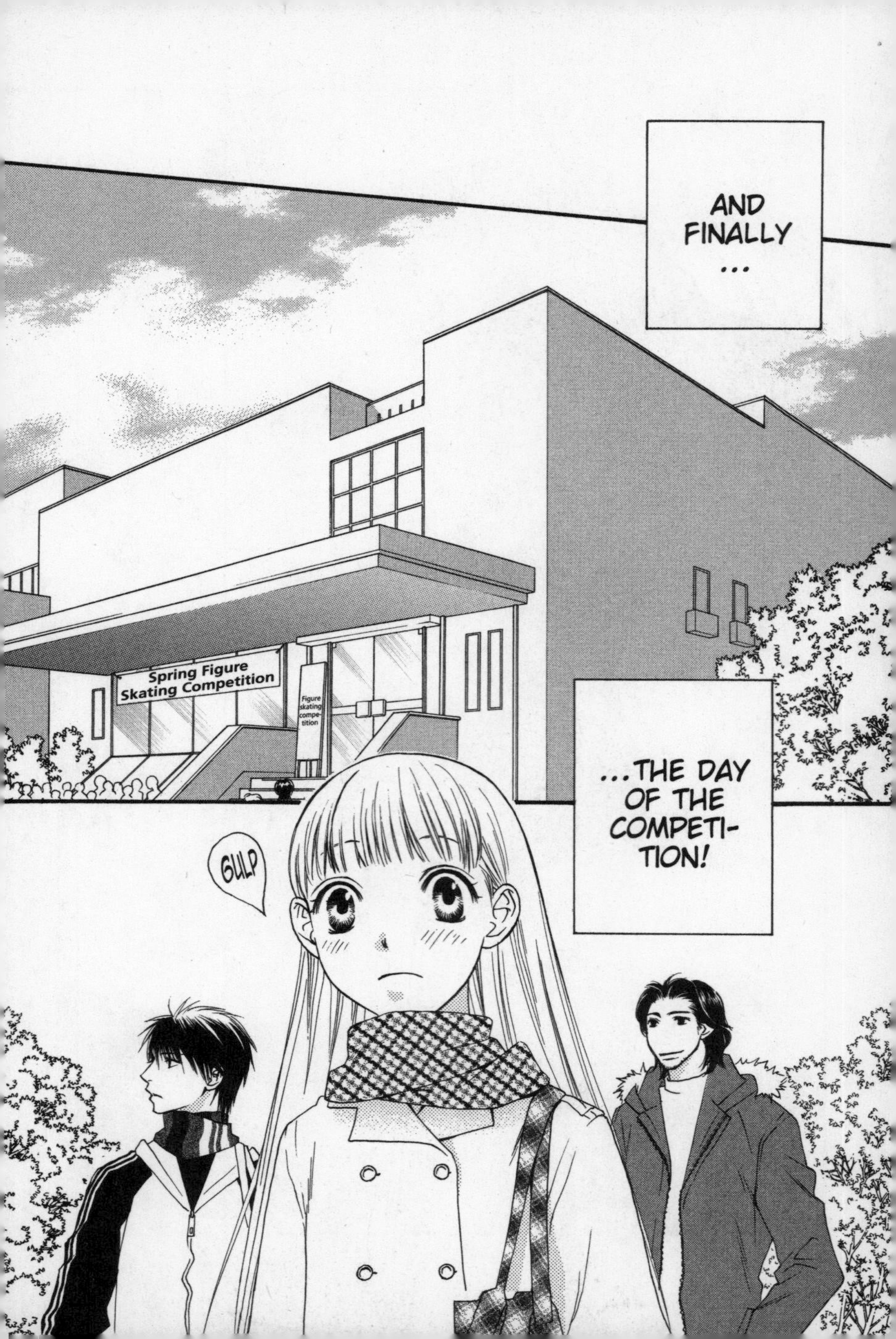
AND FINALLY ...
Spring Figure Skating Competition
Figure skating compe-tition
...THE DAY OF THE COMPETI-TION!
GULP

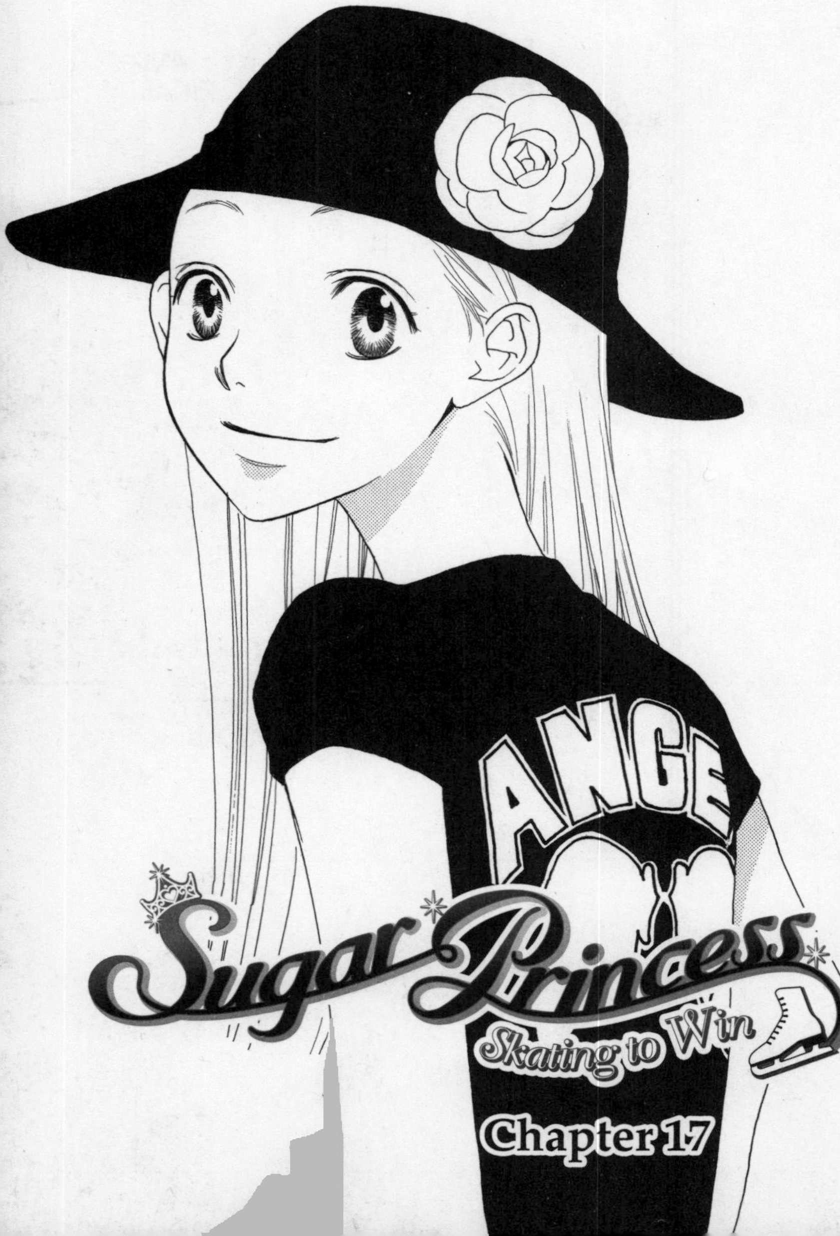
ANGE
Sugar Princess
Skating to Win
Chapter 17

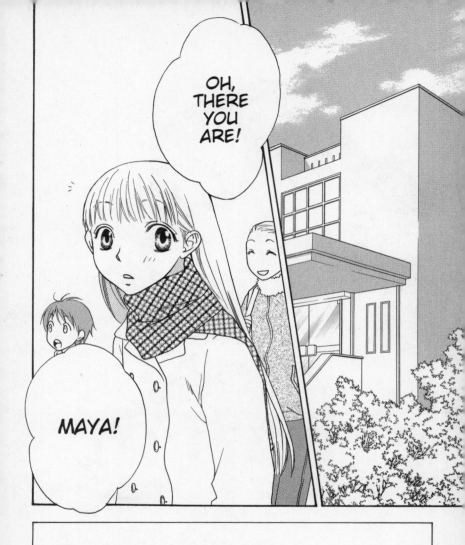

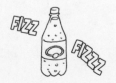

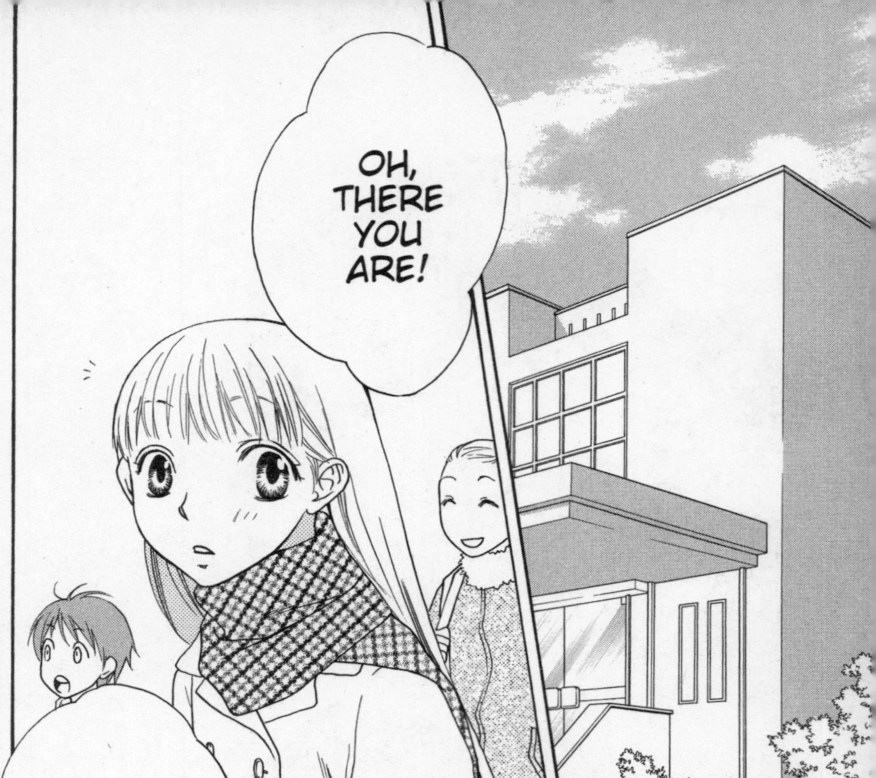
OH, THERE YOU ARE!
MAYA!

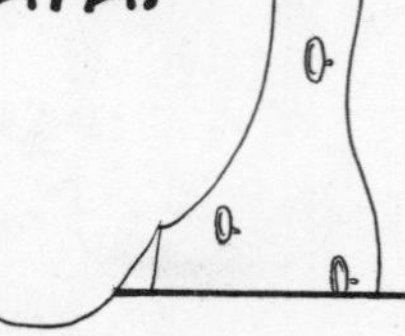
FIZZ
FIZZZ

MY RECENT CRAZE IS TO DRINK CRYSTAL GEYSER (SPARKLING WATER)!

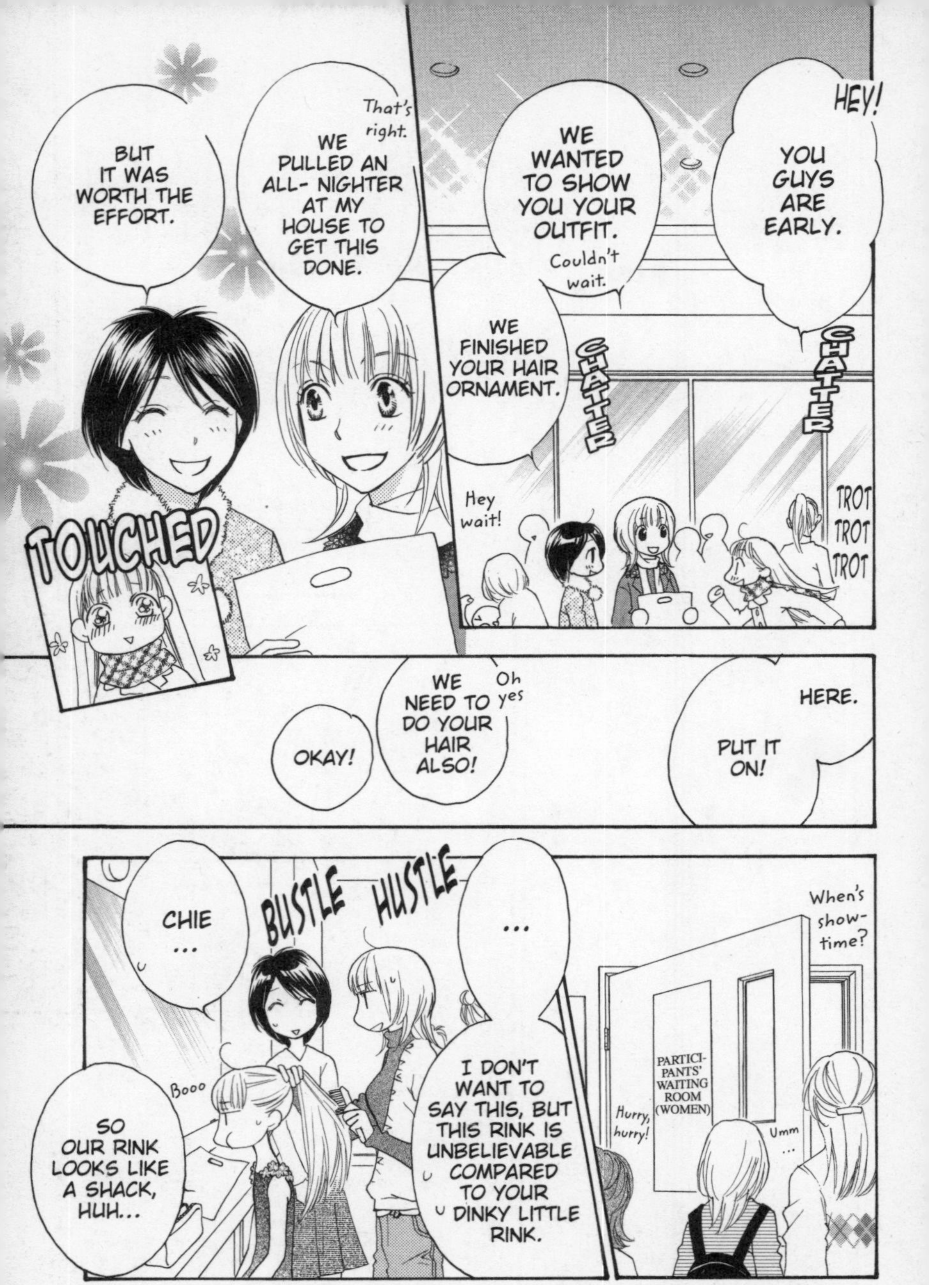
HEY!
YOU GUYS ARE EARLY.
CHATTER
WE WANTED TO SHOW YOU YOUR OUTFIT.
Couldn't wait.
CHATTER
WE FINISHED YOUR HAIR ORNAMENT.
TROT TROT TROT
Hey wait!
That's right.
WE PULLED AN ALL-NIGHTER AT MY HOUSE TO GET THIS DONE.
BUT IT WAS WORTH THE EFFORT.
TOUCHED
HERE.
PUT IT ON!
Oh yes
WE NEED TO DO YOUR HAIR ALSO!
OKAY!
When's show-time?
PARTICI-PANTS' WAITING ROOM (WOMEN)
Umm...
Hurry, hurry!
...
I DON'T WANT TO SAY THIS, BUT THIS RINK IS UNBELIEVABLE COMPARED TO YOUR DINKY LITTLE RINK.
HUSTLE
BUSTLE
CHIE...
SO OUR RINK LOOKS LIKE A SHACK, HUH...
Booo

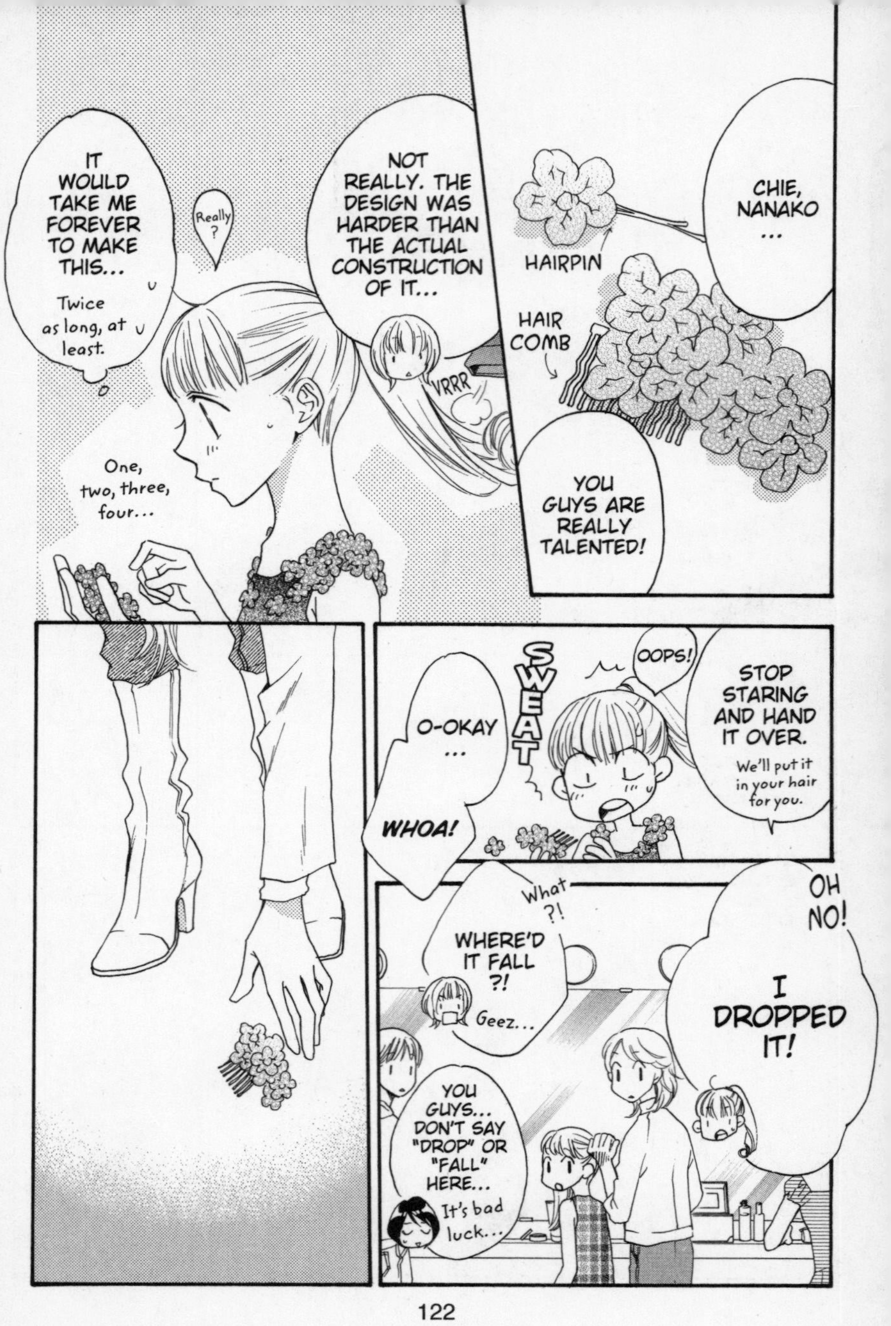
CHIE, NANAKO ...
HAIRPIN
HAIR COMB
YOU GUYS ARE REALLY TALENTED!
NOT REALLY. THE DESIGN WAS HARDER THAN THE ACTUAL CONSTRUCTION OF IT...
VRRR
Really?
IT WOULD TAKE ME FOREVER TO MAKE THIS...
Twice as long, at least.
One, two, three, four...
STOP STARING AND HAND IT OVER.
We'll put it in your hair for you.
OOPS!
SWEAT
O-OKAY ...
WHOA!
OH NO!
I DROPPED IT!
What?!
WHERE'D IT FALL?!
Geez...
YOU GUYS... DON'T SAY "DROP" OR "FALL" HERE...
It's bad luck...

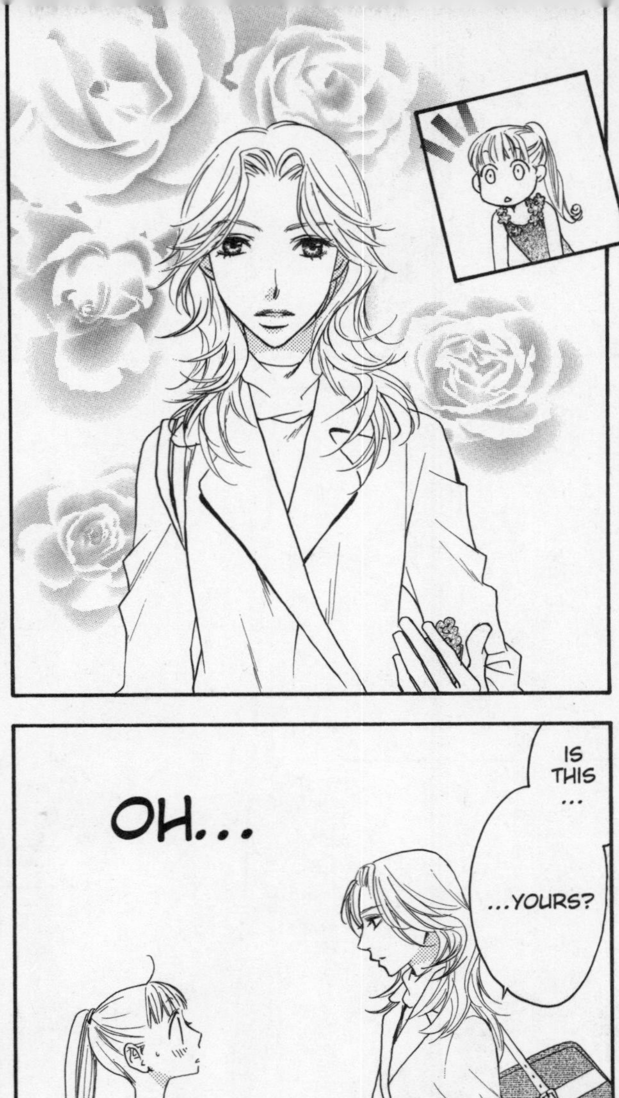

IS THIS ... ...YOURS?
OH...

ONE BIG MISTAKE...

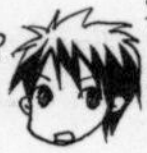

What?
SHUN'S HAIR-STYLE ...

I SHADED HIS HAIR USING A SIMILAR STYLE AS ONE OF MY PREVIOUS CHARACTERS, BUT...IT WAS QUITE LABORIOUS. (LOL)

THE PREVIOUS CHARACTER SELDOM APPEARED, SO I DIDN'T NOTICE IT THEN...

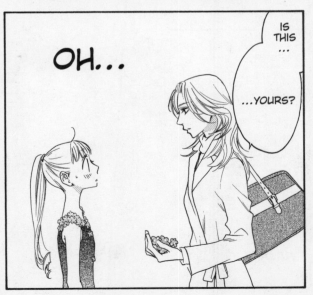

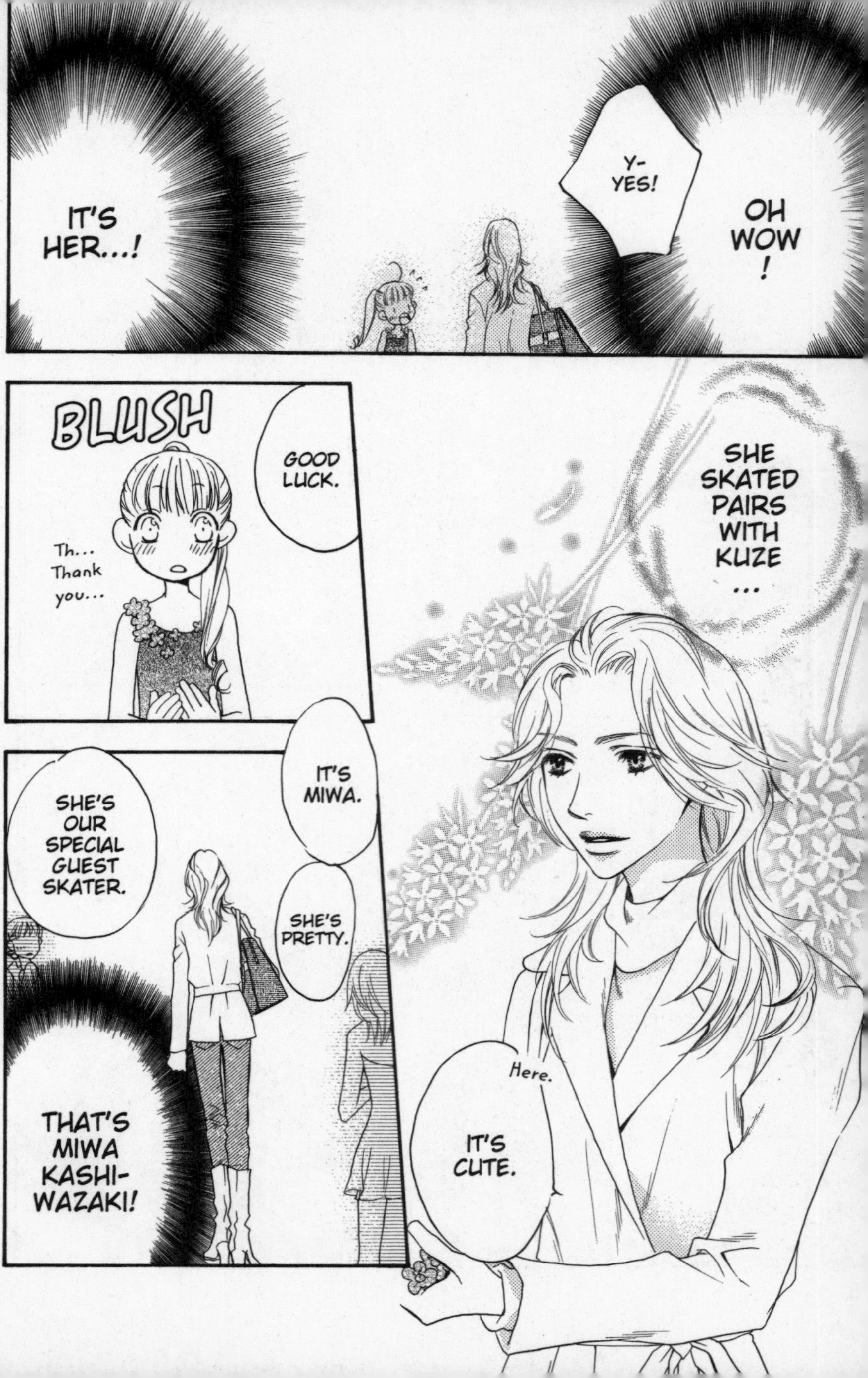

OH WOW!
Y-YES!
IT'S HER...!
SHE SKATED PAIRS WITH KUZE...
Here.
IT'S CUTE.
GOOD LUCK.
BLUSH
Th... Thank you...
IT'S MIWA.
SHE'S OUR SPECIAL GUEST SKATER.
SHE'S PRETTY.
THAT'S MIWA KASHI-WAZAKI!

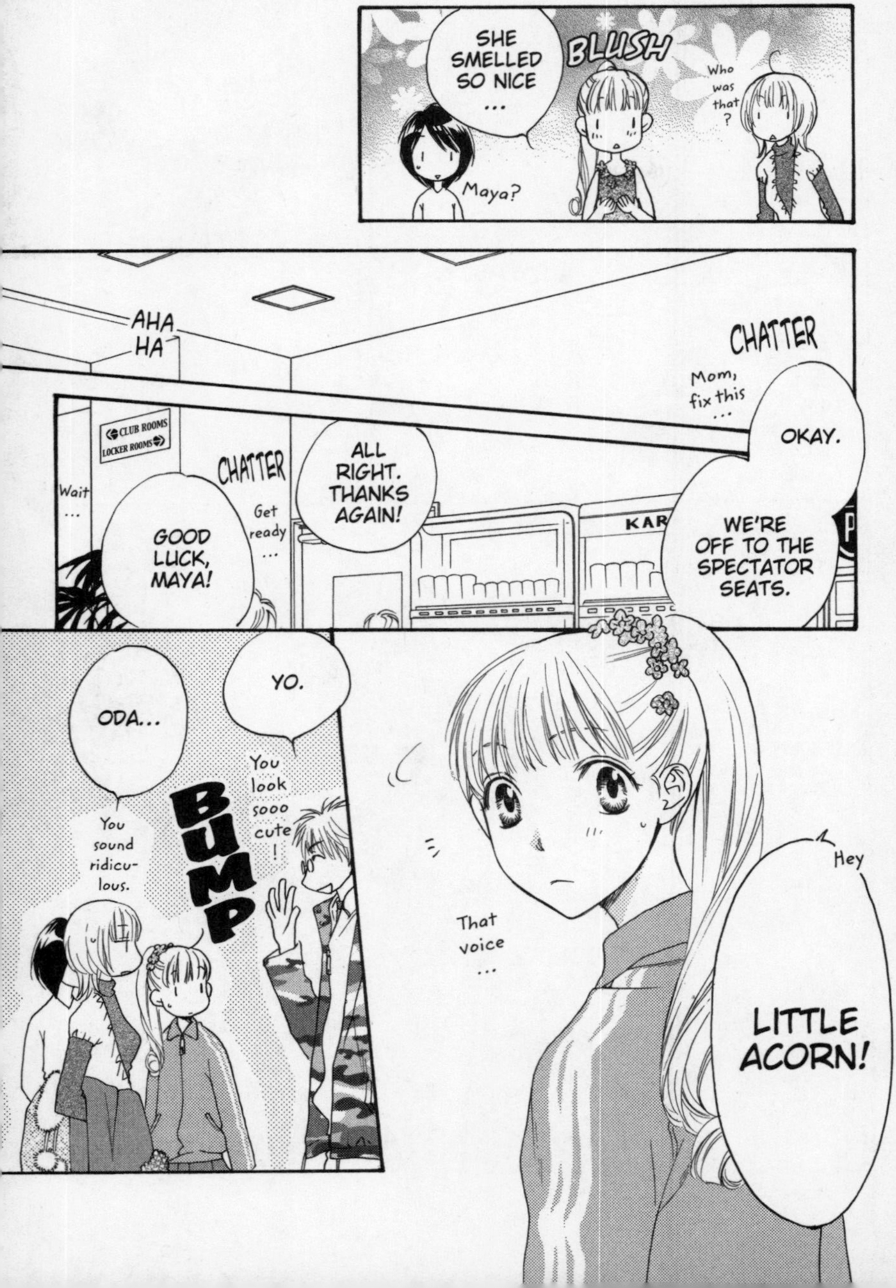
Who was that?
BLUSH
SHE SMELLED SO NICE...
Maya?
CHATTER
Mom, fix this...
OKAY.
AHA HA
WE'RE OFF TO THE SPECTATOR SEATS.
KAR
ALL RIGHT. THANKS AGAIN!
Get ready...
CHATTER
GOOD LUCK, MAYA!
CLUB ROOMS
LOCKER ROOMS
Wait...
Hey
LITTLE ACORN!
That voice...
YO.
You look sooo cute!
ODA...
You sound ridicu-lous.
BUMP

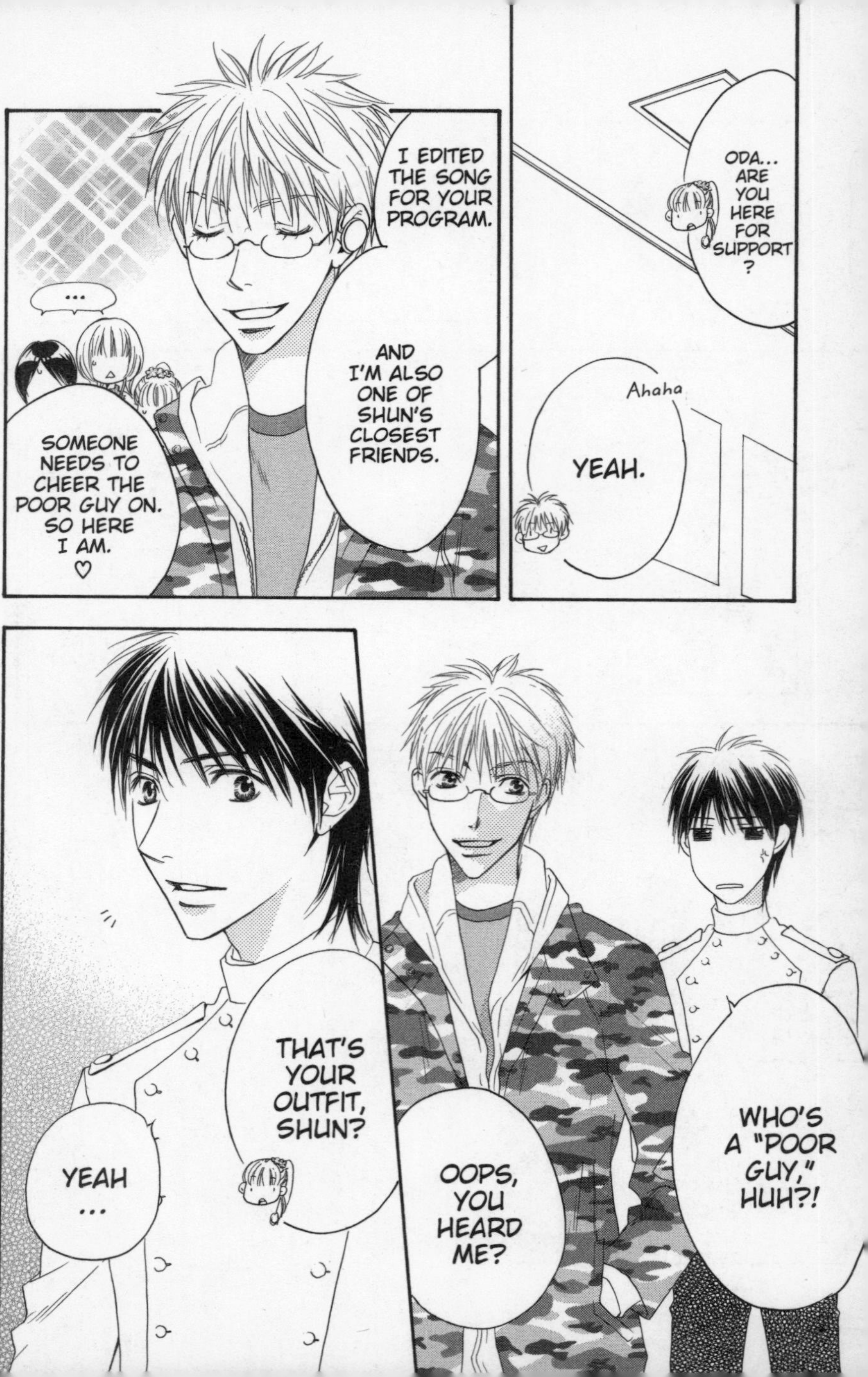
ODA... ARE YOU HERE FOR SUPPORT?
Ahaha
YEAH.
I EDITED THE SONG FOR YOUR PROGRAM.
AND I'M ALSO ONE OF SHUN'S CLOSEST FRIENDS.
...
SOMEONE NEEDS TO CHEER THE POOR GUY ON. SO HERE I AM. ♡
WHO'S A "POOR GUY," HUH?!
OOPS, YOU HEARD ME?
THAT'S YOUR OUTFIT, SHUN?
YEAH...

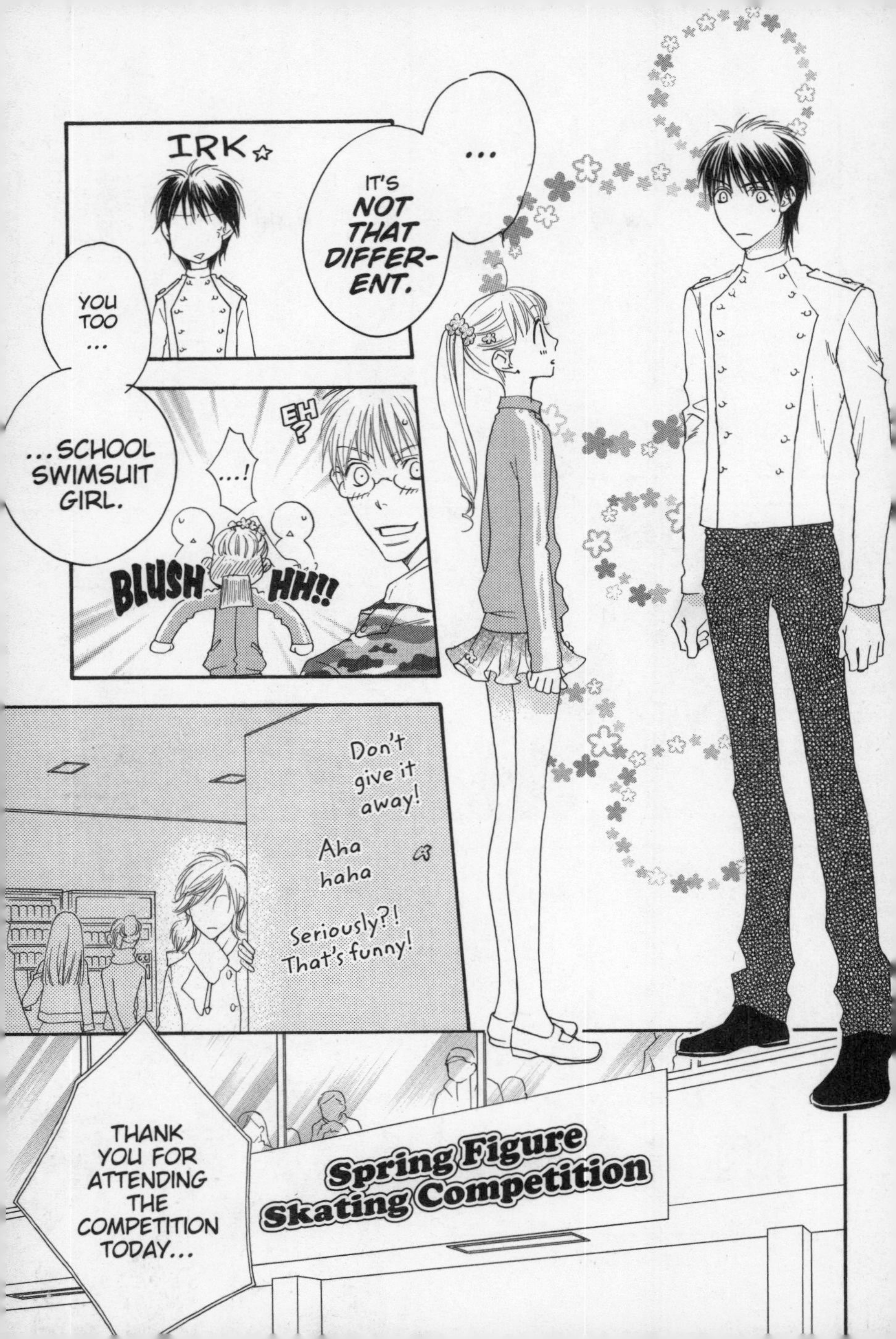
...
IT'S NOT THAT DIFFERENT.
IRK
YOU TOO ...
...SCHOOL SWIMSUIT GIRL.
EH?
...!
BLUSH~HH!!
Don't give it away!
Aha haha
Seriously?! That's funny!
THANK YOU FOR ATTENDING THE COMPETITION TODAY...
Spring Figure Skating Competition

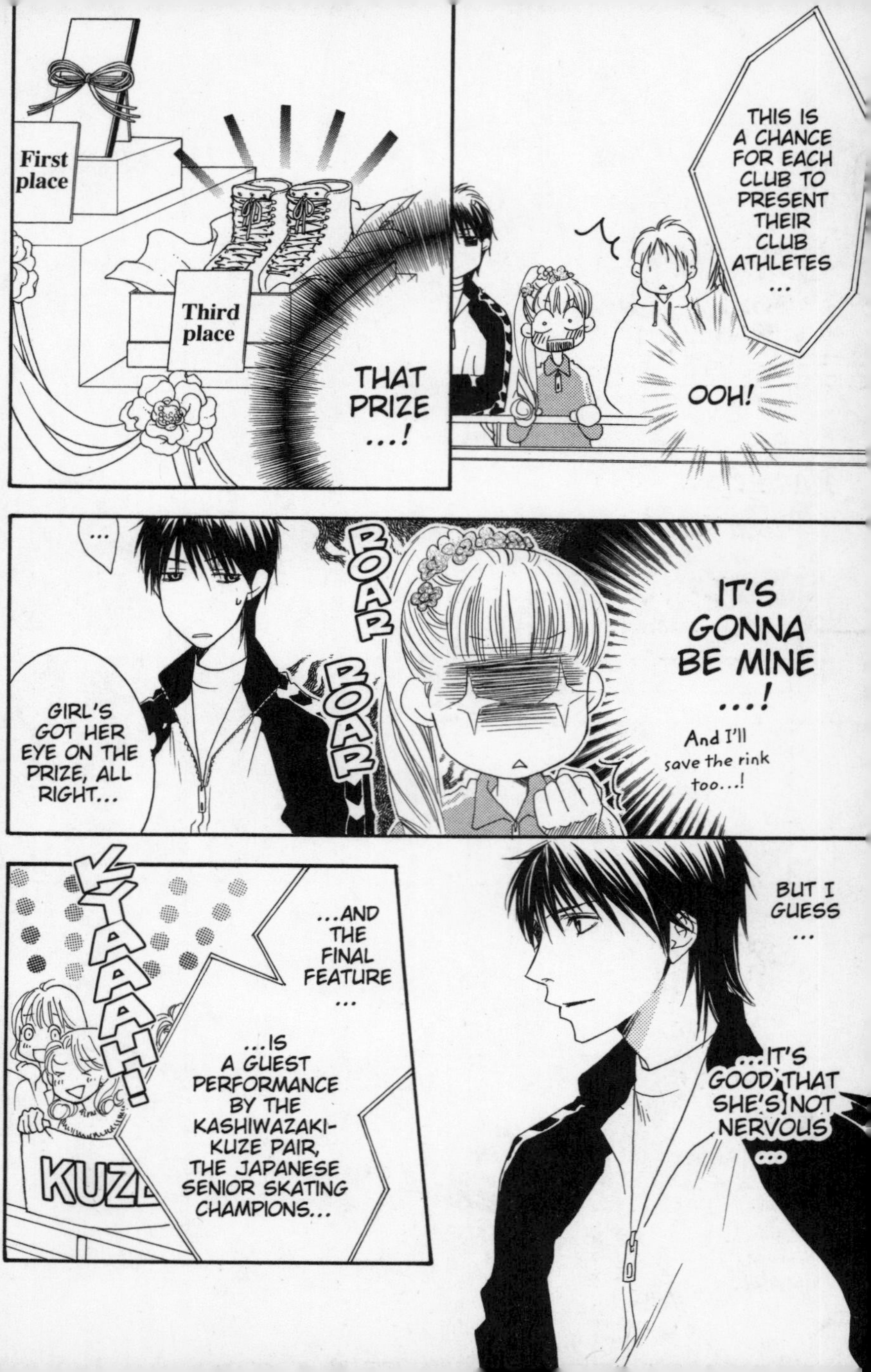

THIS IS A CHANCE FOR EACH CLUB TO PRESENT THEIR CLUB ATHLETES ...
OOH!
THAT PRIZE ...!
First place
Third place
IT'S GONNA BE MINE ...!
And I'll save the rink too...!
ROAR
ROAR
...
GIRL'S GOT HER EYE ON THE PRIZE, ALL RIGHT...
BUT I GUESS ...
...IT'S GOOD THAT SHE'S NOT NERVOUS ...
...AND THE FINAL FEATURE ...
...IS A GUEST PERFORMANCE BY THE KASHIWAZAKI-KUZE PAIR, THE JAPANESE SENIOR SKATING CHAMPIONS...
KYAAAAH!
KUZE

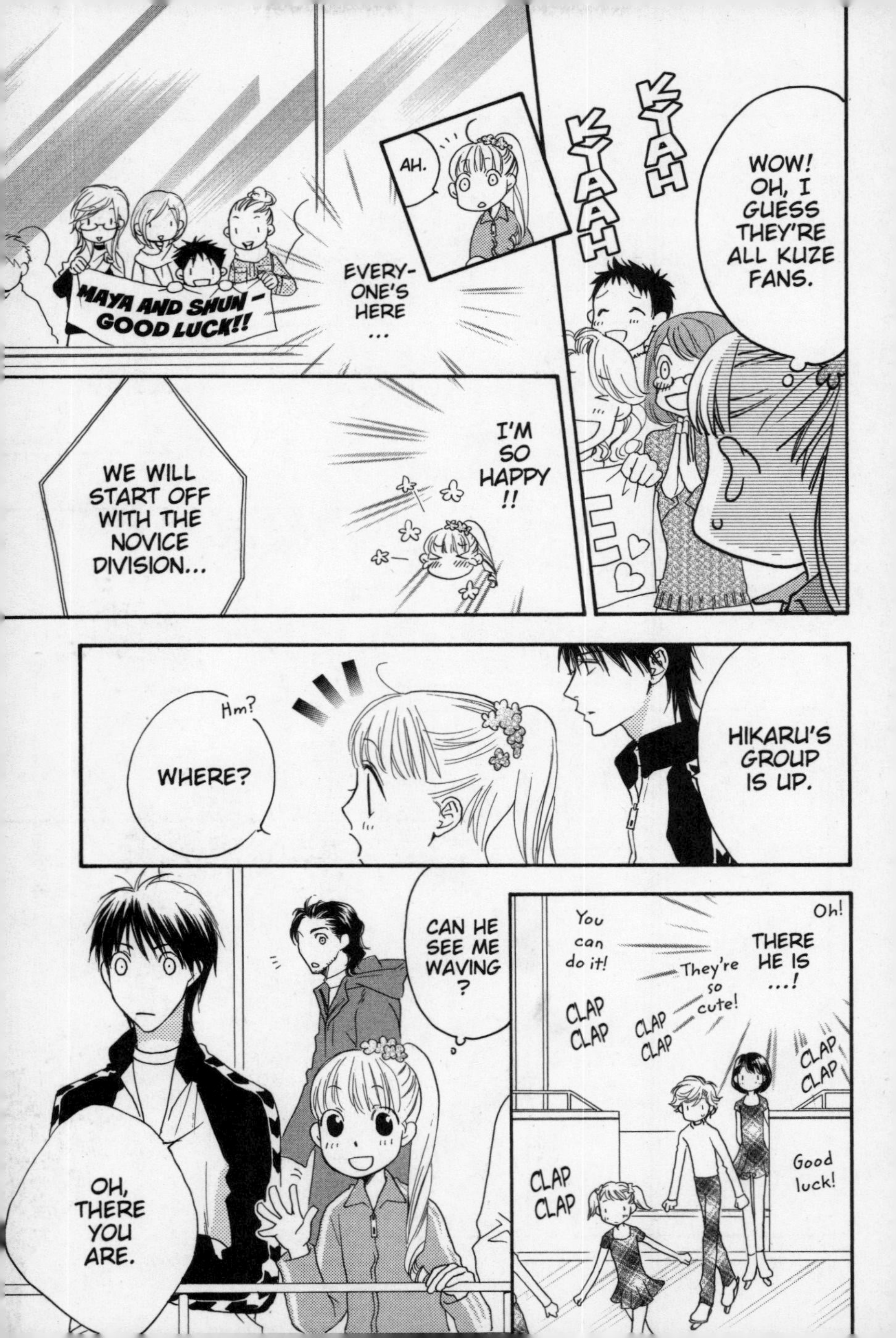
KYAH
KYAAAH
WOW! OH, I GUESS THEY'RE ALL KUZE FANS.
AH.
MAYA AND SHUN – GOOD LUCK!!
EVERY-ONE'S HERE ...
I'M SO HAPPY !!
WE WILL START OFF WITH THE NOVICE DIVISION...
HIKARU'S GROUP IS UP.
Hm?
WHERE?
Oh!
THERE HE IS ...!
Good luck!
CLAP CLAP
They're so cute!
CLAP CLAP
You can do it!
CLAP CLAP
CLAP CLAP
CAN HE SEE ME WAVING ?
OH, THERE YOU ARE.

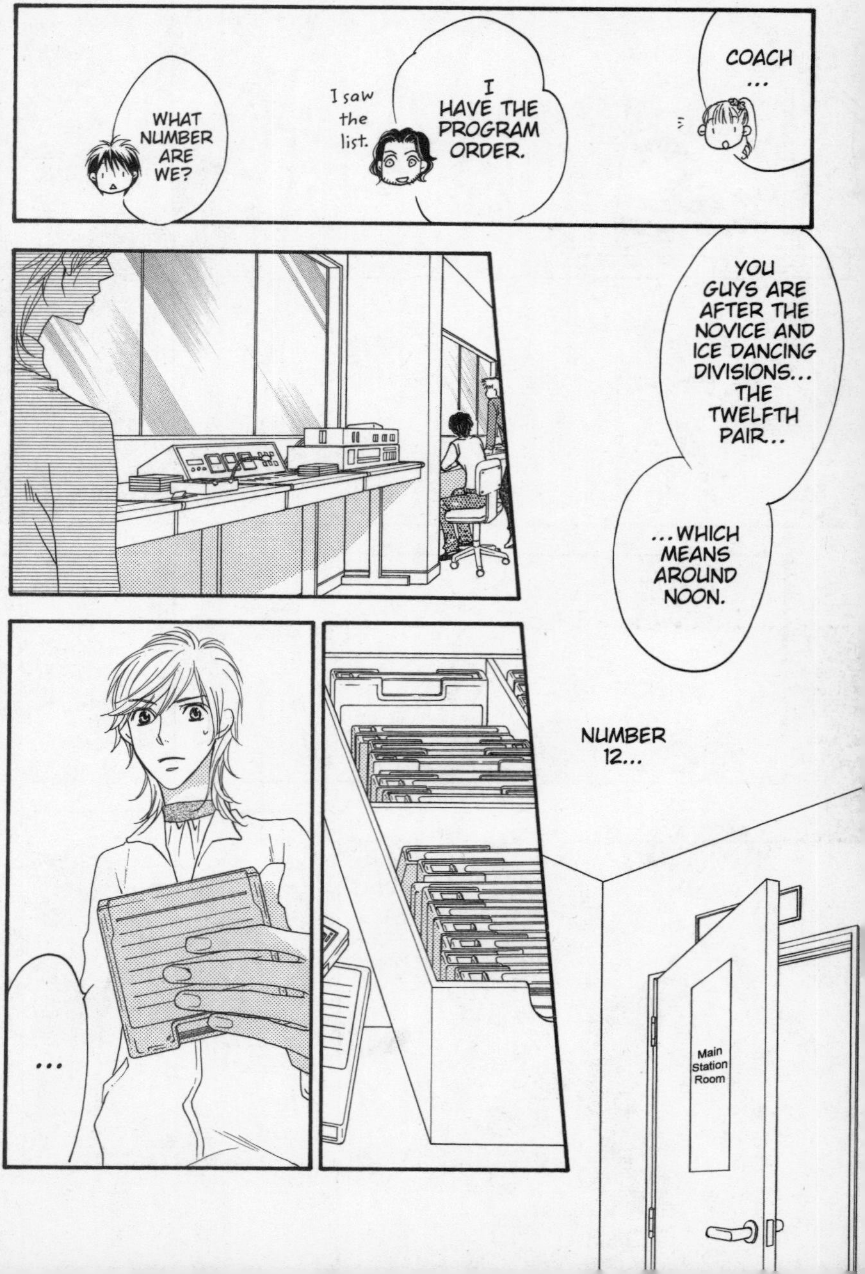
COACH...
I HAVE THE PROGRAM ORDER.
I saw the list.
WHAT NUMBER ARE WE?
YOU GUYS ARE AFTER THE NOVICE AND ICE DANCING DIVISIONS... THE TWELFTH PAIR...
...WHICH MEANS AROUND NOON.
NUMBER 12...
Main Station Room
...

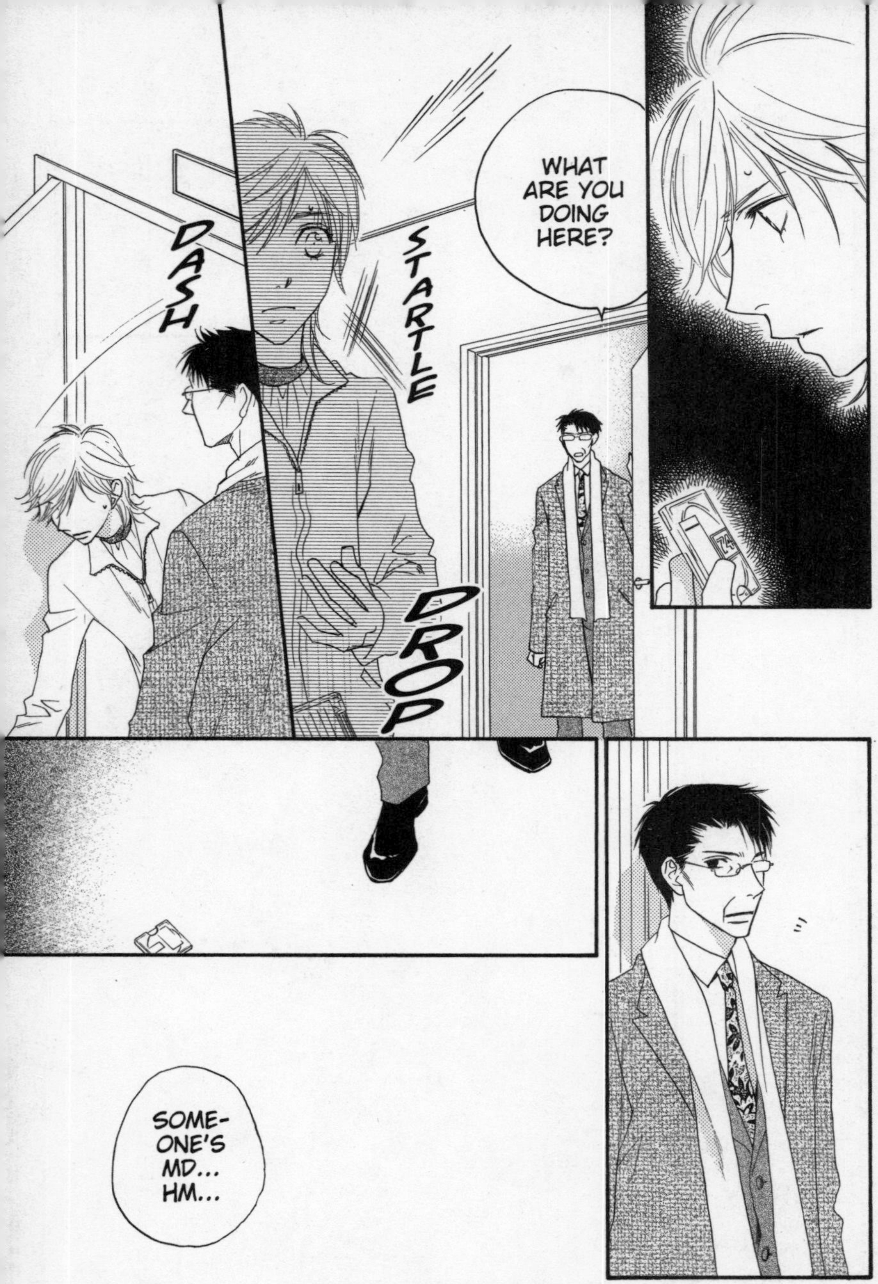
WHAT ARE YOU DOING HERE?
STARTLE
DROP
DASH
SOME-ONE'S MD... HM...

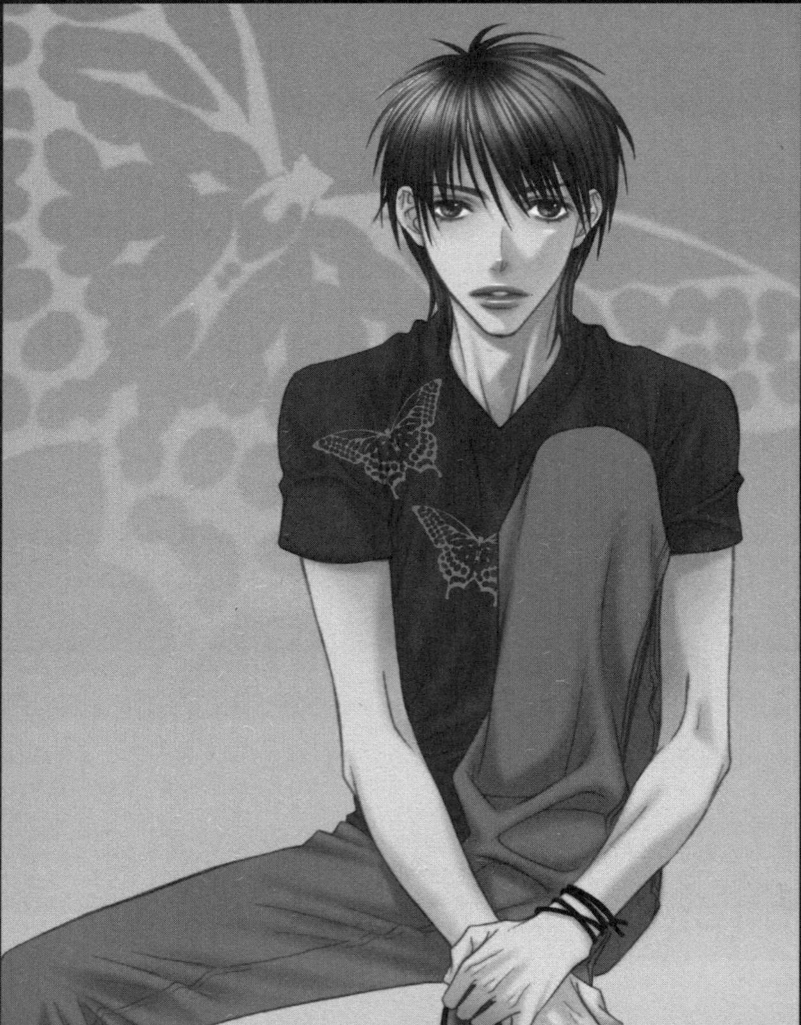

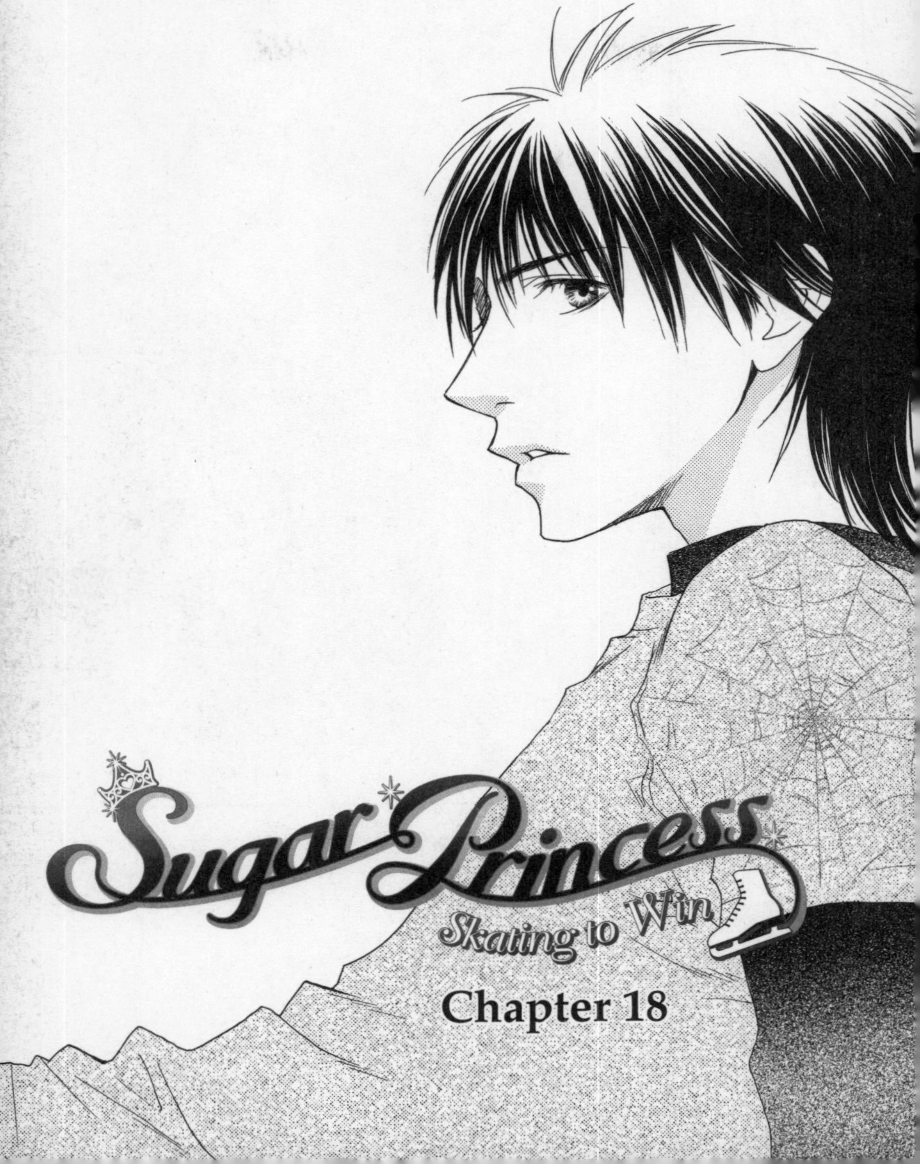
Sugar Princess
Skating to Win
Chapter 18

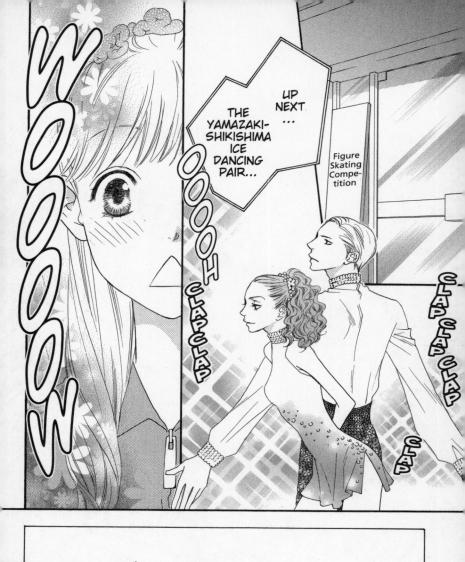

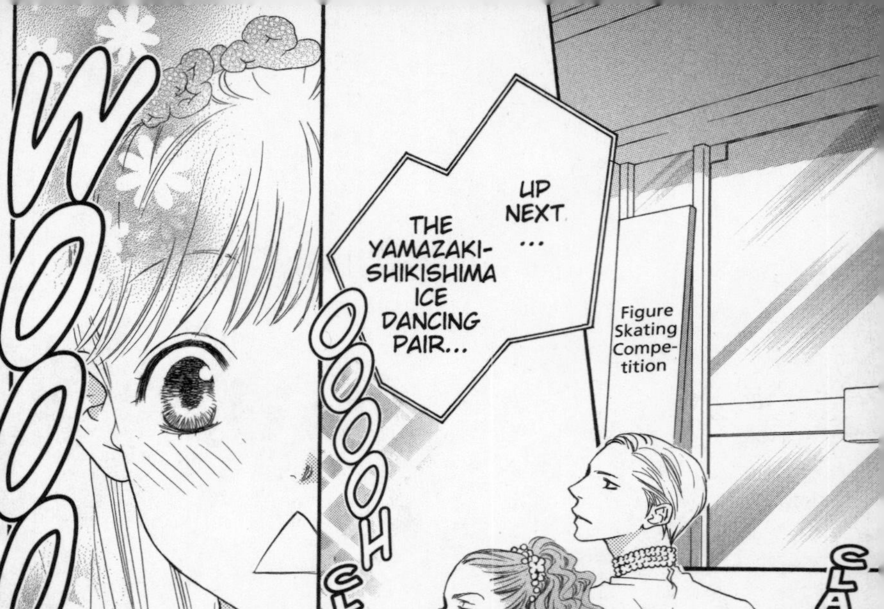
UP NEXT ...
THE YAMAZAKI-SHIKISHIMA ICE DANCING PAIR...
OOOOOH
Figure Skating Competition
CLAP CLAP
CLAP CLAP CLAP CLAP
CLAP
WOOOOOW

I LOVE PLUM WINE.

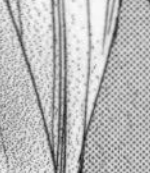
Delicious!

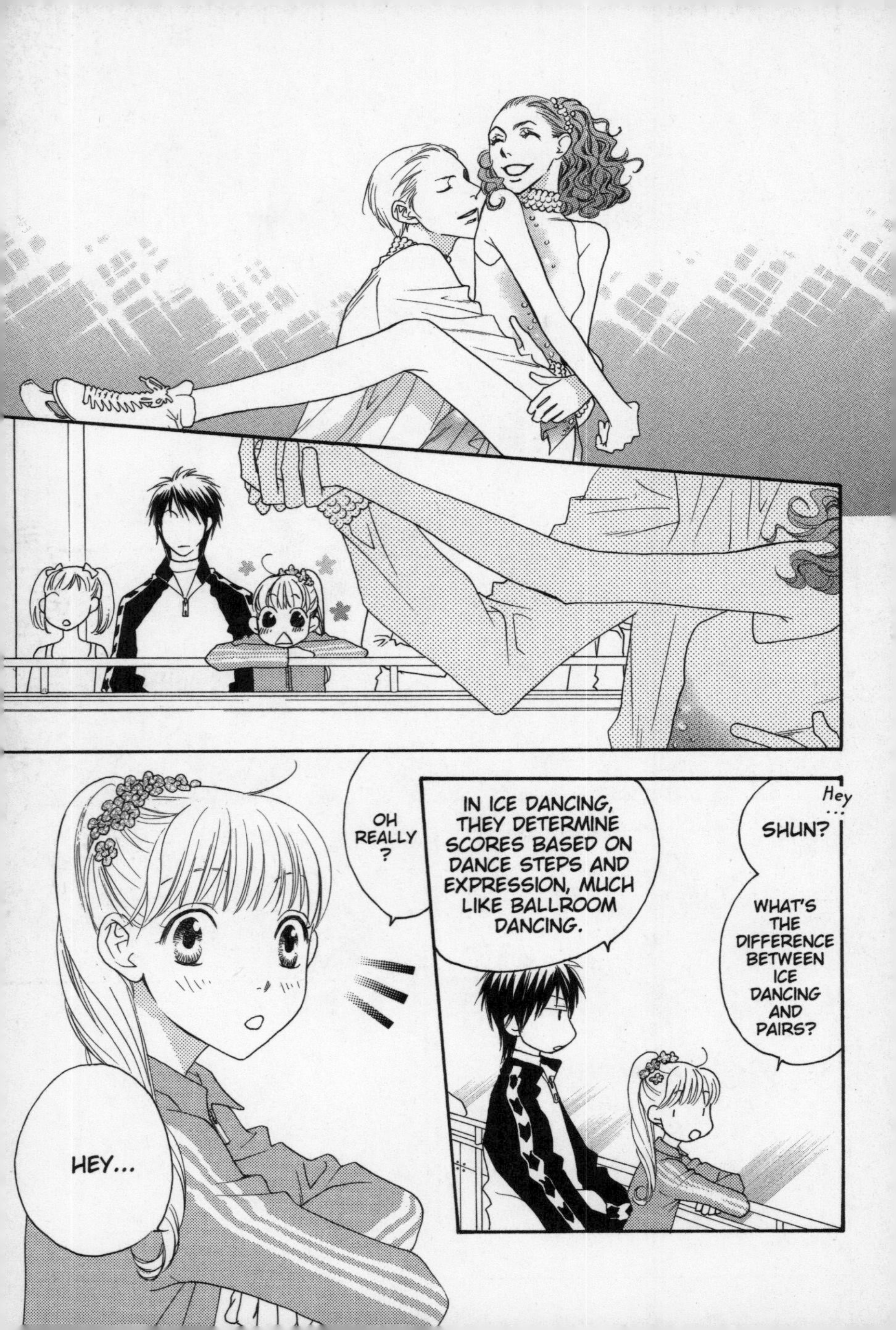
Hey...
SHUN?
WHAT'S THE DIFFERENCE BETWEEN ICE DANCING AND PAIRS?
IN ICE DANCING, THEY DETERMINE SCORES BASED ON DANCE STEPS AND EXPRESSION, MUCH LIKE BALLROOM DANCING.
OH REALLY?
HEY...

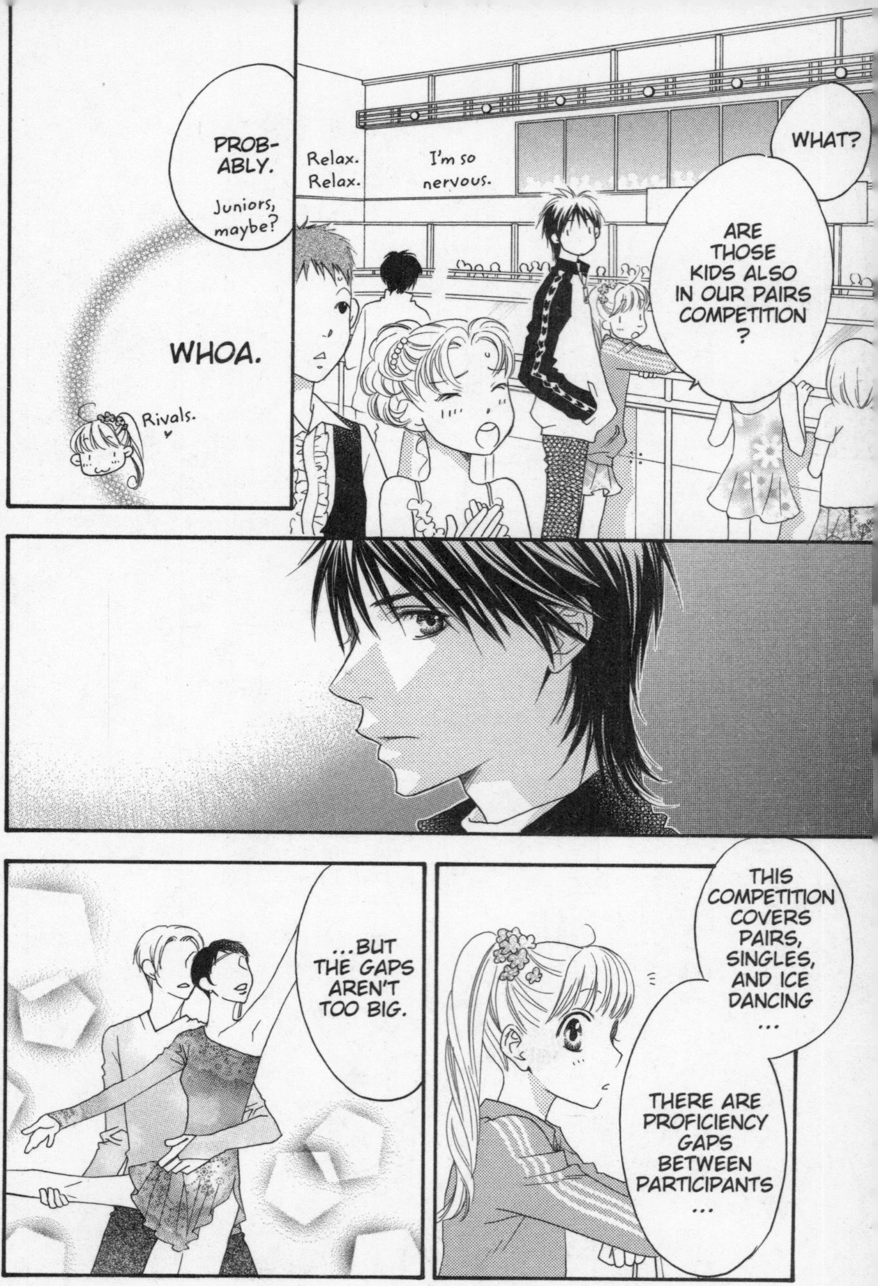
WHAT?
ARE THOSE KIDS ALSO IN OUR PAIRS COMPETITION?
I'm so nervous.
Relax. Relax.
PROB-ABLY.
Juniors, maybe?
WHOA.
Rivals.
THIS COMPETITION COVERS PAIRS, SINGLES, AND ICE DANCING...
THERE ARE PROFICIENCY GAPS BETWEEN PARTICIPANTS...
...BUT THE GAPS AREN'T TOO BIG.

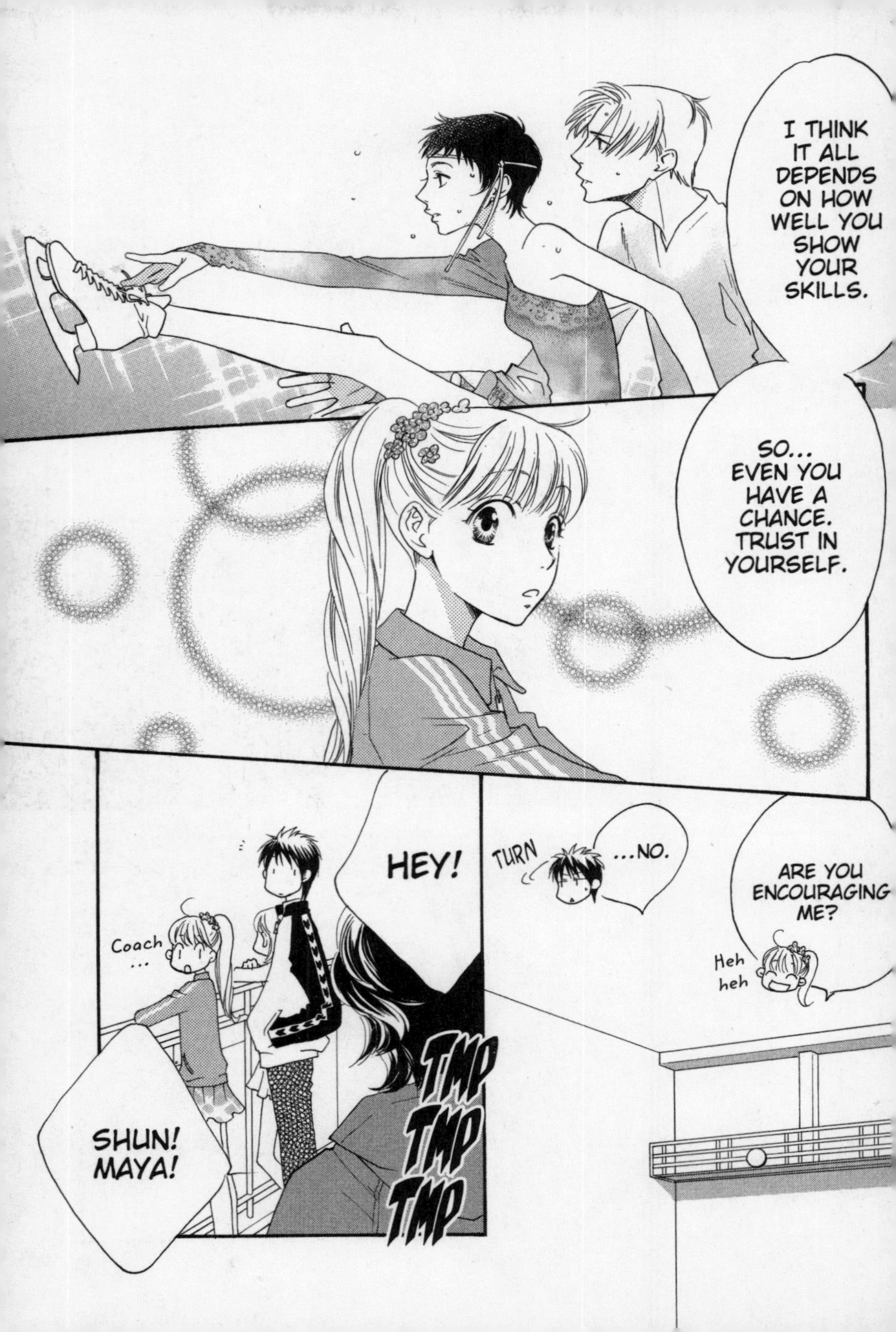
I THINK IT ALL DEPENDS ON HOW WELL YOU SHOW YOUR SKILLS.
SO... EVEN YOU HAVE A CHANCE. TRUST IN YOURSELF.
ARE YOU ENCOURAGING ME?
Heh heh
TURN
...NO.
HEY!
Coach...
TMP TMP TMP
SHUN! MAYA!

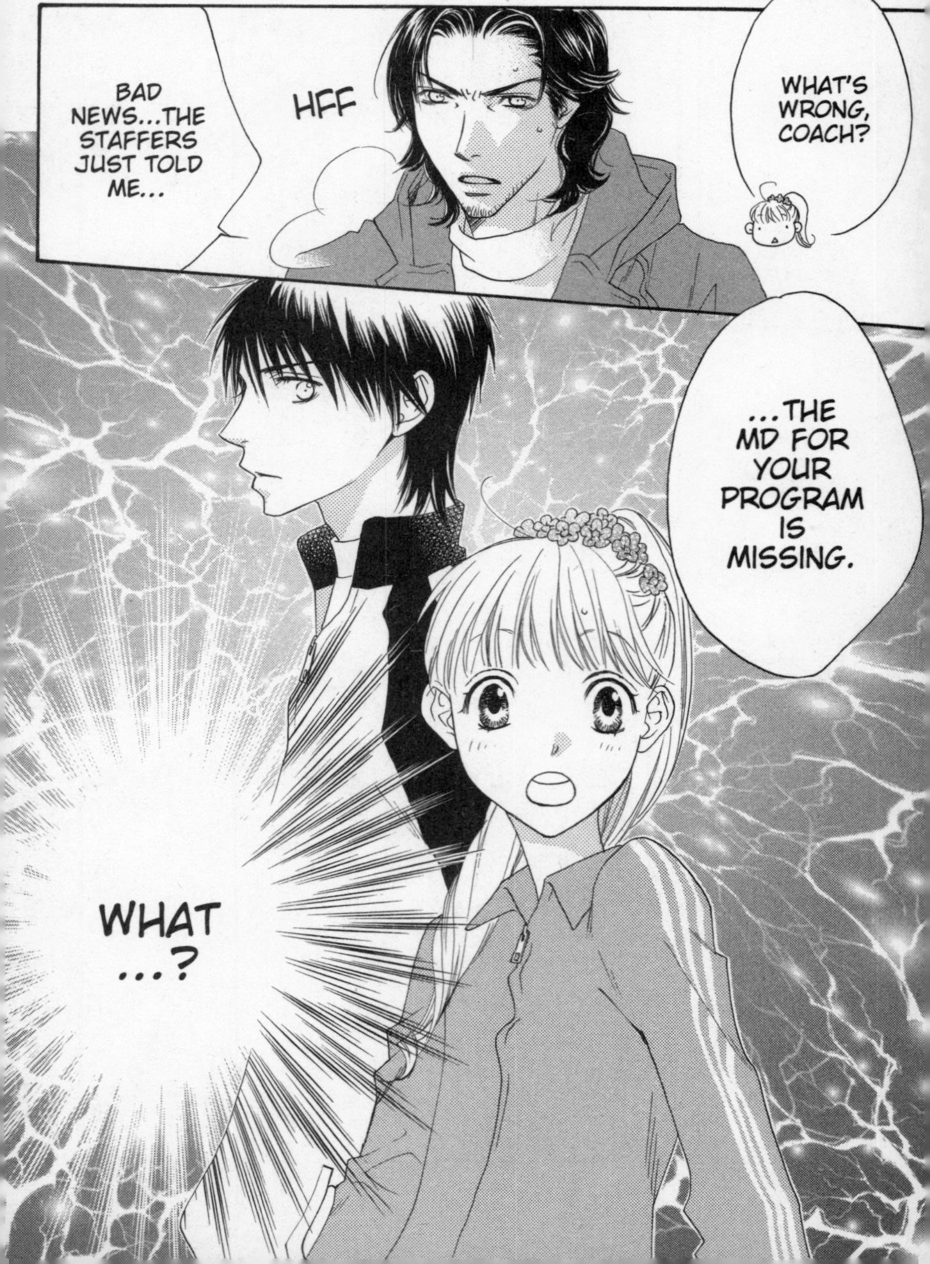
WHAT'S WRONG, COACH?
HFF
BAD NEWS...THE STAFFERS JUST TOLD ME...
...THE MD FOR YOUR PROGRAM IS MISSING.
WHAT ...?

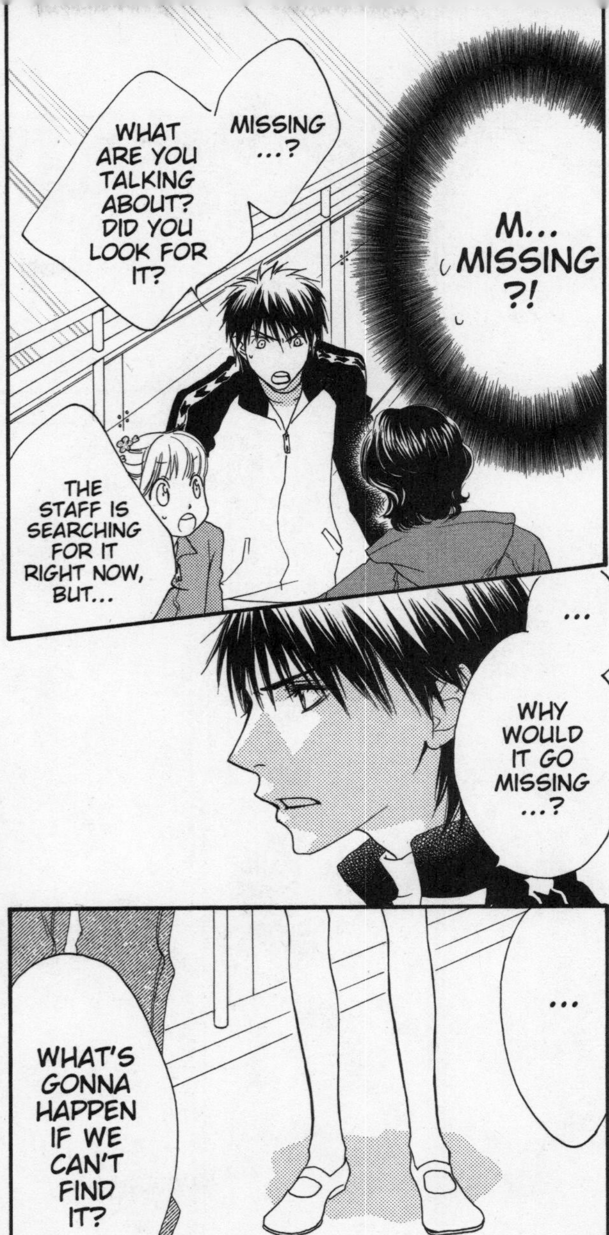
M... MISSING ?!
MISSING ...?
WHAT ARE YOU TALKING ABOUT? DID YOU LOOK FOR IT?
THE STAFF IS SEARCHING FOR IT RIGHT NOW, BUT...
...
WHY WOULD IT GO MISSING ...?
...
WHAT'S GONNA HAPPEN IF WE CAN'T FIND IT?

I FOUND AN INTERESTING MENU ITEM AT THE SKATING RINK STAND...

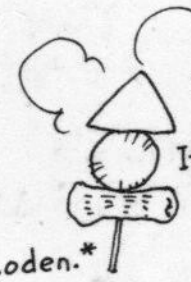
It's...
...oden.*

HOT COFFEE AND ODEN TASTE BETTER WHEN CONSUMED AT A COLD SKATING RINK.

*Oden is stewed vegetables and meat, often skewered.

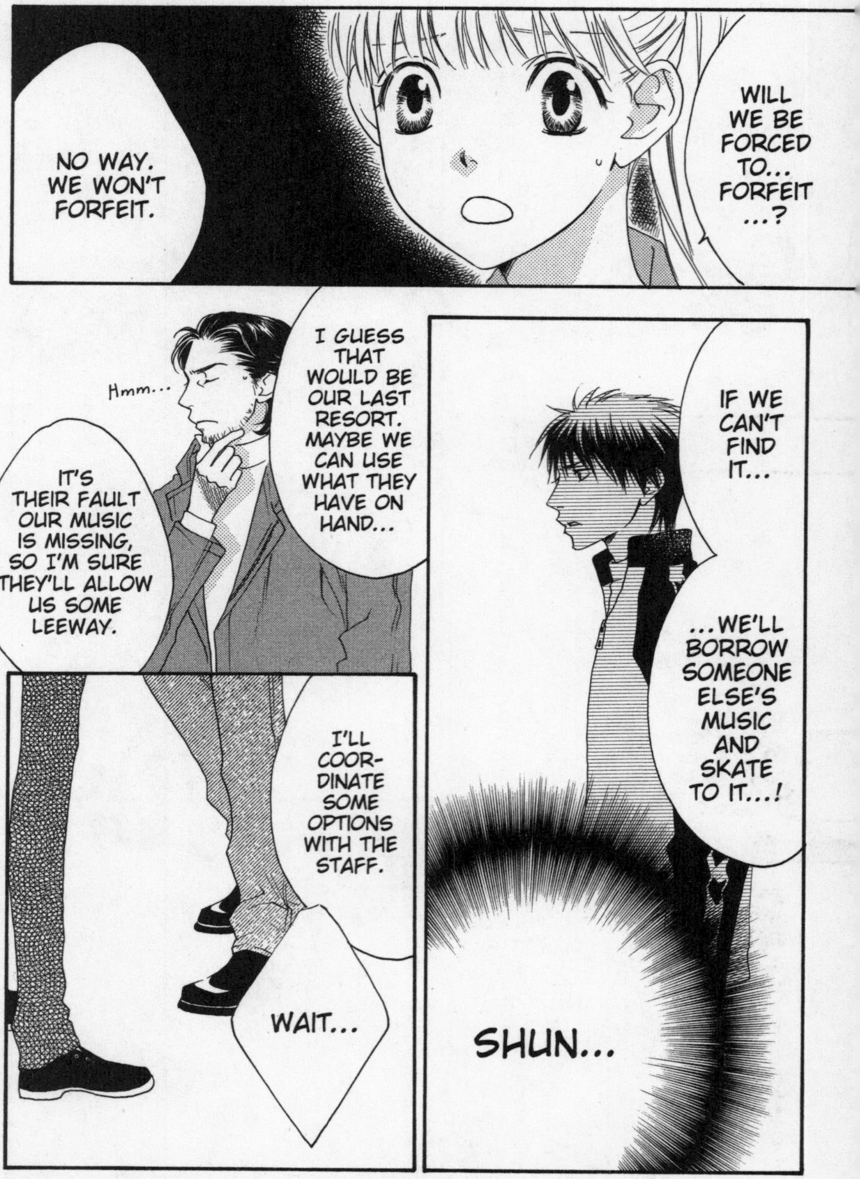
WILL WE BE FORCED TO... FORFEIT...?
NO WAY. WE WON'T FORFEIT.
IF WE CAN'T FIND IT...
...WE'LL BORROW SOMEONE ELSE'S MUSIC AND SKATE TO IT...!
SHUN...
I GUESS THAT WOULD BE OUR LAST RESORT. MAYBE WE CAN USE WHAT THEY HAVE ON HAND...
Hmm...
IT'S THEIR FAULT OUR MUSIC IS MISSING, SO I'M SURE THEY'LL ALLOW US SOME LEEWAY.
I'LL COOR-DINATE SOME OPTIONS WITH THE STAFF.
WAIT...

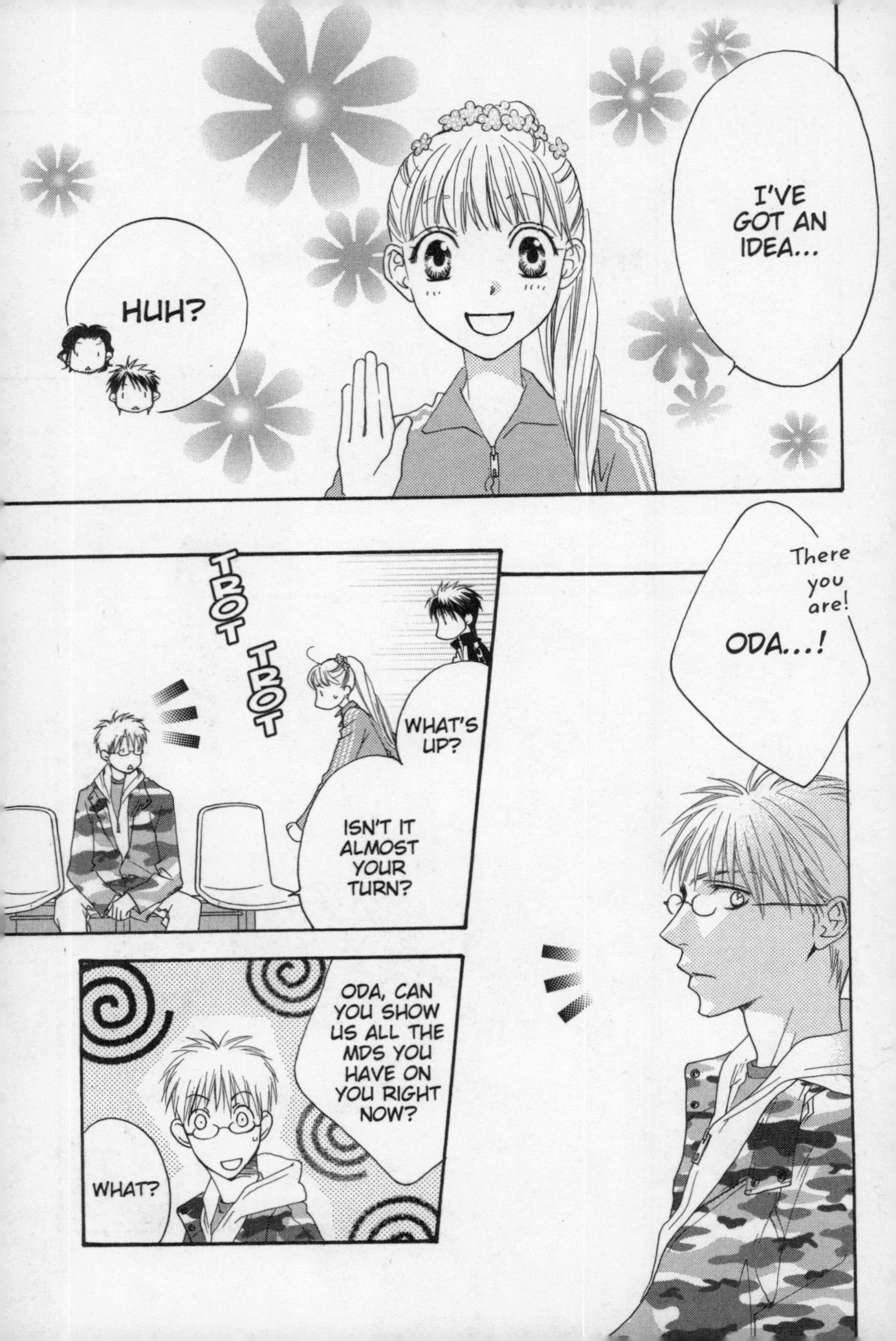
I'VE GOT AN IDEA...
HUH?
There you are!
ODA...!
TROT TROT
WHAT'S UP?
ISN'T IT ALMOST YOUR TURN?
ODA, CAN YOU SHOW US ALL THE MDS YOU HAVE ON YOU RIGHT NOW?
WHAT?

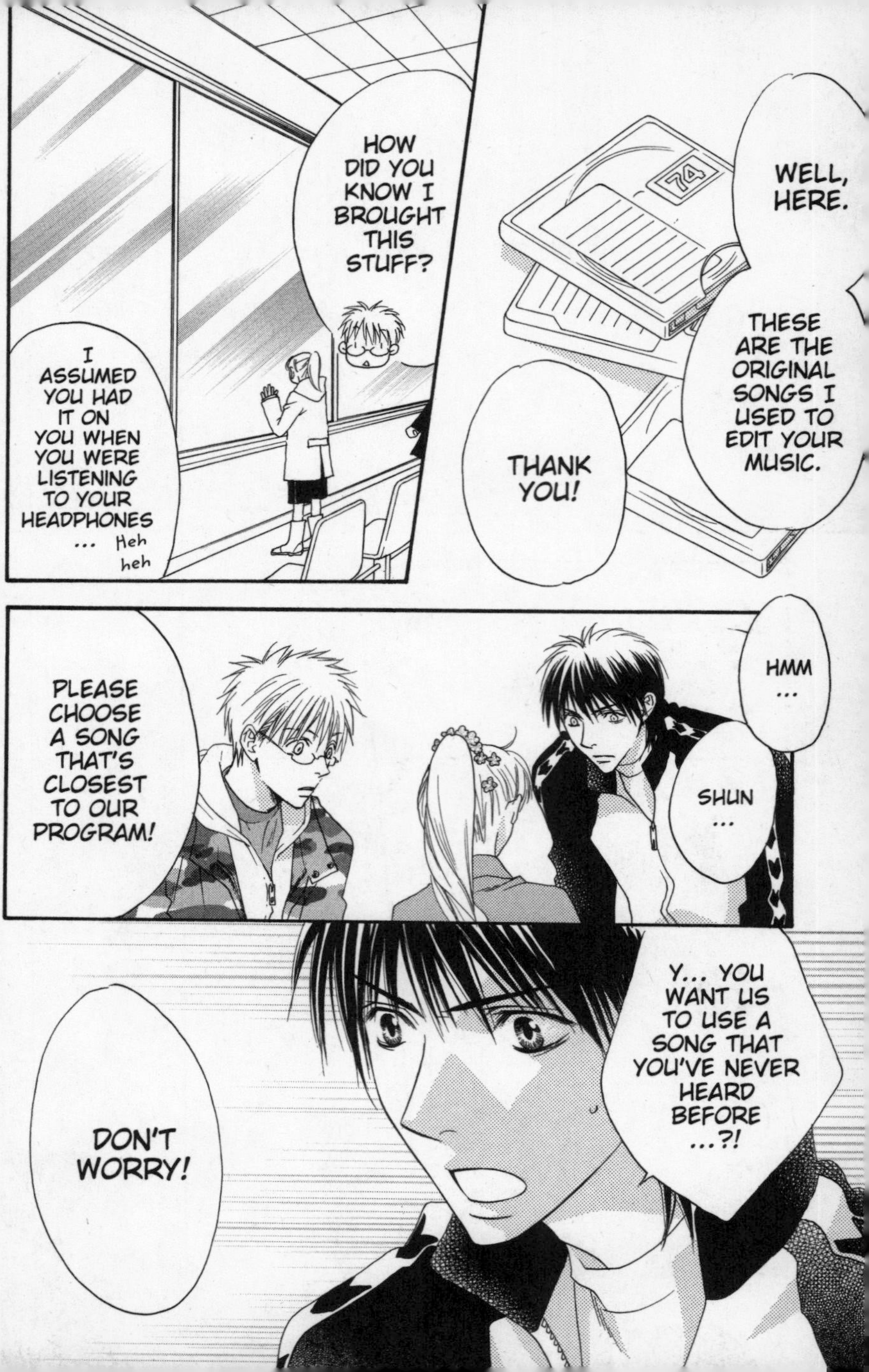
WELL, HERE.
THESE ARE THE ORIGINAL SONGS I USED TO EDIT YOUR MUSIC.
THANK YOU!
HOW DID YOU KNOW I BROUGHT THIS STUFF?
I ASSUMED YOU HAD IT ON YOU WHEN YOU WERE LISTENING TO YOUR HEADPHONES ...
Heh heh
HMM ...
SHUN ...
PLEASE CHOOSE A SONG THAT'S CLOSEST TO OUR PROGRAM!
Y... YOU WANT US TO USE A SONG THAT YOU'VE NEVER HEARD BEFORE ...?!
DON'T WORRY!

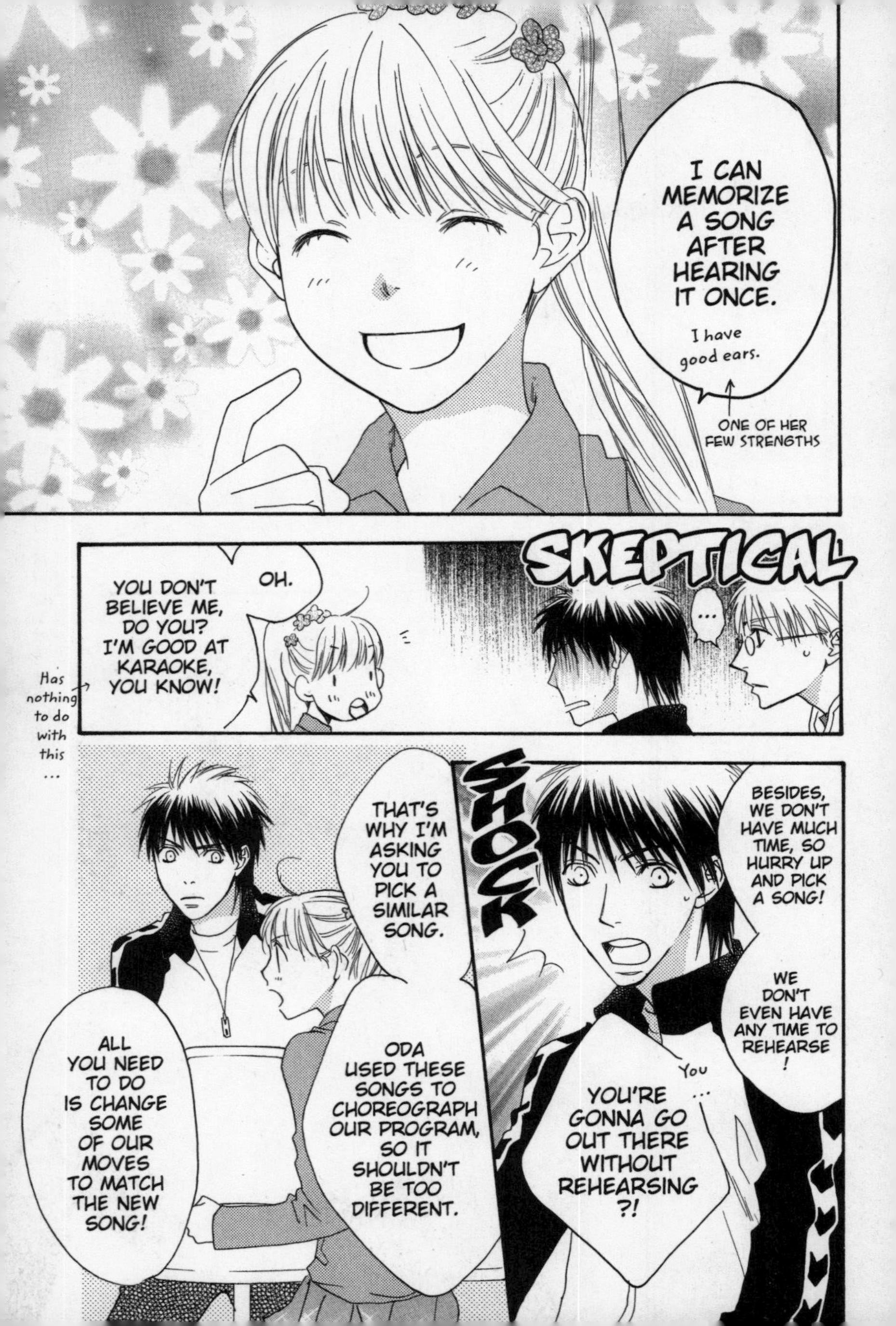
I CAN MEMORIZE A SONG AFTER HEARING IT ONCE.
I have good ears.
ONE OF HER FEW STRENGTHS
SKEPTICAL
...
OH.
YOU DON'T BELIEVE ME, DO YOU? I'M GOOD AT KARAOKE, YOU KNOW!
Has nothing to do with this ...
SHOCK
BESIDES, WE DON'T HAVE MUCH TIME, SO HURRY UP AND PICK A SONG!
WE DON'T EVEN HAVE ANY TIME TO REHEARSE!
You ...
YOU'RE GONNA GO OUT THERE WITHOUT REHEARSING?!
THAT'S WHY I'M ASKING YOU TO PICK A SIMILAR SONG.
ODA USED THESE SONGS TO CHOREOGRAPH OUR PROGRAM, SO IT SHOULDN'T BE TOO DIFFERENT.
ALL YOU NEED TO DO IS CHANGE SOME OF OUR MOVES TO MATCH THE NEW SONG!

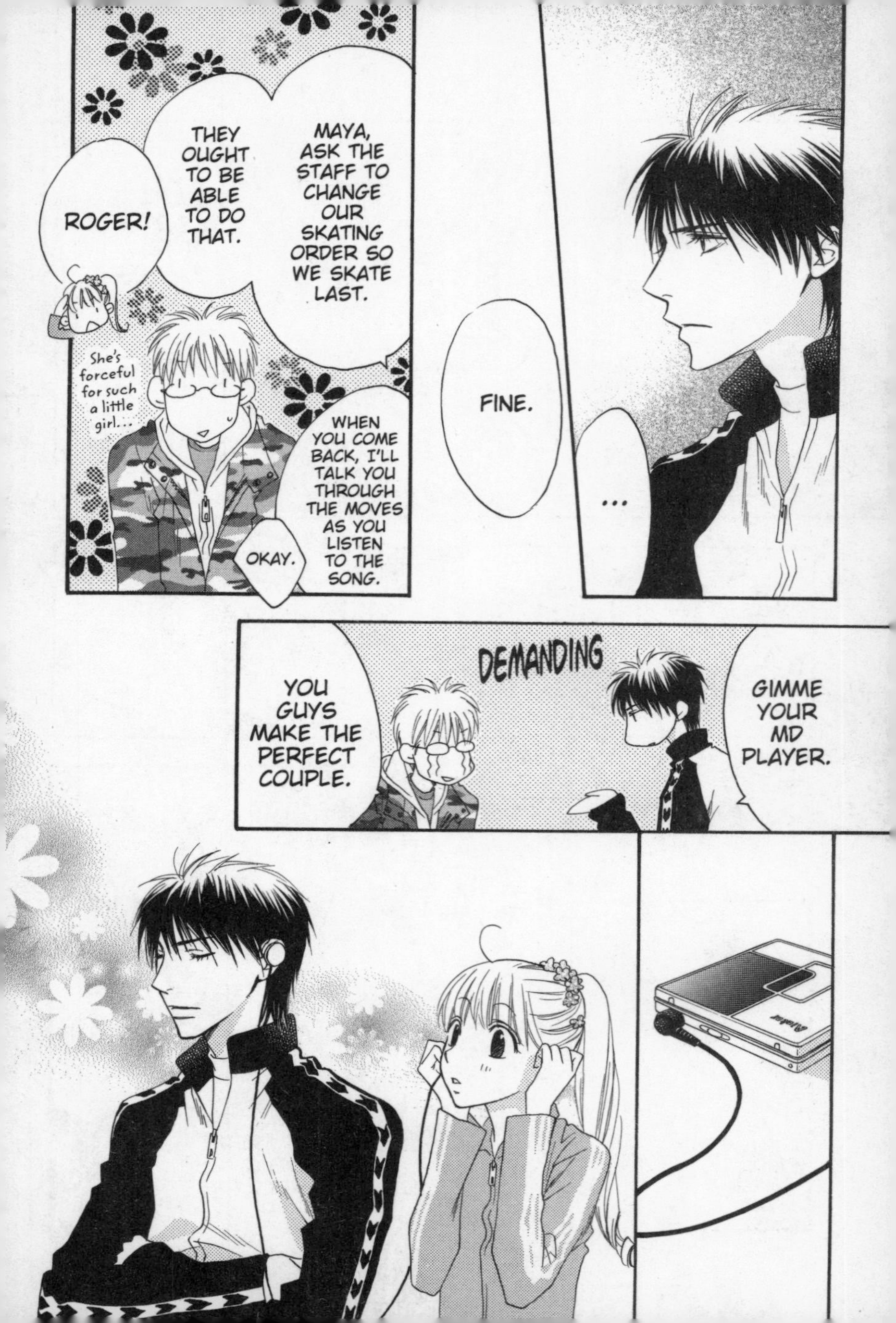
...
FINE.
MAYA, ASK THE STAFF TO CHANGE OUR SKATING ORDER SO WE SKATE LAST.
THEY OUGHT TO BE ABLE TO DO THAT.
ROGER!
She's forceful for such a little girl...
WHEN YOU COME BACK, I'LL TALK YOU THROUGH THE MOVES AS YOU LISTEN TO THE SONG.
OKAY.
GIMME YOUR MD PLAYER.
DEMANDING
YOU GUYS MAKE THE PERFECT COUPLE.

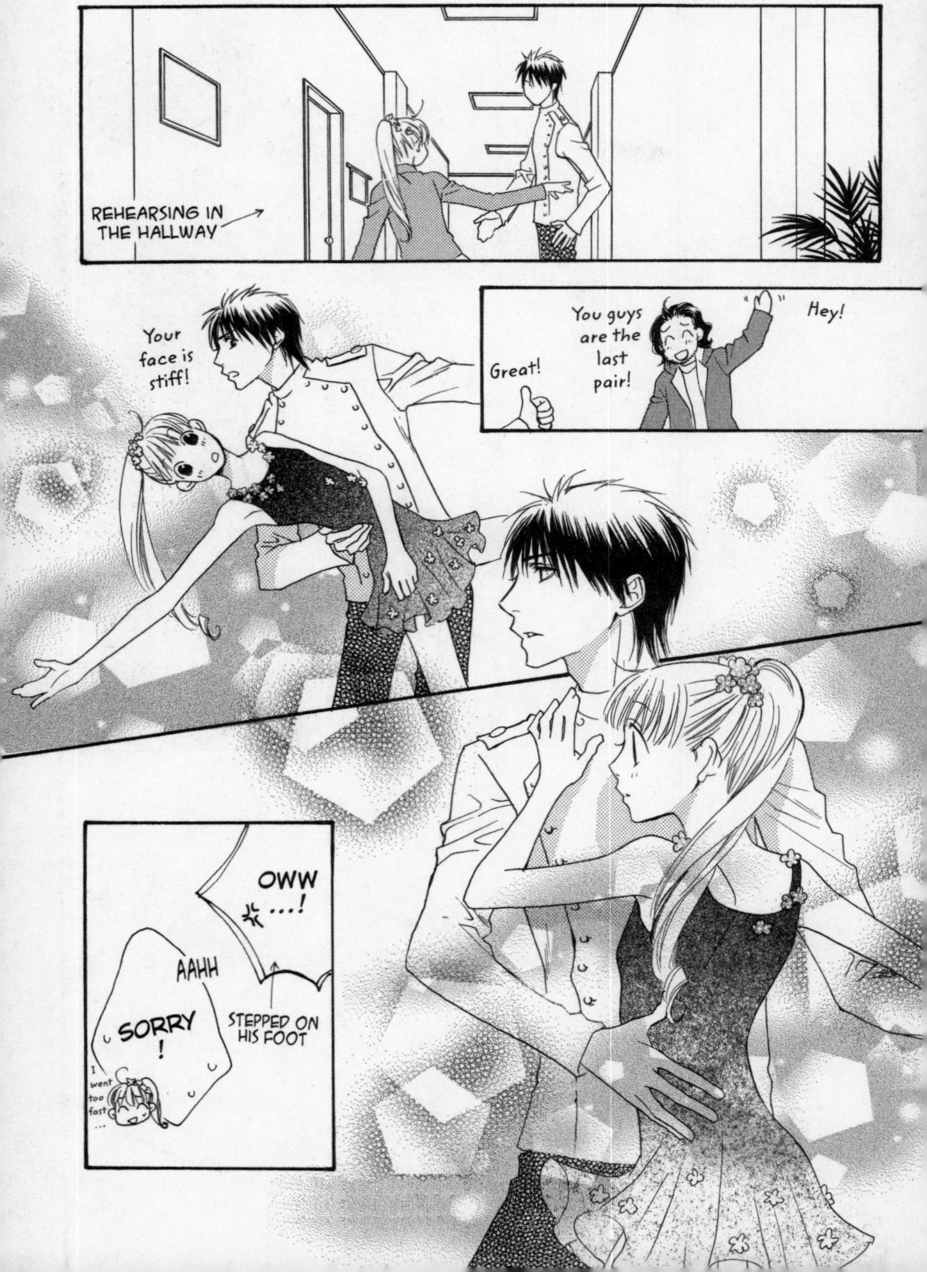
REHEARSING IN THE HALLWAY
Hey!
You guys are the last pair!
Great!
Your face is stiff!
OWW ...!
STEPPED ON HIS FOOT
AAHH
SORRY !
I went too fast ...

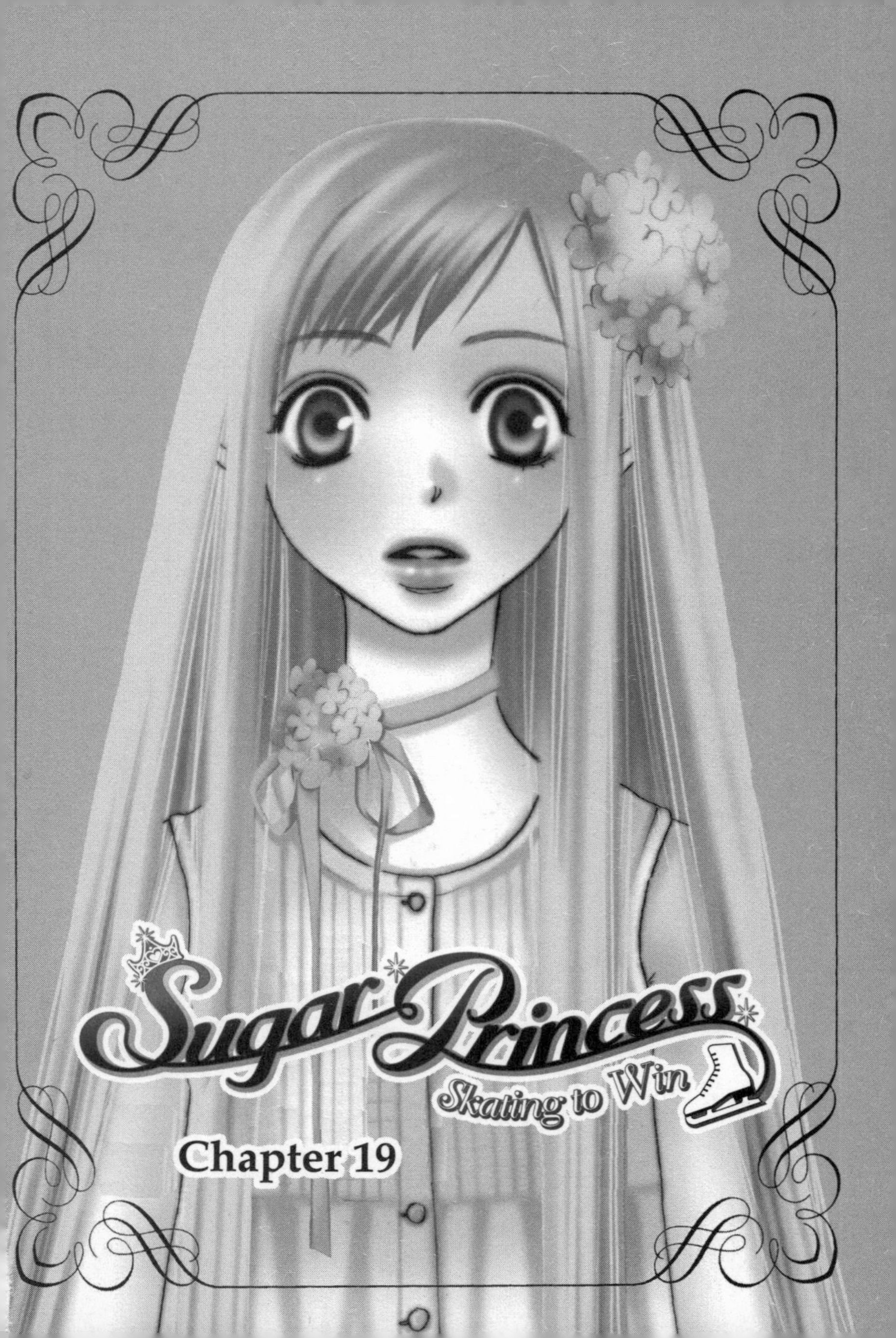
Sugar Princess
Skating to Win
Chapter 19

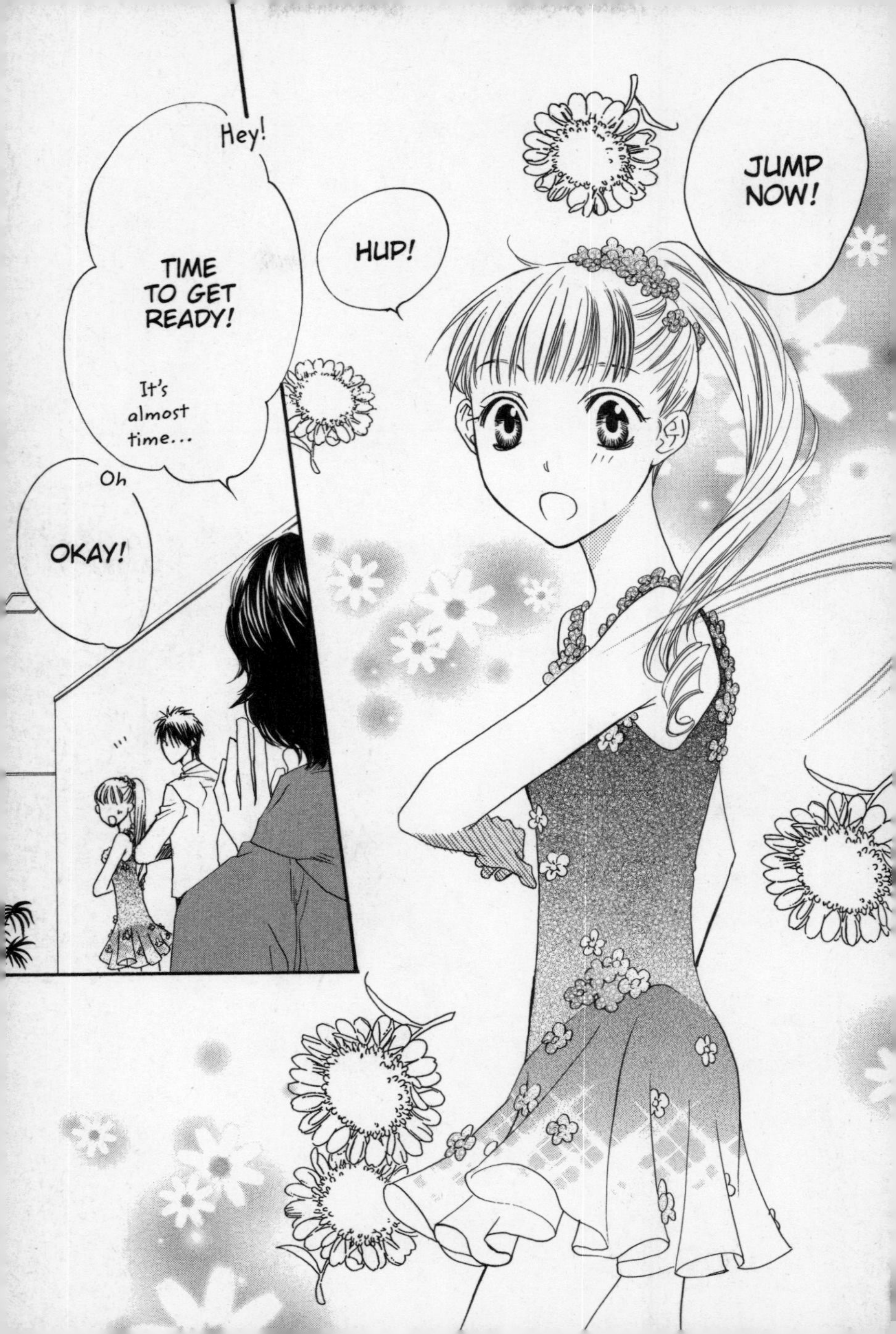
JUMP NOW!
HUP!
Hey! TIME TO GET READY! It's almost time...
Oh OKAY!

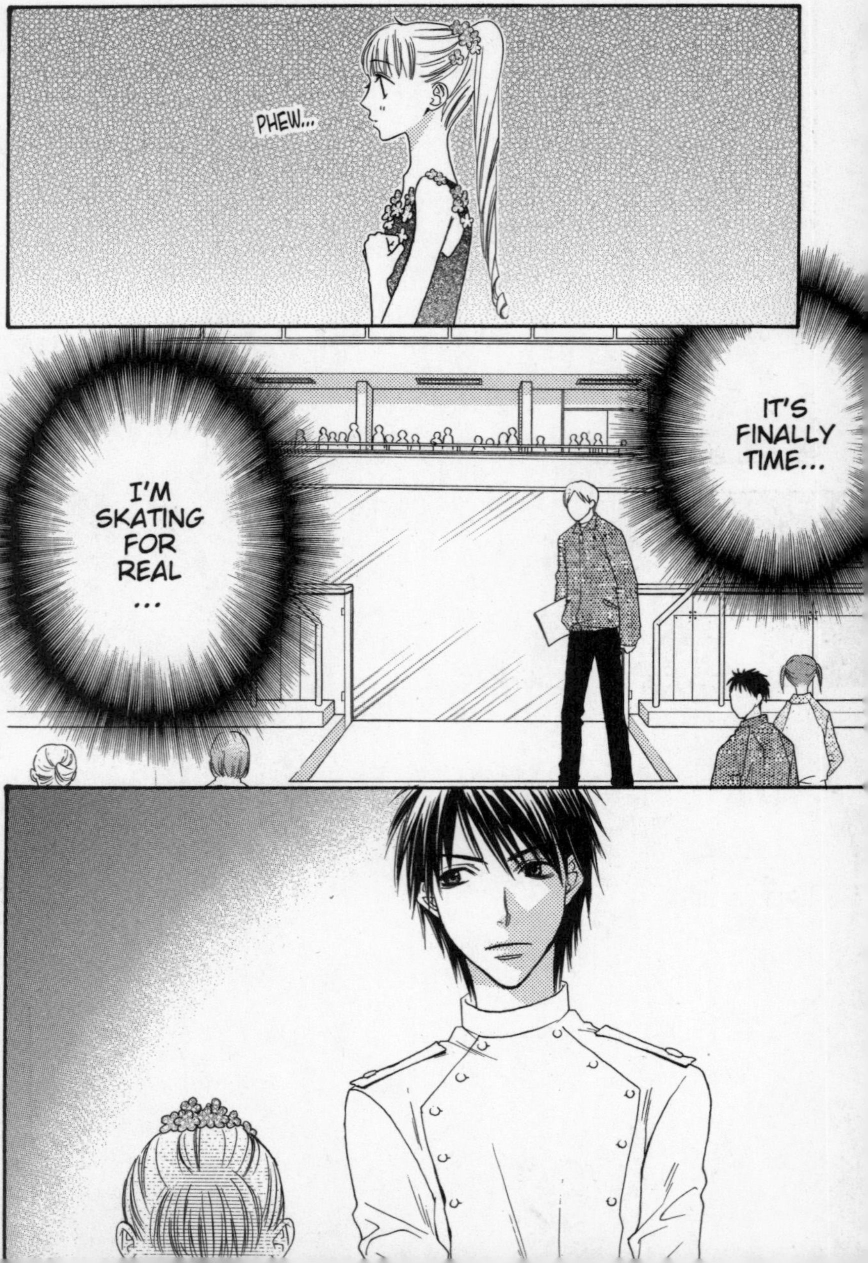
PHEW...
IT'S FINALLY TIME...
I'M SKATING FOR REAL ...

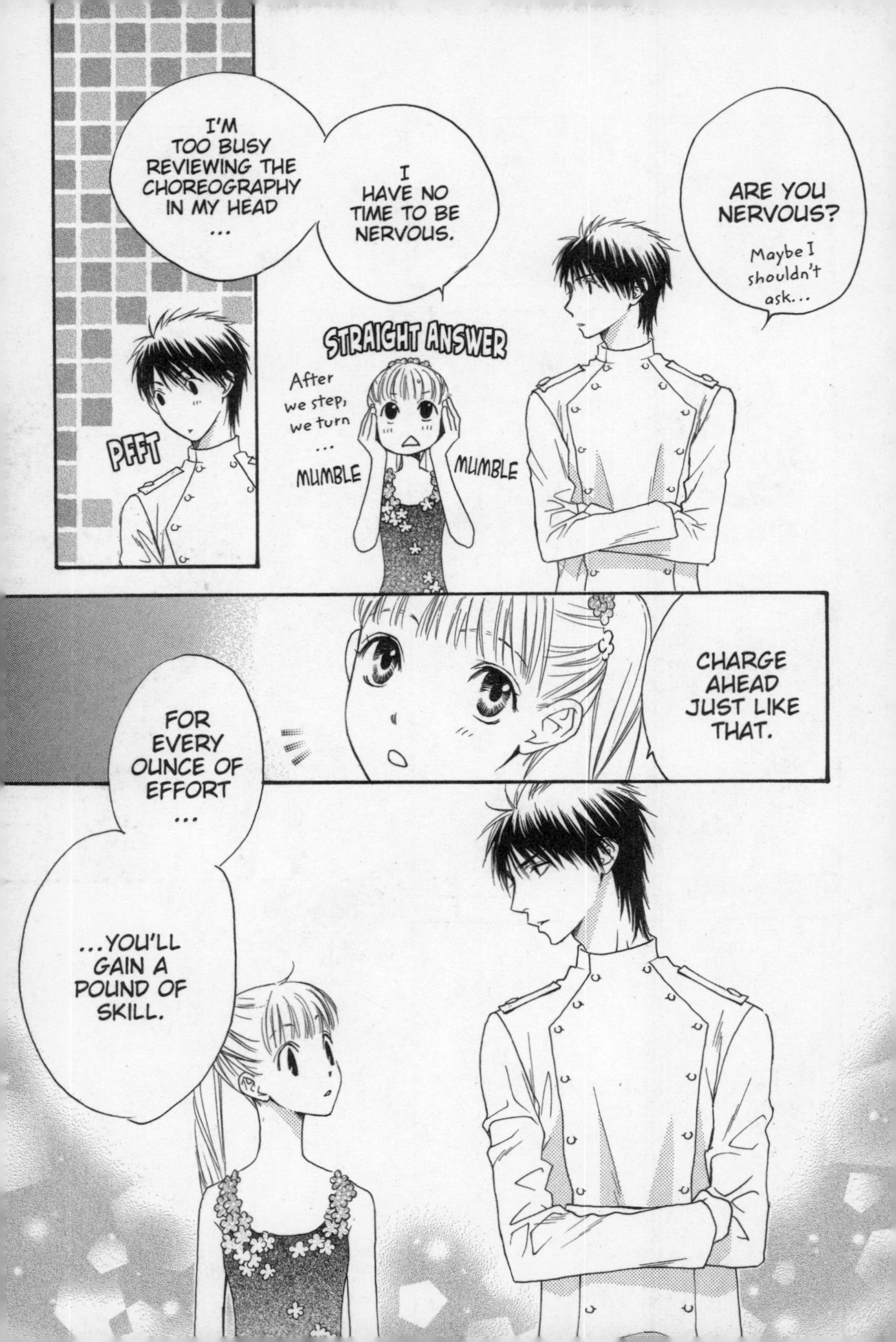
ARE YOU NERVOUS?
Maybe I shouldn't ask...
I HAVE NO TIME TO BE NERVOUS.
I'M TOO BUSY REVIEWING THE CHOREOGRAPHY IN MY HEAD ...
STRAIGHT ANSWER
After we step, we turn ...
MUMBLE
MUMBLE
PFFT
CHARGE AHEAD JUST LIKE THAT.
FOR EVERY OUNCE OF EFFORT ...
...YOU'LL GAIN A POUND OF SKILL.

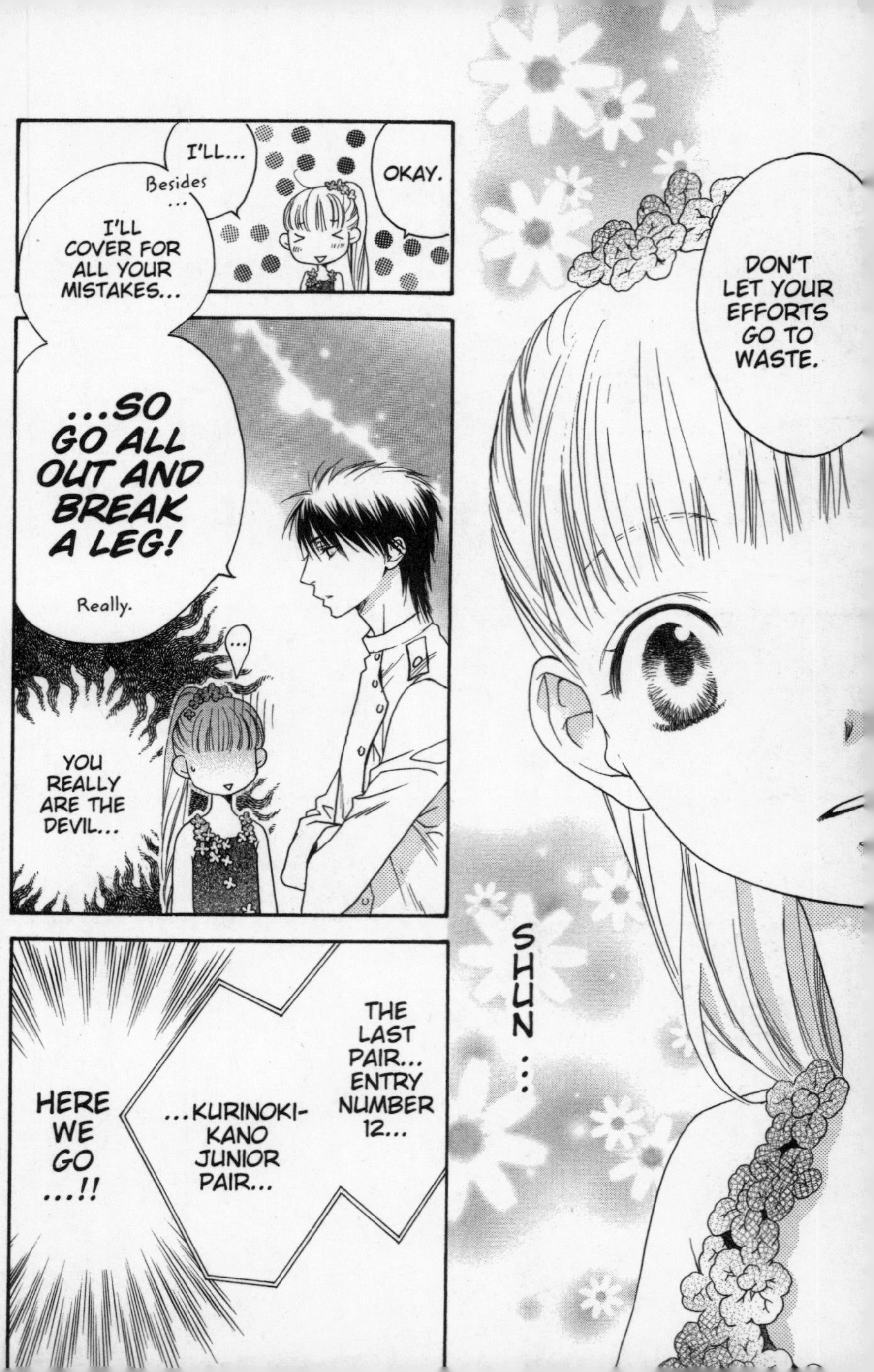
DON'T LET YOUR EFFORTS GO TO WASTE.
SHUN...
OKAY.
I'LL...
Besides...
I'LL COVER FOR ALL YOUR MISTAKES...
...SO GO ALL OUT AND BREAK A LEG!
Really.
...
YOU REALLY ARE THE DEVIL...
THE LAST PAIR... ENTRY NUMBER 12...
...KURINOKI-KANO JUNIOR PAIR...
HERE WE GO ...!!

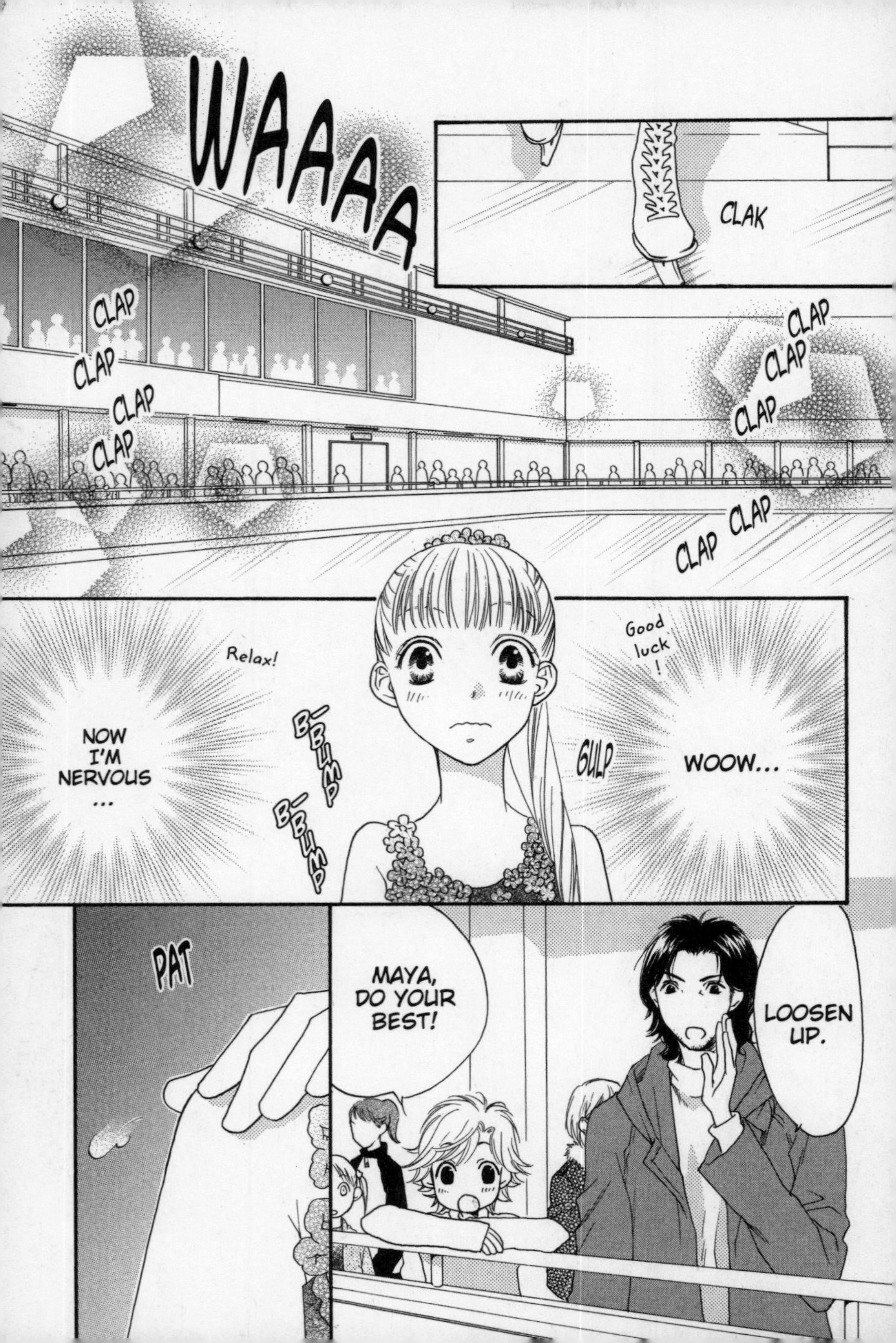
WAAAA
CLAK
CLAP CLAP CLAP
CLAP CLAP
CLAP CLAP
CLAP CLAP
Good luck!
WOOW...
GULP
B-BUMP B-BUMP
Relax!
NOW I'M NERVOUS...
LOOSEN UP.
MAYA, DO YOUR BEST!
PAT

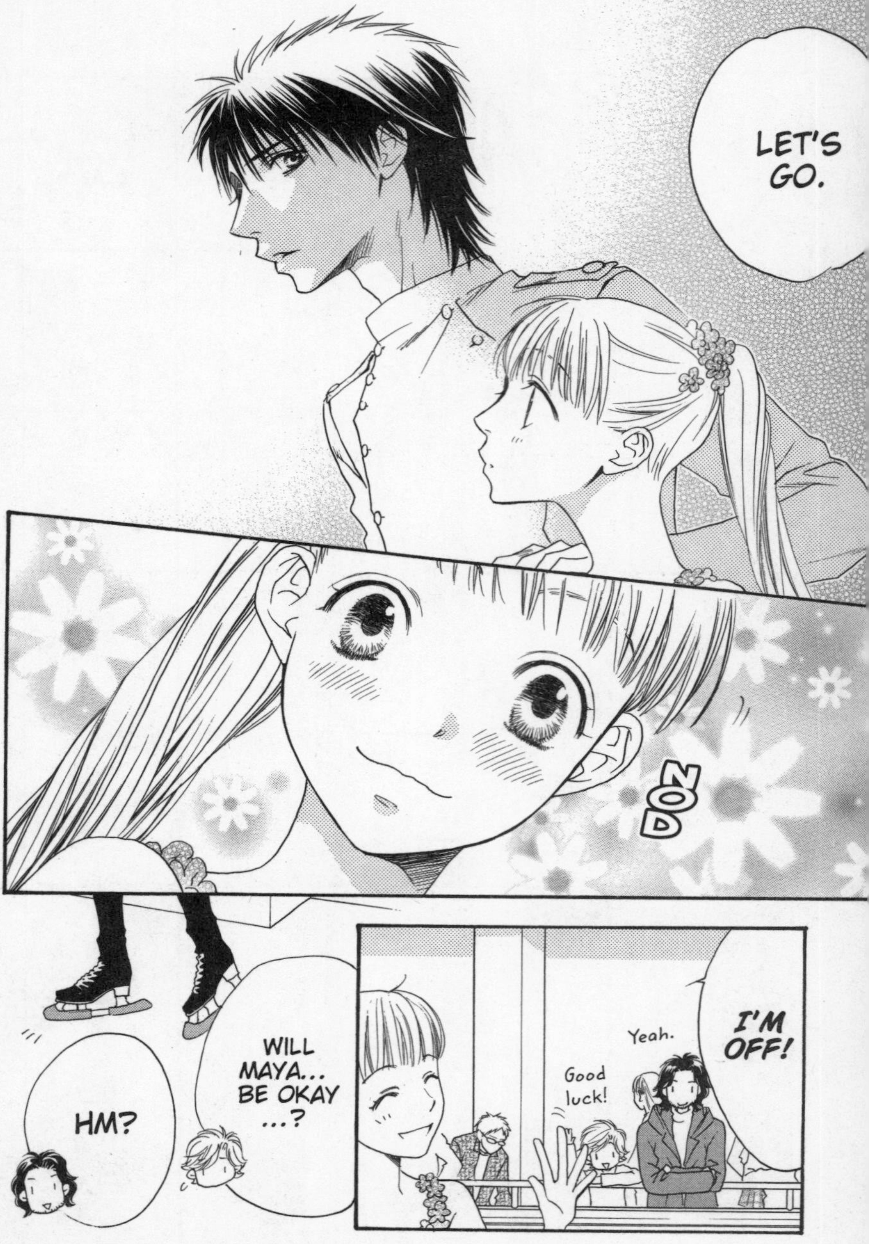
LET'S GO.
NOD
I'M OFF!
Yeah.
Good luck!
WILL MAYA... BE OKAY ...?
HM?

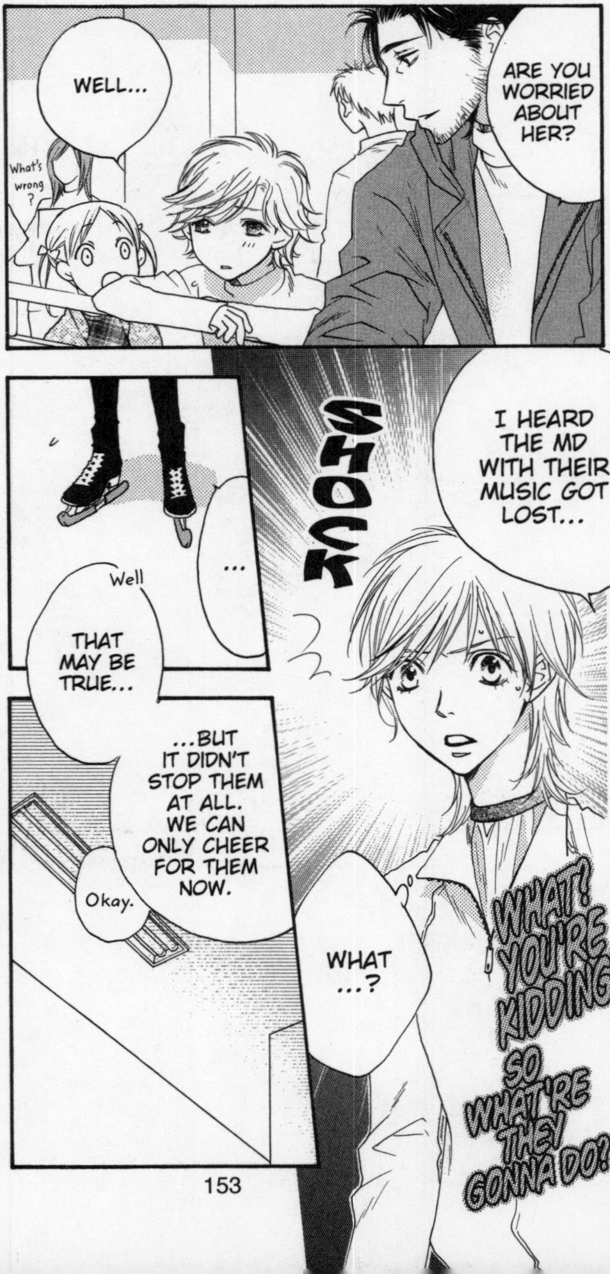
ARE YOU WORRIED ABOUT HER?
WELL...
What's wrong?
I HEARD THE MD WITH THEIR MUSIC GOT LOST...
SHOCK
WHAT ...?
WHAT! YOU'RE KIDDING!
SO WHAT'RE THEY GONNA DO?
...
Well
THAT MAY BE TRUE...
...BUT IT DIDN'T STOP THEM AT ALL. WE CAN ONLY CHEER FOR THEM NOW.
Okay.

I DON'T KNOW WHAT YOU CALL IT...

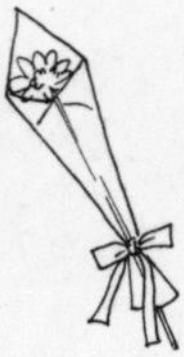

THOSE FLOWERS THAT PEOPLE GIVE THE SKATERS AFTER THEIR PERFORMANCE...

IS THERE A SPECIAL NAME FOR IT?

THROWN FLOWERS?

GIFT FLOWERS?

I WONDER IF THERE'S A SPECIFIC NAME ATTACHED TO IT IN THE FIRST PLACE... ?

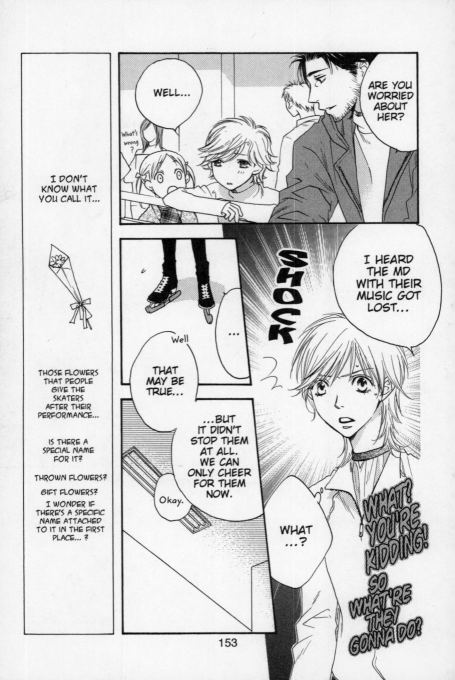

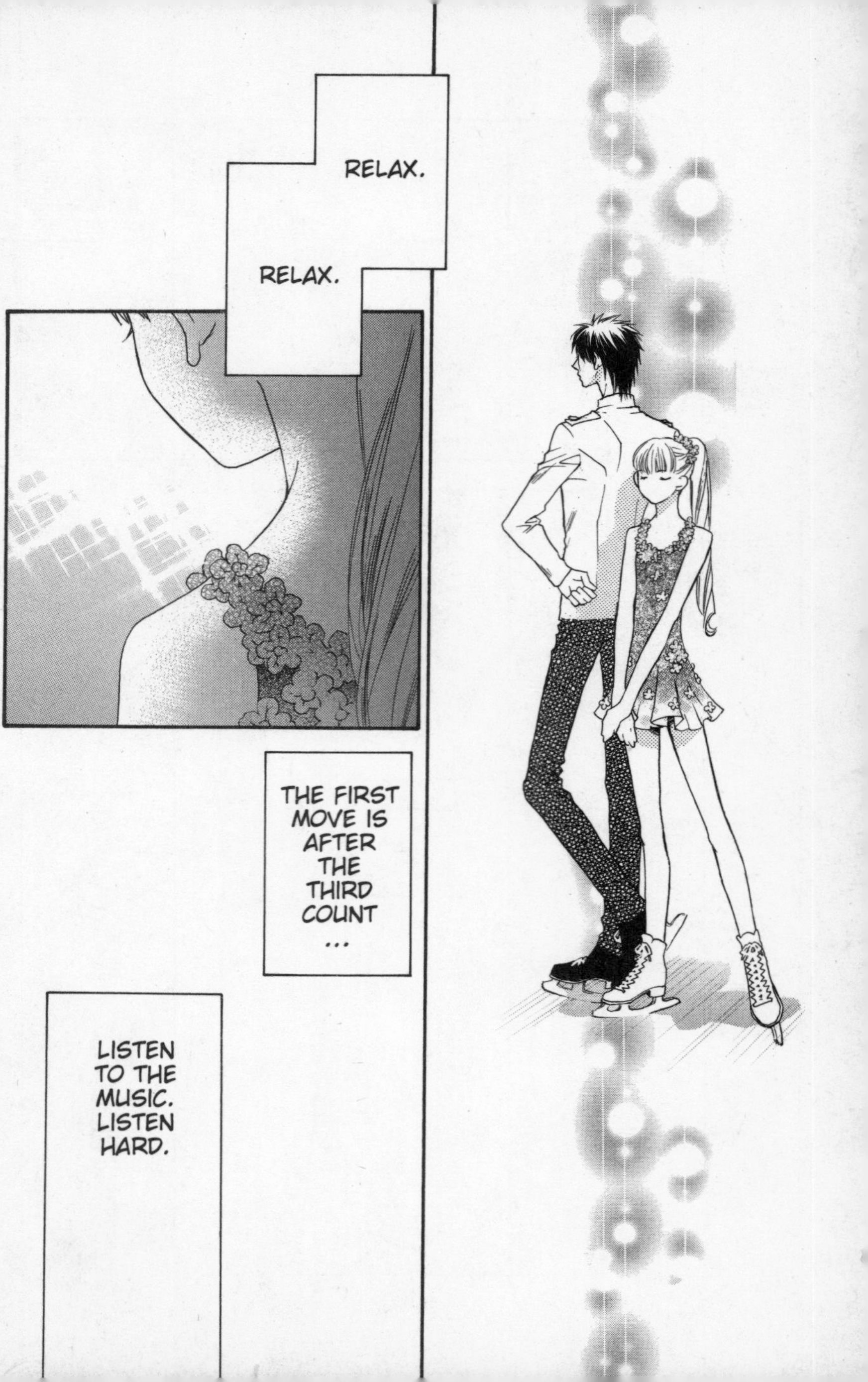
RELAX.
RELAX.
THE FIRST MOVE IS AFTER THE THIRD COUNT ...
LISTEN TO THE MUSIC. LISTEN HARD.

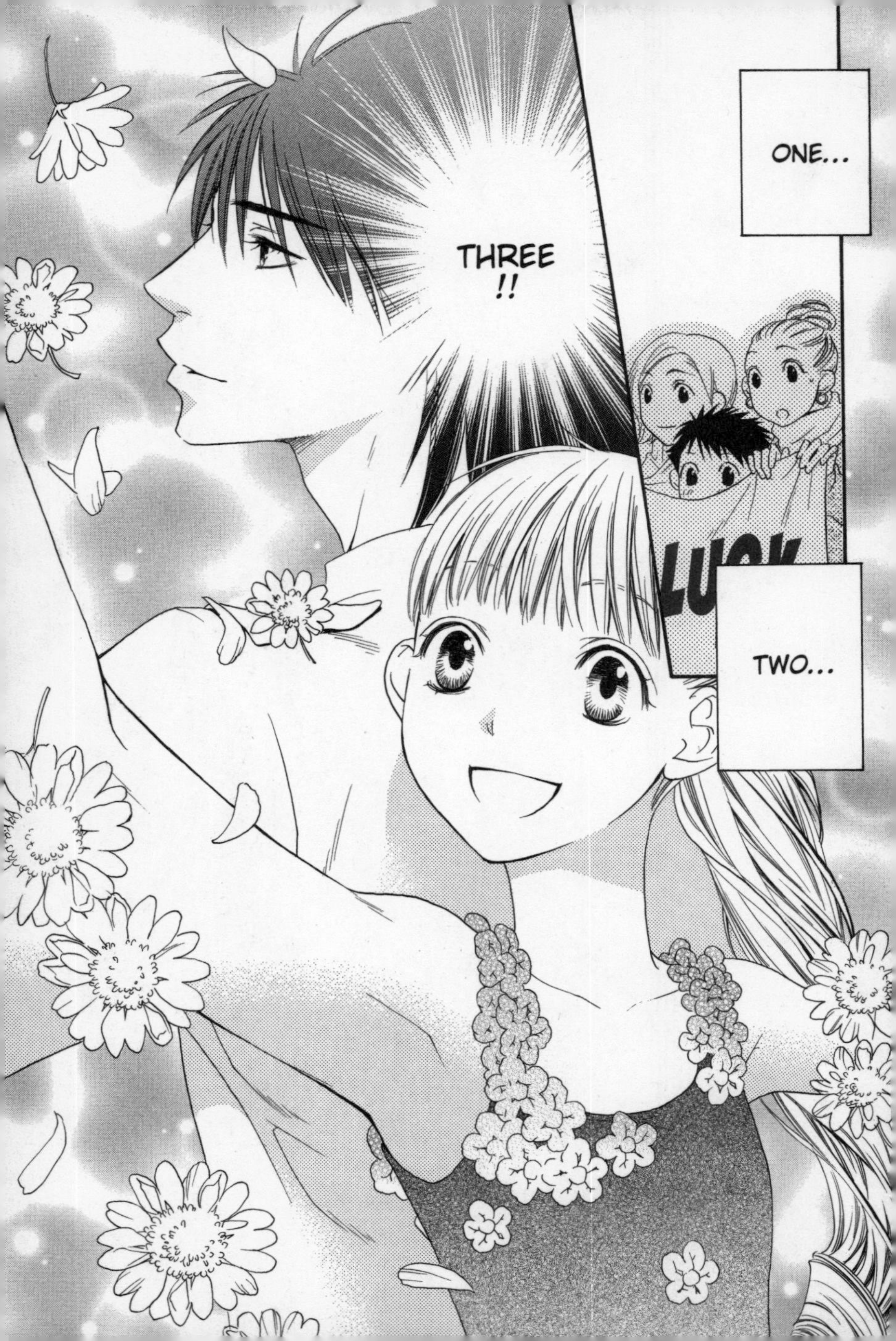
ONE...
LUCK
TWO...
THREE !!

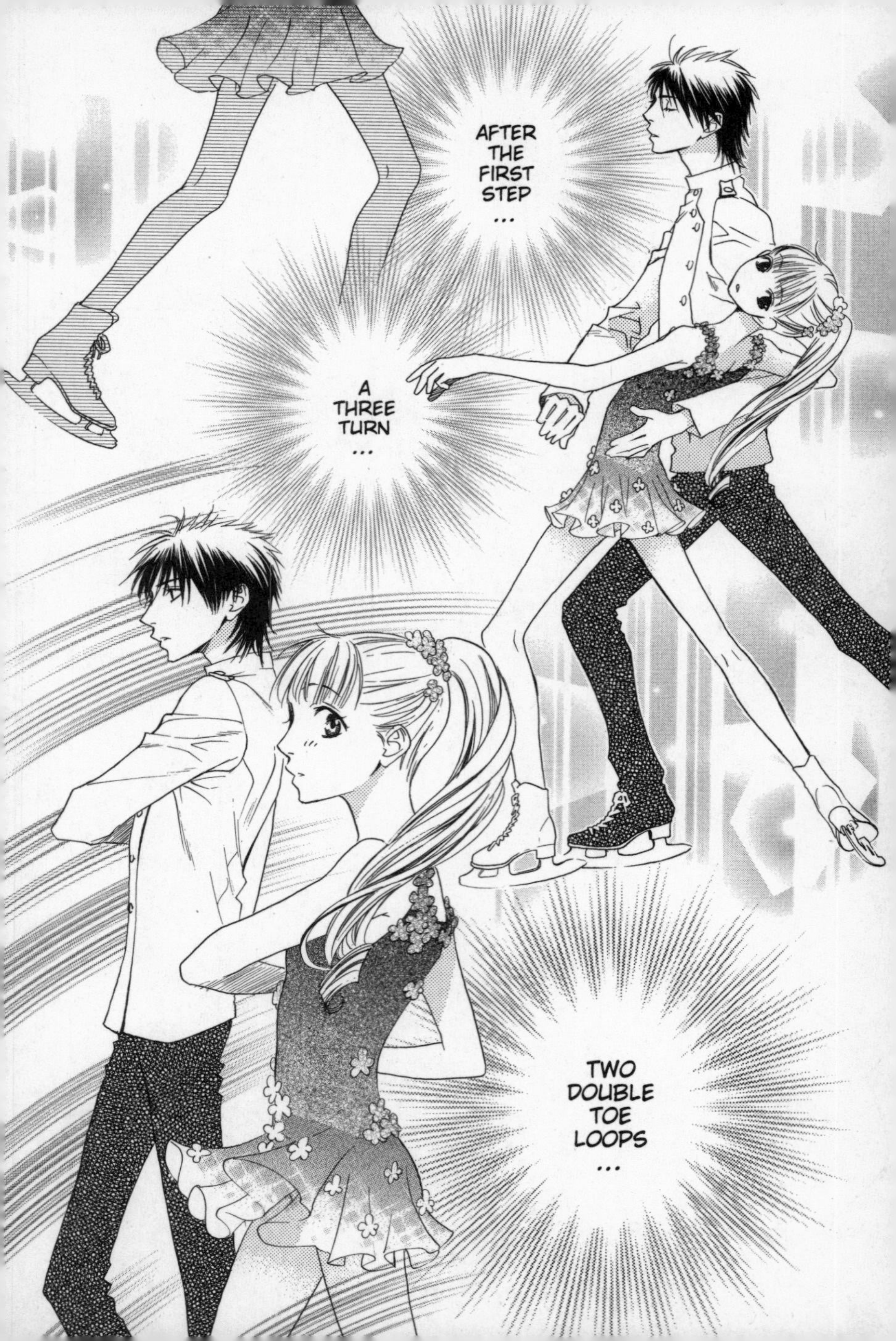
AFTER THE FIRST STEP ...
A THREE TURN ...
TWO DOUBLE TOE LOOPS ...

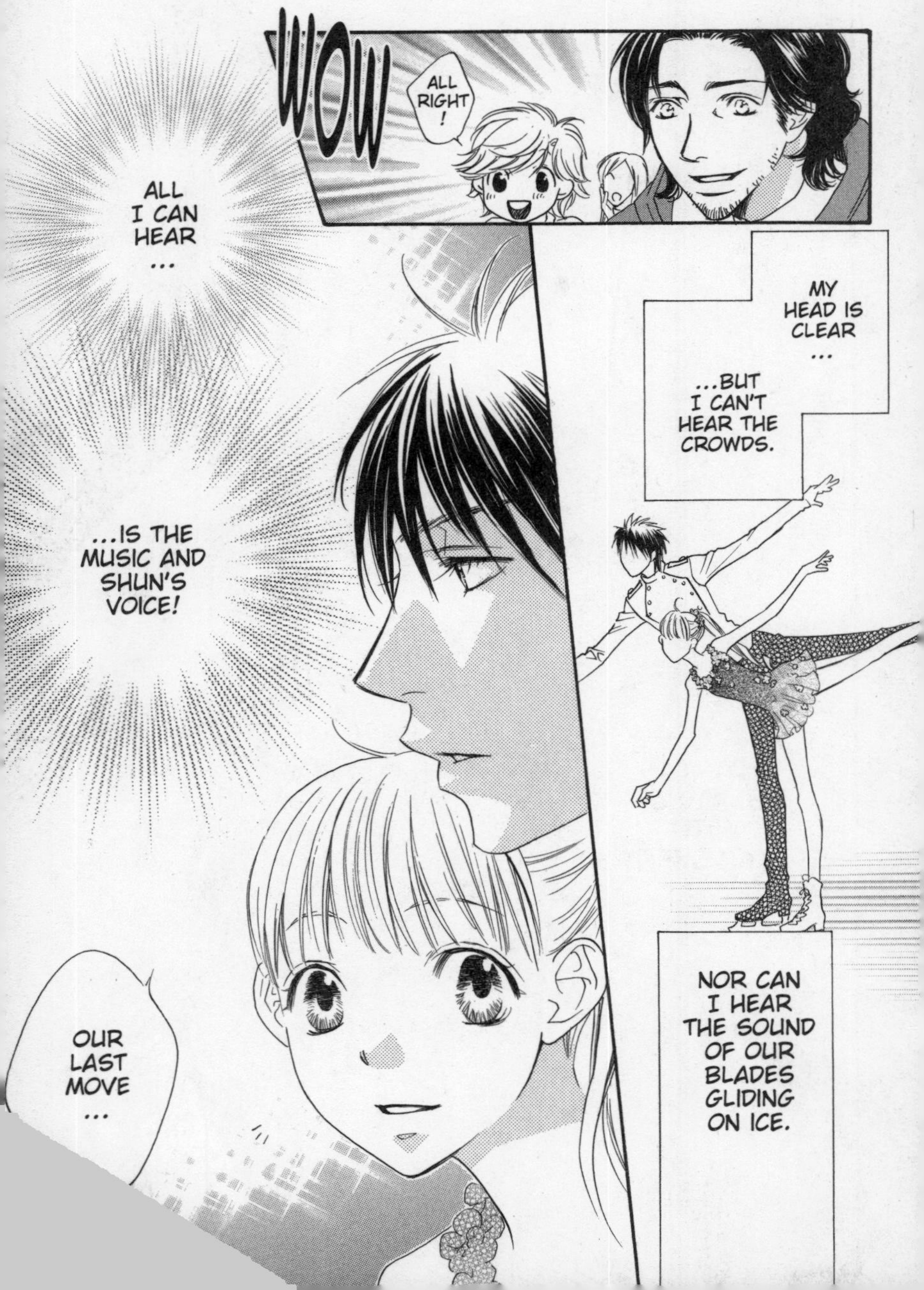
WOW
ALL RIGHT!
MY HEAD IS CLEAR...
...BUT I CAN'T HEAR THE CROWDS.
NOR CAN I HEAR THE SOUND OF OUR BLADES GLIDING ON ICE.
ALL I CAN HEAR...
...IS THE MUSIC AND SHUN'S VOICE!
OUR LAST MOVE...

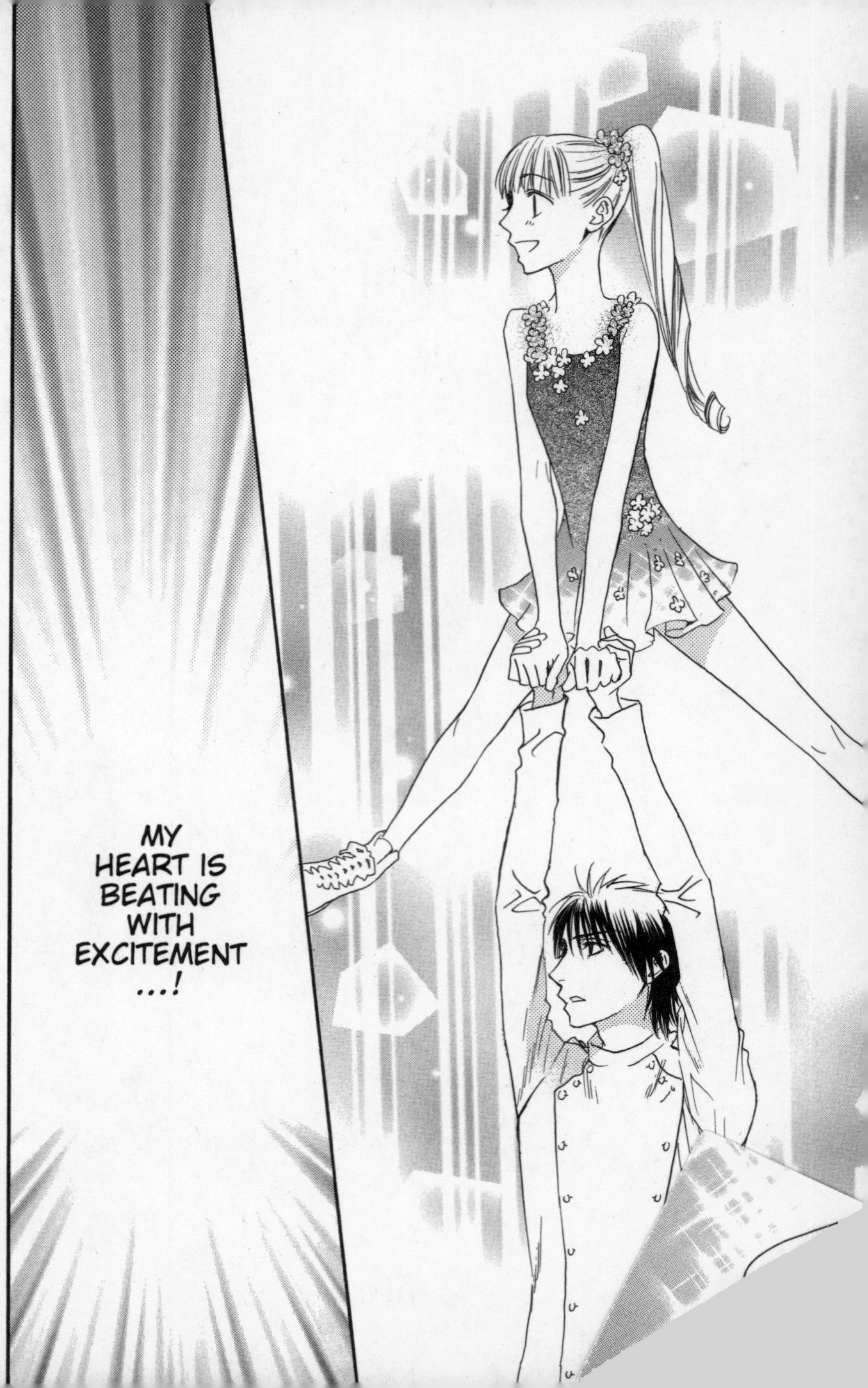
MY HEART IS BEATING WITH EXCITEMENT ...!

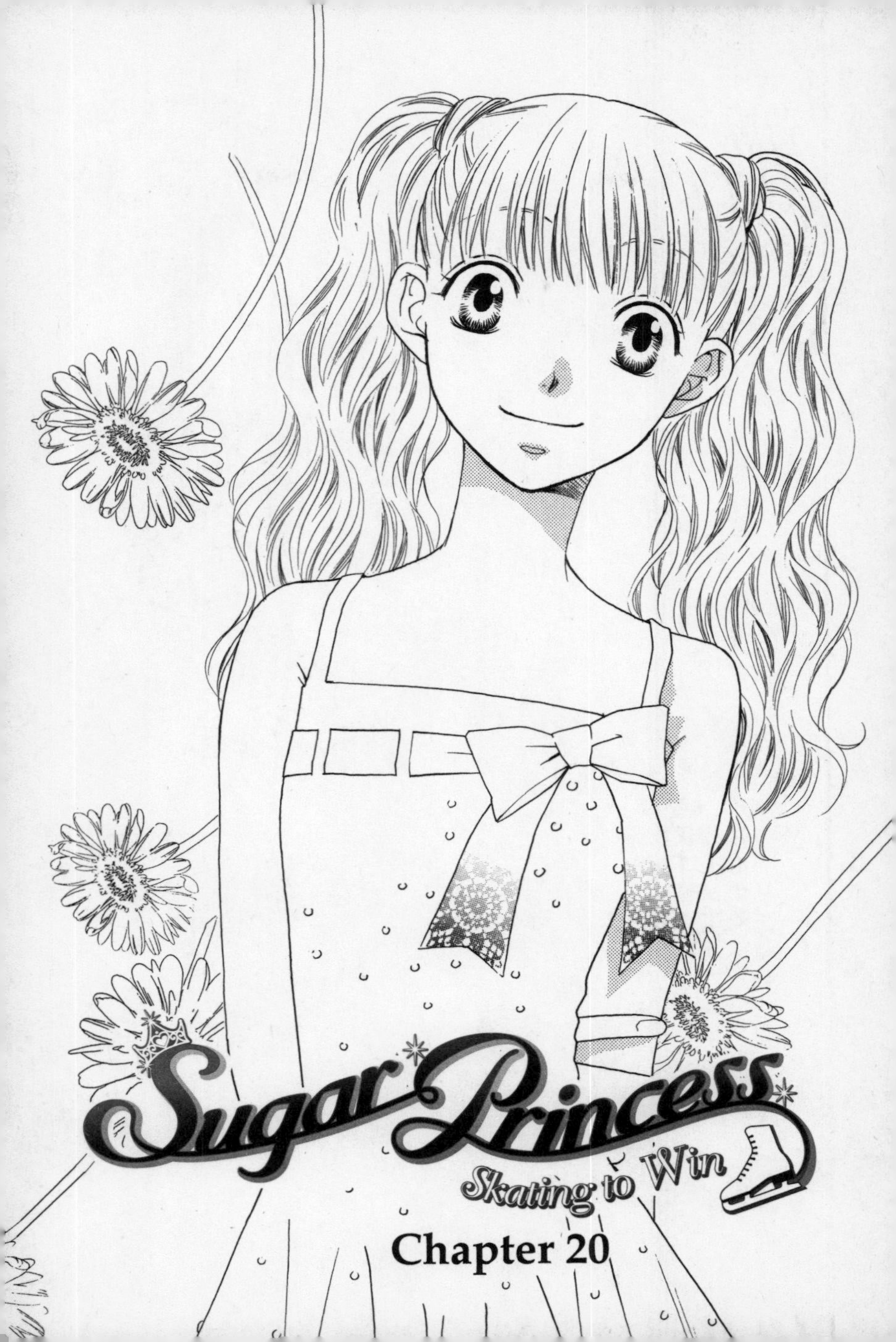
Sugar Princess
Skating to Win
Chapter 20

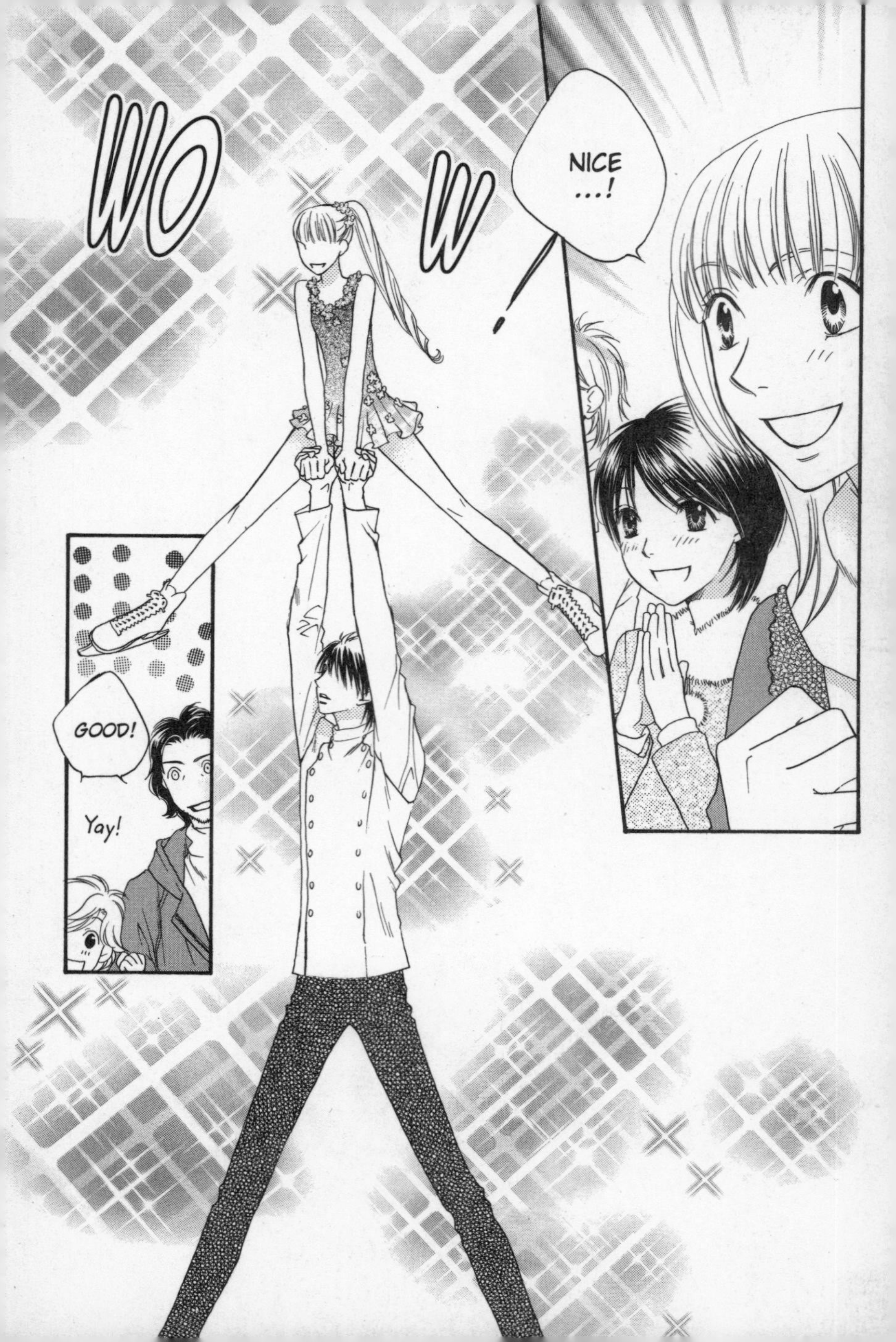
NICE ...!
WOW
GOOD!
Yay!

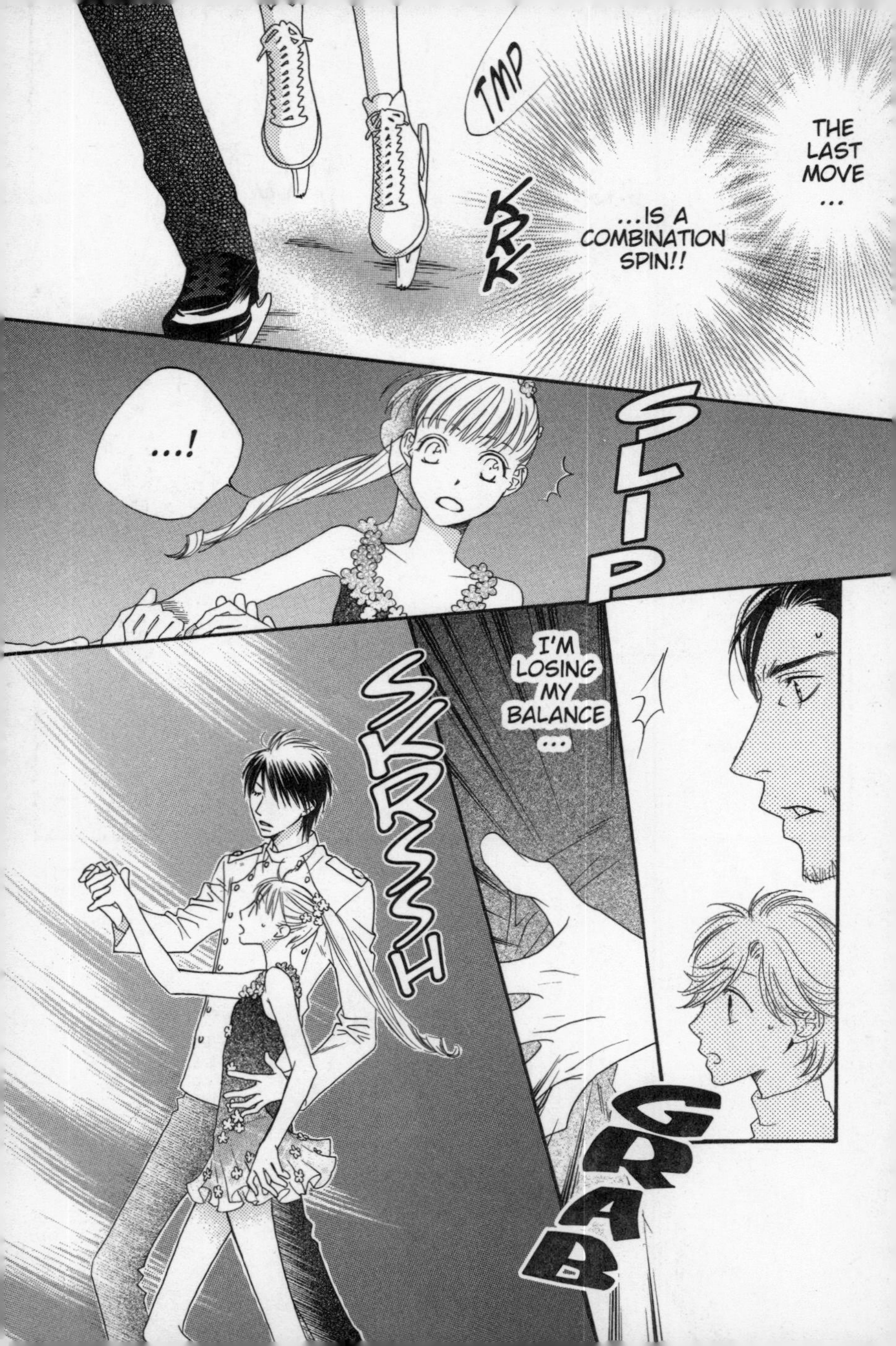
THE LAST MOVE ...
TMP
KRK
...IS A COMBINATION SPIN!!
SLIP
...!
GRAB
I'M LOSING MY BALANCE ...
SKRSSH

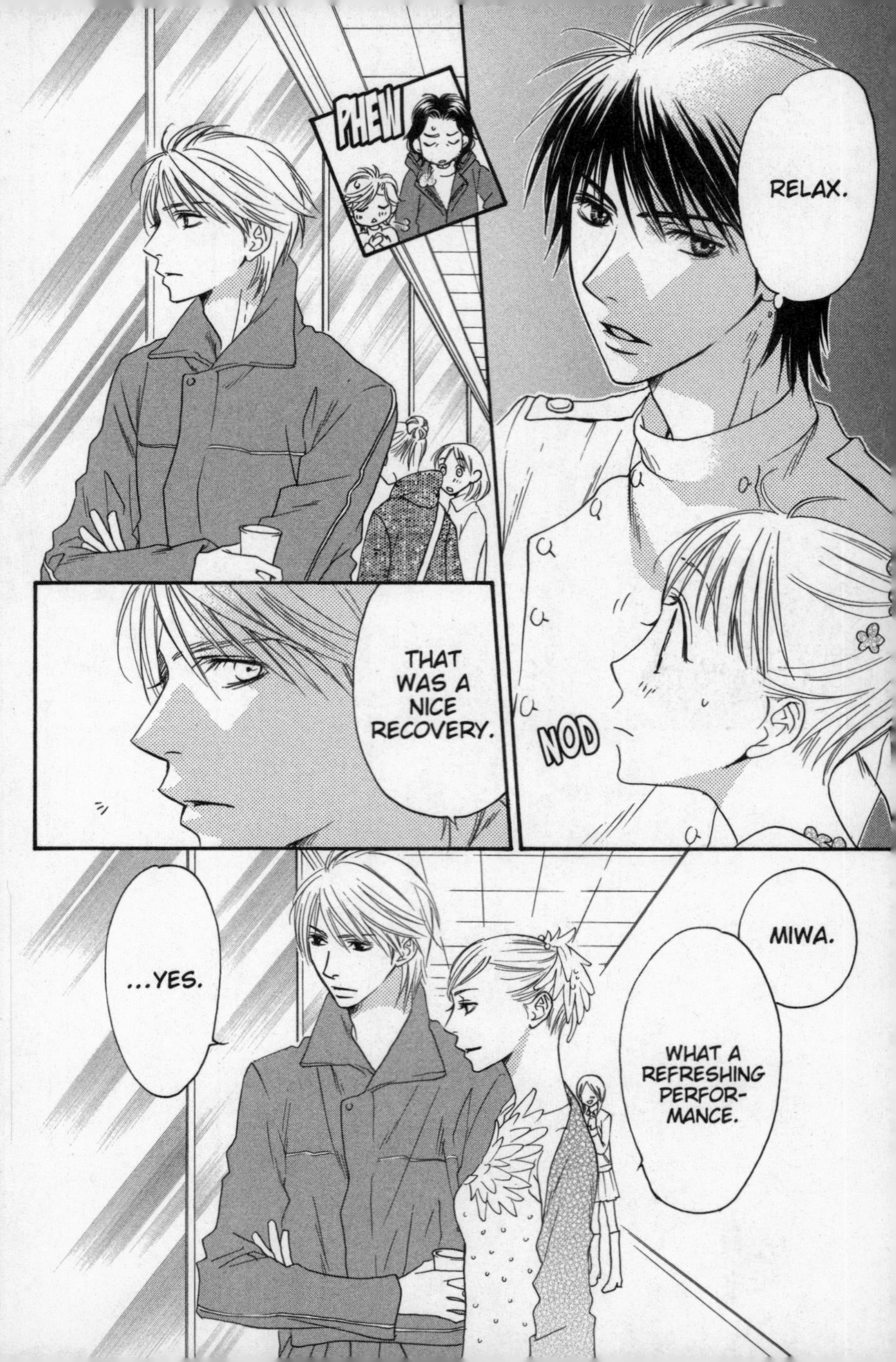
RELAX.
NOD
PHEW
THAT WAS A NICE RECOVERY.
MIWA.
WHAT A REFRESHING PERFOR-MANCE.
...YES.

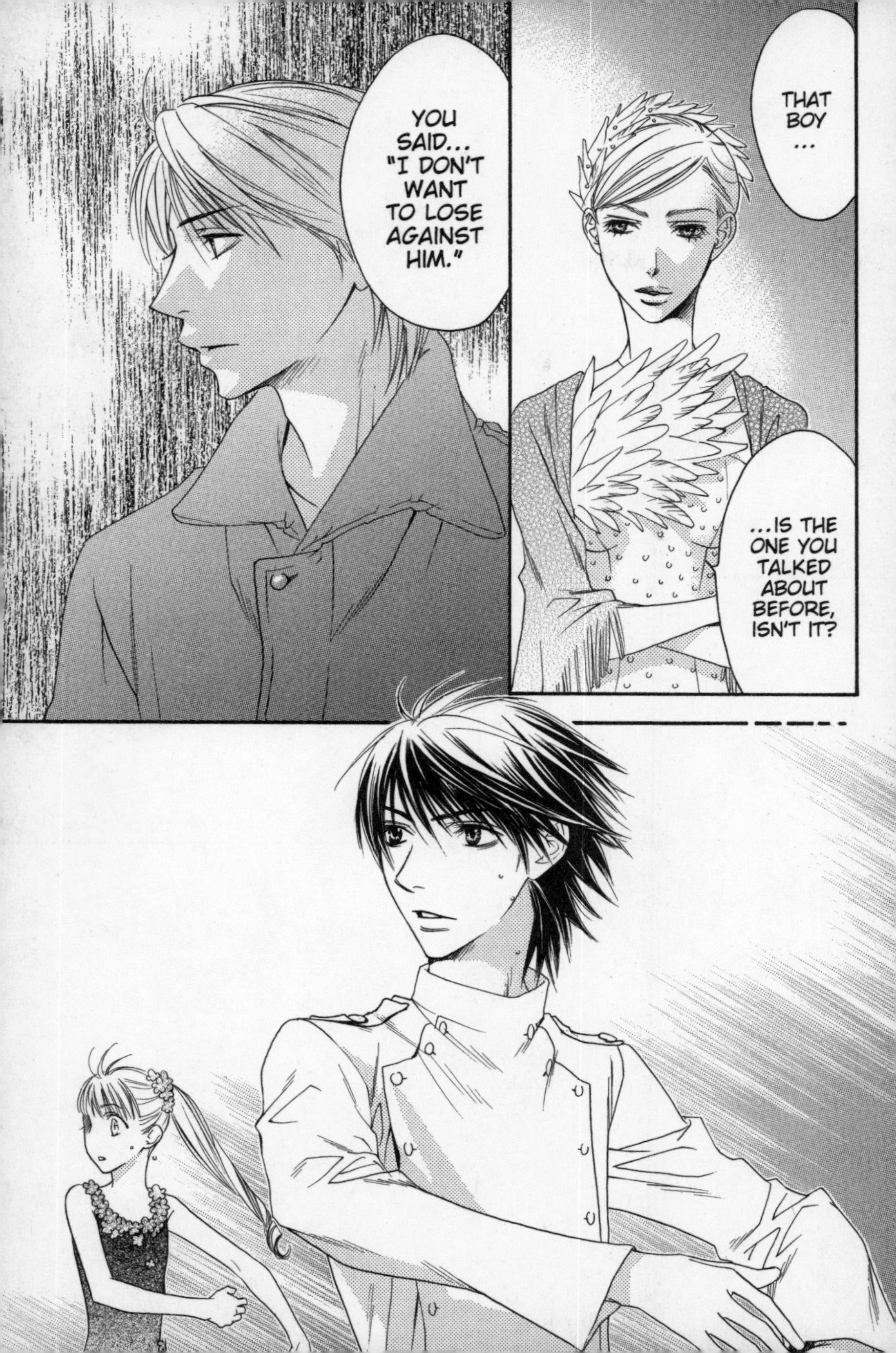
THAT BOY ...
...IS THE ONE YOU TALKED ABOUT BEFORE, ISN'T IT?
YOU SAID... "I DON'T WANT TO LOSE AGAINST HIM."

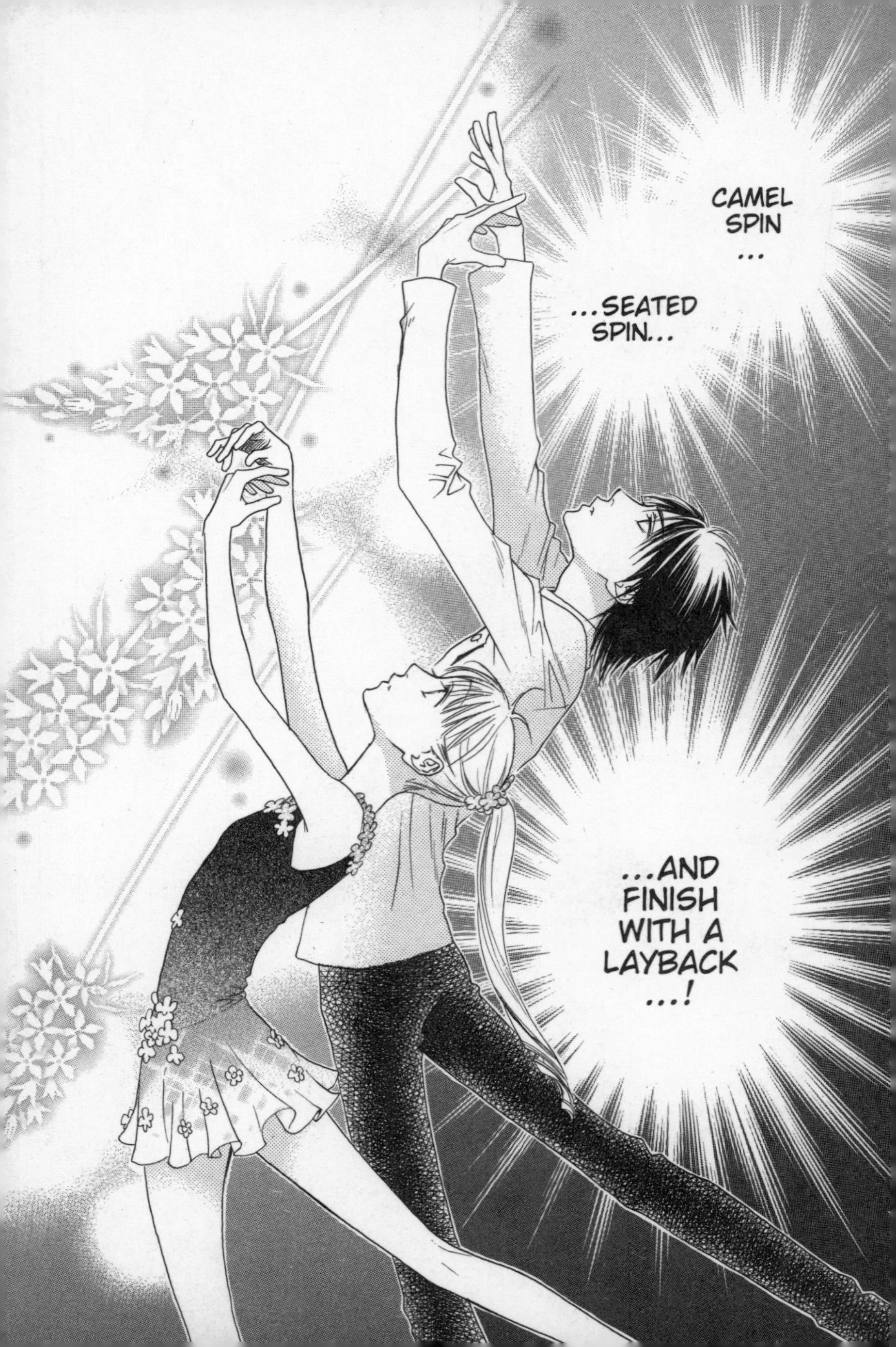
CAMEL SPIN
...
...SEATED SPIN...
...AND FINISH WITH A LAYBACK
...!

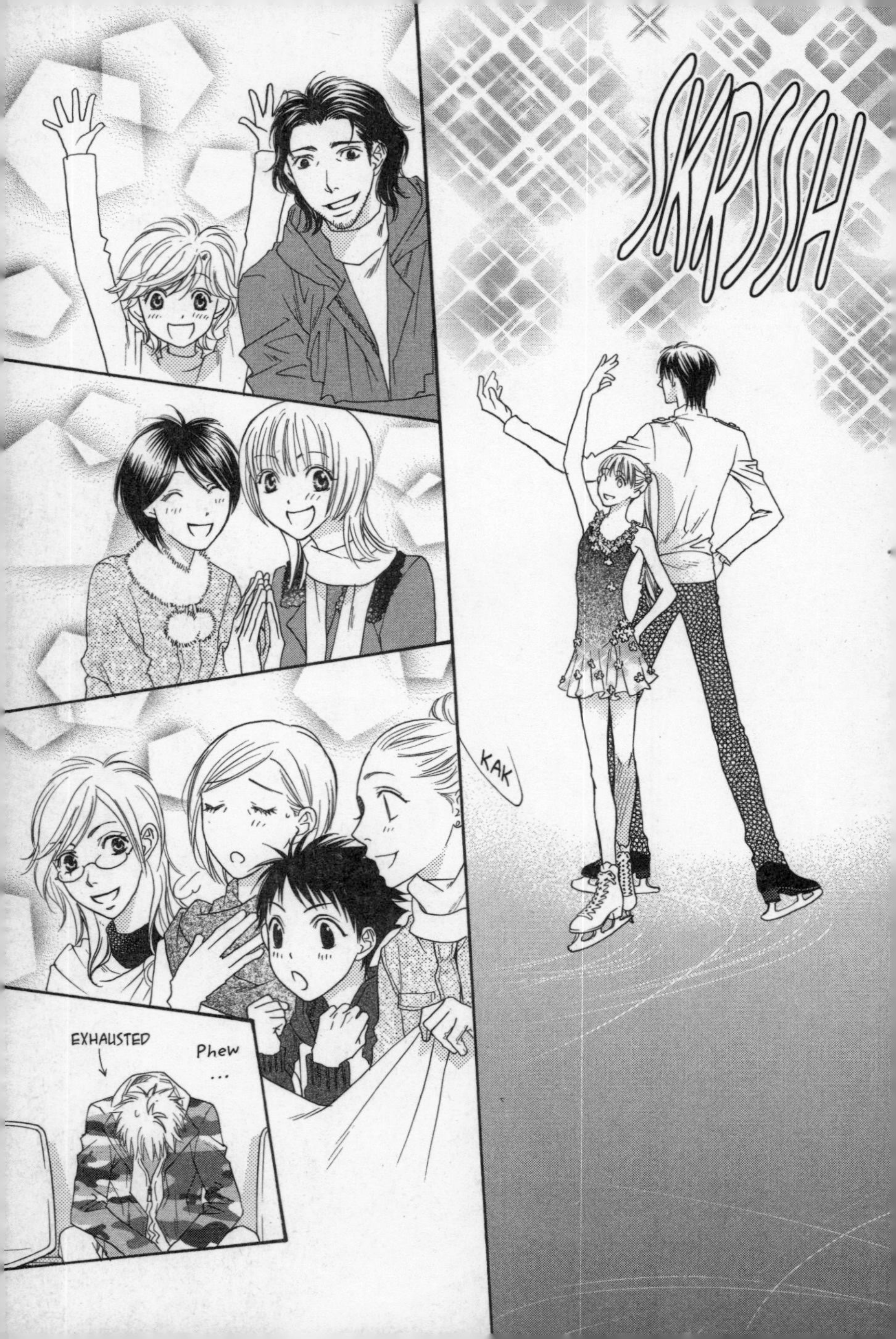
SKRSSH
KAK
EXHAUSTED
Phew
...

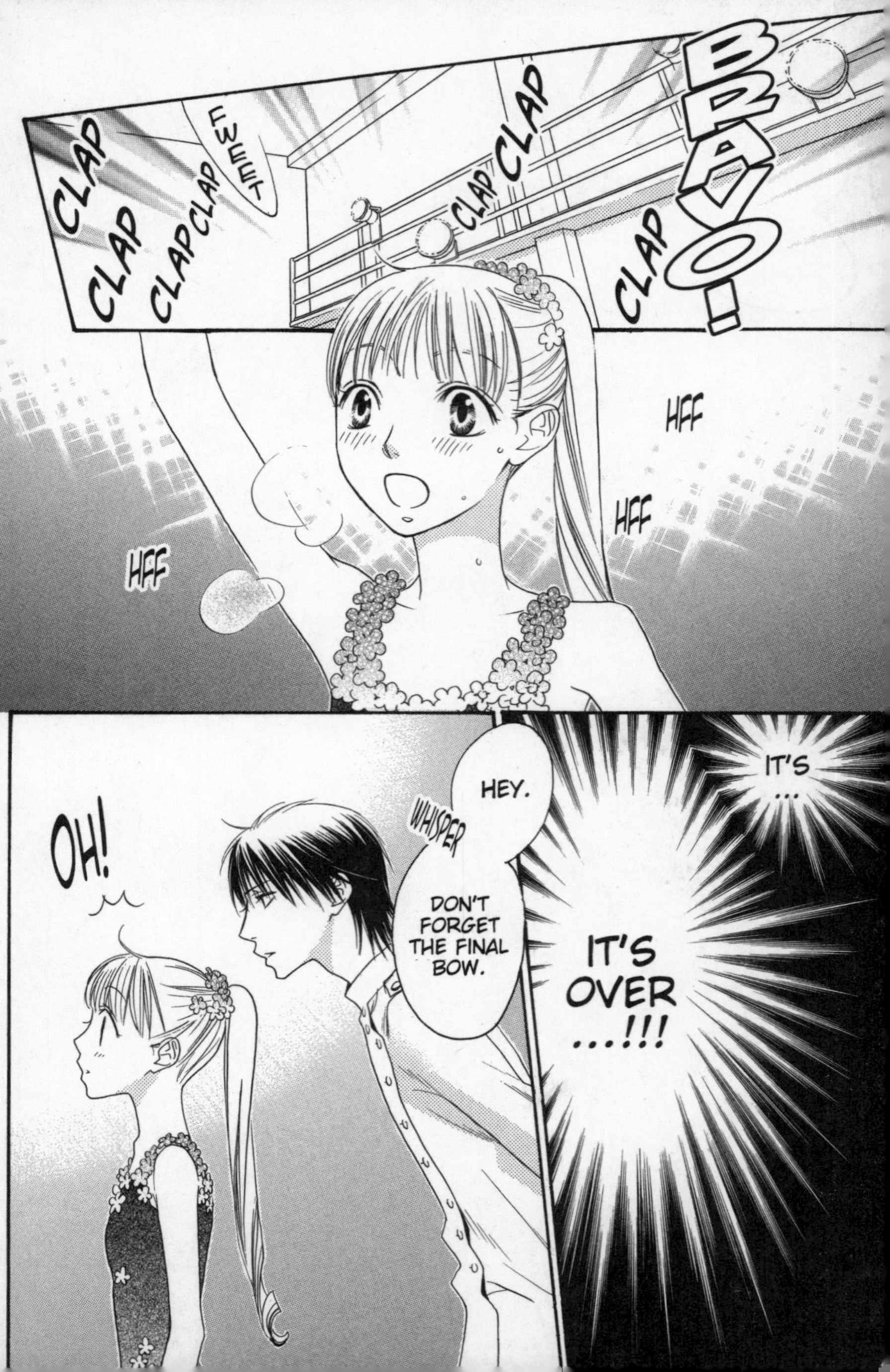
BRAVO!
CLAP
CLAP CLAP
CLAP
FWEET
CLAPCLAP
CLAP
CLAP
CLAP
HFF
HFF
HFF
IT'S ...
IT'S OVER ...!!!
HEY.
WHISPER
DON'T FORGET THE FINAL BOW.
OH!

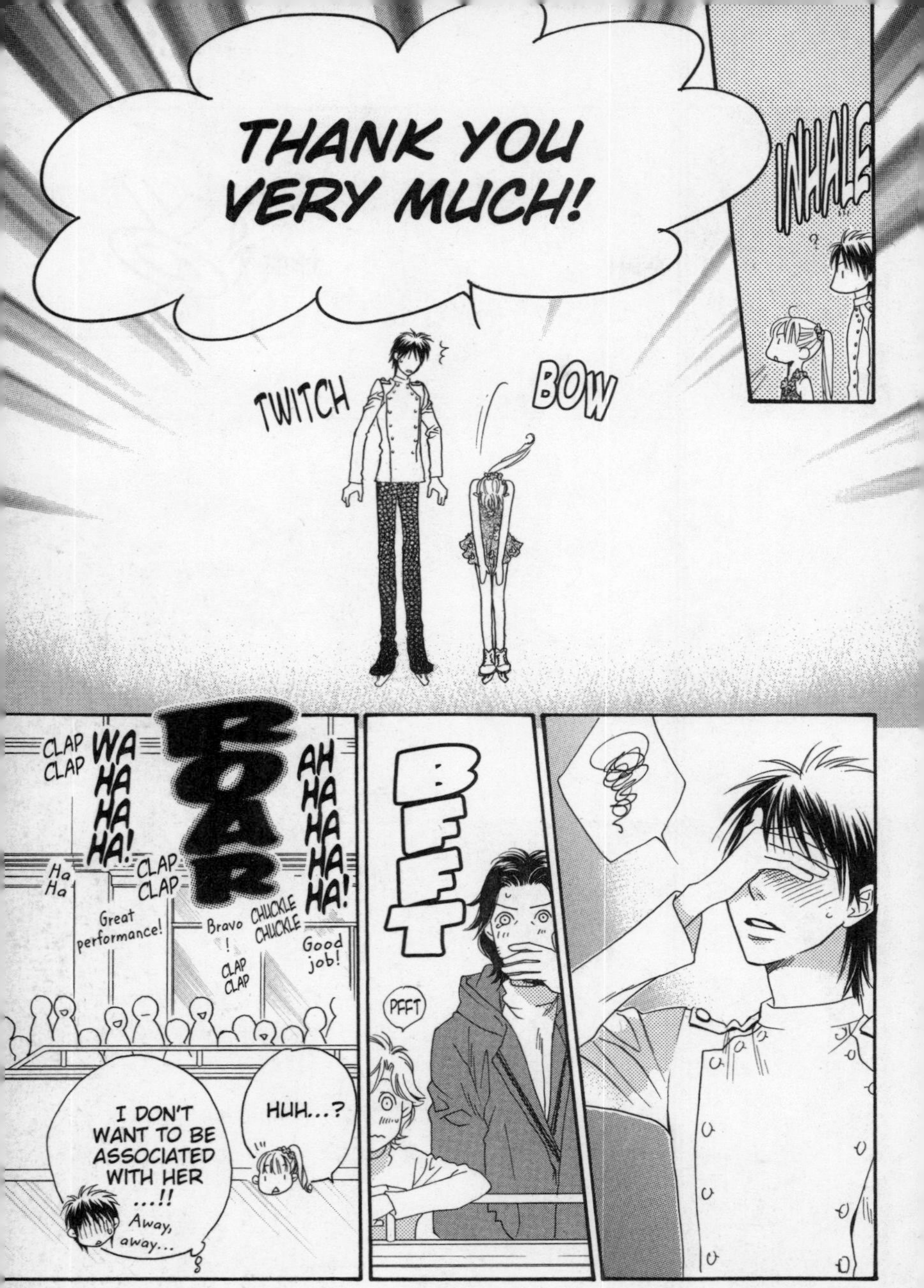
WHALE
THANK YOU VERY MUCH!
BOW
TWITCH
BFFT
PFFT
ROAR
AH HA HA HA HA HA!
WA HA HA HA!
CLAP CLAP
CLAP CLAP
Ha Ha
Great performance!
Bravo!
CHUCKLE CHUCKLE
Good job!
CLAP CLAP
HUH...?
I DON'T WANT TO BE ASSOCIATED WITH HER ...!!
Away, away...

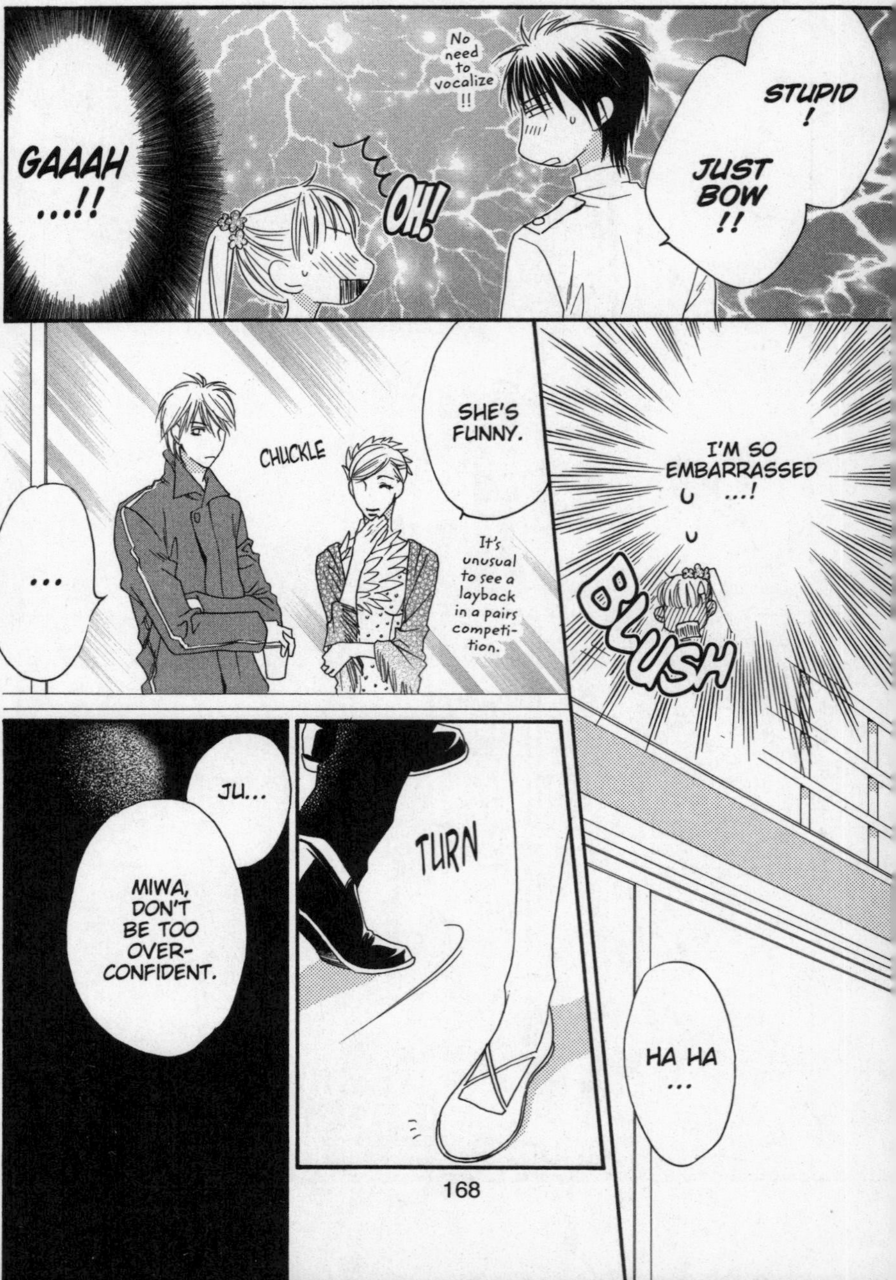
STUPID! JUST BOW!!
No need to vocalize!!
OH!
GAAAH...!!
I'M SO EMBARRASSED...!
BLUSH
HA HA...
SHE'S FUNNY.
CHUCKLE
It's unusual to see a layback in a pairs competition.
...
TURN
JU...
MIWA, DON'T BE TOO OVER-CONFIDENT.

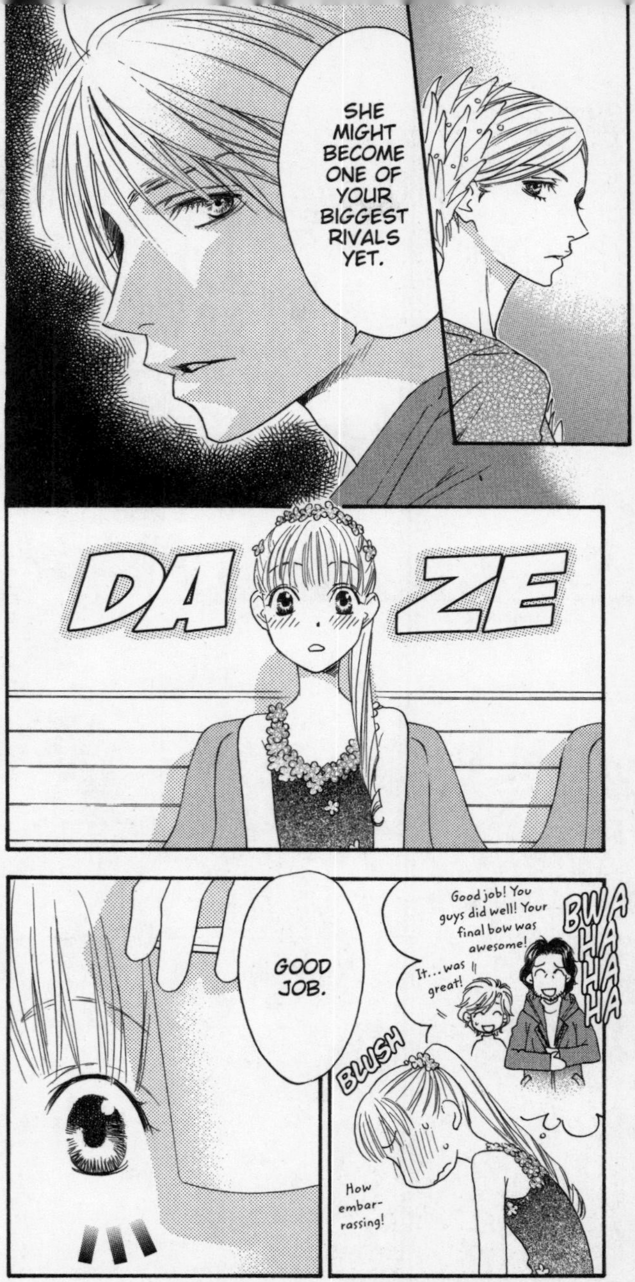
SHE MIGHT BECOME ONE OF YOUR BIGGEST RIVALS YET.
DA ZE
Good job! You guys did well! Your final bow was awesome!
BWAHAHAHA
It... was great!
BLUSH
How embarrassing!
GOOD JOB.

I BOUGHT A SANDWICH WHILE I WATCHED SKATING PRACTICE AT THE RINK, BUT...

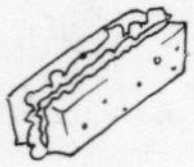

...IT WAS PARTIALLY FROZEN WHEN I BIT INTO IT. (LOL)

ESPECIALLY THE LETTUCE.

EVEN THE SPECTATOR SEATS IN THE (SKATING) RINK ARE FREEZING.

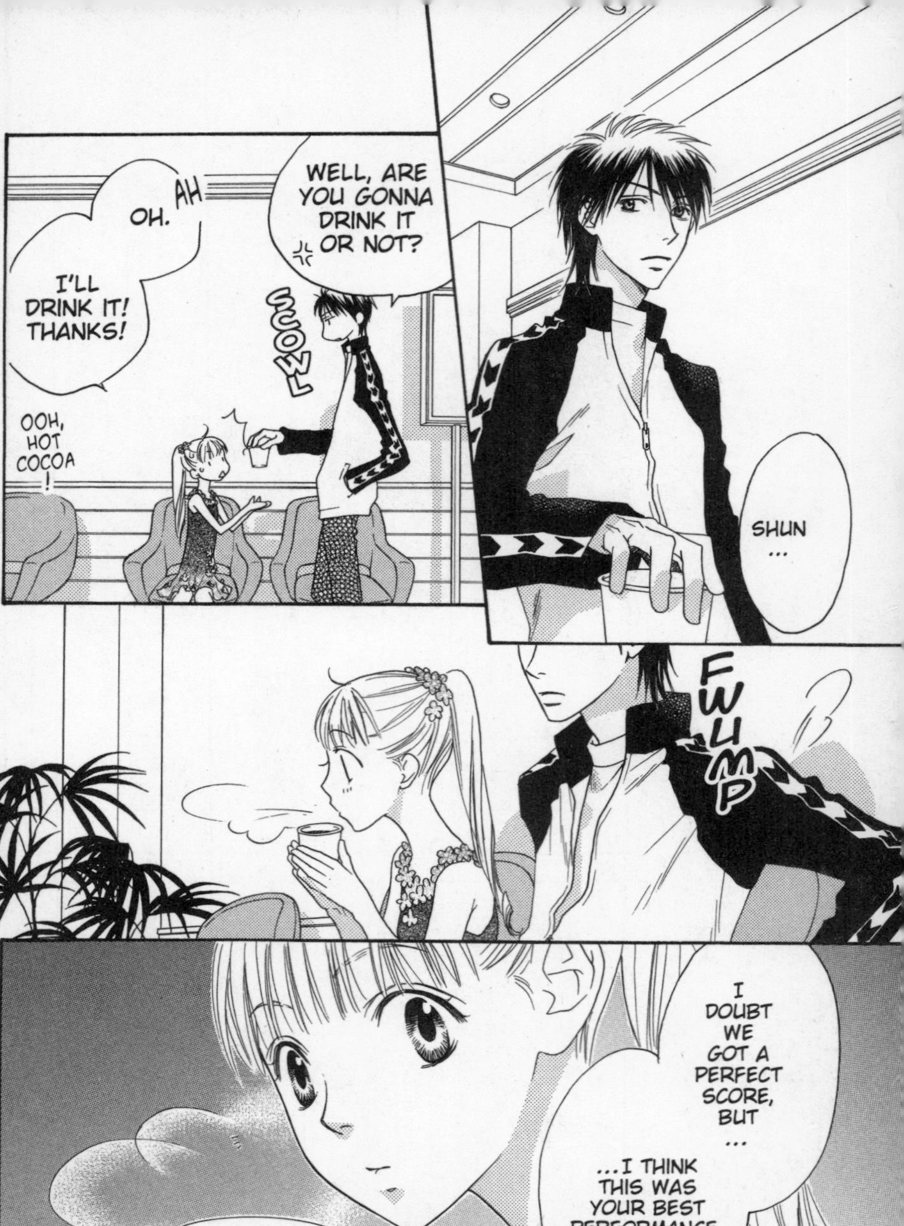
SHUN ...
WELL, ARE YOU GONNA DRINK IT OR NOT?
SCOWL
OH. AH
I'LL DRINK IT! THANKS!
OOH, HOT COCOA!
FWUMP
I DOUBT WE GOT A PERFECT SCORE, BUT ...
...I THINK THIS WAS YOUR BEST PERFORMANCE.

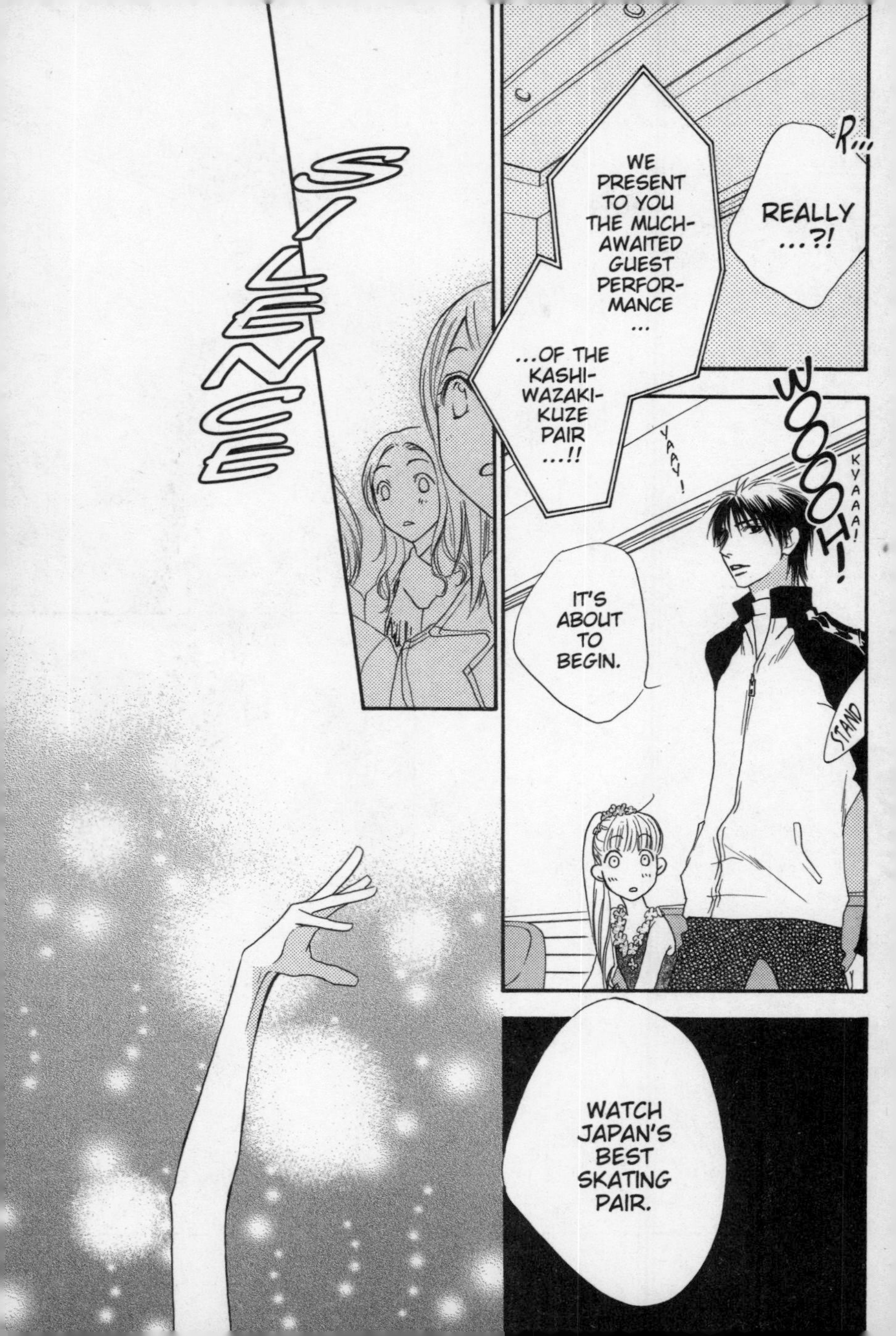
R...
REALLY ...?!
WE PRESENT TO YOU THE MUCH-AWAITED GUEST PERFORMANCE ...
...OF THE KASHI-WAZAKI-KUZE PAIR ...!!
WOOOOH!
KYAAA!
YAAY!
IT'S ABOUT TO BEGIN.
STAND
WATCH JAPAN'S BEST SKATING PAIR.
SILENCE

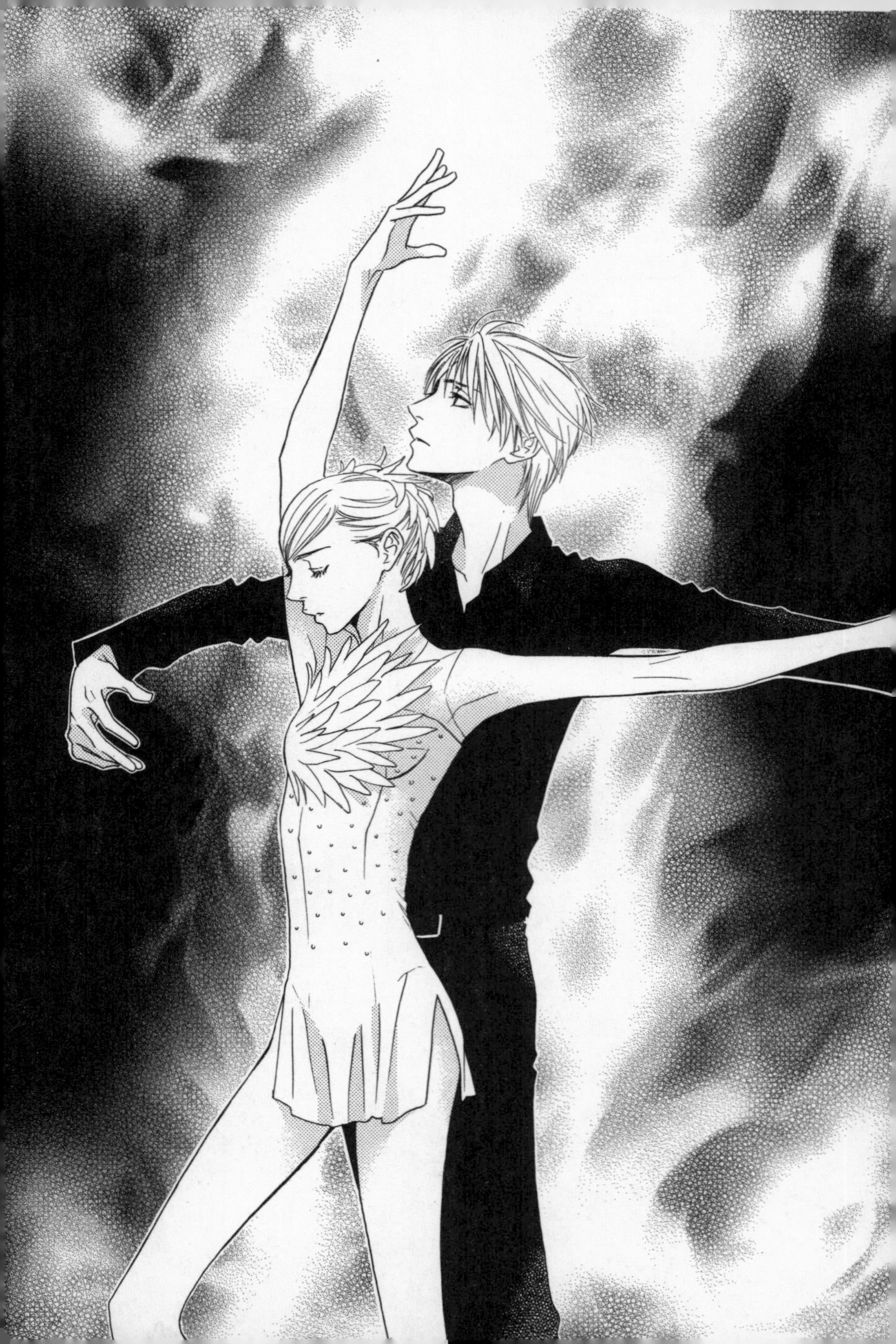

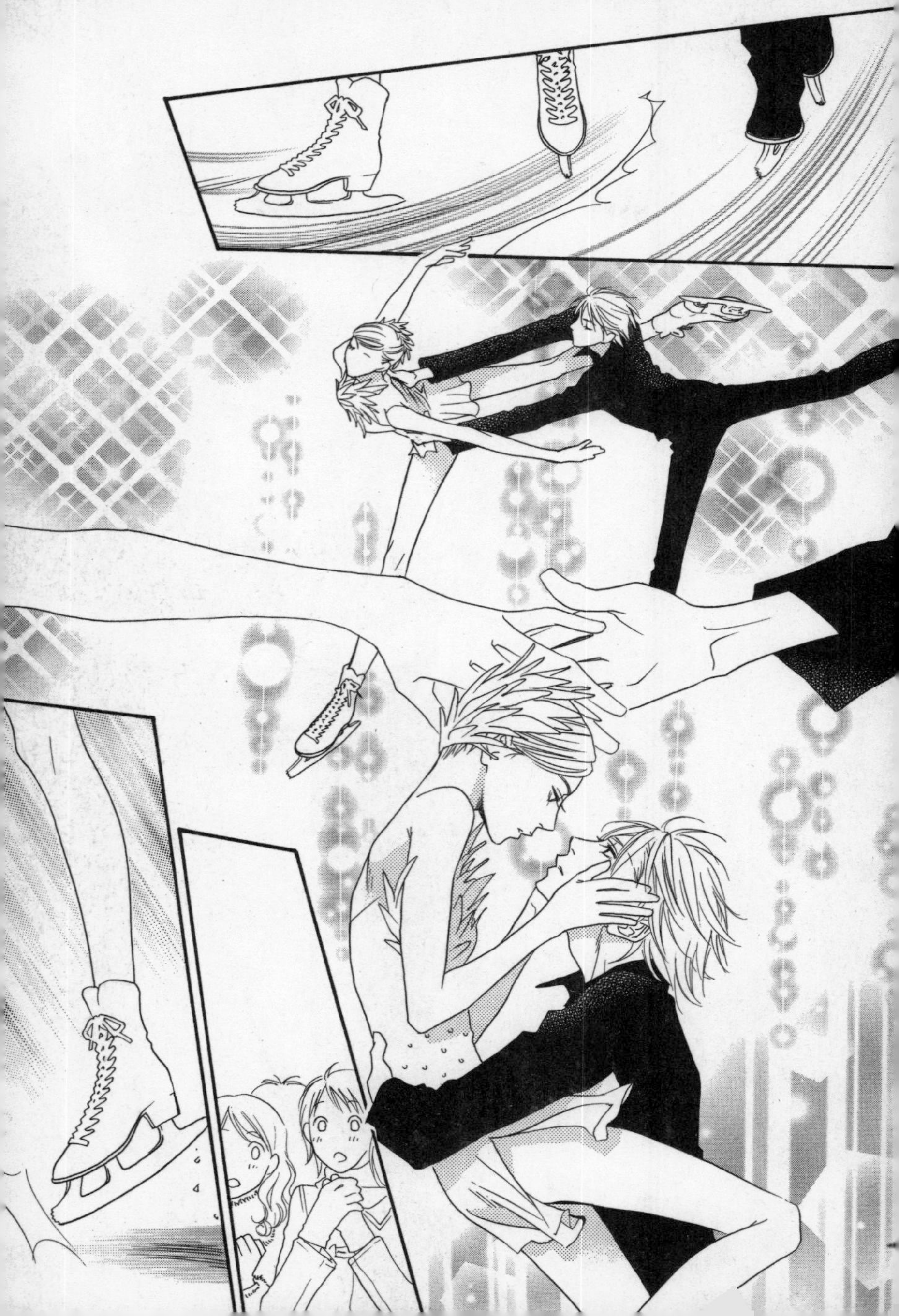

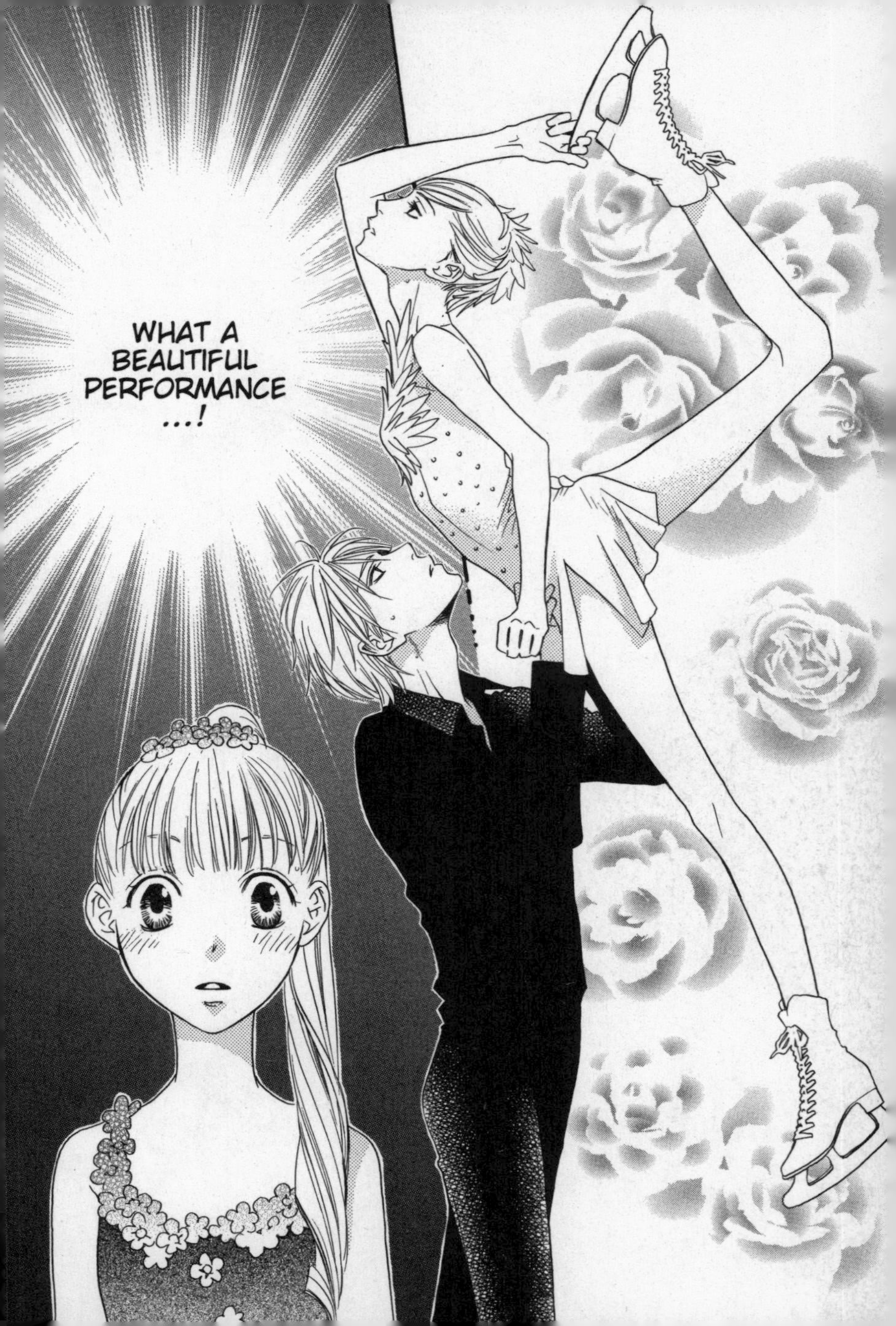
WHAT A BEAUTIFUL PERFORMANCE ...!

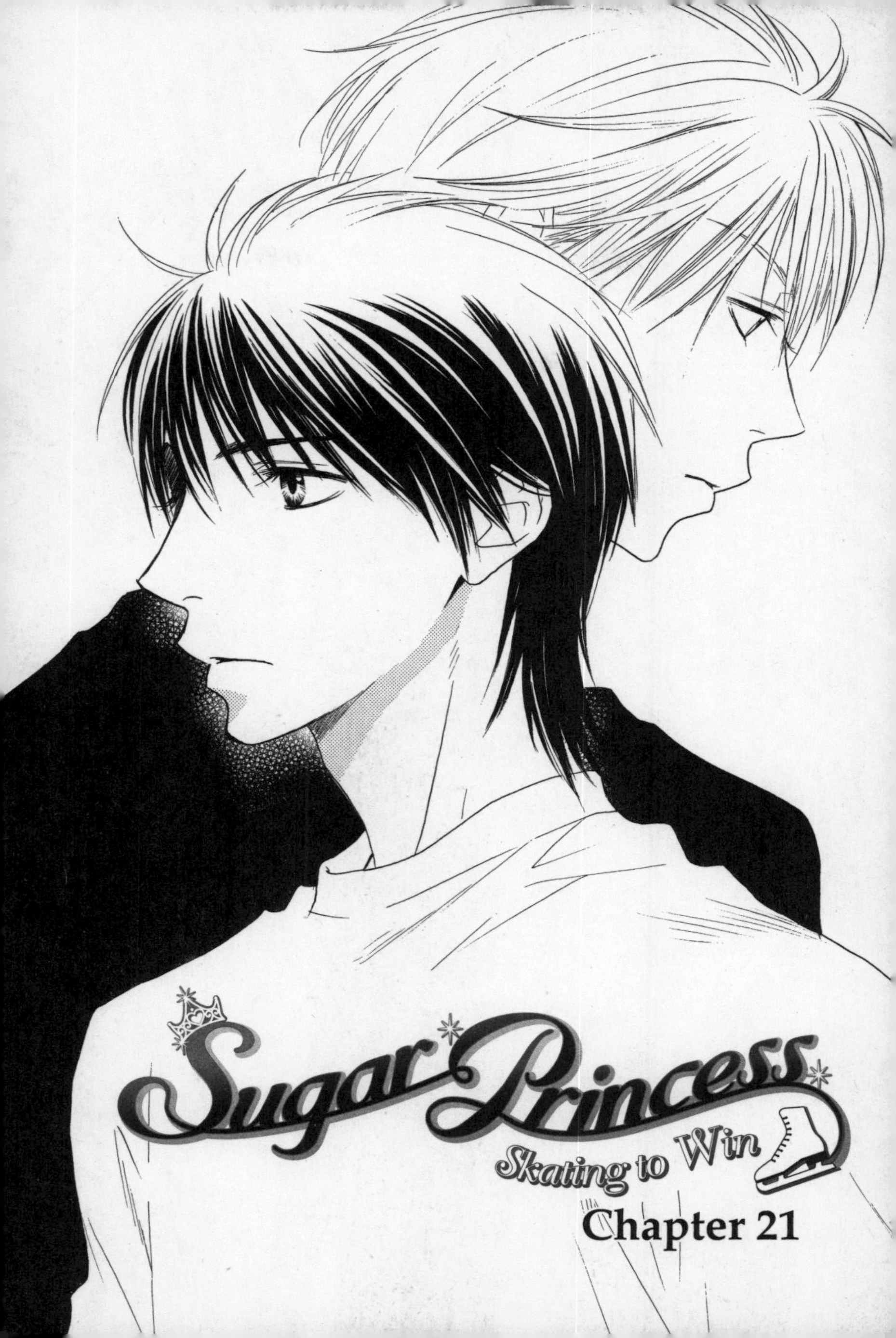
Sugar Princess
Skating to Win
Chapter 21

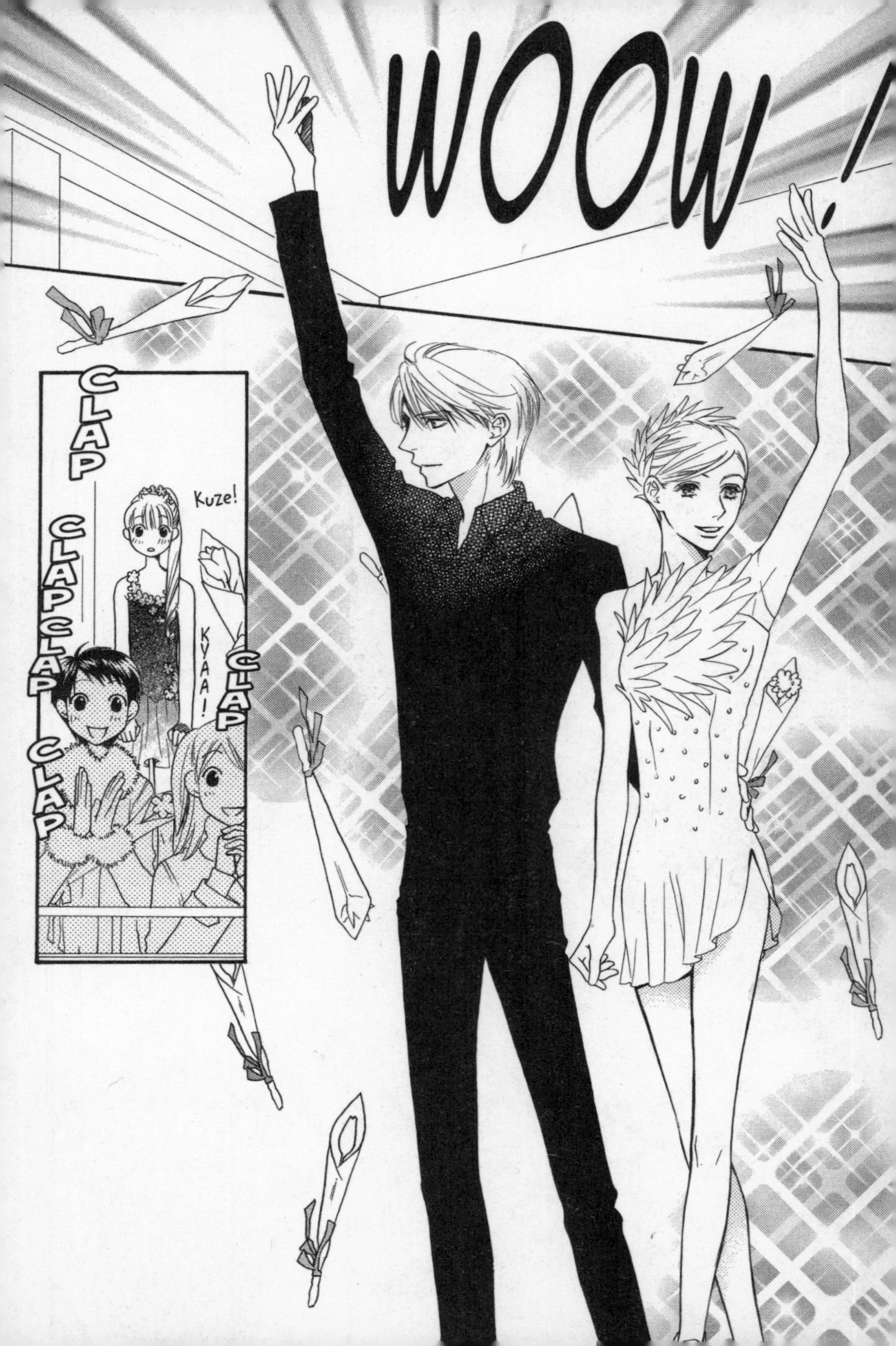
WOOW!
Kuze!
KYAA!
CLAP
CLAP
CLAP CLAP
CLAP CLAP
CLAP

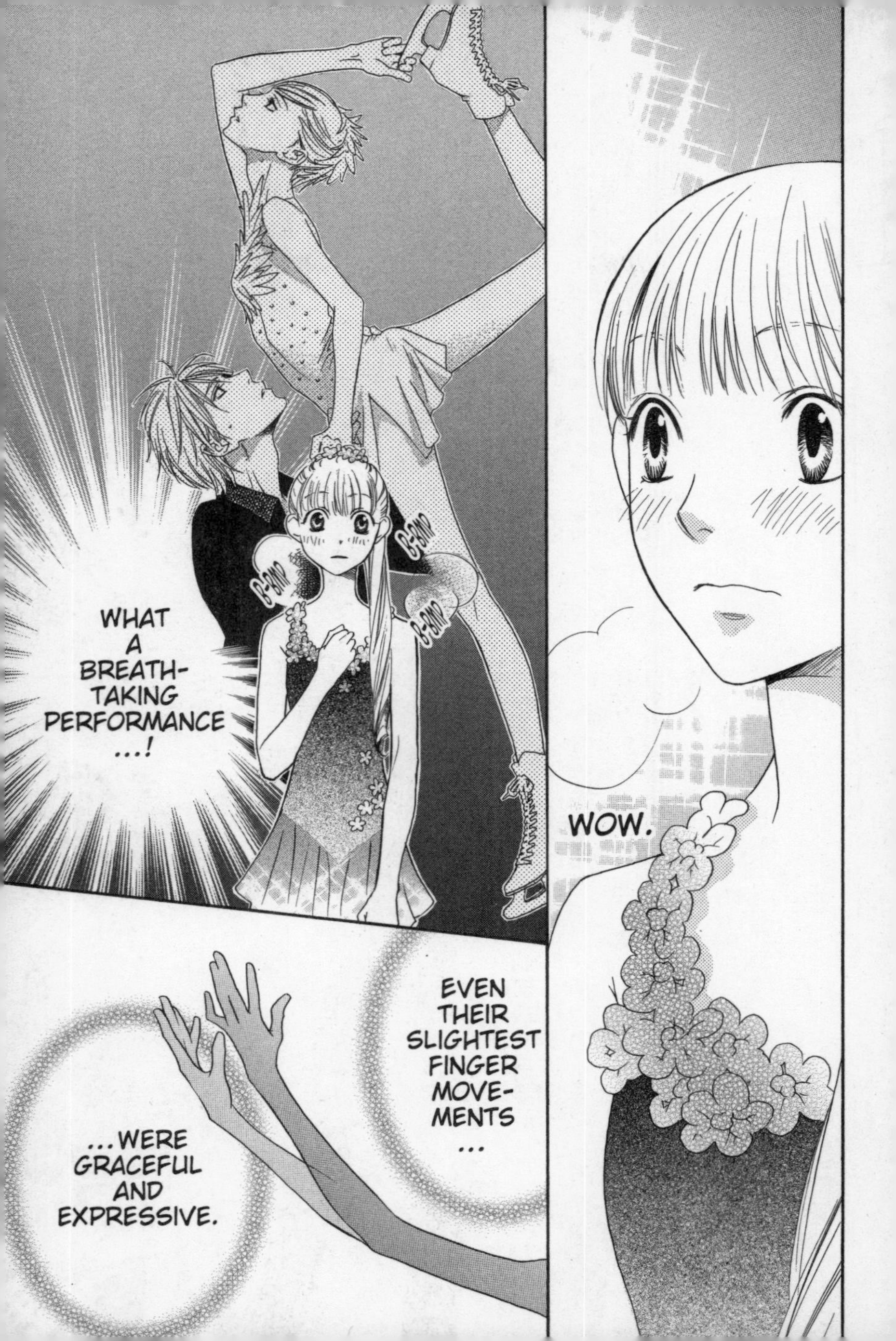
WOW.
B-BMP
B-BMP
B-BMP
WHAT A BREATH-TAKING PERFORMANCE...!
EVEN THEIR SLIGHTEST FINGER MOVE-MENTS...
...WERE GRACEFUL AND EXPRESSIVE.

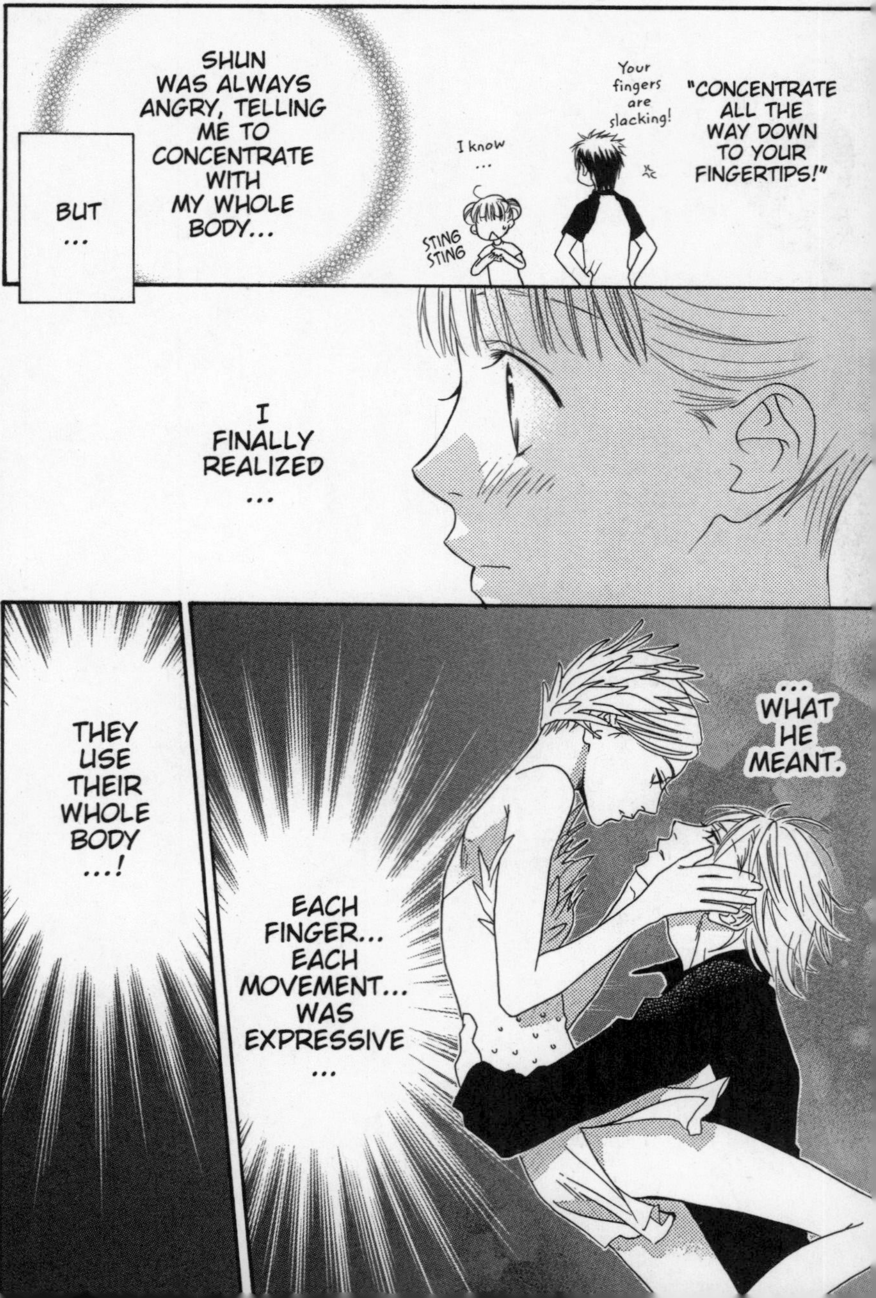
"CONCENTRATE ALL THE WAY DOWN TO YOUR FINGERTIPS!"
Your fingers are slacking!
I know ...
STING STING
SHUN WAS ALWAYS ANGRY, TELLING ME TO CONCENTRATE WITH MY WHOLE BODY...
BUT ...
I FINALLY REALIZED ...
... WHAT HE MEANT.
EACH FINGER... EACH MOVEMENT... WAS EXPRESSIVE ...
THEY USE THEIR WHOLE BODY ...!

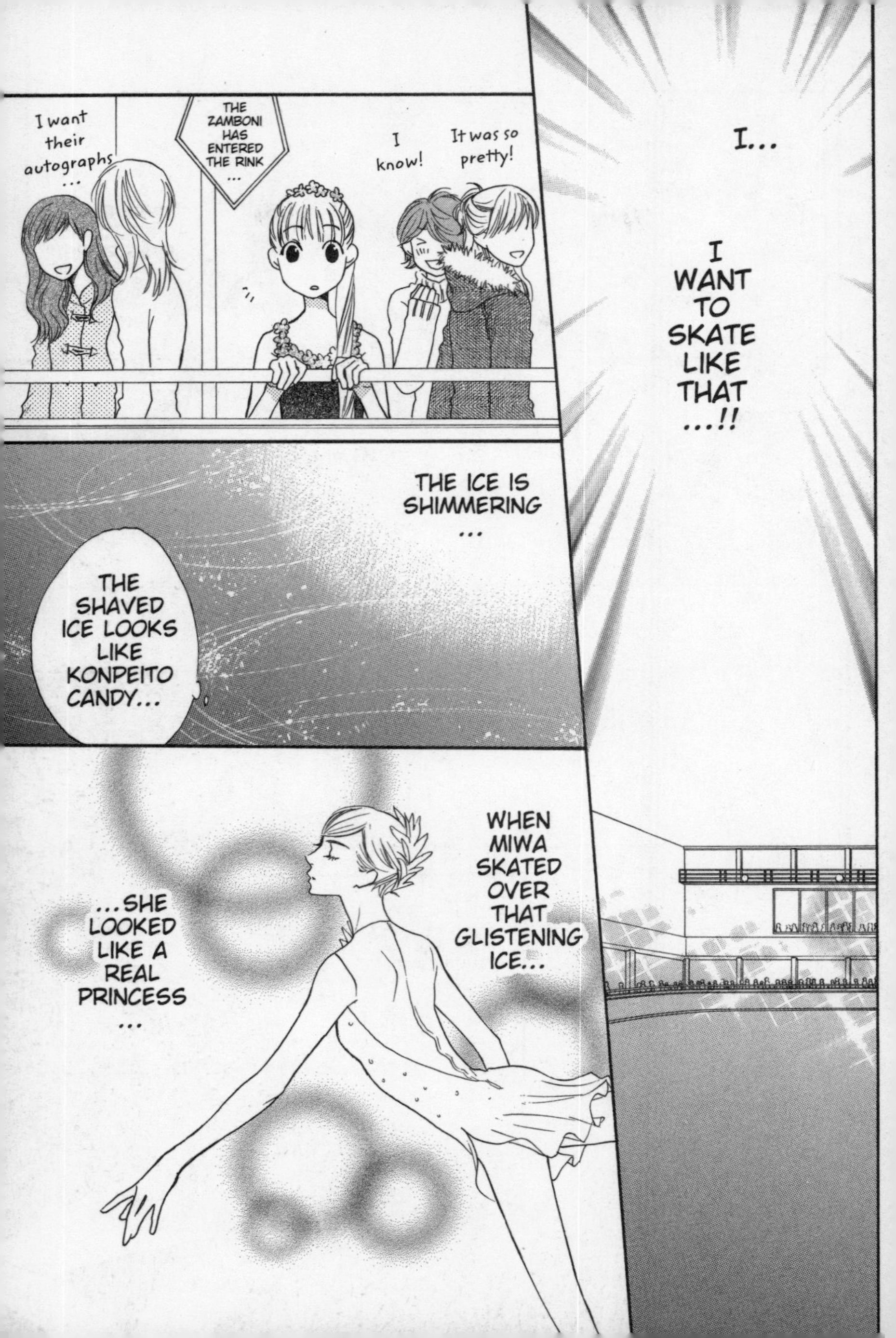
I...
I WANT TO SKATE LIKE THAT...!!
It was so pretty!
I know!
THE ZAMBONI HAS ENTERED THE RINK...
I want their autographs...
THE ICE IS SHIMMERING...
THE SHAVED ICE LOOKS LIKE KONPEITO CANDY...
WHEN MIWA SKATED OVER THAT GLISTENING ICE...
...SHE LOOKED LIKE A REAL PRINCESS...

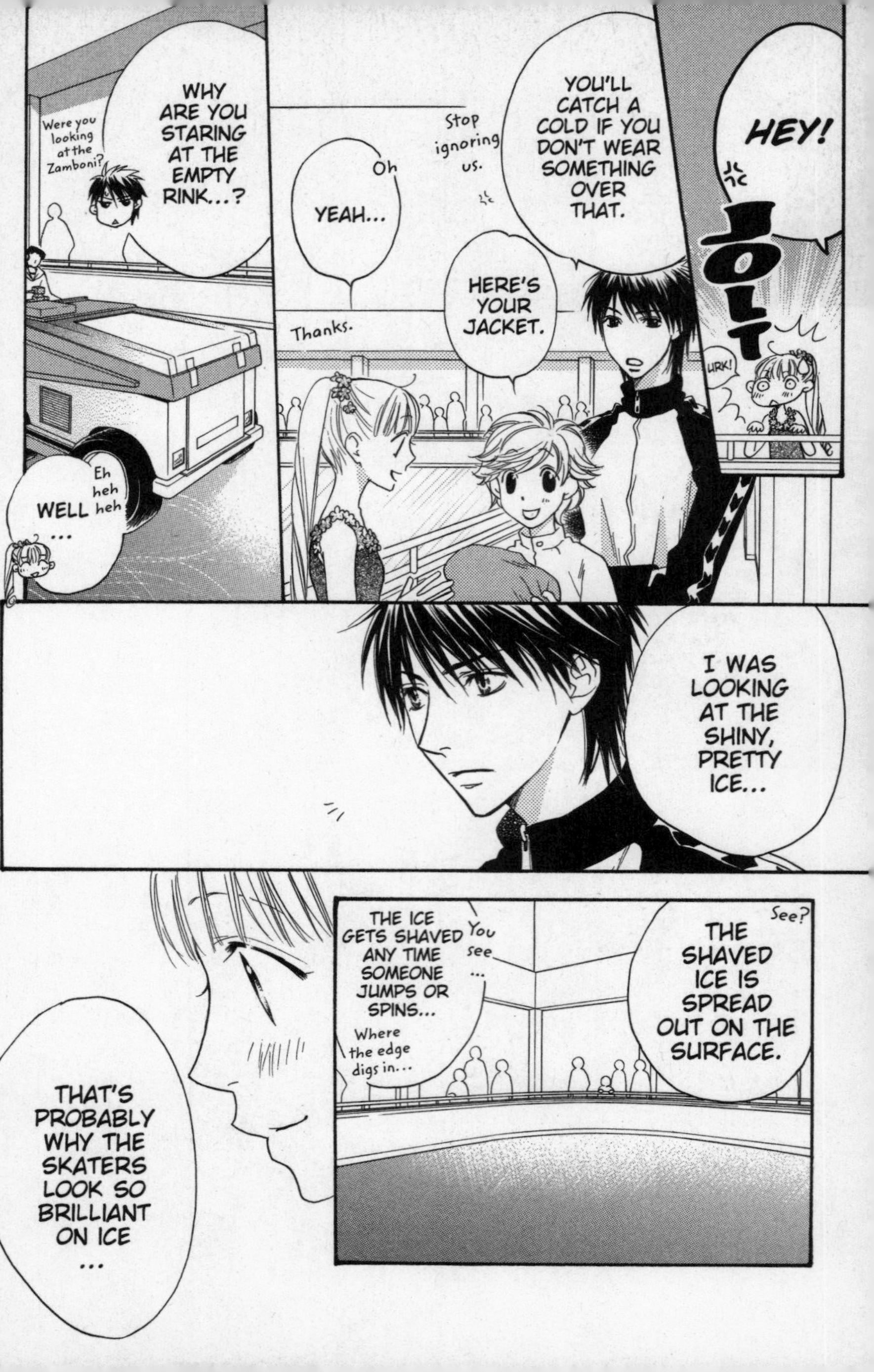
HEY!
JOLT
URK!
YOU'LL CATCH A COLD IF YOU DON'T WEAR SOMETHING OVER THAT.
Stop ignoring us.
HERE'S YOUR JACKET.
Oh
YEAH...
Thanks.
WHY ARE YOU STARING AT THE EMPTY RINK...?
Were you looking at the Zamboni?
Eh heh heh
WELL...
I WAS LOOKING AT THE SHINY, PRETTY ICE...
See?
THE SHAVED ICE IS SPREAD OUT ON THE SURFACE.
You see...
THE ICE GETS SHAVED ANY TIME SOMEONE JUMPS OR SPINS...
Where the edge digs in...
THAT'S PROBABLY WHY THE SKATERS LOOK SO BRILLIANT ON ICE...

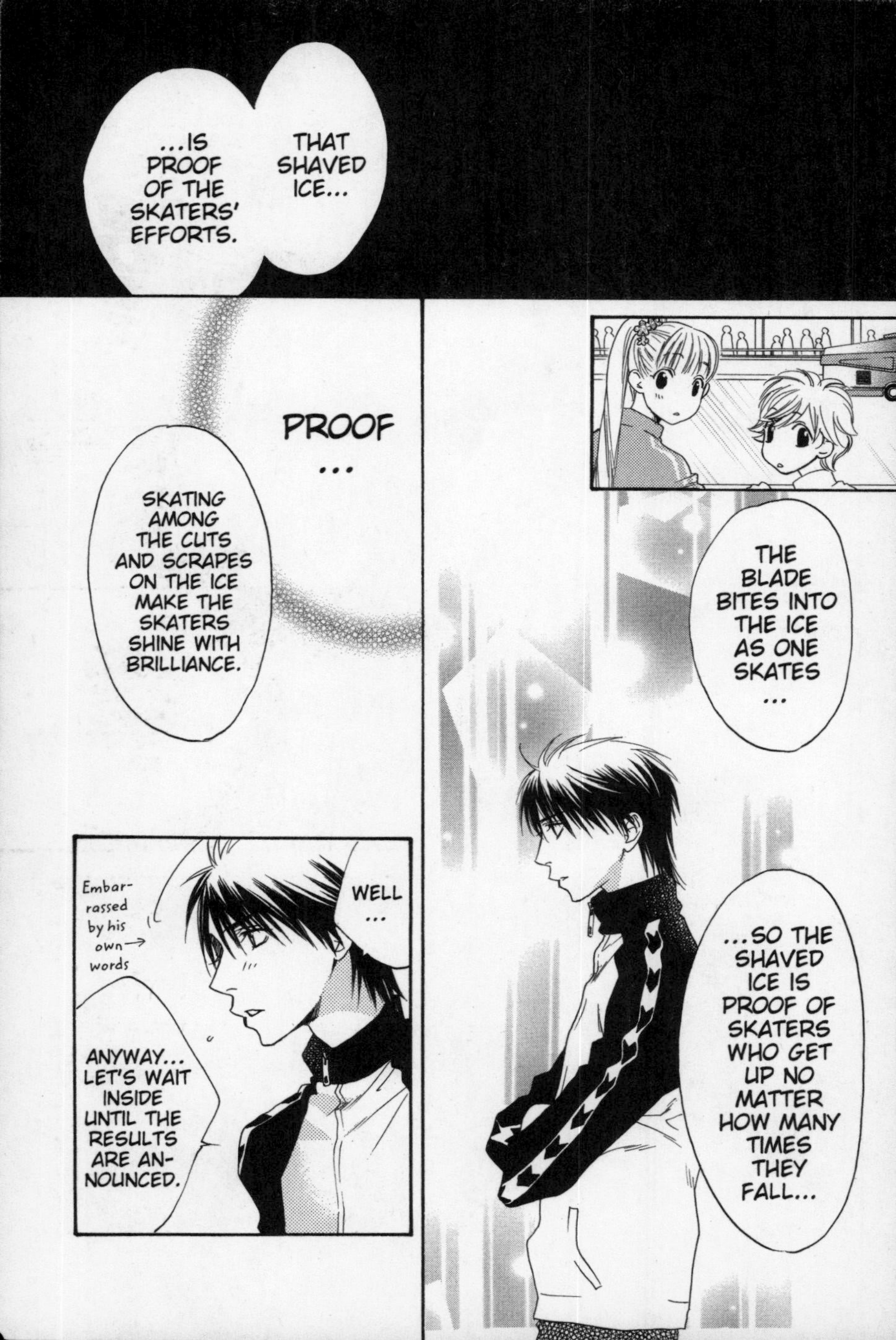
THAT SHAVED ICE...
...IS PROOF OF THE SKATERS' EFFORTS.
THE BLADE BITES INTO THE ICE AS ONE SKATES ...
...SO THE SHAVED ICE IS PROOF OF SKATERS WHO GET UP NO MATTER HOW MANY TIMES THEY FALL...
PROOF ...
SKATING AMONG THE CUTS AND SCRAPES ON THE ICE MAKE THE SKATERS SHINE WITH BRILLIANCE.
WELL ...
Embarrassed by his own words
ANYWAY... LET'S WAIT INSIDE UNTIL THE RESULTS ARE ANNOUNCED.

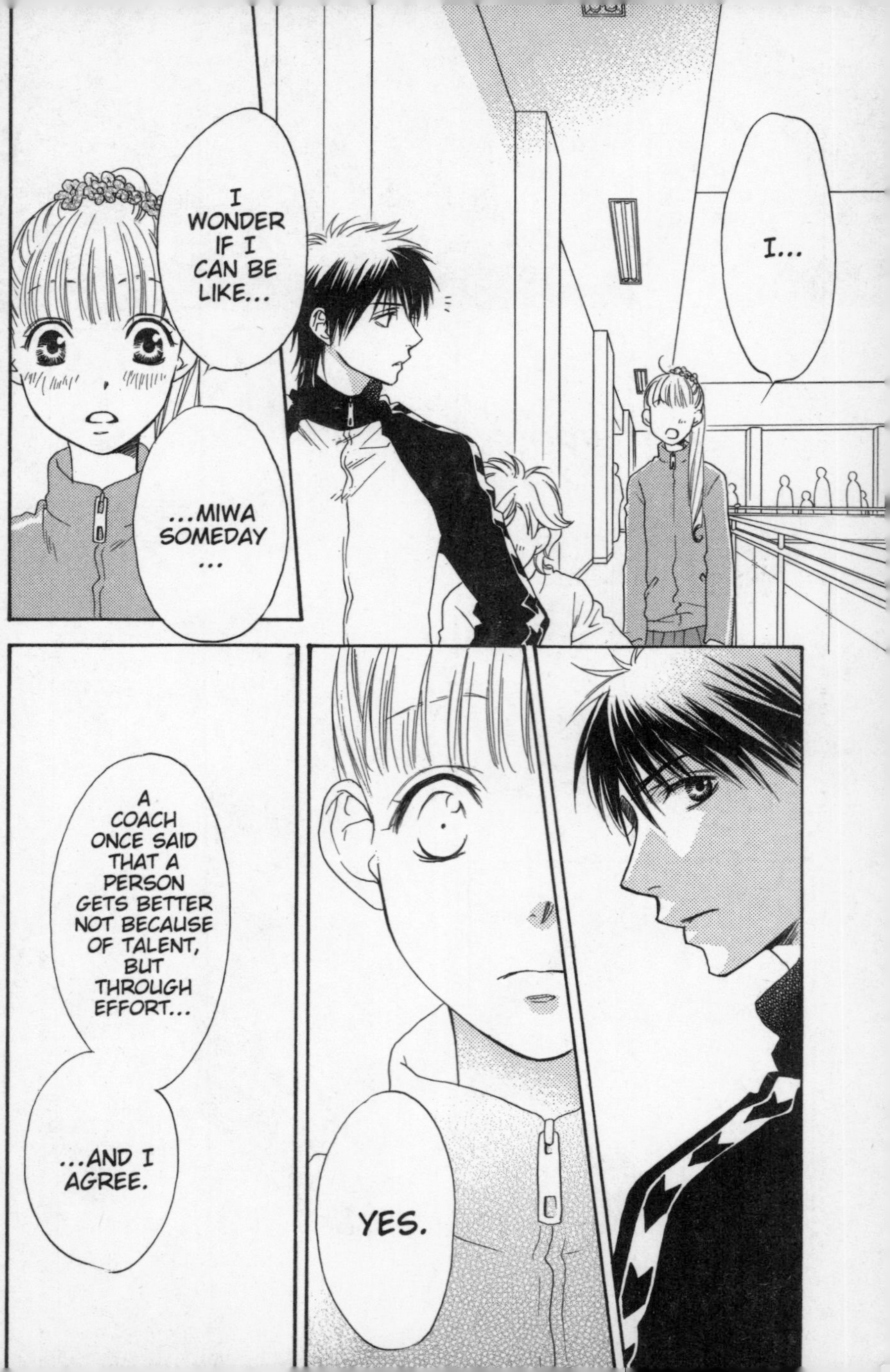
I...
I WONDER IF I CAN BE LIKE...
...MIWA SOMEDAY...
YES.
A COACH ONCE SAID THAT A PERSON GETS BETTER NOT BECAUSE OF TALENT, BUT THROUGH EFFORT...
...AND I AGREE.

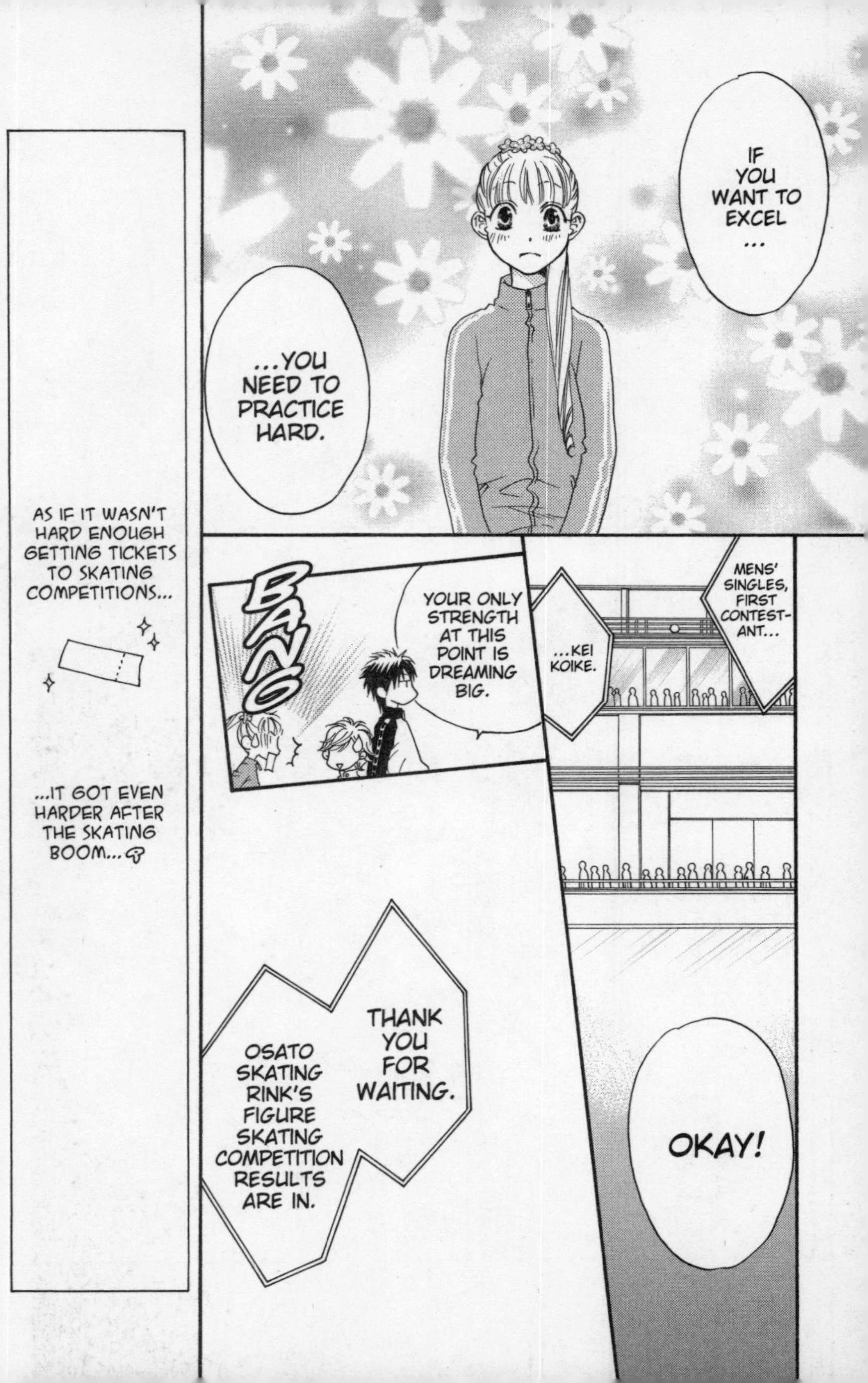
IF YOU WANT TO EXCEL ...
...YOU NEED TO PRACTICE HARD.
MENS' SINGLES, FIRST CONTEST-ANT...
...KEI KOIKE.
OKAY!
YOUR ONLY STRENGTH AT THIS POINT IS DREAMING BIG.
BANG
THANK YOU FOR WAITING.
OSATO SKATING RINK'S FIGURE SKATING COMPETITION RESULTS ARE IN.

AS IF IT WASN'T HARD ENOUGH GETTING TICKETS TO SKATING COMPETITIONS...

...IT GOT EVEN HARDER AFTER THE SKATING BOOM...

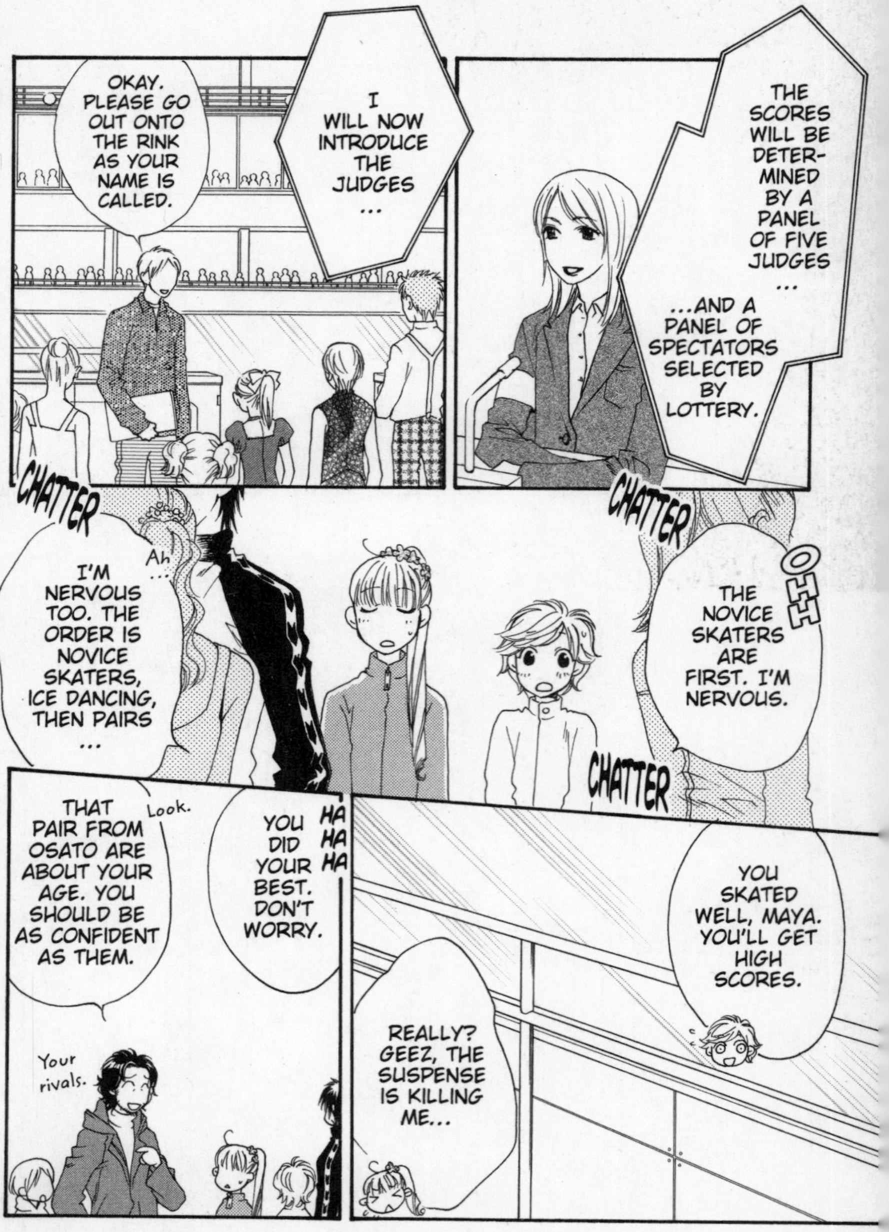
THE SCORES WILL BE DETER-MINED BY A PANEL OF FIVE JUDGES ...
...AND A PANEL OF SPECTATORS SELECTED BY LOTTERY.
I WILL NOW INTRODUCE THE JUDGES ...
OKAY. PLEASE GO OUT ONTO THE RINK AS YOUR NAME IS CALLED.
CHATTER
OHH
THE NOVICE SKATERS ARE FIRST. I'M NERVOUS.
CHATTER
Ah ...
I'M NERVOUS TOO. THE ORDER IS NOVICE SKATERS, ICE DANCING, THEN PAIRS ...
CHATTER
YOU SKATED WELL, MAYA. YOU'LL GET HIGH SCORES.
REALLY? GEEZ, THE SUSPENSE IS KILLING ME...
HA HA HA
YOU DID YOUR BEST. DON'T WORRY.
Look.
THAT PAIR FROM OSATO ARE ABOUT YOUR AGE. YOU SHOULD BE AS CONFIDENT AS THEM.
Your rivals.

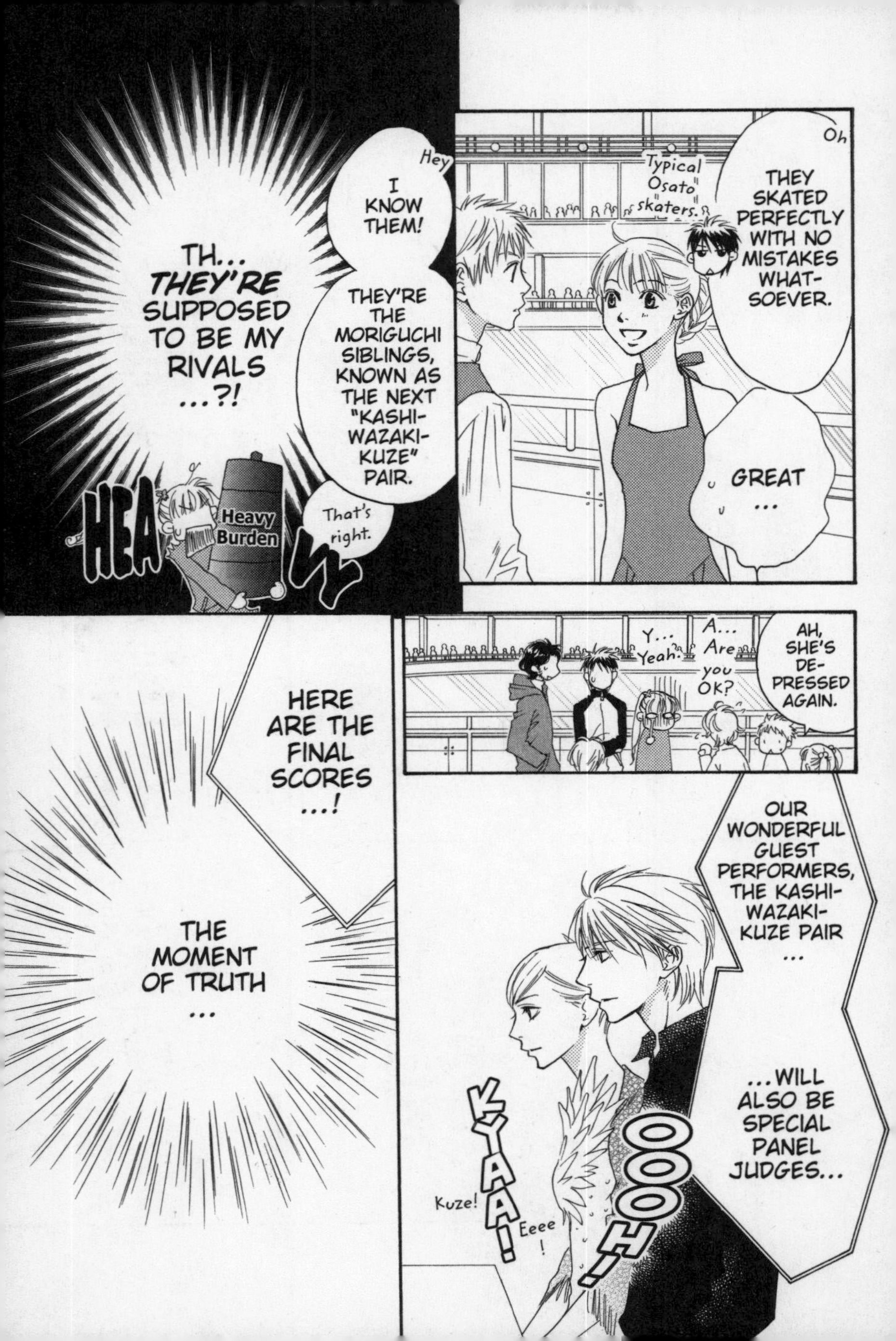
Oh
THEY SKATED PERFECTLY WITH NO MISTAKES WHAT-SOEVER.
"Typical Osato" skaters...
GREAT ...
Hey
I KNOW THEM!
THEY'RE THE MORIGUCHI SIBLINGS, KNOWN AS THE NEXT "KASHI-WAZAKI-KUZE" PAIR.
TH... *THEY'RE* SUPPOSED TO BE MY RIVALS ...?!
That's right.
Heavy Burden
HEA
AH, SHE'S DE-PRESSED AGAIN.
A... Are you OK?
Y... Yeah.
HERE ARE THE FINAL SCORES ...!
OUR WONDERFUL GUEST PERFORMERS, THE KASHI-WAZAKI-KUZE PAIR ...
...WILL ALSO BE SPECIAL PANEL JUDGES...
OOOH!
KYAAA!
Eeee!
Kuze!
THE MOMENT OF TRUTH ...

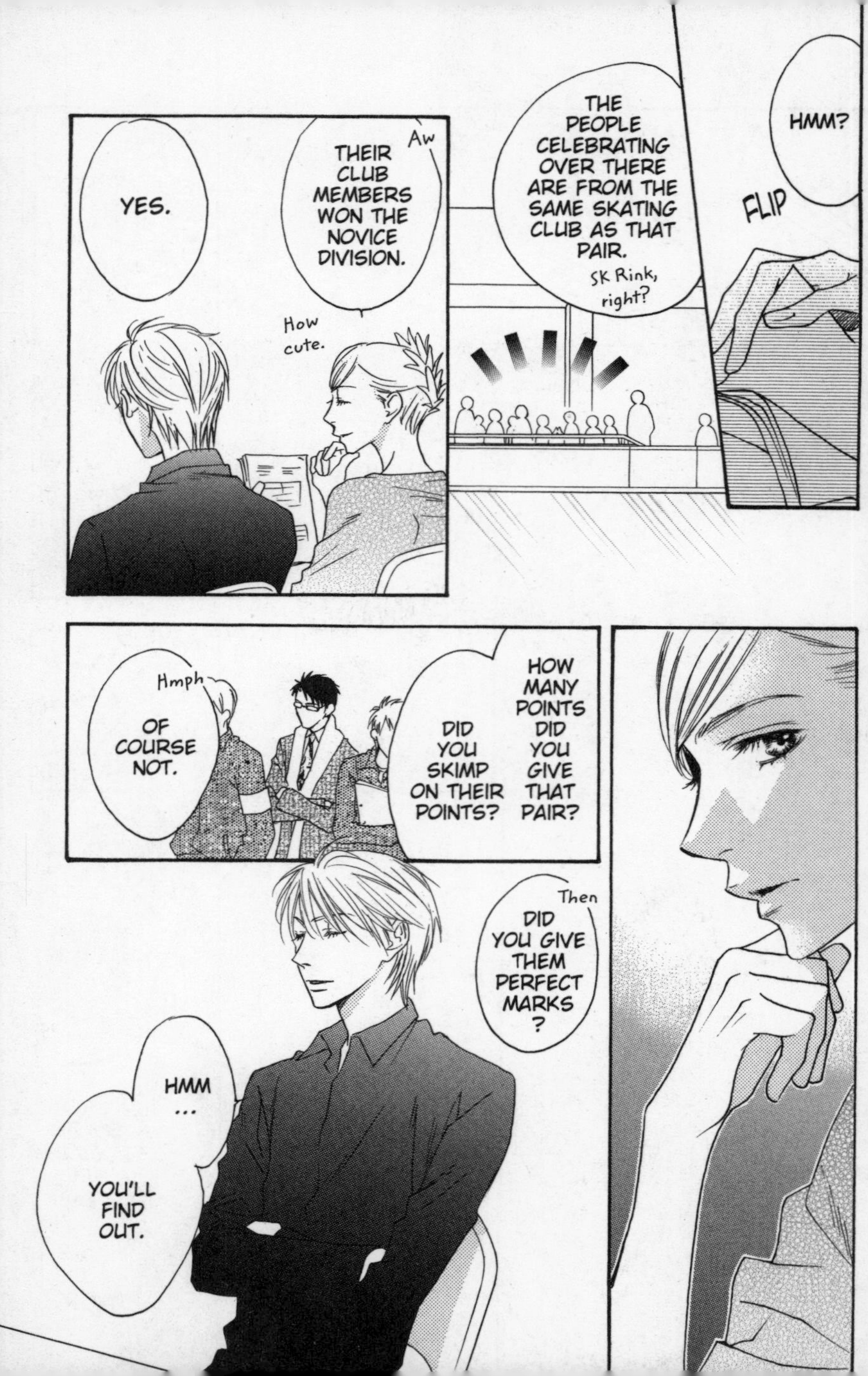
HMM?
FLIP
THE PEOPLE CELEBRATING OVER THERE ARE FROM THE SAME SKATING CLUB AS THAT PAIR.
SK Rink, right?
Aw
THEIR CLUB MEMBERS WON THE NOVICE DIVISION.
How cute.
YES.
HOW MANY POINTS DID YOU GIVE THAT PAIR?
DID YOU SKIMP ON THEIR POINTS?
Hmph
OF COURSE NOT.
Then
DID YOU GIVE THEM PERFECT MARKS?
HMM...
YOU'LL FIND OUT.

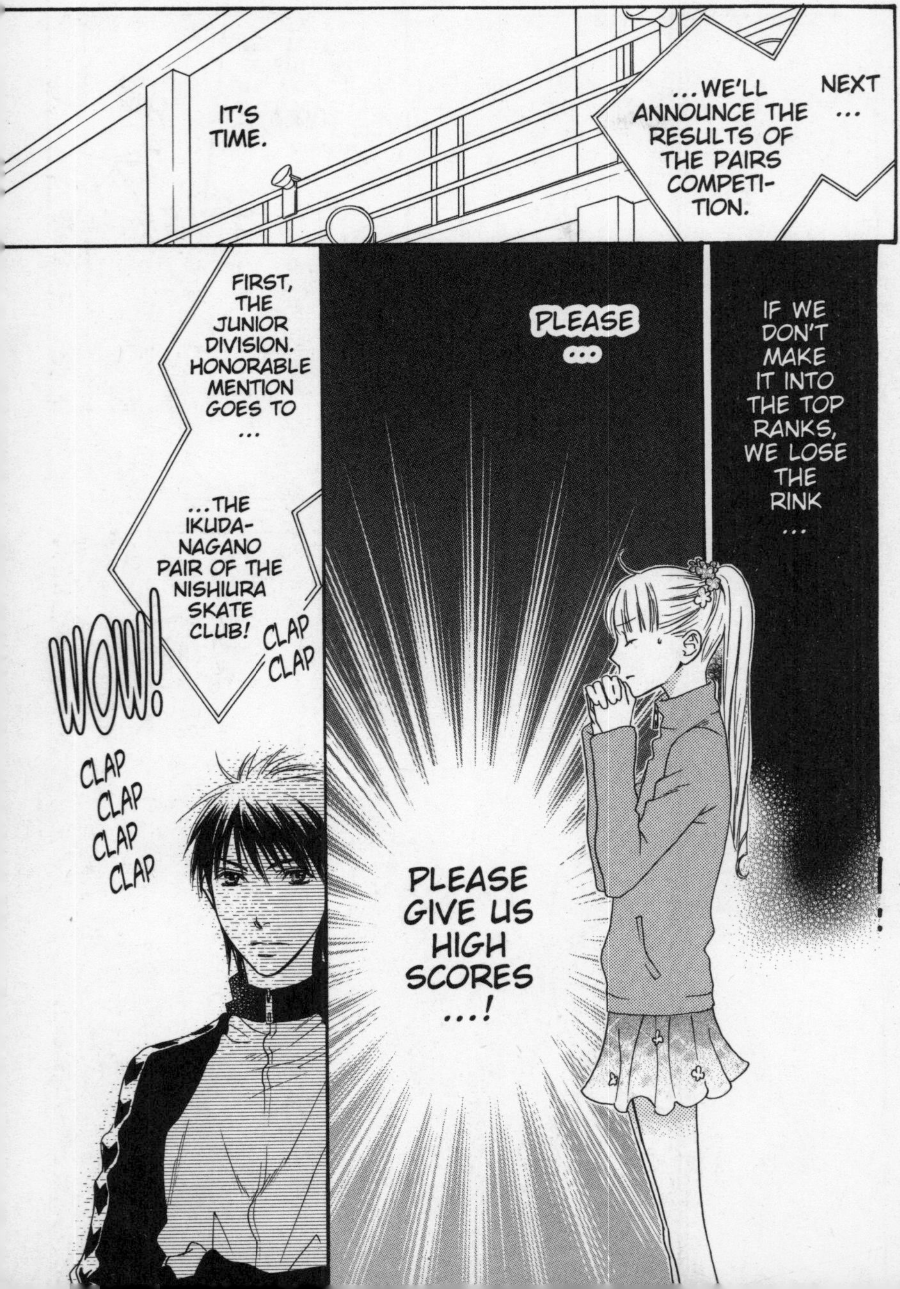
NEXT ...
...WE'LL ANNOUNCE THE RESULTS OF THE PAIRS COMPETI-TION.
IT'S TIME.
IF WE DON'T MAKE IT INTO THE TOP RANKS, WE LOSE THE RINK ...
PLEASE ...
PLEASE GIVE US HIGH SCORES ...!
FIRST, THE JUNIOR DIVISION. HONORABLE MENTION GOES TO ...
...THE IKUDA-NAGANO PAIR OF THE NISHIURA SKATE CLUB!
CLAP CLAP
WOW!
CLAP CLAP CLAP CLAP

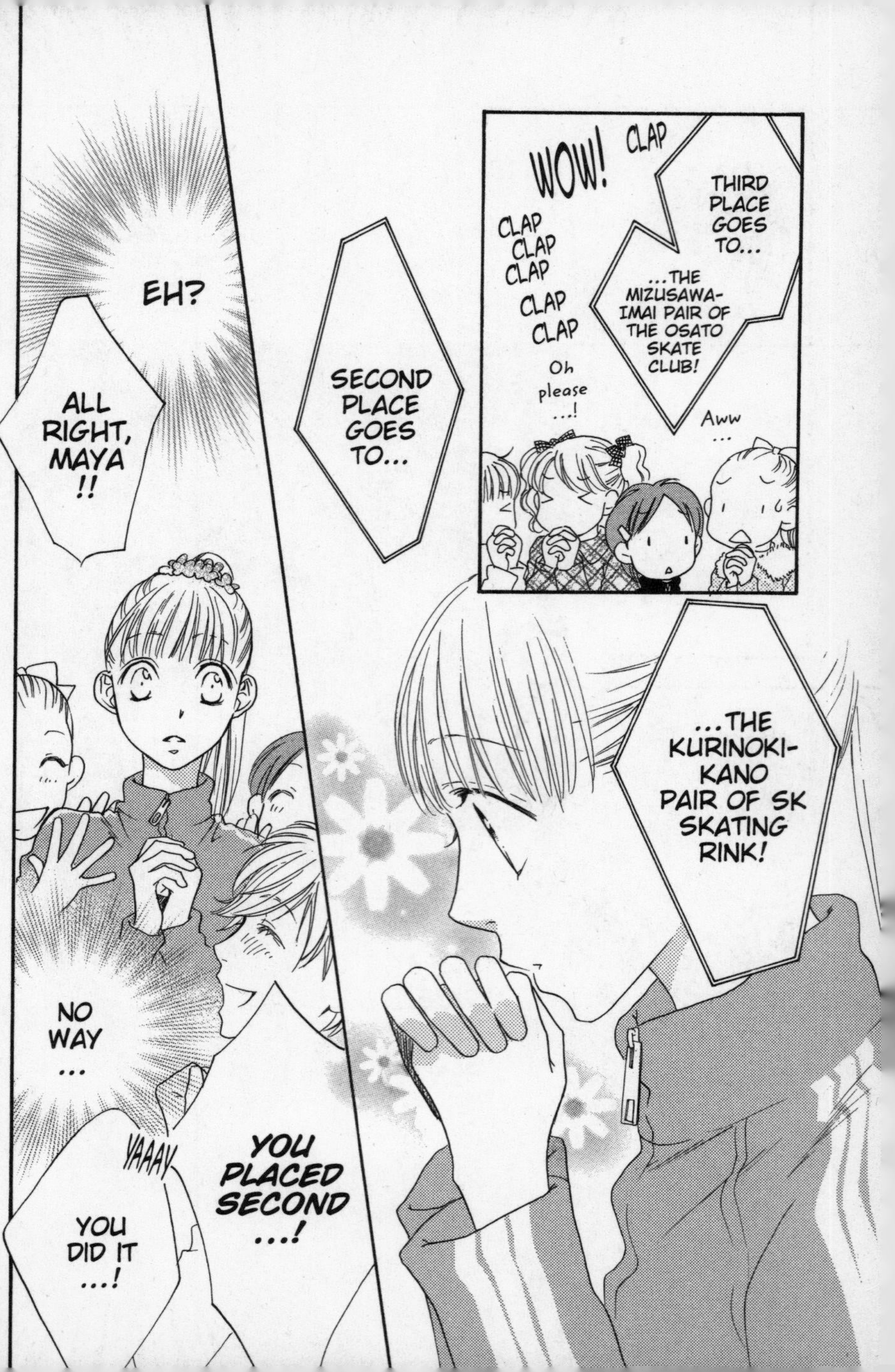
THIRD PLACE GOES TO...
...THE MIZUSAWA-IMAI PAIR OF THE OSATO SKATE CLUB!
CLAP
WOW!
CLAP CLAP CLAP CLAP CLAP
Aww ...
Oh please ...!
SECOND PLACE GOES TO...
...THE KURINOKI-KANO PAIR OF SK SKATING RINK!
EH?
ALL RIGHT, MAYA !!
NO WAY ...
YOU PLACED SECOND ...!
YAAAY
YOU DID IT ...!

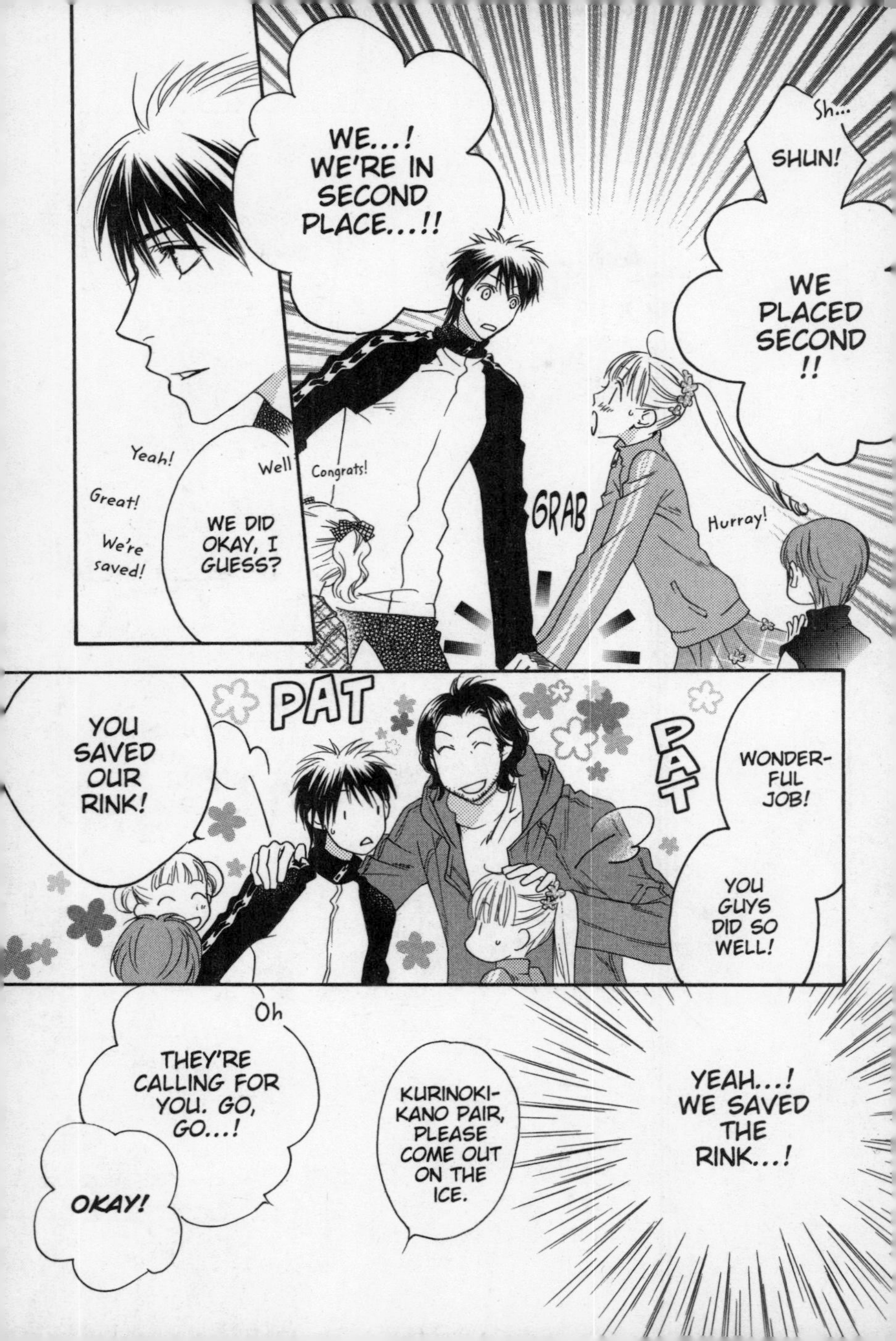
Sh...
SHUN!
WE PLACED SECOND !!
Hurray!
GRAB
WE...! WE'RE IN SECOND PLACE...!!
Congrats!
Well
WE DID OKAY, I GUESS?
Yeah!
Great!
We're saved!
WONDER-FUL JOB!
YOU GUYS DID SO WELL!
PAT
PAT
YOU SAVED OUR RINK!
YEAH...! WE SAVED THE RINK...!
KURINOKI-KANO PAIR, PLEASE COME OUT ON THE ICE.
Oh
THEY'RE CALLING FOR YOU. GO, GO...!
OKAY!

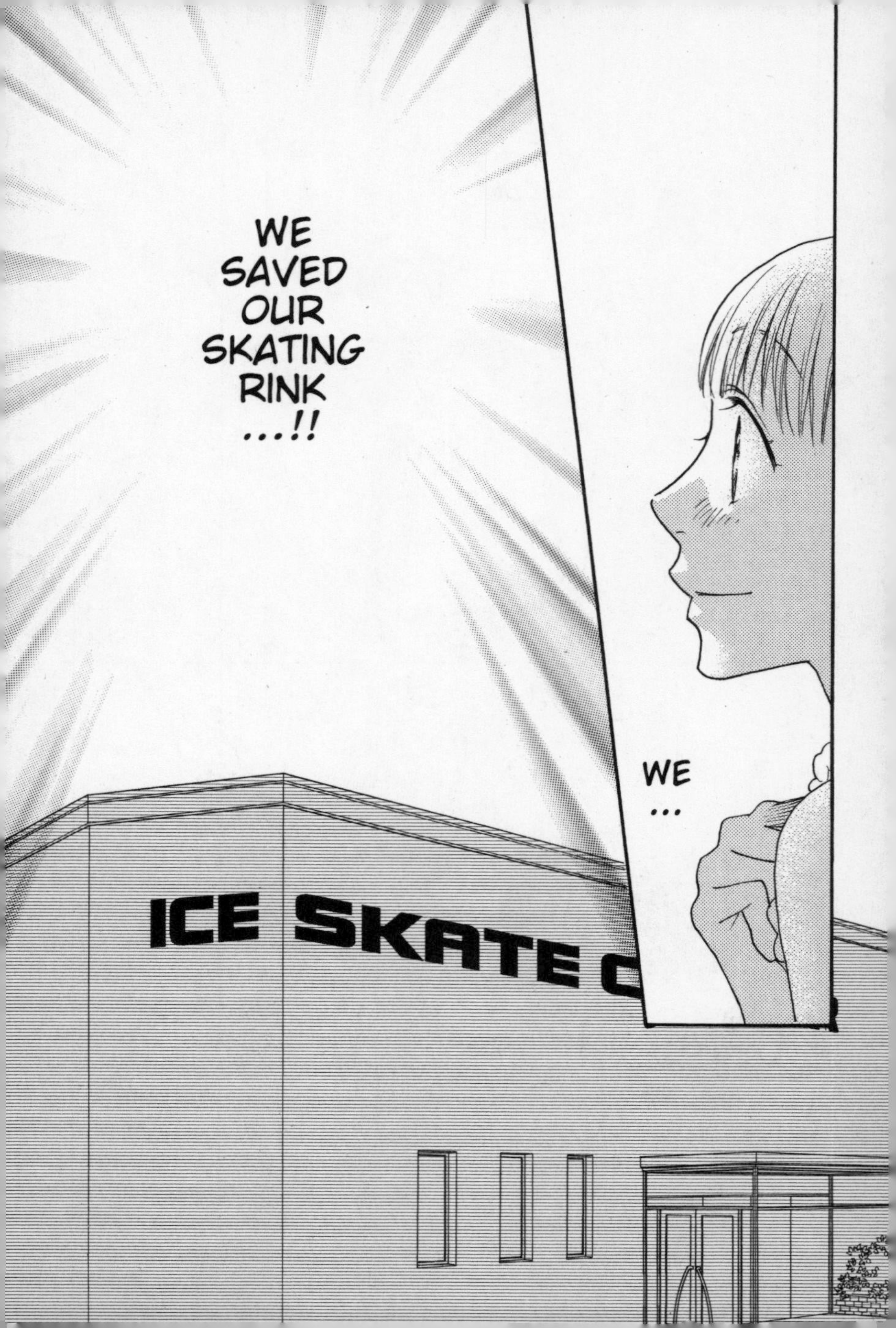
WE ...
WE SAVED OUR SKATING RINK ...!!
ICE SKATE

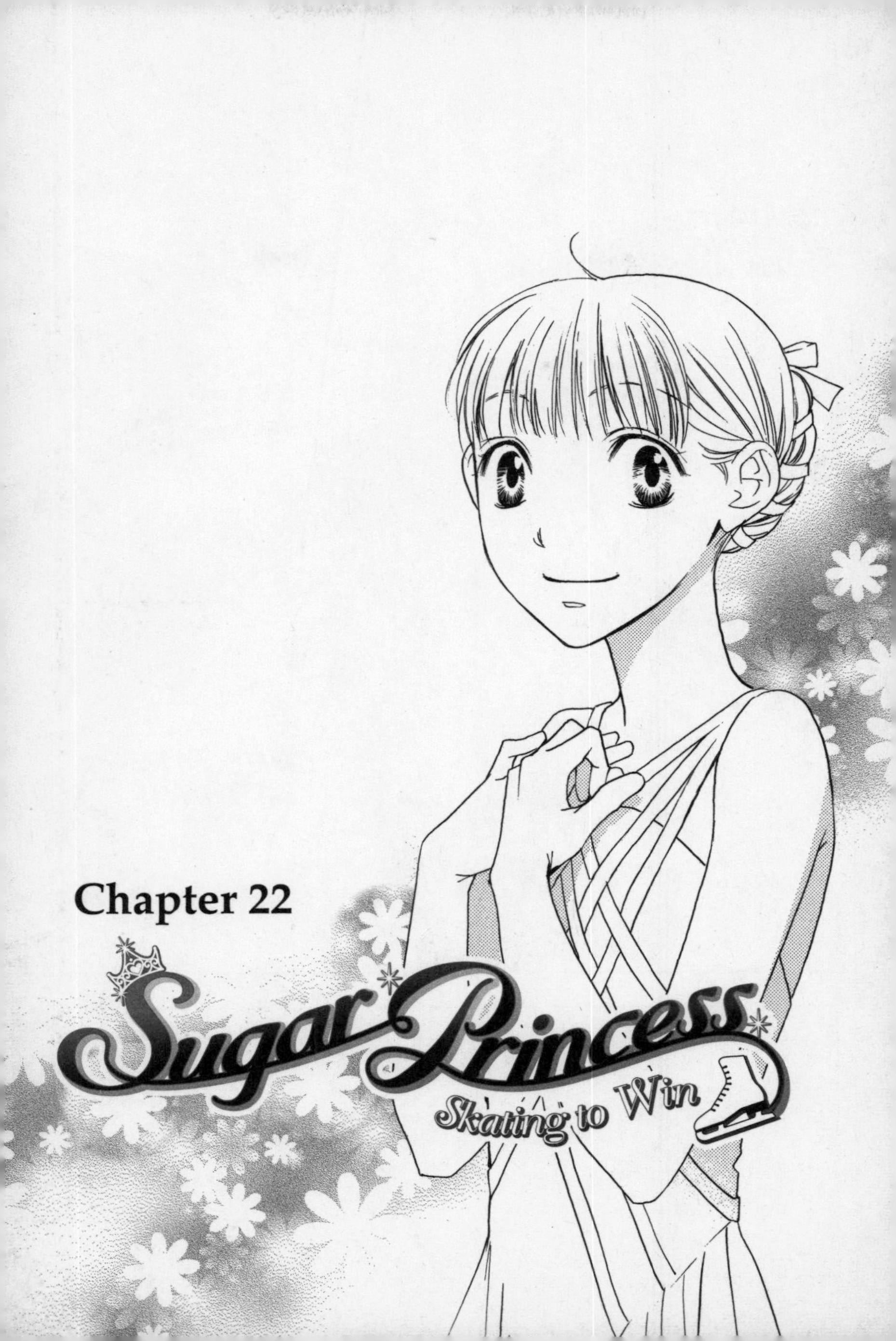
Chapter 22
Sugar Princess
Skating to Win

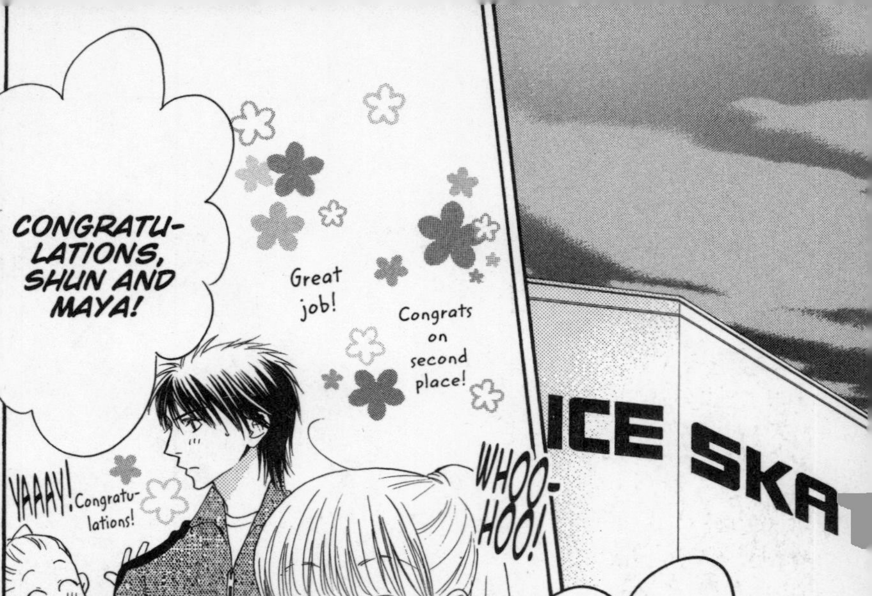
ICE SKA
Congrats on second place!
Great job!
CONGRATULATIONS, SHUN AND MAYA!
WHOO-HOO!
CONGRATULATIONS!
YAAAY!
Congratulations!
HURRAY!
EH HEH HEH
THANK YOU, THANK YOU!

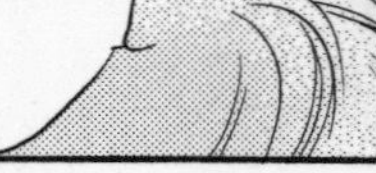

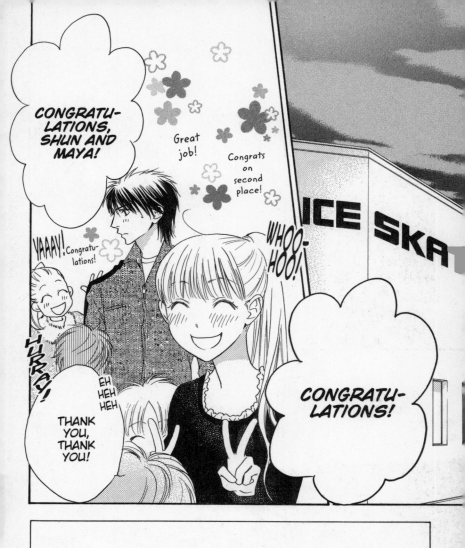

I HAVEN'T BEEN ABLE TO READ MANGA MUCH THESE DAYS. (LOL)

CAN SOMEONE RECOMMEND SOME TITLES TO ME?

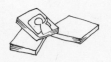

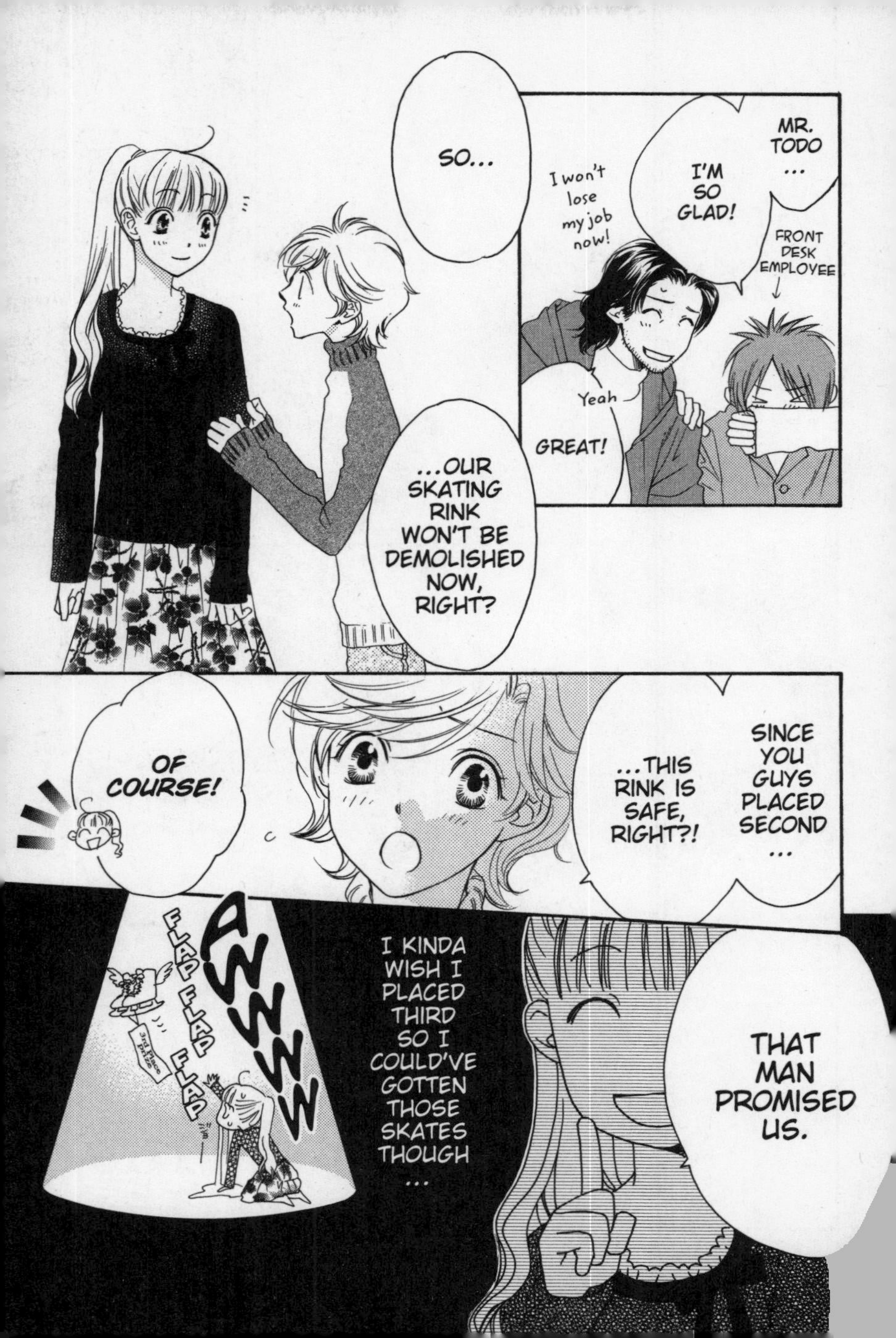
MR. TODO ...
I'M SO GLAD!
I won't lose my job now!
FRONT DESK EMPLOYEE
Yeah
GREAT!
SO...
...OUR SKATING RINK WON'T BE DEMOLISHED NOW, RIGHT?
SINCE YOU GUYS PLACED SECOND ...
...THIS RINK IS SAFE, RIGHT?!
OF COURSE!
THAT MAN PROMISED US.
I KINDA WISH I PLACED THIRD SO I COULD'VE GOTTEN THOSE SKATES THOUGH ...
AWWWW
FLAP FLAP FLAP
3rd Place prize

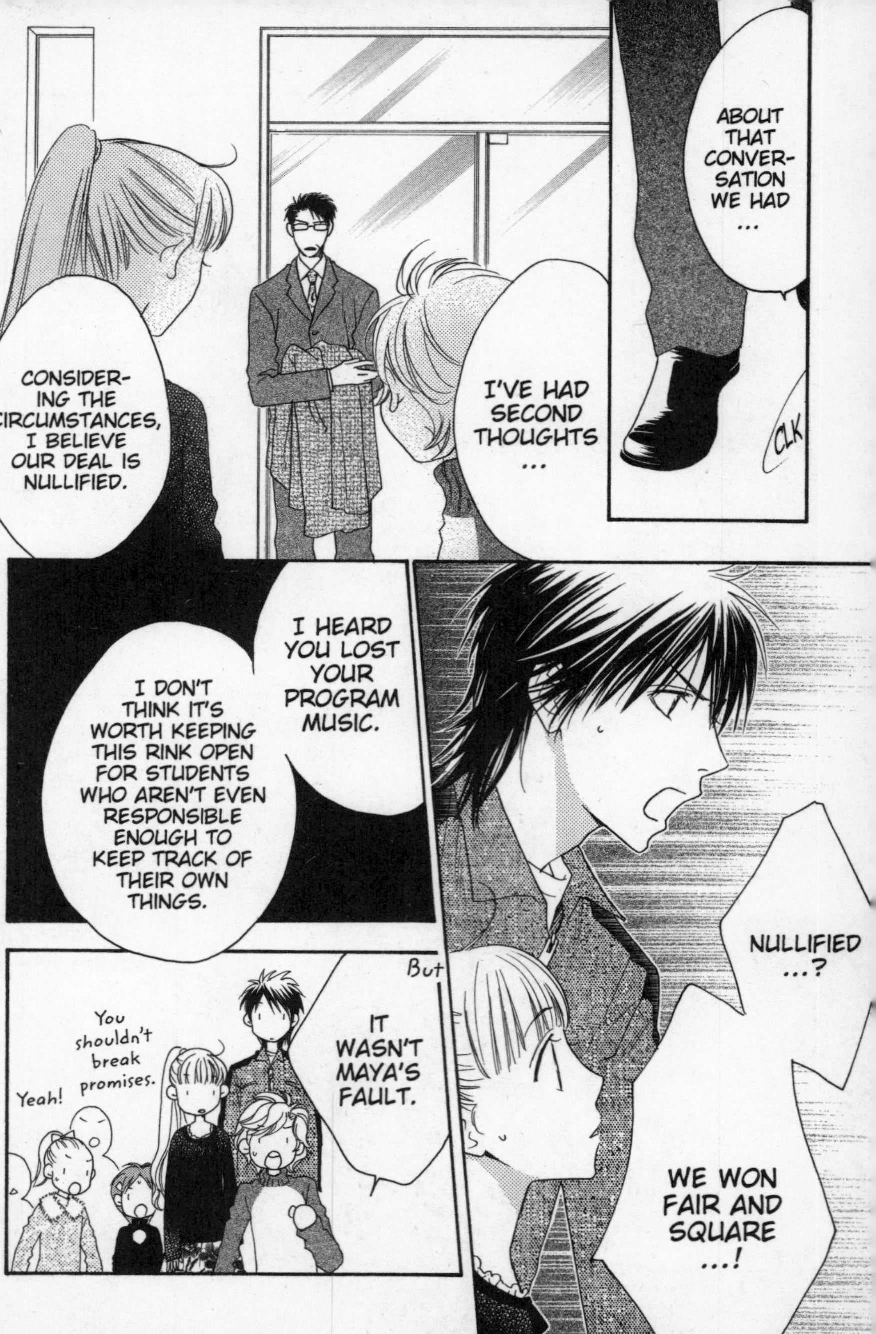

ABOUT THAT CONVER-SATION WE HAD ...
CLK
I'VE HAD SECOND THOUGHTS ...
CONSIDER-ING THE CIRCUMSTANCES, I BELIEVE OUR DEAL IS NULLIFIED.
NULLIFIED ...?
WE WON FAIR AND SQUARE ...!
I HEARD YOU LOST YOUR PROGRAM MUSIC.
I DON'T THINK IT'S WORTH KEEPING THIS RINK OPEN FOR STUDENTS WHO AREN'T EVEN RESPONSIBLE ENOUGH TO KEEP TRACK OF THEIR OWN THINGS.
But
IT WASN'T MAYA'S FAULT.
You shouldn't break promises.
Yeah!

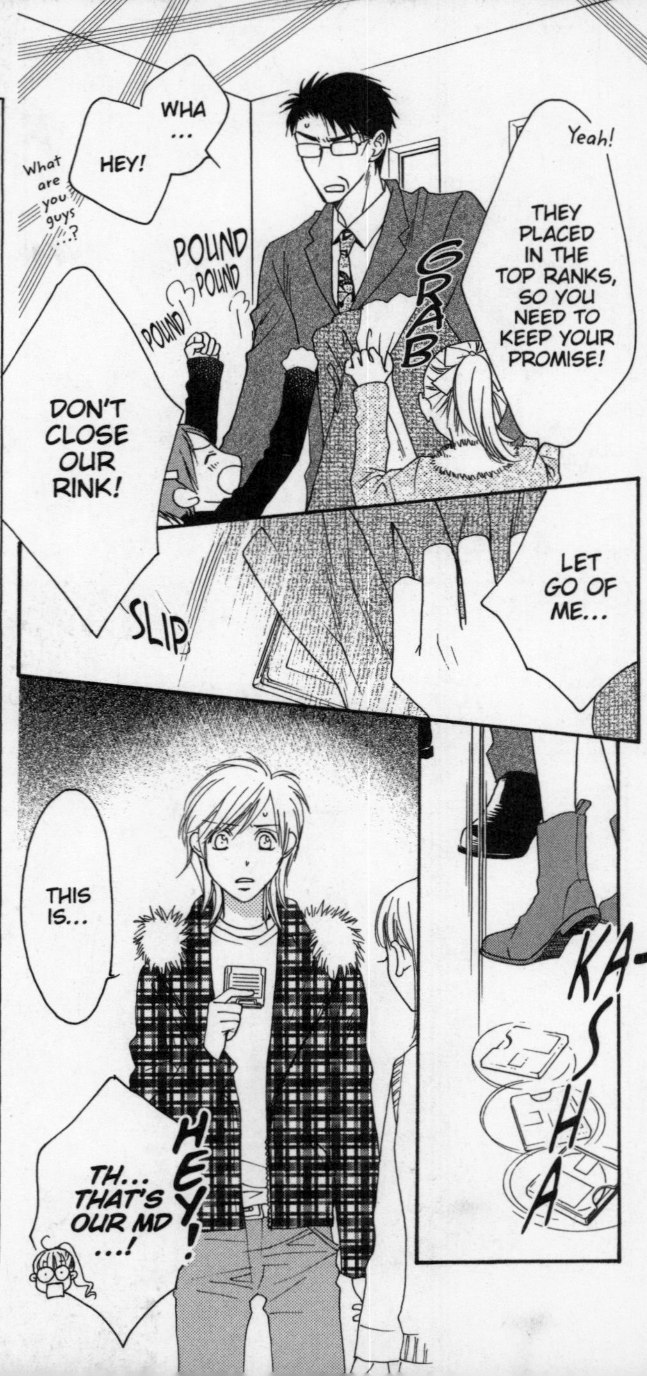
Yeah!
THEY PLACED IN THE TOP RANKS, SO YOU NEED TO KEEP YOUR PROMISE!
GRAB
DON'T CLOSE OUR RINK!
POUND POUND POUND
WHA... HEY!
What are you guys...?
LET GO OF ME...
SLIP
KA-SHA
THIS IS...
HEY!
TH... THAT'S OUR MD...!

SEE YOU!

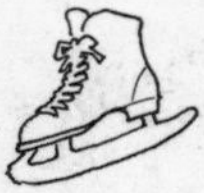

VIVA! FIGURE SKATING!

2007 / NAKAJO

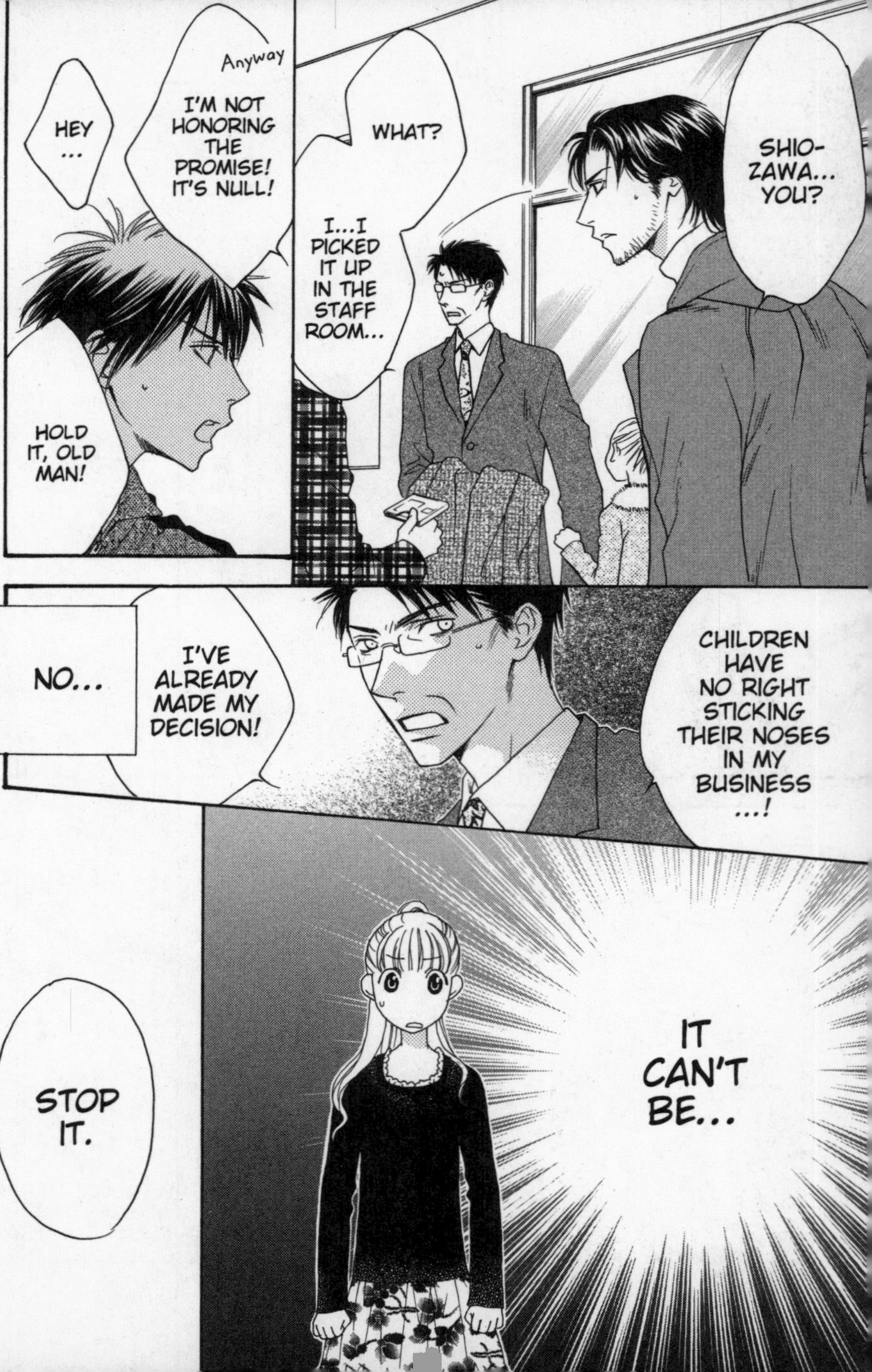
SHIO-ZAWA... YOU?
WHAT?
I...I PICKED IT UP IN THE STAFF ROOM...
Anyway
I'M NOT HONORING THE PROMISE! IT'S NULL!
HEY ...
HOLD IT, OLD MAN!
CHILDREN HAVE NO RIGHT STICKING THEIR NOSES IN MY BUSINESS ...!
I'VE ALREADY MADE MY DECISION!
NO...
IT CAN'T BE...
STOP IT.

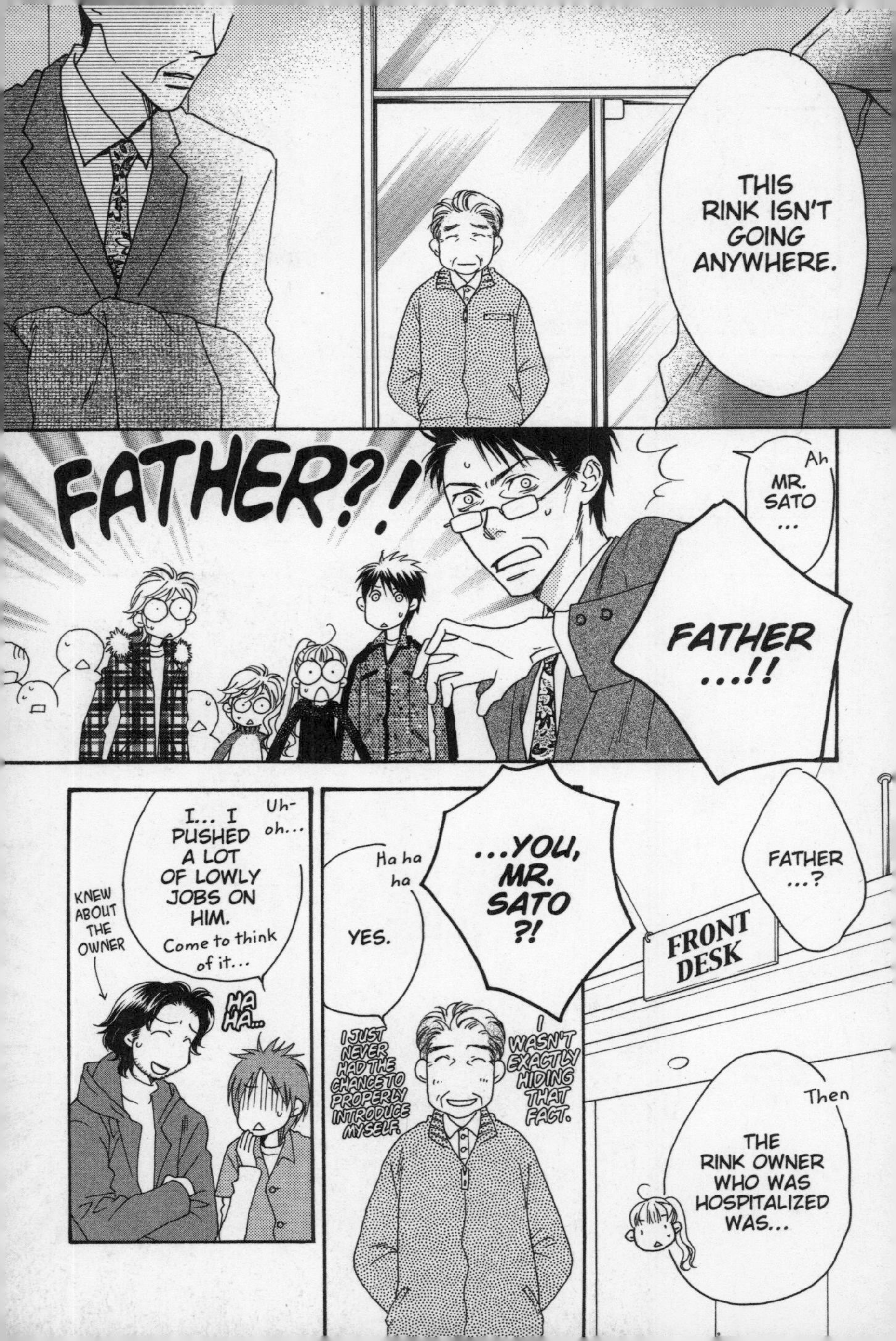
THIS RINK ISN'T GOING ANYWHERE.
Ah MR. SATO ...
FATHER ...!!
FATHER?!
FATHER ...?
FRONT DESK
Then
THE RINK OWNER WHO WAS HOSPITALIZED WAS...
...YOU, MR. SATO ?!
I WASN'T EXACTLY HIDING THAT FACT.
Ha ha ha
YES.
I JUST NEVER HAD THE CHANCE TO PROPERLY INTRODUCE MYSELF.
Uh-oh...
I... I PUSHED A LOT OF LOWLY JOBS ON HIM.
Come to think of it...
KNEW ABOUT THE OWNER
HA HA...

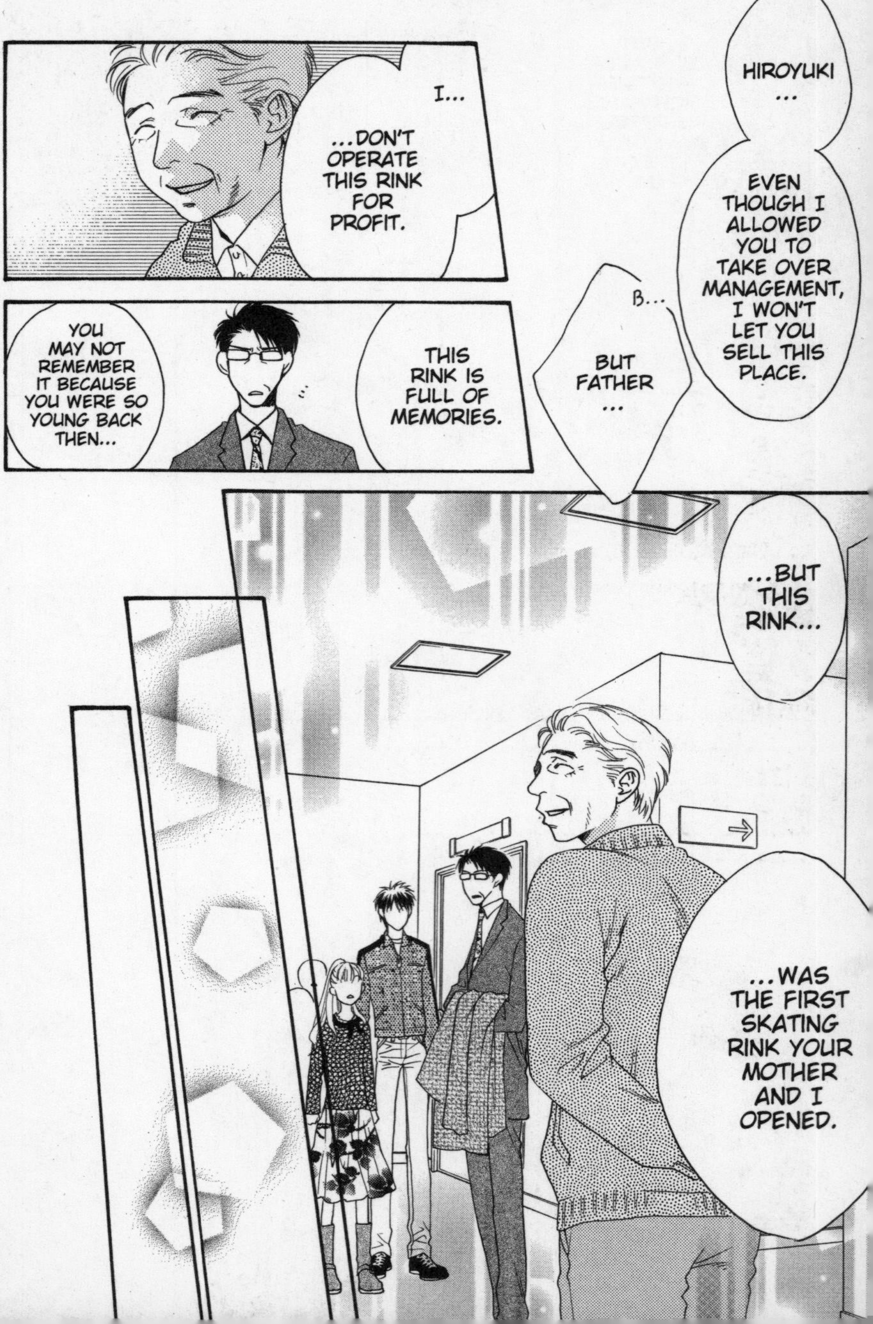
HIROYUKI ...
EVEN THOUGH I ALLOWED YOU TO TAKE OVER MANAGEMENT, I WON'T LET YOU SELL THIS PLACE.
B...
BUT FATHER ...
I...
...DON'T OPERATE THIS RINK FOR PROFIT.
THIS RINK IS FULL OF MEMORIES.
YOU MAY NOT REMEMBER IT BECAUSE YOU WERE SO YOUNG BACK THEN...
...BUT THIS RINK...
...WAS THE FIRST SKATING RINK YOUR MOTHER AND I OPENED.

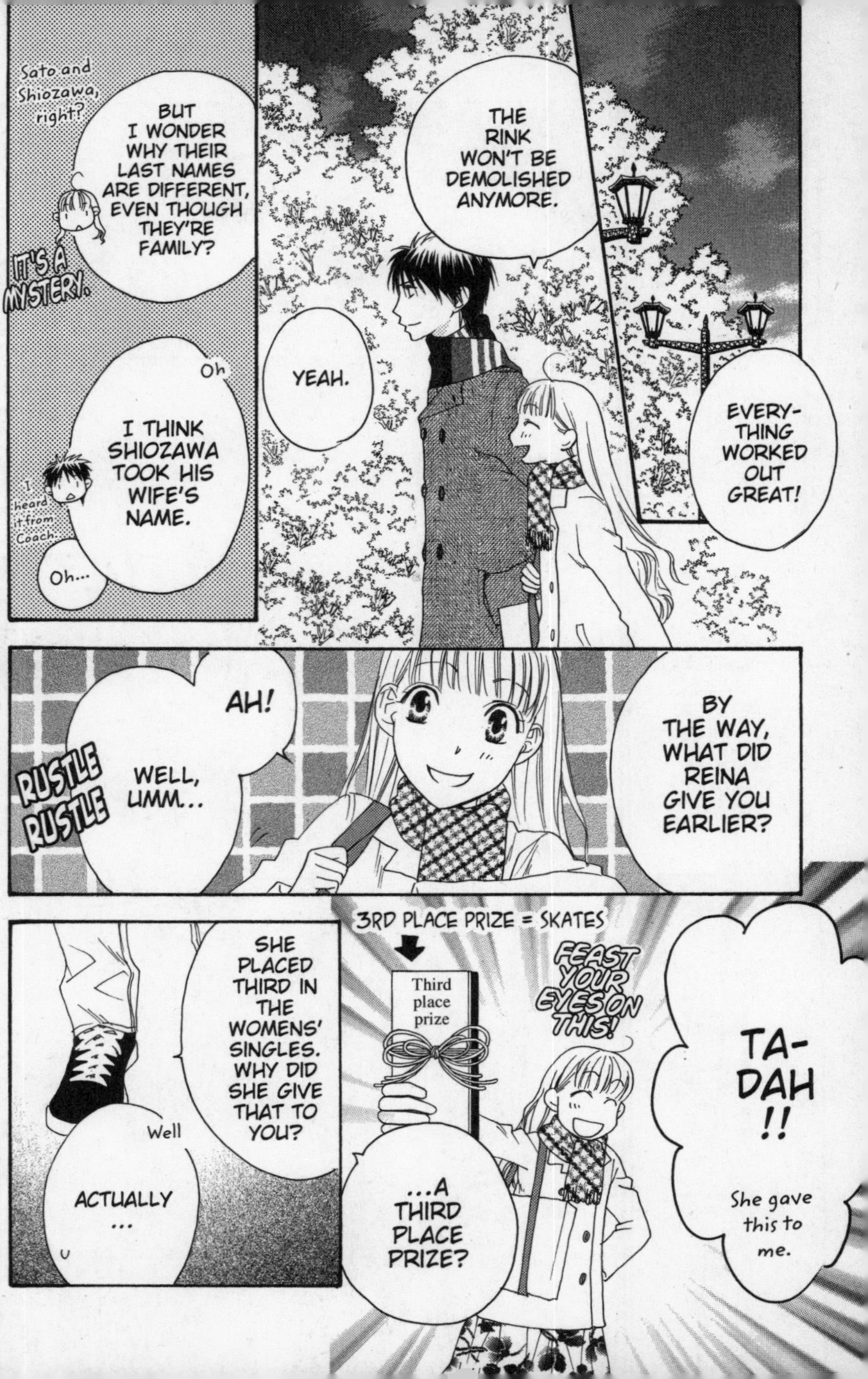
EVERY-THING WORKED OUT GREAT!
THE RINK WON'T BE DEMOLISHED ANYMORE.
YEAH.
BUT I WONDER WHY THEIR LAST NAMES ARE DIFFERENT, EVEN THOUGH THEY'RE FAMILY?
Sato and Shiozawa, right?
IT'S A MYSTERY.
Oh
I THINK SHIOZAWA TOOK HIS WIFE'S NAME.
I heard it from Coach.
Oh...
BY THE WAY, WHAT DID REINA GIVE YOU EARLIER?
AH!
WELL, UMM...
RUSTLE RUSTLE
TA-DAH!!
She gave this to me.
FEAST YOUR EYES ON THIS!
3RD PLACE PRIZE = SKATES
Third place prize
...A THIRD PLACE PRIZE?
SHE PLACED THIRD IN THE WOMENS' SINGLES. WHY DID SHE GIVE THAT TO YOU?
Well
ACTUALLY...

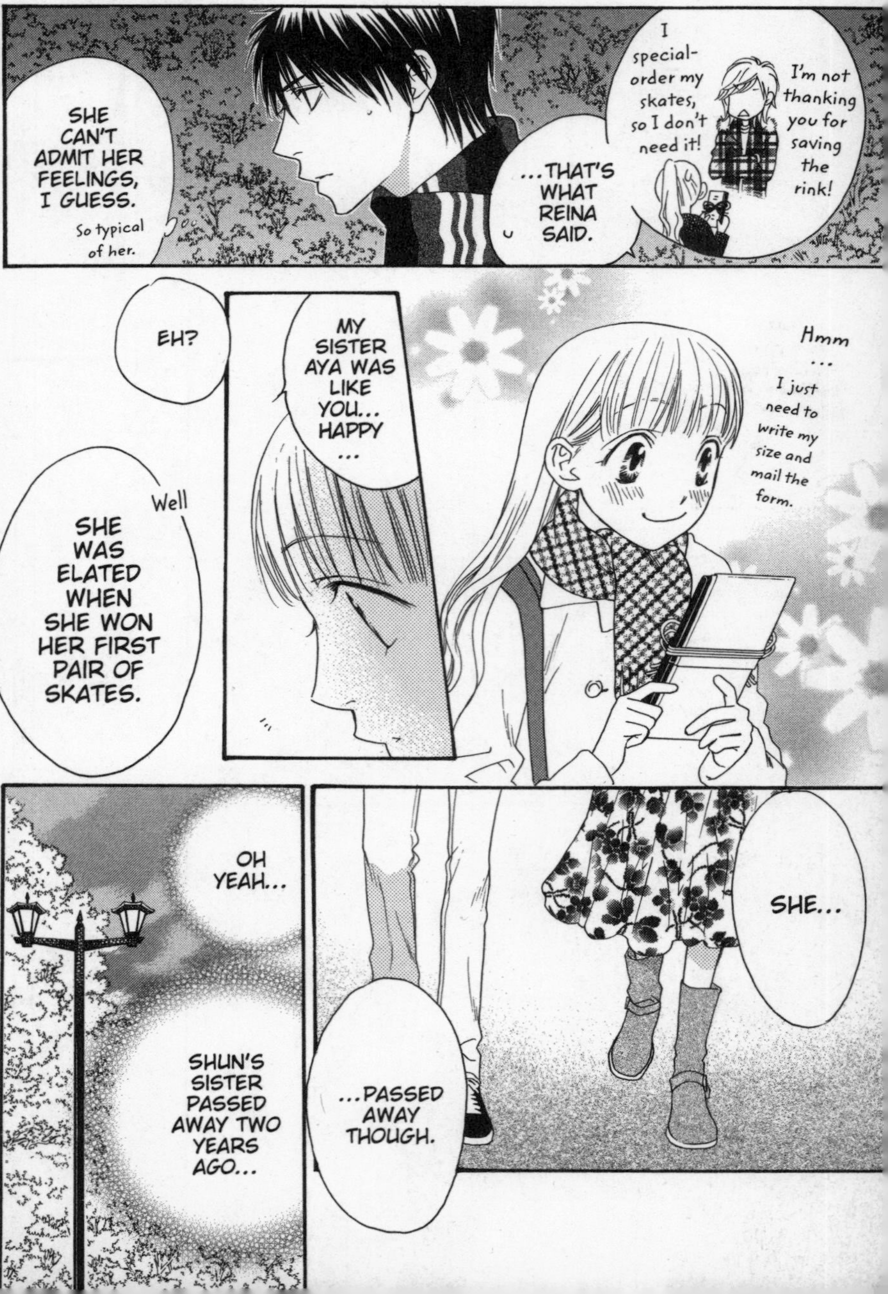
I'm not thanking you for saving the rink!
I special-order my skates, so I don't need it!
...THAT'S WHAT REINA SAID.
SHE CAN'T ADMIT HER FEELINGS, I GUESS.
So typical of her.
Hmm... I just need to write my size and mail the form.
MY SISTER AYA WAS LIKE YOU... HAPPY...
EH?
Well
SHE WAS ELATED WHEN SHE WON HER FIRST PAIR OF SKATES.
SHE...
...PASSED AWAY THOUGH.
OH YEAH...
SHUN'S SISTER PASSED AWAY TWO YEARS AGO...

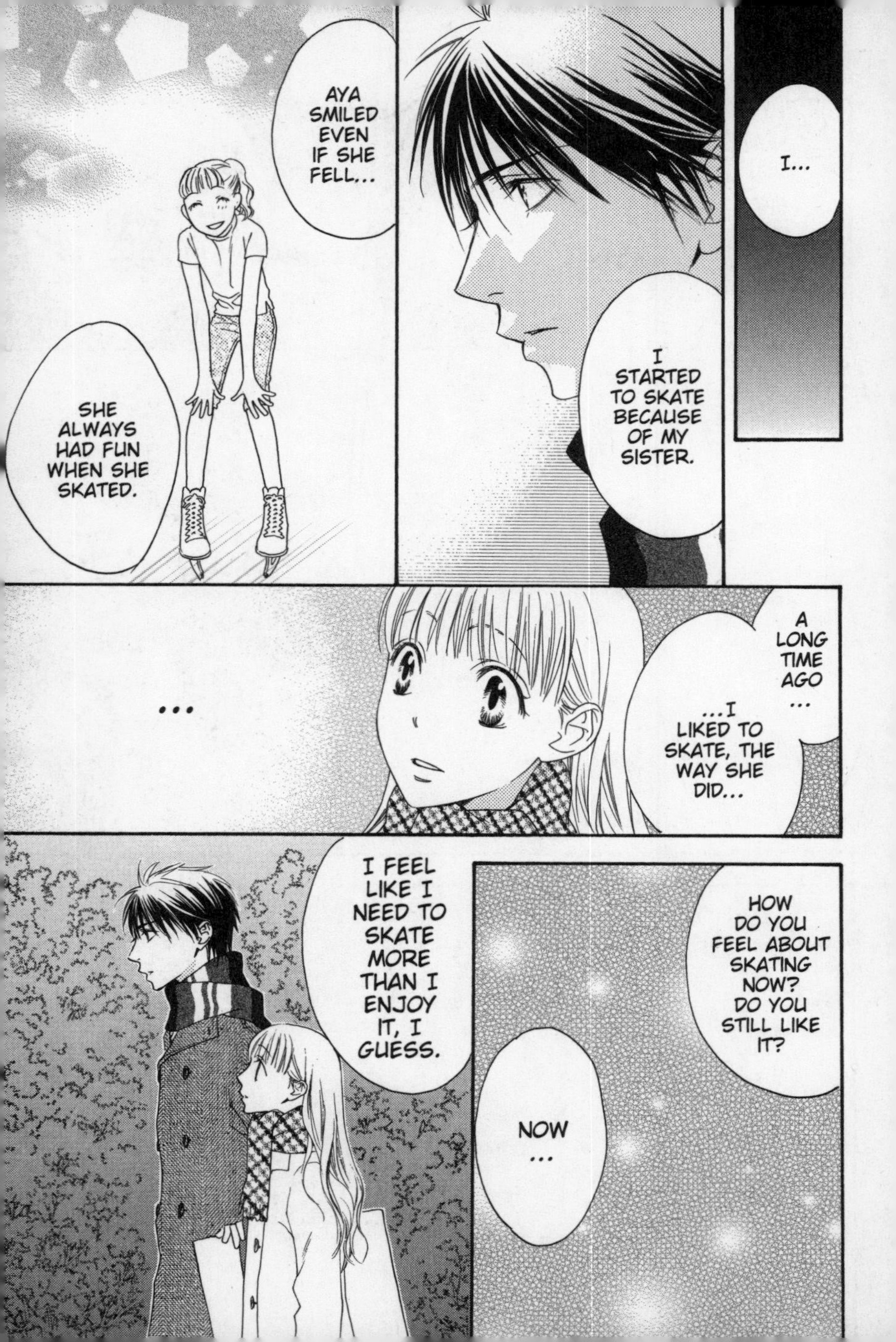

I...
I STARTED TO SKATE BECAUSE OF MY SISTER.
AYA SMILED EVEN IF SHE FELL...
SHE ALWAYS HAD FUN WHEN SHE SKATED.
A LONG TIME AGO...
...I LIKED TO SKATE, THE WAY SHE DID...
...
HOW DO YOU FEEL ABOUT SKATING NOW? DO YOU STILL LIKE IT?
NOW...
I FEEL LIKE I NEED TO SKATE MORE THAN I ENJOY IT, I GUESS.

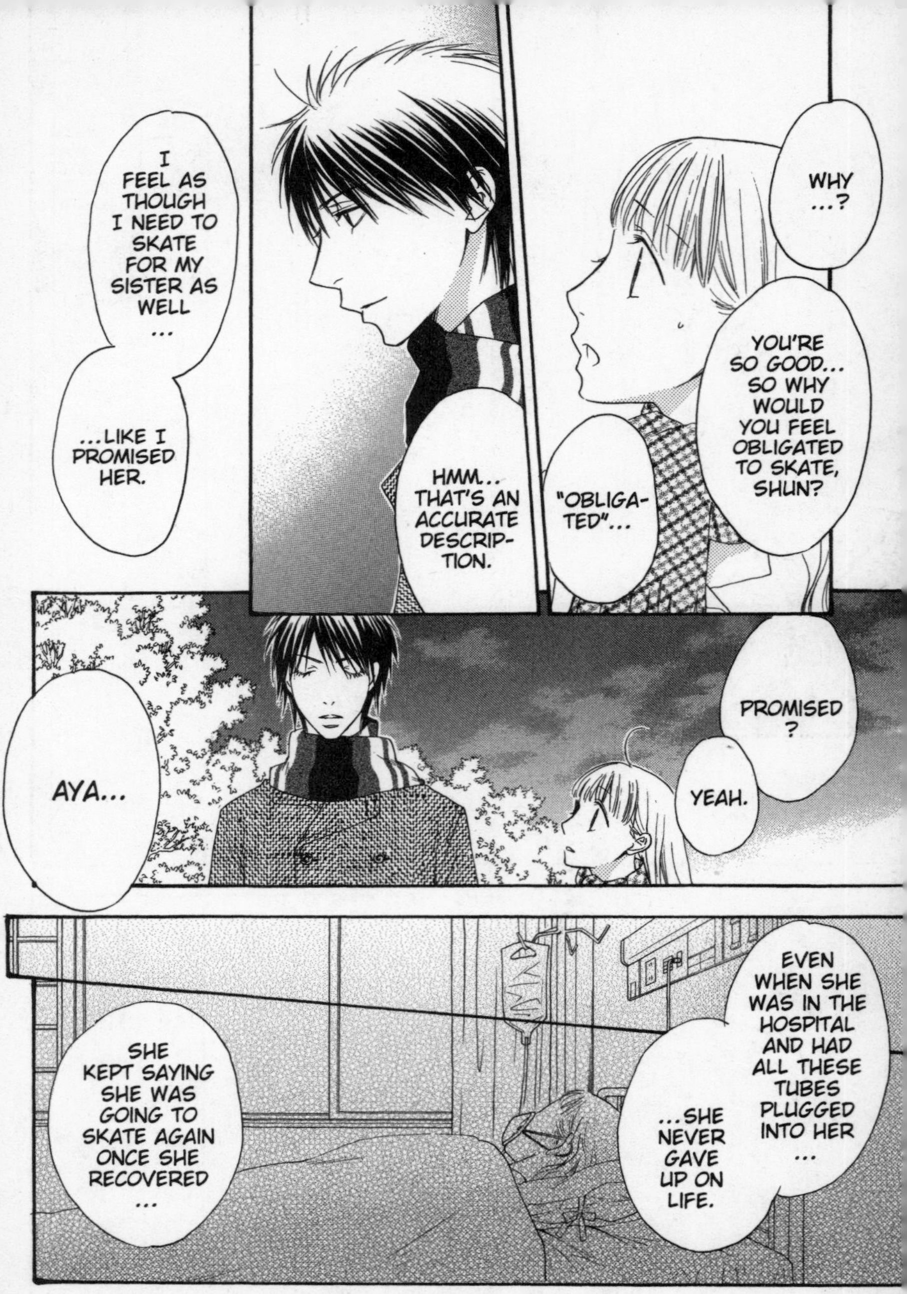
WHY...?
YOU'RE SO GOOD... SO WHY WOULD YOU FEEL OBLIGATED TO SKATE, SHUN?
"OBLIGATED"...
HMM... THAT'S AN ACCURATE DESCRIPTION.
I FEEL AS THOUGH I NEED TO SKATE FOR MY SISTER AS WELL...
...LIKE I PROMISED HER.
PROMISED?
YEAH.
AYA...
EVEN WHEN SHE WAS IN THE HOSPITAL AND HAD ALL THESE TUBES PLUGGED INTO HER...
...SHE NEVER GAVE UP ON LIFE.
SHE KEPT SAYING SHE WAS GOING TO SKATE AGAIN ONCE SHE RECOVERED...

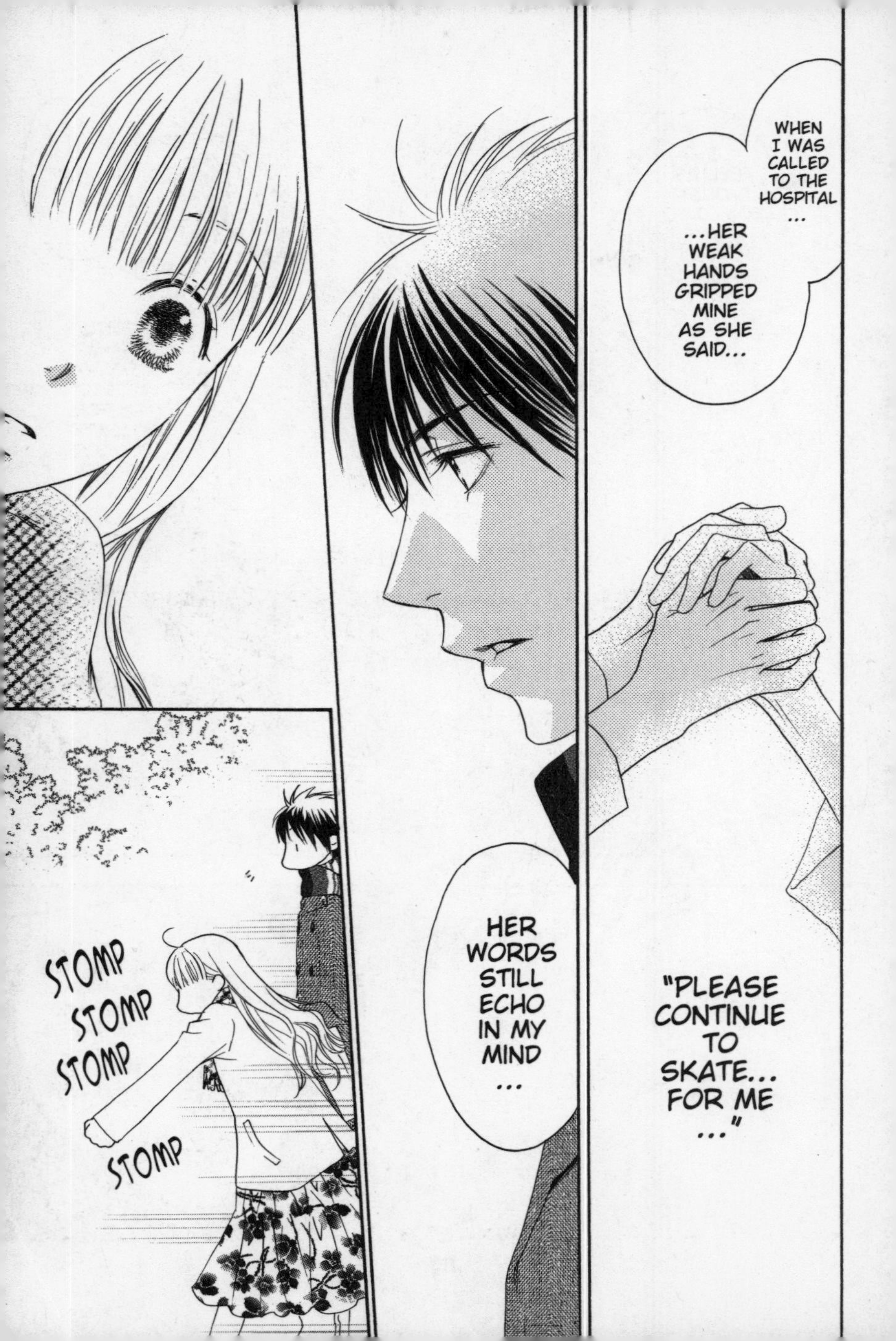
WHEN I WAS CALLED TO THE HOSPITAL...
...HER WEAK HANDS GRIPPED MINE AS SHE SAID...
"PLEASE CONTINUE TO SKATE... FOR ME..."
HER WORDS STILL ECHO IN MY MIND...
STOMP STOMP STOMP
STOMP

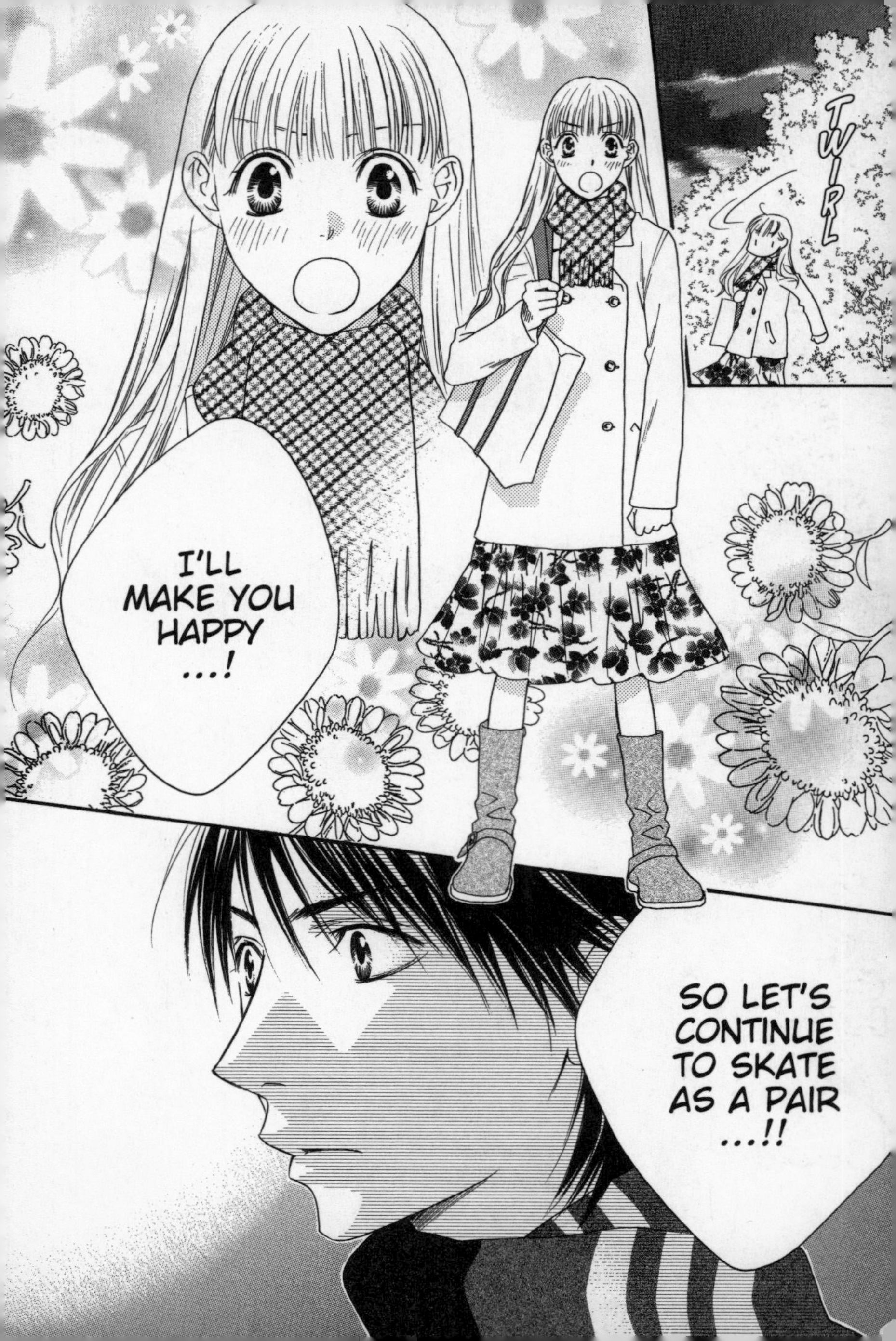
TWIRL
I'LL MAKE YOU HAPPY ...!
SO LET'S CONTINUE TO SKATE AS A PAIR ...!!

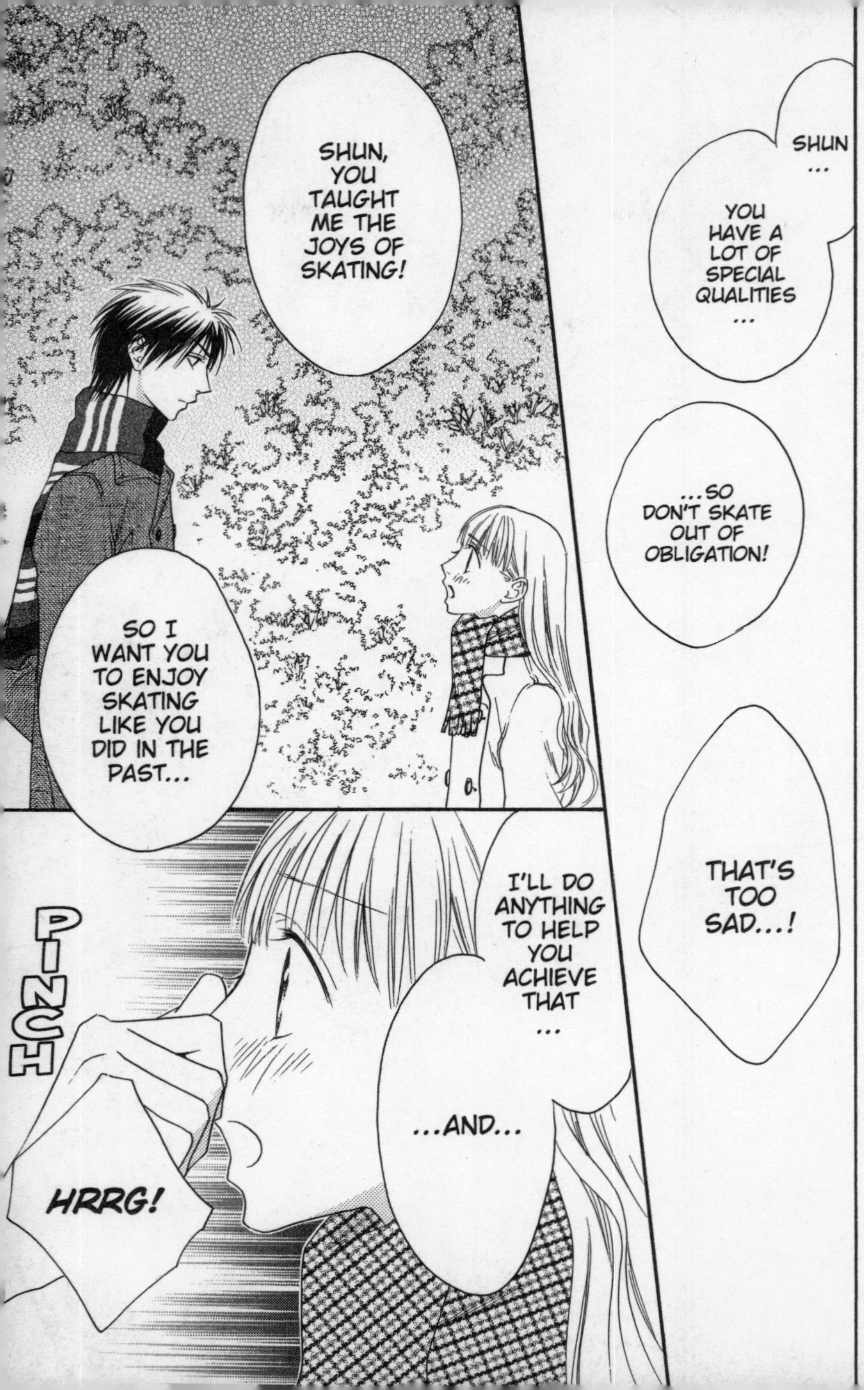
SHUN ...
YOU HAVE A LOT OF SPECIAL QUALITIES ...
...SO DON'T SKATE OUT OF OBLIGATION!
THAT'S TOO SAD...!
SHUN, YOU TAUGHT ME THE JOYS OF SKATING!
SO I WANT YOU TO ENJOY SKATING LIKE YOU DID IN THE PAST...
I'LL DO ANYTHING TO HELP YOU ACHIEVE THAT ...
...AND...
PINCH
HRRG!

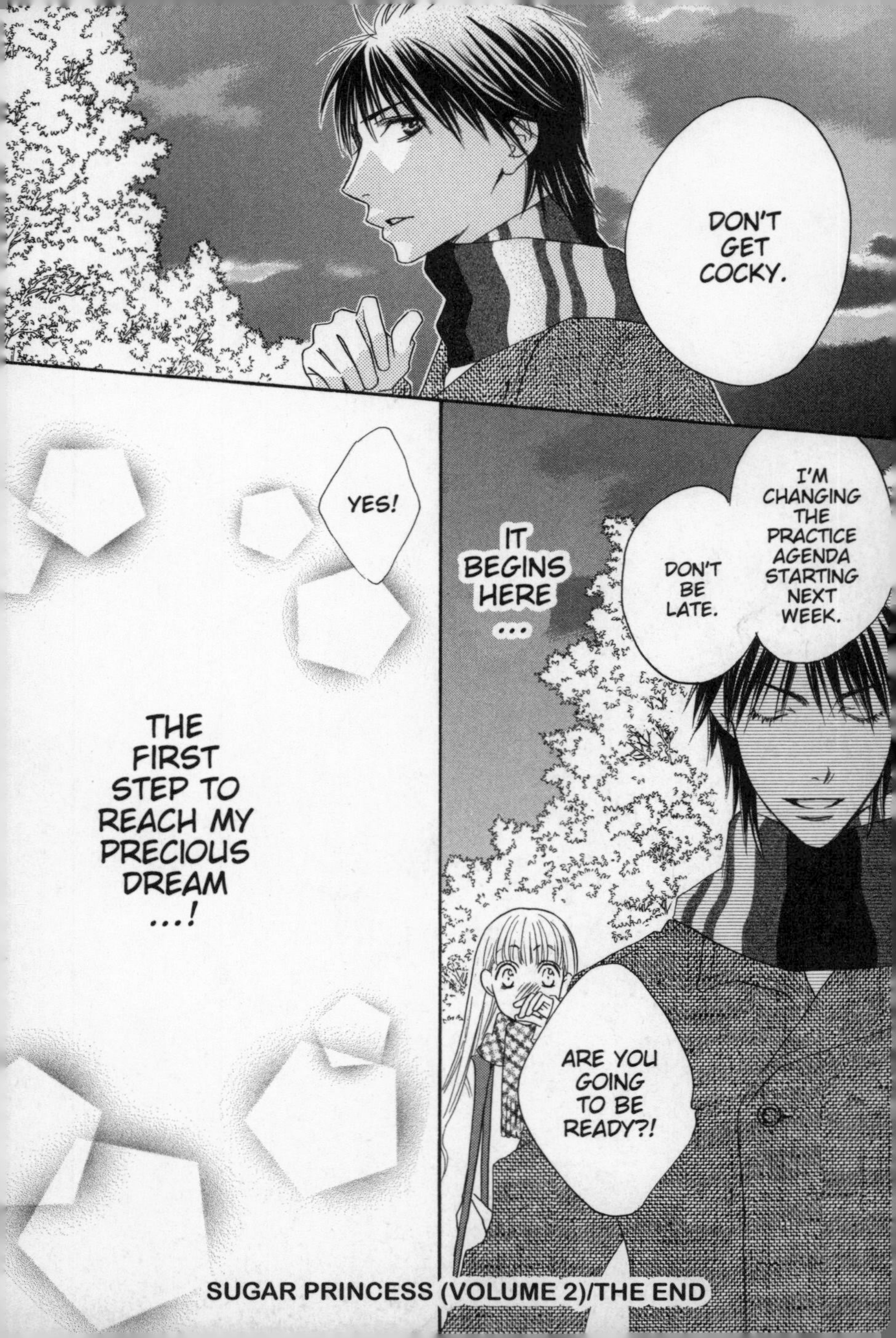
DON'T GET COCKY.
I'M CHANGING THE PRACTICE AGENDA STARTING NEXT WEEK.
DON'T BE LATE.
IT BEGINS HERE...
ARE YOU GOING TO BE READY?!
YES!
THE FIRST STEP TO REACH MY PRECIOUS DREAM ...!
SUGAR PRINCESS (VOLUME 2)/THE END

Hisaya Nakajo's manga series *Hanazakari no Kimitachi he* (For You in Full Blossom, casually known as *Hana-Kimi*) has been a hit since it first appeared in 1997 in the shojo manga magazine *Hana to Yume* (Flowers and Dreams). In Japan, a *Hana-Kimi* art book and several drama CDs have been released. Her other manga series include *Missing Piece* (two volumes) and *Yumemiru Happa* (The Dreaming Leaf, one volume).

Sugar Princess
Vol. 2
The Shojo Beat Manga Edition

STORY & ART BY
HISAYA NAKAJO

Translation & Adaptation/Anastasia Moreno
Touch-up Art & Lettering/Rina Mapa
Design/Izumi Hirayama
Editor/Amy Yu

Editor in Chief, Books/Alvin Lu
Editor in Chief, Magazines/Marc Weidenbaum
VP of Publishing Licensing/Rika Inouye
VP of Sales/Gonzalo Ferreyra
Sr. VP of Marketing/Liza Coppola
Publisher/Hyoe Narita

Printed in Canada

Published by VIZ Media, LLC
P.O. Box 77010
San Francisco, CA 94107

Shojo Beat Manga Edition
10 9 8 7 6 5 4 3 2 1
First printing, November 2008

www.viz.com

store.viz.com

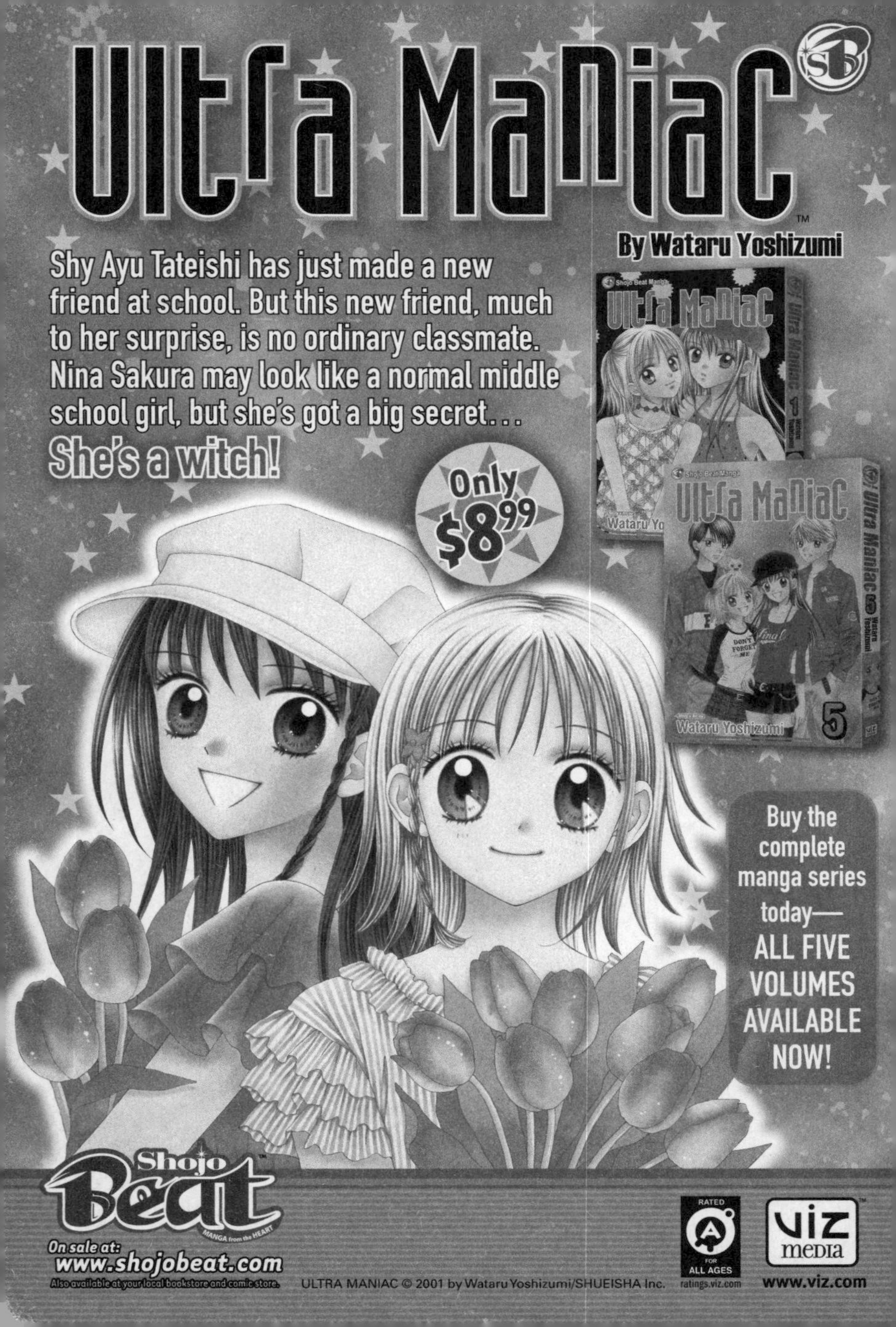
Ultra Maniac™
By Wataru Yoshizumi
Shy Ayu Tateishi has just made a new friend at school. But this new friend, much to her surprise, is no ordinary classmate. Nina Sakura may look like a normal middle school girl, but she's got a big secret...
She's a witch!
Only $8.99
Buy the complete manga series today— ALL FIVE VOLUMES AVAILABLE NOW!
Shojo Beat™
MANGA from the HEART
On sale at:
www.shojobeat.com
Also available at your local bookstore and comic store.
ULTRA MANIAC © 2001 by Wataru Yoshizumi/SHUEISHA Inc.
RATED A FOR ALL AGES
ratings.viz.com
VIZ media
www.viz.com

The
gripping
story —
in **manga**
format

Get the complete *Be With You* collection—
buy the manga and fiction today!

www.viz.com

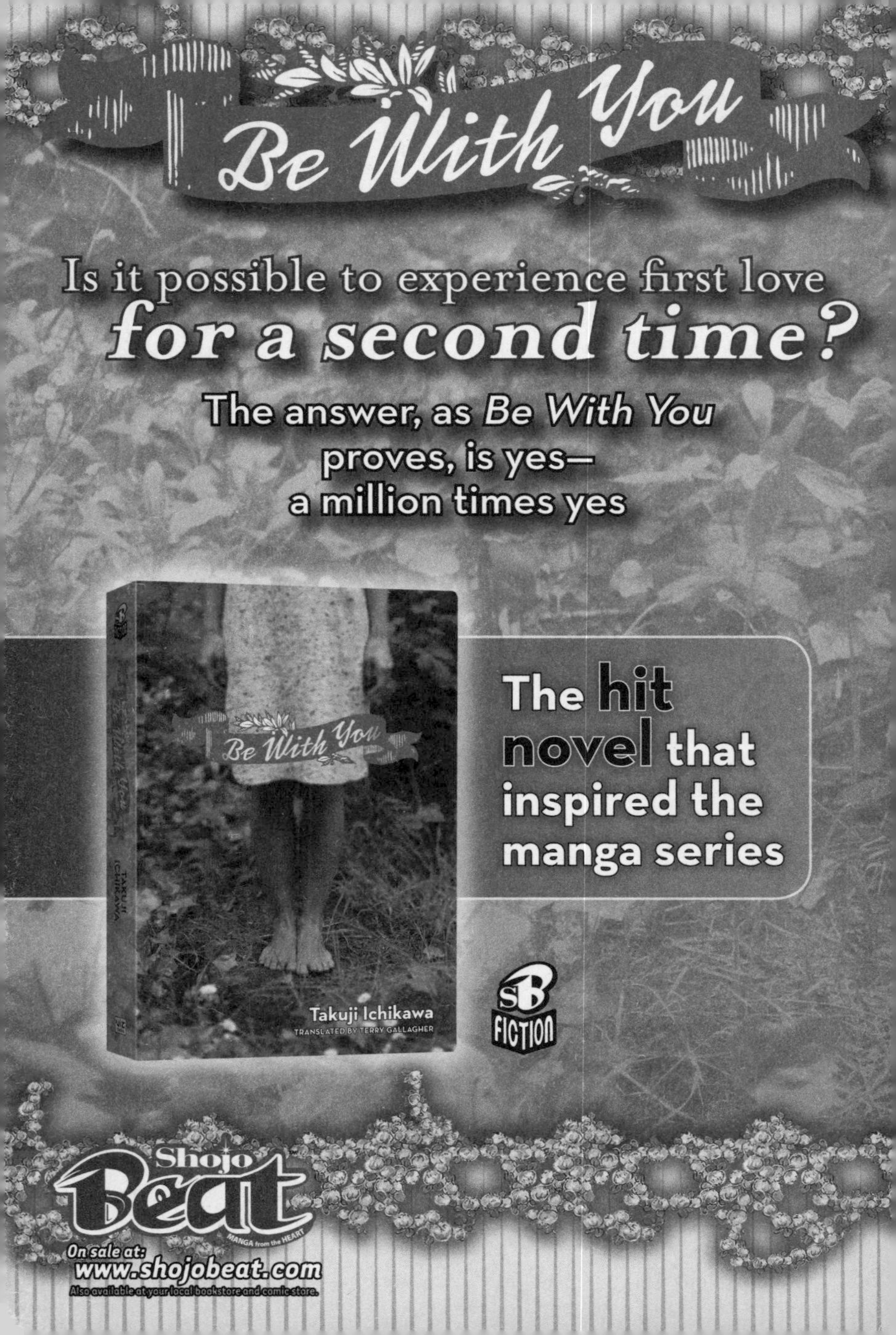
Be With You
Is it possible to experience first love
for a second time?
The answer, as Be With You proves, is yes—
a million times yes
Be With You
Takuji Ichikawa
TRANSLATED BY TERRY GALLAGHER
The hit novel that inspired the manga series
SB FICTION
Shojo Beat
MANGA from the HEART
On sale at:
www.shojobeat.com
Also available at your local bookstore and comic store.

Art book featuring 216 pages of beautiful color images personally selected by Tanemura

Read where Mitsuki's pop dreams began in the manga—all 7 volumes now available

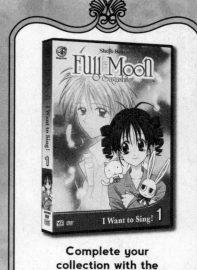

Complete your collection with the anime, now on DVD

RATED
T
FOR
TEEN
ratings.viz.com

www.viz.com